THE
BLUE-EYED
SHEIKS

THE BLUE-EYED SHEIKS

The Canadian
Oil Establishment

PETER FOSTER

Collins Toronto 1979

To My Mother and Father

First published 1979
by Collins Publishers
100 Lesmill Road, Don Mills, Ontario

© 1979 by Peter Foster

Canadian Cataloguing in Publication Data

Foster, Peter, 1947 —
   The blue-eyed sheiks

ISBN 0-00-216608-9

1. Petroleum industry and trade — Canada. I. Title.

HD9574.C22F68   338.2′7′2820971   C79-094657-2

Printed in Canada

Contents

Acknowledgements 7
Foreword 9
Introduction 11

Part One 17
Petroleum and Politics: And the Last Shall be First

Chapter One 19
OPEC and the World — The Genie Becomes the Master

Chapter Two 27
Canada and the U.S. Sticking It to Uncle Sam

Chapter Three 35
Alberta and Ottawa: Settling Old Scores

Part Two 47
Petroleum and Corporate Power: Big Oil's Troubled Decade

Chapter Four 49
Big Oil in Canada

Chapter Five 57
Imperial Oil — The Biggest Target

Chapter Six 70
Imperial's Sisters: The Bumpy Road to the Tar Sands

Chapter Seven 88
The "Invisible" Oil Companies: Brickbats for Mobil and Bouquets
   for Chevron

6   *Chapter Eight   106*
Blair and Bloody Noses

Chapter Nine   123
Shoot Out at the Cody Corral

Chapter Ten   139
PetroCan

Chapter Eleven   144
Maurice Strong — The Reluctant Millionaire

Chapter Twelve   165
A "Riverboat Man in a Gambler's Industry"

Part Three   185
Making Money in Petroleum: They Never Had It So Good

Chapter Thirteen   187
McMahon & Brown: The Old Timers Had It Tough

Chapter Fourteen   196
Canadian Hunter: Making a Myth as Natural Gas Fuels the
    Canadian Initiative

Chapter Fifteen   214
The Newest and Largest Fortunes: Gas and Land

Chapter Sixteen   233
Ringing Out the Good News: The Financial Boom

Part Four   251
Petroleum and the New Alberta

Chapter Seventeen   253
Peter Lougheed: The Bucks Stop Here

Chapter Eighteen   265
The Empire Builders

Chapter Nineteen   278
Calgary

Postscript   298
Appendix   302
Index   314

Acknowledgements

The idea for this book came while I was covering the petroleum industry for the *Financial Post* during 1977 and 1978. At the beginning of 1979 I commenced an eight month leave of absence to work full time on the project. I have to thank Neville Nankivell, editor of the *Post*, and Don Rumball, its business editor, for giving me both the time and encouragement to undertake the venture. Most of all I have to thank my publisher, Nick Harris, for seeing the topicality of the project and making the financial act of faith to support my efforts. Among others at Collins, particular thanks are due to Michael Worek, my editor, for his encouragement and assistance, and to Margaret Paull.

I spent the first half of 1979 in Calgary, and my thanks are due to a number of cherished friends and colleagues who both provided assistance and made my hard-working stay a very pleasant one. In particular, I would like to thank Richard Osler, the *Financial Post's* Calgary editor, and his wife Cathy; John Howse, the business editor of the *Calgary Herald*, and Inger, Kimmie, Kari, Joseph and Jason Howse; Tom Kennedy, the *Globe & Mail's* Calgary correspondent, and his wife Mary; Stan Roberts, Andrew Brown, Mike Voelcker, Ed Cott, Dave Yager, Suzie Kurtz and Delton Campbell. In Toronto, special thanks goes to Norm Frazer for his help and encouragement, Robert Robinson for his inspiration, and Jane Cottrell for her unselfish help and understanding.

My thanks are due to a large number of others whom I refrain from mentioning either because they appear in the text or else because they have requested that their assistance go unsung.

A great deal of this book is based on personal interviews with the people who appear in it. They were, in general, both generous with their time and open with their opinions. I hope they are not too offended with the results of their co-operation.

8   I have made extensive use of articles from the *Financial Post* and the Toronto *Globe and Mail,* as well as a large number of government documents, annual reports and company releases. My thanks are particularly due to the staff of the *Financial Post* library for their help in locating many of these. The following is a brief list of books that I found particularly useful in proving both information and inspiration:

Anthony Sampson, *The Seven Sisters* (New York, Viking, 1975).

Philip Smith, *The Treasure Seekers* (Toronto, Macmillan, 1978)

Robert Engler, *The Brotherhood of Oil* (Chicago, University of Chicago Press, 1977)

Earle Gray, *The Great Canadian Oil Patch* (Toronto, Maclean-Hunter 1970)

Earle Gray, *Super Pipe* (Toronto, Griffin House, 1978)

Donald Peacock, *People, Peregrines and Arctic Pipelines* (Vancouver, J. J. Douglas, 1977)

Peter C. Newman, *The Canadian Establishment* (Toronto, McClelland and Stewart, 1975)

Bob Considine, *Larger Than Life. A biography of the remarkable Dr. Armand Hammer* (London, W. H. Allen, 1975)

Allan Hustak, *Peter Lougheed* (Toronto, McClelland and Stewart, 1979)

Oil in the Seventies. Essays in Energy Policy (Vancouver, The Fraser Institute, 1977)

Our Industry Petroleum (London, British Petroleum Company, 1977)

The Big Tough Expensive Job, ed. James Laxer and Anne Martin (Toronto, Press Porcepic, 1976)

Foreword

In June of 1978, Sheik Ahmed Zaki Yamani, the Saudi Arabian oil minister and one of the most powerful men in world oil, addressed the Canadian Society of Petroleum Geologists in Calgary. He delivered a scholarly economic dissertation projecting a short term world oversupply of oil that could exert a downward pressure on prices into the early 1980's. Within a year, the average official oil price had increased by more than 50%.

If a man who is not only a great authority on oil but also one of the protagonists in setting its price can be so overtaken by events, then mere observers of the petroleum scene should obviously approach the topic with great care and humility.

The end of the decade seems an appropriate time for an assessment of Canadian petroleum in the light of profound changes in the control of international oil in the 1970's. However, neither the Canadian industry nor the politics of energy seems to show any desire to stand still for a snapshot.

My aim has been to trace how the momentous events in world petroleum — from the first "OPEC crisis" of the winter of 1973-74 to the Iranian revolution and the further disruptions of the first half of 1979 — have had a profound effect in Canada on much more than the price we pay for gasoline. I have, as briefly as possible, attempted to outline the evolution of the Canadian oil industry and of federal oil policy. This sets the scene for Alberta's struggle for — and success in winning — many of the financial fruits of the OPEC crisis.

I have outlined the problems of big oil in Canada in the past decade, both in terms of corporate strategy and political acceptability, concluding that although they may be little loved, they are still, at least statistically, the lords of Canadian oil.

Most of all, I have tried to recount the amazing ascendency in the 1970's of Canadian petroleum entrepreneurs — from the most

10   financially oriented to the most politically aware — in an industry previously dominated by the international oil companies.

This book is not intended to be a comprehensive review of the Canadian petroleum industry. Many large companies have received barely a mention while producers less than one-tenth their size have received considerable attention. This is because, at a time of great change, I am attempting to outline where things are going rather than where they are now. I have concentrated on companies like Alberta Gas Trunk Line, Dome Petroleum and federally-owned PetroCanada because of their initiative and because they are the shape of things to come. In looking at the major oil companies I have attempted to emphasise their all-too-human character rather than clinically dissecting their vast operations. In looking at Alberta, I have attempted to provide some insight into the people involved in politics, business and money.

Rather than writing separate sections on the important topics of Canada's petroleum supply situation and its prospects, I have interwoven details and projections where they fit into the corporate and personal stories told. For example, the importance of the tar sands belongs with the major oil companies. The significance of Canada's abundant gas supplies and the complexities of the highly-politicized gas pipeline business belong with the entrepreneurs who have made the major finds in recent years and with the Canadians who now dominate the gas transmission business.

P.W.F.
Toronto, September, 1979

Introduction

Early in May, 1979, the shirtsleeved dealers in Geneva who carry out the bulk of trading on the world oil "spot market" found their telephones overheating. The market was going mad. Spot-market oil, accounting for about 10% of world production, is any oil not under contract to the major companies. Its price is a sensitive indicator of the balance of world supply and demand. In the final two weeks of May and the first week of June a dramatic movement in price showed that there had been a major change in that delicate balance. The spot price of oil doubled to almost $40 US a barrel. The unseen commodity in which the traders dealt — huge tanker-loads of oil, many of them already steaming across the world's oceans — were changing hands at an unprecedented rate. Fever-ish bidding on behalf of desperate countries, most notably South Africa and Israel, which had been boycotted by the Arabs, was adding millions of dollars to the value of these cargoes within a few nautical miles.

The prime cause of all this activity lay three thousand miles to the east of Geneva, in Iran, where a revolution had caused a sharp cutback in oil exports. This cutback not only manifested itself in a rocketing spot-market oil price, it also demonstrated itself four thousand miles west of Geneva, in the gasoline stations of the United States.

As the Geneva dealers tried to talk on four telephones at once, Canadians on the other side of the globe watched televised reports of their brethren south of the border losing their tempers as they lined up for gasoline. The substance that fueled the North American dream was, once again, turning it into a nightmare. Reports of shootings in American gas stations sent a shudder through the umbilical cord that links Canadians with their automobiles.

For the second time in six years, OPEC had sent mighty tremors down the San Andreas fault of world economic growth. However, both the significance and the impact of OPEC price increases go far beyond an enormous inflation in the world's most important energy source. What they mean is that the world's most powerful fuel has been turned into its most potent economic weapon. For Canadians, that thought is, not surprisingly, a frightening one. But perhaps more frightening is the realization that petroleum has been used as a political weapon not only by the distant and dimly-understood nations of OPEC. It has been wielded within the boundaries of Canada.

The global shift in the control of oil from its consumers, represented by the major oil companies, to its producers, the nations of OPEC, has been perfectly mirrored within Canada. Here, there has been an enormous shift of both economic wealth and political power to Canada's major producing province, Alberta, from the federal government and the consuming provinces of the East. It represents the most significant turnabout in political relationships since the birth of Confederation.

There are no statues in Calgary to Sheik Yamani, but it is ultimately to the Saudi Arabian oil minister, the brains behind OPEC, that Alberta owes most of the fabulous increase in both wealth and power that the 1970's brought it. OPEC's actions, under Yamani's guidance, have been termed blackmail by a petroleum-hooked world that literally runs on oil. Yet Peter Lougheed, the iron-willed Premier of Alberta, and the whole Canadian oil industry have clearly aligned themselves with Yamani. In the autumn of 1979, despite a fourfold increase in domestic oil prices within five years to $13.75 a barrel, Lougheed and most Albertans claimed that they were "subsidizing" the rest of Canada by not charging the full world price.

The fruits of Alberta's uncompromising attitude are more than obvious today. As it moves into the 1980's, it is the richest province in Confederation. Revenues from oil and gas are flowing into provincial coffers at the astonishing rate of more than $6,000 a minute, and it has $5 billion accumulated in a rapidly growing savings account, the Heritage Fund, that it literally does not know how to employ. More individual multi-millionaires have been created by Alberta's oil boom than at any time or in any place in Canadian history. But the truly astonishing fact is that the boom in the 1980's promises, or more appropriately threatens, to be even bigger. The source of all this wealth lies in the movement of Canadian domestic oil and gas prices towards world levels, and yet by the end of the 1970's Albertan prices were further below OPEC prices than at any time during the decade. By mid 1979, although Albertan oil was selling for four times its level at the beginning of the decade, it was still more than $10 below the world price. That, inevitably, was where it was heading.

The price of oil in Canada has to move towards world levels as a matter of economic necessity, since the country still imports very sizable volumes of petroleum. The cost of these imports is subsidized by the federal government. The $10 by which Albertan oil is cheaper than imports is the same amount Ottawa has to pay importers to bring imported oil down to domestic levels. In the wake of the Iranian crisis it was becoming an intolerable burden. Thus, in the fall of 1979, the new federal Conservative Government was having to think about a faster acceleration towards world price levels than their Liberal predecessors. Nobody was arguing about the necessity of that movement. The issue, as it had been since OPEC first struck in the fall of 1973, was: who gets the fruits of higher domestic oil prices? Is it reasonable that one part of a country should press the assertion of its constitutional "rights" under quite unforseen circumstances to a degree which threatens the whole economic and political well-being of the country? Just how much right does Peter Lougheed have to behave like the bluest of blue-eyed Sheiks?

Alberta can claim similarity to Saudi Arabia in a number of ways. The Albertans, like the Saudis, produce far more petroleum than they can consume themselves — almost 90% of Canada's oil and gas; like the Arabs, they "export" most of it from their provincial jurisdiction; and finally, just like the Arabs, they have reaped a bonanza from the enormous petroleum price increases since the winter of 1973-1974.

In the summer of 1978, Lougheed seemed to receive the ultimate accolade, a visit from the Mephistophelean Yamani himself. Lougheed did not adopt the burnous, but as the two men walked together through the Syncrude tar sands plant or were seen entering dinners with their wives, they seemed very much to be speaking as one sheik to another.

But there are in fact considerable differences in their positions. Indeed, Yamani, despite being at the root of the greatest threat to world postwar economic growth, seems in many ways far more "reasonable" than his Albertan counterpart.

In a unique way, Yamani has adopted the twin roles of Islamic Satan and saviour to the world economy. On the one hand, the quadrupling of world oil prices he helped bring about at the end of 1973 and the beginning of 1974, and the further increases he has presided over since, have been seen as a cardinal sin against the western world's religion of economic growth. At the same time they have been praised as necessary, indeed essential, douches of cold common sense to an energy-hooked world headed for disaster.

The ambivalent attitude towards Yamani has arisen from basic contradictions within the system itself. Economic growth has been treated as the highest good, and yet it has become increasingly obvious that economic growth fueled by finite supplies of cheap petroleum cannot go on forever. OPEC's actions have caused a very necessary, if painful, reassessment.

Yamani thus can preach the doctrine of conservation for the "good" of the whole world. Lougheed, by contrast merely wants to establish the much less exalted creed of provincial ownership. The Albertan premier can indeed claim constitutional control over the province's resources, but that status does not appear as unassailable as that of the Saudis, who can claim their vast oil reserves as a legacy from Allah. Lougheed's somewhat more recent constitutional status has become increasingly resented as he has used it as a bludgeon. Indeed, Lougheed has never claimed exalted objectives in his fight for the spoils of higher oil prices. His actions have been dictated by the, for him, valid goal of asserting provincial rights within Canada. By the end of the decade, it was not so much that such a goal looked short-sighted, rather that it seemed now to have been more than adequately achieved. Moving into the 1980's, the creed was beginning to look more like greed.

The discrepancy in the relative wealth of the provinces has obviously always been a source of resentment. Ontario, with its industrial "golden triangle", the commercial might of Toronto and the political power of Ottawa, have been the natural focus for this resentment throughout most of the twentieth century. Now, however, the focus has shifted west, and the Heritage Fund provides a bullseye target.

The fund, based on Alberta's petroleum revenue, is like some horrendous gasoline pump with dials clocking up $2,000 a minute. It is projected to grow to $10 billion by 1983 and $35 billion by 1990. More and more, it is becoming the focus of squabbling within the province and jealousy from outside. Many prominent Albertans regard it as a dangerous tool in the hands of the provincial government, even a Conservative one, and accuse Edmonton of mismanagement. Eastern energy consumers increasingly regard it as a rip-off, while Ottawa sees it as the symbol of a dangerous shift of economic power to the West.

Few Albertan oilmen acknowledge Sheik Yamani as their ultimate benefactor since it is not the nature of businessmen to dwell on the ultimate political causes of any set of economic circumstances. For the red-blooded entrepreneur, it is taking advantage of the circumstances that is his driving imperative. Albertan businessmen have seized the opportunities presented by the OPEC crisis and Peter Lougheed's intransigence with both hands.

Petroleum has always been a boom-and-bust business, but OPEC has changed things. It has made Alberta a boom-and-boom province, and Calgary is the huge but roughly finished gem in the province's towering business crown. Calgary has pursued the business of petroleum intermittently throughout this century and

virtually fulltime for the past thirty years since the find at Leduc
near Edmonton heralded the modern age of Canadian petroleum. Nothing has changed about the essential orientation of the business. Calgary is still a permanent base camp for an enormous hunt, where hundreds of companies send out thousands of expeditionary parties every year in pursuit of their elusive petroleum prey. But what has changed, and changed forever, is the importance of the prey and the financial rewards for tracking it down.

Calgary as a physical entity has been almost completely swamped by the boom of the past five years. Now Canada's fastest growing city, it appears like some no-expense-spared rush job to construct a huge metropolis from scratch. Anything architecturally pre-OPEC looks either sadly out-of-date or like a valuable relic. The mansions of Calgary's Mount Royal and the down-home cosiness of 17th Avenue's credit unions, animal hospitals and funeral parlours —although far from old — provide an almost stately contrast to the frenetic building and business activity going on ten blocks away.

There, deals are spun off at great speed, like atoms at the heart of a nuclear reactor. Indeed, "downtown core" in this context seems peculiarly appropriate. However, beneath all this surface wheeling and dealing, Calgary is a city of dreams. Geologists, whose minds are like time machines roaming the pre-historic earth, dream of striking the motherload of petroleum; empire builders see their corporate ambitions outlined by their minds eye on the panelled walls of plush-carpeted boardrooms; entrepreneurial carpetbaggers dream of the big killing. They come in all shapes and sizes, and from all sorts of backgrounds — tough farmboys from Saskatchewan, canny little Scotsmen, urban Dutchmen in velvet waistcoats, charming Frenchmen, big, enveloping Americans — to seek their fortune. It does not take them long to become Calgarians because being a Calgarian is not a matter of geographical origin, it is a state of mind.

For those with the right state of mind, the required total commitment, and just a little luck, the rewards have been great. Multimillionaires abound in Calgary. There are possibly more per capita than in any other town in Canada. However, what is most significant is that the majority of them have achieved that status in the past decade, and many of them in the latter half of the 1970's.

But the OPEC crisis has brought about far more than an enormous transfer of power and wealth to the province and businessmen of Alberta. It has also produced great changes within the Canadian petroleum industry. The past decade has seen an inevitable fall from political grace by the multi-national oil companies that previously ruled Canadian oil. In statistical terms, foreigners still control more than three-quarters of Canada's oil industry, but a significant part of the initiative in new energy schemes has now moved back to Canada.

Two men, so different in personality but so similar in corporate drive, have spearheaded this move: Jack Gallagher, the uniquely persuasive and charming chairman of Dome Petroleum, and Bob Blair, the dour and aggressive president of Alberta Gas Trunk Line. Significantly, both are based in Alberta. As empire-builders, they rank head and shoulders above even Calgary's dynamic business elite. Gallagher is in many ways an outstanding example of the classic old-time promoter, a man with a petroleum dream seeking funds to pursue it. What makes him unique is his skill in promoting that dream. Blair, however, appears like a whole new evolutionary form within the corporate jungle. Supremely entrepreneurial and yet with a much broader perspective on business than merely the "bottom line" of profits, his national, and nationalistic, approach to energy matters is undoubtedly the one for the times in Canada.

This book is about Blair, Gallagher, Lougheed and the other individuals that have either helped shape, or taken advantage of, the revolutionary changes in Canada's post-OPEC petroleum scene.

PART ONE

Petroleum and Politics: And the Last Shall Be First

"The problem of the energy crisis is in the end a problem of political power. The two meanings of the word "power" — the power of energy and the power of politics — are coming much closer together."

ANTHONY SAMPSON

"Who holds not his foe away from the cistern with sword and spear, it is broken and spoiled: Who uses not roughness him shall men wrong."

THE MUALLAQAT, VI

1 | OPEC and the World—The Genie Becomes the Master

In the wake of the OPEC crisis, a nagging question shot around the world. It ran down every pipeline, into every giant tanker, into every automobile and jet aircraft, into every home with an oil-based heating system: did we control oil, or did oil control us?

The substance that provided both the battleground and the weapon for the revolutionary changes of the 1970's is the richest and most powerful of nature's hidden treasures, petroleum.

Petroleum is like a genie. Hunched in infinite blackness, often miles below the surface of the earth, it offers both wealth and power to those who can release it by pricking its cage of rock. But the beast is strangely formed and strangely found. Its creation is still not fully understood. However, the genie's bounty, quite literally, fuels the modern world.

Without this peculiar substance, which appears at the surface of the earth in a range of forms from a heavy liquid to a gas, most means of transportation would grind to a halt, production machinery would stop, and a ghastly chill would come into our cosy, centrally-heated lives. If religion was once the emotional opiate of the masses, so, now, the entire developed world is economically hooked on petroleum. The OPEC crisis of 1973-1974 first brought home the terrible vulnerability of our situation, but did little to change it. That became readily apparent during the summer of 1979.

The genie petroleum, like the genies of the Arabian Nights, is often unpredictable. Moreover, although it can bestow great economic and political power, it can also overwhelm a weak master. In the wake of the OPEC crisis, a nagging question shot around the world. It ran down every pipeline, into every giant tanker, into every automobile and jet aircraft, into every home with an oil-based heating system: did we control oil, or did oil control us?

By the 19th century, oil seeps in various forms had been used for many thousands of years. Asphalt and pitch had been used as a binding and embalming material in Biblical times. Moses' burning bush was quite probably a gas seep that had somehow been ignited, as was the "eternal flame" at the Delphic Oracle. The Chinese were piping natural gas (in bamboo) a thousand years before Christ was born.

But the modern oil age was first heralded, literally, by a flickering flame. Despite the rapid development of industrialization through steam, dependable lighting was still a problem in the mid 19th century. Another key requirement of the time was lubrication for the proliferation of machinery. Light was provided by candles and by smelly and smoky lamps fueled by whale oil. Lubrication also came from whale oil and from other equally objectionable fish, animal and vegetable oils. Captain Ahab in Herman Melville's *Moby Dick* may well have been a vengeful character at the centre of a religious parable. But he was also, somewhat more mundanely, a key part of the 19th century's lighting and lubricating business!

Pioneer work by a Canadian, Dr. Abraham Gesner, into turning both coal and asphalt into illuminating oils paved the way for an explosion in the development of processes for distilling and refining oil products.

Once a use had been found for oil, the search began to find more of it. This peculiar substance began to develop an obsessive grip on the minds of men. An explosive increase in the search, and a tightening of the grip, came with the invention of the internal combustion engine and, later, with the advent of air travel. Oil also became increasingly used in industry. The 20th century was to become the great age of petroleum.

But if petroleum was to prove among the most useful of the earth's mineral treasures, a cornucopia of enormous technological potential, its essential unpredictability also sometimes proved an economic nightmare.

Whereas man's search for metals and the coal to fuel the industrial revolution had taken him burrowing beneath the ground like an animal, tunneling beneath millions of tons of threatening rock to bring out his prize, petroleum was quite different. Once the genie had been found, it came to its new master, often in great abundance. Needless to say, with uncertain markets and only rudimentary transportation systems, a big oil strike sometimes caused financial chaos.

In the earliest days of the oil industry in the northeastern United States and southwestern Ontario, and later as the industry moved to the giant finds in Texas that made the U.S. for many years the world's greatest oil producer, oil's development was marked by enormous fluctuations in price. These occurred as new discoveries appeared and, sometimes literally, flooded the market. In the 1860's in Ontario, for example, discoveries caused the price of oil to fall from $11 a barrel to 40¢ a barrel in a matter of months. Whatever the benefits of free enterprise economics, under a free market system, oil was capable of wreaking havoc.

It was John D. Rockefeller who established himself as oil's first master before the turn of the century. Rockefeller saw oil as a commodity of enormous commercial value, but troublesome because its supply depended on unpredictable "strikes". He felt that if he controlled transportation and refining, he could impose some order to the terrible disorder that free markets implied for a product with such unpredictable supply patterns.

But Rockefeller's business tactics, and the ultimate size of his empire, did not appeal to the free enterprise economic philosophy of the United States, and opposition sparked the antitrust movement and the disbanding of the Standard Oil Trust that had become his flagship.

Nevertheless, it was the "children" of John D. Rockefeller — most notably Exxon, Mobil and Standard Oil of California — in concert with two other American companies, Gulf and Texaco, and two European companies, Shell and British Petroleum, that were to carry out Rockefeller's plan to "tame" oil for the first 70 years of the 20th century. These "Seven Sisters", as the major oil companies came to be called, ringed the globe in their search for oil and markets. They found abundant supplies, built giant, efficient marketing networks and held down the price to consumers. It was the fruits of their efforts that enabled petroleum, in its various forms, to stimulate the growth of the 20th century. By the end of the 1970's, they were the most hated and distrusted companies on earth. During that decade, the genie petroleum made the Seven Sisters its slave, and proved that petroleum was not the servant of oil-consuming nations, it was their master.

World oil production and use doubled every ten years from 1880 onwards, but by 1960, the absolute figures were growing enormous. In that year, more than one billion tonnes of crude oil was produced. By 1970, the world was producing 2.3 billion tonnes, or 47.8 million barrels every day. Yet, surprisingly, few people seemed to question whether that sort of growth could go on forever.

Perhaps the other astonishing fact about oil was that the price of a barrel of crude oil in 1970, at $1.80, was about the same as it had been in the 1920's, and much less than it had been in the 1860's when the price of Pennsylvania crude was $9.59 a barrel.

For the first 90 years of the modern petroleum age, from 1860 to 1950, the United States dominated world production. In 1950, the United States produced one half of the world's oil. Her production continued to grow for another 20 years, but other huge sources of oil were also being found around the world, most notably among the Arab nations of the Middle East. By 1965, the Middle East as a whole had overtaken the United States as an oil producer. However, even in 1970, the United States was still the world's single largest oil producing country. But then, as the 1970's opened, United States domestic oil production peaked. Suddenly, the giant of the world economy developed an overwhelming thirst for imported oil. The stage was set for a momentous change.

The abundance of new oil finds throughout the world in the 1950's and 1960's led to a complacency among consumers. But in late 1973 they were to relearn a lesson revealed in the Arabian Nights and taught to the earliest oil explorers: releasing genies from either bottles or oil reservoirs can prove a highly dangerous act.

The Roots of the OPEC Crisis

The Canadian government was not one but two steps removed from the events that led to the OPEC crisis of 1973-1974 and the profound change in the control of the world's oil that it brought. Even the mighty United States found itself one step removed. The reason national governments found these events so hard to control was that the crisis was not essentially a confrontation between oil producing and consuming countries, but between the producing countries and the major oil companies. The rivalry of these companies, said British author Anthony Sampson in his brilliant book *The Seven Sisters*, "had been a long subplot to modern history, financing whole nations, fueling wars, developing deserts".

All of the seven, Exxon, Shell, British Petroleum, Texaco, Gulf, Mobil and Standard Oil of California (Socal), had major subsidiaries in Canada, and it was mainly through these subsidiaries that Canada received the hefty imports it needed for the eastern markets of Quebec and the Maritimes. Hence the Canadian government's two step removal. It was not responsible for buying oil from overseas. Neither, in most cases, were Canada's largest, foreign-owned, oil companies. It was their parents who were mainly responsible for pushing oil Canada's way.

As long as the world had a surplus of oil, as it had throughout the 1950's and the 1960's, this arrangement worked well, because the major companies represented the interests of the consumer. They may have formed a giant cartel, but, at least, the cartel was on our side, with the objective of building up supplies while holding down prices.

A long chain of events led up to the OPEC crisis, but perhaps the critical starting point was the year 1960. In that year, Exxon forced down the world price of oil, OPEC* was created, and Canada's

---

* The Organization of Petroleum Exporting Countries had five founding members: Saudi Arabia, Iran, Iraq, Kuwait and Venezuela.

government, under John Diefenbaker, announced the country's first real oil policy. Both the creation of OPEC and Canada's decision to continue to rely heavily on imports into eastern Canada, despite the abundance of supplies in the West, were related to the low world prices Exxon was enforcing. OPEC was created to oppose these bargain basement prices. The Canadian national oil policy was, at least partially, formulated to take advantage of them.

It seems more than ironic today that the creation of OPEC was in response to *falling* prices. However, a measure of the producing countries' lack of power at that time was that the oil companies completely ignored the Organization and continued to deal with its members separately. Playing off one against the other, "punishing" those who — like dusky Oliver Twists — asked for more, and acting in secret concert, the major oil companies showed a seemingly impregnable united front.

The majors retained the whip hand throughout the 1960's. When Israel invaded Egypt in 1967, the Arabs imposed an embargo, the first real attempt to use oil as a weapon. But the embargo failed because of lack of unity among producers. In fact, the Shah used the embargo as an opportunity to increase Iranian output to pay for his own expensive and grandiose plans.

Although this attempt failed to win higher prices it should have provided a little *memento mori* for the Sisters, reminding them that their vast commercial empires rested on the shifting sands of increasing Arab nationalism and militancy. The cloud on the horizon, no bigger than an oil minister's hand, was a forthcoming storm that would spread from the desert all over the world.

The first critical showdown over oil control came in Libya, by this time an OPEC member, in 1969. In the late 1960's, Libya had leaped to stardom in the world supply scene. Its oil was of high quality and it was very close to major west European markets, whose oil-thirsty economies were just a short hop across the Mediterranean. By 1969, Libya was supplying one-quarter of total European needs. Then, suddenly, a coup in the country sent a collective shiver of anticipation down consumers' backs. The new ruler of Libya was a fanatic revolutionary, Colonel Muamer Qaddafi. Worse, he was intent on using oil as a weapon against Israel. The company he decided to push for higher prices was not one of the Seven Sisters but the fast growing independent, Los Angeles-based Occidental Petroleum. Much of Occidental's meteoric growth had been due to its success in Libya, founded on the concessions won there by its head, the "remarkable" Dr. Armand Hammer.*

---

* Reviewing Hammer's biography, the *New York Times Book Review* described him as: ". . . a character so versatile and unbelievable that most writers of topical-events fiction would be embarrassed to put him in a novel."

Hammer, who was to appear briefly on the Canadian scene in 1977 and 1978 with abortive bids for Bridger Petroleum and Husky Oil, was, and indeed still is, a man of many talents.* Part statesman, part buccaneer, part art connoisseur, he did not even enter the oil business until he was in his 50's. As a shrewd businessman and an inveterate globetrotter, he soon found himself very much at home in the world of multinational oil. He charmed Libya's ruler, King Idris, into giving him concessions in 1966, much to the chagrin of the Sisters, and then proceeded to make mammoth strikes. Soon, "Oxy" oil was all over Europe.

However, the Sisters' concern over Hammer was not just that he was a competitor. It was also that he was vulnerable. Since he was overwhelmingly dependent on Libyan oil, he couldn't play the Sisters' favorite game of shifting supply sources around in order to quell restless natives. Following the revolution in 1969, Qaddafi set about putting the majors' worst fears into reality demanding more money from Occidental. Hammer turned to the biggest of the sisters, Exxon, for help; but Exxon's head, Ken Jamieson, a Canadian from Medicine Hat, Alberta, wouldn't give him the favorable terms he wanted. In the end, Hammer had to capitulate, agreeing to what seems now like a pathetically small increase, of 30¢ a barrel, with an agreement to pay another 2¢ a barrel annually over the following five years.

However, the capitulation was the pivot in the subsequently rapid shift in power towards OPEC. There was a perceptibly more militant mood at the Organization's meeting in Caracas in late 1970. The oil companies tried to agree on a common front, but failed. With growing confidence, as their oil became more important to world markets and global supply tightened, OPEC acted alone. In February 1971, under the Teheran agreement, it imposed price increases of 30¢ a barrel, rising to 50¢ by 1975. On April 2, 1971, in Libya, the Tripoli agreement was signed, and Libya gained even more favorable terms from the fifteen multinationals operating there. With the Teheran and Tripoli agreements, the majors seemed to have suffered a major defeat. But of course, the world had seen nothing yet. Over the following two and a half years the rout gathered momentum. Producing nations, flexing their newfound muscles, began to demand participation in the profits earned from their oil; the world oil glut of the sixties was rapidly turning into a shortage as the United States' production peaked and its massive demand for oil became the major factor in world markets. Meanwhile, the Arab-Israeli crisis was steadily worsening.

---

* Occidental has a Canadian subsidiary, Canadian Occidental Petroleum Ltd., which is 82% owned through Oxy subsidiary Hooker Chemical Corp.

By the autumn of 1973, the stage was set for another major confrontation. In September, world market prices for oil had, for the first time, risen above "posted prices", an extremely significant event. Posted prices had first been published in the Middle East in the early 1950's. Their chief significance had been as the notional prices on which the producing countries' taxes and royalties were set. They were deliberately fixed at an "artificially" high level, and had little relevance to real oil market transactions. They had, in fact, about as much significance as a price tag in a casbah — if such a thing can be imagined. They were armslength prices, but oil is not an armslength business. Actual prices depend on constant under-the-counter bargaining between the producers and the companies. Until 1973 the companies had long held the advantage in any bargaining. However, the movement of the market price above the posted price meant the proverbial boot had just decisively switched feet.

OPEC "invited" the companies to join them on October 8, 1973, to discuss a "substantial increase" in the price of oil. Just before the meeting, Egypt and Syria invaded Israel. Arab militancy was running high when the two sides met in Vienna. The OPEC side was led by the oil ministers of Saudi Arabia and Iran, Sheik Yamani and Jamshid Amouzegar. Yamani began by asking for a doubling of the price, to $6 a barrel. George Piercy, the Exxon engineer who led the five-man company delegation, offered a 15% increase. Yamani came down to $5 but Piercy had no mandate to go beyond 25%. A price rise of the magnitude put forward by Yamani would have profound economic consequences and could not be countenanced without government consultation. For once, the oil companies acknowledged that oil was a far too important matter to be left to them alone. The negotiations were called off as the company men asked for a two week postponment.

With the middle east war still raging, the Organization of Arab Petroleum Exporting Countries, OAPEC, the Arab group within OPEC, began openly to discuss using oil as a weapon of war. Shortly afterwards OAPEC met in Kuwait and decided unilaterally to raise the price to $5.12 a barrel, a 70% increase. But worse was to come. On the second day of their meeting, they decided to impose a production cut of 5% monthly until Israel withdrew from what they considered to be Arab lands. At the same time, the Saudi foreign minister was in Washington delivering a similar message. Shortly after the Kuwait meeting, Saudi Arabia announced a 10% production cutback and a total embargo on oil shipments to the United States and the Netherlands.

It is still uncertain how far the oil price increase and the embargo were designed to work together, but whatever the intention, their impact was devastating. The embargo, in what was already a shortage situation, forced market prices higher and higher. Nobody really understood what was happening. On December 16, an auction of "spot" oil in Iran fetched a price of $17 a barrel. The climax followed a few days later in Teheran.

The attitude of the Shah of Iran — a man as overweaning when he had the whip hand as he has subsequently proved spineless in defeat — indicated the completeness of the OPEC victory. With an intellectual conversion that only the promise of wealth can bring, the Shah had become the world's greatest conservationist almost overnight. He did not just talk about wasting oil. He pontificated about it.

In speech that, in the light of subsequent events, would rank as a classic example of "hubris" in a Greek drama, the pride that cometh before a fall, the Shah said: "Eventually all those children of well-to-do families who have plenty to eat at every meal, who have their own cars, and who act almost as terrorists and throw bombs here and there, will have to rethink all these privileges of the advanced industrial world. And they will have to work harder . . ."*

At the Teheran meeting there was a fundamental conflict between the grab-as-much-as-possible approach of the Shah and the more moderate approach of Sheik Yamani. However, it was not big enough to split the OPEC ranks, and although the Shah had originally wanted $14 a barrel, the eventual imposition of a price of $11.65 — to take effect from January 1, 1974 — was still seen as a victory of Iranian militancy over Saudi "moderation".

The world economy had just received its most unwanted Christmas present ever. The price of oil had quadrupled in just three months, and there had been a decisive shift of control away from the giant oil companies and toward oil exporting nations.

---

* *Middle East Economic Survey*, Dec. 28, 1973.

2 | Canada and the U.S. Sticking It to Uncle Sam

The events of the winter of 1973-74 enabled Can-
ada, at least briefly, to acquire more than nui-
sance value. It achieved this by its decision to
charge the U.S. world prices for its Canadian oil.
Canada, for just a brief while, was able to push
the realization that it really was a separate
country into the great egocentricity that is the
U.S. national consciousness.

When the history of the 20th century is written, that massive
shift of power will stand as perhaps the great watershed in global
economic relations in our time. Within a matter of months, control
of the world's most important source of energy had passed from its
greatest consumers, represented by the major oil companies, to its
largest exporters, the nations of the Organization of Petroleum Exporting Countries. The very conspicuous evidence of that shift was
a quadrupling of its price.

The huge interconnected world marketing system built by the
Seven Sisters meant the result of that momentous change quickly
found its way into every pipeline and storage tank in the world.
The flow of petroleum down pipelines was suddenly matched by
an enormous increase in wealth and power flowing in the opposite
direction. In Canada, all pipelines led to Alberta.

The discovery of the Leduc field, 18 miles southwest of Edmonton, in 1947, marked the beginning of Canada's rise as a significant
oil producer. Between that discovery and the beginning of the
1970's, Albertan producers had one overwhelming problem with
their oil: nobody wanted to buy it.

Alberta's involvement with oil goes back before the turn of the
century. Periodic bouts of excitement had swept through the
streets of Calgary as the Turner Valley, west of the city, had un-
veiled a series of discoveries, but production nowhere near kept
pace with the growing petroleum demands of Canada's economic
development. That situation changed dramatically in the late
1940's and throughout the 1950's.

In 1947, domestic production, almost all of it in Alberta, provided only 10% of Canadian needs. The overwhelming majority of imports came from Venezuela and, ironically, from the United States. In 1947, more than 10 years had gone by without a significant find. Imperial had drilled 133 consecutive dry holes when, in a mood of virtual desperation, it stumbled across the gusher at Leduc.

In 1947, Canadian oil had provided only 19,500 of the 211,000 barrels a day used by Canadian refineries. By 1957, shipments to refineries had increased threefold, to 654,000 barrels a day, but the Canadian element had increased almost twenty-fold to 347,500 barrels a day. Imports still provided almost half Canada's oil, but this was highly desired, because imports were cheaper than domestic oil. Over the same decade, Venezuelan oil came to dominate the import market and American imports were gradually phased out.

The discovery of Albertan oil effectively led to the division of Canada into two energy halves. The west could now easily supply all the western provinces, but for the east, imported oil remained preferable because it was cheaper. In order to find markets for its oil production, Alberta looked to the United States. Pipelines were built to take Alberta's oil to market. One steel ribbon went west and replaced Californian oil in the British Columbian market and also supplied oil to the northwest United States. Another main artery went east, to Regina and then on to Sarnia, Ontario. It was in the Ontario market that Albertan oil met the challenge of cheap foreign competition. Alberta's markets in the United States were subject to the same challenge.

A National Oil Policy Is Born

Towards the end of the 1950's, Albertan oil producers clamoured for the federal government to protect them against cheap imported oil. Their concerns perfectly mirrored those of domestic producers south of the border who were not among the charmed circle of the Seven Sisters. John Diefenbaker's Conservative government had come to power in 1957, and he had appointed a Toronto businessman, Henry Borden, to look into Canada's energy situation. One of the main issues to which the Borden Inquiry addressed itself was how far domestic Canadian markets should be reserved for "expensive" Albertan oil.

The five American Sisters south of the border were disliked by other domestic oil producers because they were responsible for producing and importing cheap foreign oil. The situation in Canada was very similar. Canada's largest oil companies were mainly subsidiaries of the Seven Sisters. They were also the biggest producers of Alberta crude.

However, they had little desire to push Albertan crude into eastern markets. Their interests were fundamentally different from
those of the native Albertan producers because the predominant
part of their business was not producing oil, it was refining and
marketing it. Their refineries, mostly in the Montreal region, were
provided with cheap foreign crude funnelled to them through their
huge multi-national parents. Their interests were not sinister, they
were purely commercial. They didn't care where their crude came
from, as long as it was cheap. Albertan oil wasn't cheap.

Native Albertan producers, on the other hand, wanted secure
markets, and they realized that the only hope of a large secure
market was eastern Canada. Securing those markets, however,
would require a federal government decision to limit the import of
cheap foreign oil. A loose coalition of Albertan independent producers approached Ottawa and suggested that the cost of Albertan
oil in eastern markets could be brought down by reducing the wellhead price and constructing a more efficient pipeline than the existing Interprovincial line from Alberta to Ontario. However, even
with these changes, an import tariff on imported oil was still felt to
be necessary to make Albertan oil competitive in Montreal. There
would, also, of course, have to be a new pipeline built to carry the
oil east beyond Toronto.

For Borden, the imposition of a tariff would have presented a
problem. A tariff would not have made Albertan oil more competitive, rather it would have made imported oil less competitive by increasing the price to all consumers.

Some of the big oil companies stated flatly that they would not
take Albertan oil in their Montreal refineries, but in the end it was
the interests of the eastern consumer that prevailed over the demands of the western producer. Canadian oil would not be
pumped into Montreal.

Nevertheless, the Albertan producer did receive a major conces-
sion. Borden recommended that oil imports should be restricted,
but that the barrier should not be an economic one. Rather, the
Commission said, it should be a physical limit to foreign oil's pene-
tration into Canada. Thus an artificial commercial barrier was
erected along the Ottawa Valley, the so-called Ottawa Valley Line.
All markets west of this line, said Borden, should be reserved for
Albertan oil. Borden also said, however, that Albertan producers
should aggressively pursue new markets in the United States. He
suggested that the replacement of foreign oil in the Ontario market, plus new exports, should enable Albertan producers to
achieve output of 700,000 barrels a day by 1960.

In 1960, the same year in which OPEC was formed to stop the
Seven Sisters forcing world oil prices any lower, the Diefenbaker
government introduced its national oil policy. Setting a further
production target of 800,000 barrels a day by 1963, George Hees,

the Cabinet Minister responsible for the policy, pointed out that this target was in fact as high as if a pipeline had been extended to Montreal. Most of Alberta's independent producers were pacified.

Indeed, it is worth pointing out, since Alberta today is fond of painting its economic history as one of being an underdog to eastern interests, that from 1960 onwards, consumers in Ontario were forced by the federal government to pay higher prices for their oil than their Quebec neighbours, who enjoyed cheap imports. They paid these higher prices so that Alberta might have a market. This effective and real subsidy by Ontario consumers tends to be conveniently forgotten today both by the Albertan government and its oil industry, which persist in the claim that they are "subsidizing" the rest of Canada by not charging the same price as OPEC.

The Diefenbaker government's national oil policy undoubtedly facilitated the growth of Canadian production, although most of the growth went into exports. Between 1959 and 1968, while domestic use of Canadian oil showed a respectable increase from 415,000 barrels a day to 615,000 barrels a day, exports shot ahead from 92,000 barrels a day to a massive 457,000 barrels a day. Nevertheless, the growth of these markets still did not keep pace with the western industry's continued success in finding oil. By 1968 Alberta had well over 600,000 barrels a day of shut-in capacity. Moreover, this was almost exactly the level of imported oil into eastern Canada at the time.

Once again, in 1969, representatives of the Canadian producers, who by now had organized themselves into the Independent Canadian Petroleum Association, went to Ottawa to ask the federal government to make more of the Canadian market available to them by further limiting cheap imports. The four-man IPAC delegation was led by Carl O. Nickle, founder of *Nickle's Daily Oil Bulletin*, former federal Member of Parliament, art connoisseur, oil expert, wheeler-dealer and outspoken proponent of the western oil business.

In the late 1950's, the independents had suggested a completely new line into Montreal. Now they were recommending a more modest extension of the Interprovincial line from Sarnia to supply 150,000 to 200,000 barrels a day to Montreal by the fall of 1970. In what seems, with 20-20 hindsight, like a sweepingly accurate indictment of Canadian energy policy at the time, IPAC's brief said: "Canada is the only nation capable of self-sufficiency which gives only limited priority to domestic oil; permits a drain of hundreds of millions of dollars for overseas oil; leaves half the nation totally dependent on overseas supplies, thus ignoring the problem of security in emergencies; and leaves it to another nation — the United States — to provide the lion's share of market growth for a Canadian resource."

However, the government told IPAC that Venezuela had to be protected as a source, that the Canadian industry's oil was just too expensive, and that it should concentrate its efforts on selling to the American midwest. In so many subsequently highly-embarrassing words, the still relatively new and shining Trudeau Liberal government — embodiment of Gallic logic and rational decision making — was saying: "Go sell your oil elsewhere. We don't want it, or need it."

Ultimately, IPAC's motivation was self-interest, but subsequently events were to prove that self-interest can sometimes be extremely prescient.

Since the early 1950's, the federal government had considered the United States the appropriate place for Alberta to sell a great deal of her oil. Borden spoke of Canada's exemption from United States oil import controls in the late 1950's as possibly "the first step leading towards the development of a continental policy with respect to crude oil . . . we feel that care should be taken to ensure that Canada, by its actions and commitments now, does not jeopardize the subsequent possible development of such a policy."

That thinking had dominated Canadian energy policy for a decade. Petroleum was treated as being no different from wood or nickle or zinc. It was just a commodity. The only difference was that there usually seemed to be too much of it.

That situation was soon to change. Throughout the 1950's and 1960's, the balance of world oil production had gradually shifted from the United States to the nations that were to form OPEC. In 1950, the United States provided half world production. In 1960, it provided one third, and in 1970 one-fifth. Then, in 1972, United States production peaked. Its demand for oil, however, did not.

Uncle Sam Develops a Massive Thirst

The first nation to feel the impact of that tremendous thirst for oil that could no longer be supplied from within was not Saudi Arabia, or Iran or Libya. It was Canada. At the beginning of the 1970's, a time of distinctly blunt American economic policies and a resurgence of the concept of "fortress America", President Nixon had imposed tariffs on Canadian oil. However, the import duty was soon removed as American demand began to greatly outdistance domestic supplies. Then the United States began to grab all the Canadian oil it could get.

1972 was a record year for the Albertan industry. Following the easing of American import controls, Canadian exports to the United States leaped to a million barrels a day, up 22% vs the previous year, as total Canadian production rose to 1.85 million barrels a day. But, by early 1973, bombarded by constant news about the American energy shortage and faced by a pronounced firming of prices, more and more questions were being asked about a Canadian "sell-out".

Energy rapidly became the focal point for long pent-up feelings about United States "domination", based on American ownership of Canadian industry and on the fact that two thirds of Canada's merchandise trade was with the United States. At its best, this relationship was seen as a symbiosis in which we needed them far more than they needed us — a feeling that is never good for the national ego. Now Canada was being portrayed as the frightened beaver on the back of a hungry tiger. The United States hadn't been giving the country a lift, it had just been carrying around its lunch!

Energy was a particularly good focal point for nationalistic resentments. As a raw material, oil fitted into the "hewers of wood and drawers of water syndrome". Although in 1973 only a little over a fifth of exports to the United States were raw materials, the feeling prevailed that Canada's industrial sophistication was being held back by its role in serving the raw material needs of the Americans. Also, 90% of the Canadian oil industry was controlled by foreigners, overwhelmingly by the major United States oil companies like Exxon, Gulf, Texaco, Mobil, Socal and Amoco. The cry "economic colonialism" resounded as it had never done before.

However, perhaps the greatest irony, and the greatest irritant to Canadian nationalist feelings, was that the vast majority of Americans remained blissfully ignorant of these sentiments. Most Americans, insofar as they bothered to consider their northern neighbour at all, thought of Canadian resources as part of the great North American weal, freely available for their use. As James McKie, professor of economics at the University of Texas, said: "The U.S. treated energy policy towards Canada almost abstractedly — a very odd approach in view of the fact that Canada was its second largest supplier and a much more important one at the time than the Middle East countries with which its policymakers were preoccupied."*

If there was a growing mutual suspicion between the United States and Canada, it was, as in all their relationships, a lopsided affair. Canada's suspicion bordered on paranoia. For the United States it was a slight nagging in its peripheral vision.

What caused the greatest suspicion in Canada was that, at the beginning of the 1970's, the predominantly American controlled oil industry had told the government that Canada had enough oil and gas to last well into the next century. It was on this assumption that the very same companies were allowed to ship unprecedented

---

* "United States and Canadian Energy Policy," *Oil in the Seventies. Essays in Energy Policy* (Vancouver, The Fraser Institute, 1977).

amounts of oil over the border, making Canada by 1972 second only to Venezuela as a source of United States imported oil. As the fateful winter of 1972-1973 approached, the murmur of suspicion that Canada had been duped grew to a roar.

Following the October 1972 election, the New Democratic Party had held the balance of power in Ottawa while the minority Liberal government attempted to rule. The NDP, most notably through its strident energy critic Tommy Douglas, had expressed increasing concern about a "sell out" on energy, and the events of 1972 and 1973 were providing plenty of ammunition for the attack.

Late in 1972, the National Energy Board produced a dramatic warning in its projections for Canadian supply and demand, stating that Canadian production would not be able to cope with potential domestic and export markets after 1973. In early 1973, Liberal energy minister Donald Macdonald, the brilliant but blunt lawyer — nicknamed "The Thumper" because of his tendency to pound on table tops —who was shortly to find himself at the eye of both Canada-United States and federal-provincial hurricanes, mentioned the possibility of legislation to ensure "domestic priority" for supplies, and in March imposed export controls. Oil was still flowing south at well over 1 million barrels a day, so Macdonald's move did not even rank as bolting the stable door. Rather it amounted to closing the door just enough so that the horse could only squeeze through! Nevertheless, the move was treated by Alberta's Premier Lougheed as a "flagrant breach of faith" — an indication of the bad feelings to come.

The events of the winter of 1973-1974 enabled Canada, at least briefly, to acquire more than nuisance value. It achieved this by its decision to charge the United States world prices for Canadian oil. Canada, for just a brief while, was able to push the realization that it really was a separate country into the great egocentricity that is the American national consciousness. South of the border, the issue became highly emotionally charged. Here were the Canadians, virtually blood relatives, allowed to live quietly — but well —in the American attic all these years. And now, suddenly, they were turning around and financially screwing their best friend and ally. How could the Canadian people be so ungrateful!

A vote of censure on Canada was moved in Congress. "Highly-placed", but unnamed, officials of the Washington administration were quoted in the *Financial Post* as saying —"more in sadness than anger" — "we just can't rely on Canada any more".

Macdonald, never one to be reticent when he thought someone with whom he was negotiating had things all wrong, headed for Washington to disabuse his opposite number, United States Energy Secretary Bill Simon, of the idea that Canada was "exploiting" the United States.

Macdonald pointed out quite simply that Canada had major import requirements as well as export sales. Canada had to pay world prices for its imports, so did it look rational to charge lower prices for its sales to the United States and then subject the Canadian consumer in the East to the cold douche of higher oil prices while effectively subsidizing American consumers?

Simon quickly got the message and publicly came out in support of the Canadian policy, openly contradicting the hard line being taken by the U.S. State Department.

The remainder of Macdonald's message presumably did not come as good news to the United States. It was that Canada, under the changed global energy situation, could not be expected any more to "roll out the barrel". Macdonald told Simon that Canada would, among other things, be phasing itself out of the oil export business completely within 10-15 years; that the United States should not expect a massive development of the Athabasca tar sands and that any such development would be geared to Canadian needs only; that gas exports too were destined to become much more expensive; and that the United States could expect to continue to pay world prices for Canadian oil.

The message said that the Canadian energy ship was in sound condition, but it just wasn't big enough to take the floundering American economy on board.

This was a completely logical stance from a political point of view, but there is no doubt that a great many Canadians took a more or less concealed delight in declaring "We're all right Sam!".

In American eyes, Canada seemed to have lined up with OPEC. Canadians had become the "blue-eyed Arabs". But things north of the border weren't quite that simple. In terms of its oil trade, Canada was both beneficiary and victim of the OPEC crisis. Beneficiary because, in the early 1970's, it was exporting huge amounts of oil to the United States. Victim, because it also imported large amounts of oil for its eastern markets. However, the decision had now been made to phase out exports. That meant that domestic supplies assumed much greater importance.

3 | Alberta and Ottawa: Settling Old Scores

"The east is used to us Westerners coming to them on bended knees. Now we are holding the high cards in terms of energy and we plan to use them."

As far as the Albertan-centred Canadian oil industry was concerned, cheap foreign imports into Eastern Canada had, for more than twenty years, been the reason why they could not "crack the market" to a greater degree. After the quadrupling of prices, Albertan oil suddenly looked far more attractive in the east, not only for price but also for security reasons. The implications were not lost on the Albertans. Albertan producers, who had often felt a little unwanted by the eastern consumer, suddenly found themselves in great demand. This about-face was a typical example of the dramatic change in relationships between oil producers and consumers that was going on throughout the world.

The oil producers of OPEC had for too long been meek. Now, in true Sermon-on-the-Mount fashion, they had inherited the earth. It was their turn to hold the whip, intellectually armed with the impregnable doctrine of conservation. Alberta, too, suddenly saw its chance. Feeling too-long ignored by consumer vote-conscious Ottawa, looked down upon by the financial community's Toronto-Montreal axis, and discriminated against by the East's grip over national transportation, the province suddenly realized that its time had come. The aspirations and accumulated resentments of Alberta stood embodied in one man, the recently-elected Provincial Premier, Peter Lougheed. His ensuing fight with Ottawa was to prove one of the most bitter in the history of confederation.

For the Albertan oil industry, which had emerged over 25 years as a significant factor in the whole North American market, OPEC's actions, from a purely economic point of view, looked like wonderful news. A quadrupling of the price meant that the industry's oil reserves in the ground were suddenly worth four times as much! What's more, these reserves weren't beneath the sands of some unstable sheikdom. They were beneath the soil of good, solid

36   Alberta. Also, with national security suddenly a top priority, the companies could be sure that their production would now receive priority. Things, however, weren't going to be quite that straightforward.

From an American point of view, all Canadians in 1974 were blue-eyed Arabs, but within Canada, there was a struggle going on as to just who was the *more* Arab.

The Albertan tribe, responsible for producing almost 90% of the country's oil and gas, was quite prepared to accept the slur of being blue-eyed Arabs, along with the burden of the great wealth that it implied. But the Ottawa tribe, which some said ruled this disparate land, wanted a goodly share of both blame and wealth for themselves. In the winter of 1973, both tribes mounted their camels and prepared to do battle.

Peter Lougheed: An Image Looking for a Cause

The Albertans were led by a relatively new sheik, Peter Lougheed, a man who had enjoyed a meteoric rise to stardom. Within a few short years he had revived the moribund provincial Conservatives and, in August 1971, snatched power from a Social Credit party that had controlled Alberta for 36 years.

The political roots of Lougheed's rise to power could partly be traced to the movement of Albertans away from the land and to the growth of a strong middle class within the province. But also, following the retirement of Ernest Manning, Social Credit's bible-thumping leader, the lines of age had begun to show severely on his party. It was time for a change — not so much a radical change of policies, but rather a change of image. Lougheed, a young, good-looking lawyer, was the man for the times.

Until the OPEC crisis, Lougheed was, to a degree, an image looking for a cause. He found that cause in the dispute with Ottawa over just who had the right to the enormous windfall benefits that the OPEC struggle brought. The bitter battle with Prime Minister Trudeau's federal Liberal government tempered Lougheed into the iron man of federal-provincial politics.

It remains uncertain just how much of Alberta's modern-day wealth can be attributed to Lougheed's trenchant bargaining stance. The OPEC crisis, by quadrupling oil prices, would have made the province much richer whoever had been in power, but his intransigence has led to him being inseparably linked with the province's fortune. In the eyes of many Albertans, it is Lougheed who has made the province the wealthiest and fastest growing in Canada.

As a student, the young Lougheed proved to be not brilliant, but assiduous. At the University of Alberta, where he studied law, his main love seems to have been sport, but he also was very active in student affairs and developed a close knit group of friends. This seemingly constant need to have a "team", of which he is the undisputed captain, has led to charges of "croneyism" by those outside Lougheed's charmed circle.

He briefly ran back punts for the newly-formed Edmonton Eskimoes football team and then went to Harvard, where he earned an MBA. When he returned to Alberta he joined the Mannix Corporation, one of the West's largest, most inaccessible, privately-owned companies — a giant group controlling assets of close to half a billion dollars in the construction, coal, pipeline and oil business. He left Mannix as a vice-president and director in 1962 to move into private legal practice with Marvin McDill and John Ballem.*

Then politics began to interest Lougheed. In 1965 he thought long and hard about entering the federal political scene, but was eventually persuaded to try and revive the ailing provincial Conservative Party after its strong-willed leader, Calgary lawyer Milton Harradance (nicknamed Milton Arrogance) stepped down. Following his election to the party leadership, Lougheed began to set about building a machine that could challenge the Socreds.

Social Credit had been in power in Alberta for as long as most people could remember. It had its roots in agricultural populism and religious fundamentalism, concepts that by the late 1960's were, to say the least, looking tired. The party had risen to power under William Aberhart, an outstanding showman and a firm believer in the Bible. During campaigns, Aberhart's party would stage horse races at country fairs. There would be a Liberal horse, a Conservative horse and a Social Credit horse, and somehow, the Social Credit horse would always come from behind to win. The message was blunt, but it worked. The good work (and the Good Book) was upheld by Aberhart's successor, Ernest Manning, who combined shrewd political judgment with regular doses of fire and brimstone over the radio.

Lougheed was both more secular and more technically advanced. His bible was Theodore White's *Making of the President 1960*, the book about John F. Kennedy's rise to power. His chosen battlefield was television. While Ernest Manning was still delivering his "Back to the Bible" sermons every week on the radio, Lougheed was working in the television studio, brushing up on his electronic sincerity in order to deliver a more worldly message. To provide funds, the Lougheed Club was formed by personal invitation only with 150 members, each of whom paid $100 annually.

In the 1967 election, the Progressive Conservatives put up a creditable performance, returning six members to the provincial legislature. Lougheed won Calgary West with the largest majority of any member in the election, and became official leader of the opposition.

---

* Ballem, in his spare time, writes "racy" novels in which topical subjects, like native rights and the Beaufort Sea are mixed up with liberal helpings of sex and violence.

In the late 1960's, Lougheed's most powerful line of attack, somewhat ironically in the light of subsequent events, was the uncertain nature of the oil industry and the Socreds failure to diversify into a more industrialized and secure economy. The irony lies not only in Alberta's subsequent unprecedented oil boom but in the fact that Lougheed himself has found diversification an elusive aim. The oil industry has been expanding at such a rate that, despite massive expenditures in petrochemicals, there just isn't "room" in the economy to accommodate much diversification.

At the time, however, weight was added to Lougheed's claims by a pull-out of the major oil companies from Alberta. Their departure was inspired by the giant oil discovery in 1968 at Prudhoe Bay off the north coast of Alaska. The oil industry thought that the 1970's would be the decade of the "frontiers", specifically the Arctic Islands, the Mackenzie Delta and the Beaufort Sea, along with the east and west coasts. It looked as if Alberta's brief blossoming as the focus of the Canadian oil industry might be drawing to a close. All the signs were there. Wildcat drilling, that is, high risk exploration away from known existing oil deposits, fell by 40% between 1969 and 1971, while the province's share of exploration expenditures dropped from three quarters of the Canadian total in 1966 to little more than a half by 1970.

Lougheed never seemed to trust the big oil companies, perhaps surprising since his own elder brother, Don, was a member of the upper echelon of the largest of them all, Imperial Oil. His objection was the politically obvious one that their interests were not the interests of Alberta. They could pull up and move out any time prospects looked better elsewhere. However, he did promise incentives to the smaller, independent Canadian-owned and run companies, who had for years struggled to eke out an existence in the shadows of the foreign-controlled giants.

The big oil companies began to sense a basic hostility in Lougheed that worried them. Shortly before the election, Lougheed invited Arne Nielsen — who had achieved hero status by becoming the first Canadian to head up a subsidiary of one of the major oil companies, Mobil, and was then also chairman of the Canadian Petroleum Association — to lunch at the Ranchmans Club, the wood-panelled home of Calgary's "old" money. Why, Lougheed wanted to know, weren't the oil companies coming through with campaign contributions? Nielsen, a squat, square-shouldered little man with the looks of a benign troglodyte, was a little embarrassed. He pointed out that this was obviously an issue for each company to decide, but then, deciding to be quite frank, he pointed out that the industry was quite happy with the government it had already! "But of course," Nielsen subsequently told the author, "we never suspected that he was going to win."

Indeed, the industry did have every reason to be contented with Social Credit. Manning strongly believed in consultation before

making any moves in oil. The royalty system, the government's
basic "take" from oil production, was reviewed only once every
ten years, and Manning saw the provincial government's role as
basically providing a stable political background and letting the industry get on with it. In Manning's view, what was good for the industry, and that, essentially, meant the foreign-controlled industry, was good for Alberta.

As the 1971 election approached, however, it was not oil but
rather social issues that dominated Lougheed's precision-run campaign. The basis of Lougheed's attack was a Federal study, "Social
Futures: 1970-2005", in which a bleak outlook was painted for the
West.

Rather than control of oil, the really pressing question seemed to
be, what do we do when the oil runs out?

Meanwhile the Socreds were showing signs of advanced decay.
Manning, a man who had made an entire career out of being Premier of Alberta, retired in 1967, leaving Harry Strom, a gentleman
farmer, to take his place. Strom possessed all the good, honest
qualities associated with his profession, but his essentially goofy
appearance was no match for the much-practised Lougheed when
it came to television. Lougheed was now beginning to wear the
province's television sets like a comfortable old glove.

While Strom puttered around the province in the Stromobile,
Lougheed's team descended on towns like a blitzkrieg. The wily
old Manning knew what the problem was. He had perhaps once
seen Lougheed as a successor to himself in a Social Credit party revived by amalgamation with the Conservatives. But now he attacked Lougheed's "Madison Avenue Glamour Boy Image", with
all the implications of Sodom and Gommorah that such an image
held.

But it was no use.

NOW, boomed the Conservative slogan; and now was the time.
The shift of economic power from the countryside to the towns had
taken place with the growth of the urban middle class, eighteen-
year-olds had the vote, and to both of these groups, Lougheed
seemed like the knight in shining pin-stripe suit that the province
needed.

On the night of August 30, 1971, the old order changed. Mounting bedlam reigned at the Conservatives' party headquarters at the
Westgate Hotel in Calgary as it became clear that the party had
done it, and done it convincingly, taking 49 seats to Social Credit's
25. Somewhat belatedly by 20th century standards, the cathode ray
tube had finally conquered the Bible in Alberta. Form had perhaps
had as much to do with Lougheed's victory as substance, but the
image was soon to be bolstered by the oil crisis. Within three years,
Lougheed would establish himself as a true political heavyweight,
and, in doing so, give the oil companies the fright of their lives!

Almost immediately after the election, it became clear that on ergy was going to be the battleground on which Lougheed would fight the case for Albertan self-assertiveness. OPEC was to provide the great clash, but the skirmishes began at once.

Energy Becomes the Battleground

Speaking to the National Press Club in Ottawa in November 1971, Lougheed demanded a greater say in national energy policy and an observer status at negotiations on oil and gas trade between Canada and the United States. "If Alberta poker chips are involved at the poker table," he declared, "we will be at that table." The federal government had other ideas. Cabinet Minister Jean-Luc Pepin stated bluntly that Lougheed's demands were out of the question. Lougheed, the federal Liberals felt, was overstepping the mark. The provinces did have undisputed ownership of their natural resources, but jurisdiction over that ownership passed to the Federal government once those products moved over the provincial border. Exports to the United States were thus none of Lougheed's business. To prove the point, the National Energy Board, the independent body set up in 1960 to licence and oversee exports, overruled the decision by its provincial counterpart, the Alberta Energy Resources Conservation Board, to allow another $1 billion-worth of gas exports.

Back in Alberta, however, Lougheed was able to assert himself, and he determined to correct the imbalance he saw in the share the province was getting from the sale of its oil and gas. He set about this first by reviewing the royalty arrangements with the industry, and second by determining to haul up the price of the gas Alberta sold to the East through the TransCanada PipeLine. Both the oil companies and Ontario, by far the largest user of Alberta gas, began to shift uneasily in their seats. Lougheed's government carried out legislative hearings in which royalties were reviewed, and ordered an inquiry into what was a "fair" price for the province's gas.

In July 1972, the Conservatives told the industry that they could have a choice — "between a rock and a hard place", one senior executive said at the time — between a royalty increase from 16-2/3% to 21% or a tax on reserves in the ground. However, there were incentives in the scheme under which exploration expenditures could be written off against the new royalties. Although the industry, predictably, set up the usual bleating chorus of complaint, the imposition was, within a couple of years, to look like an extremely mild one.

Lougheed eventually managed to negotiate the gas price upwards by threatening to cut off supplies to the East. Premier Davis of Ontario was obviously deeply concerned at the impact on inflation that his fellow Conservative premier was trying to impose. At least, he couldn't afford to be seen to be unconcerned, so in January, 1973 he flew to Alberta to make a visit that obviously carried great significance for Lougheed. Said the Albertan Premier: "The east is used to us Westerners coming to them on bended knees. Now we are holding the high cards in terms of energy and we plan to use them."

These ominous words were the prelude to the critical card game the province was going to sit down and play with the federal government — a card game in which OPEC's actions suddenly quadrupled the size of the pot.

But in early 1973, few people in Canada realized the immense forces building up in the world market for oil.

When Imperial had announced a wellhead price increase of 40¢ a barrel in August, 1973, there had been an uproar. The increase brought the total rise in the price of Canadian oil over the previous nine months to 95¢ a barrel, or a massive 32%. The federal government had still not clearly worked out what its price policy should be. But then nobody was aware what was going to happen to prices before the end of the year. In September, however, Pierre Trudeau foreshadowed a major policy change, announcing that the federal government would now be seeking to put Albertan oil into Montreal, and called for a crash study of an oil pipeline extension from Sarnia. This was inspired not by any sudden conversion to the long-stated arguments of Alberta's independent producers, but rather was due to the realization that if world prices were in for further increases, Ottawa was in a much better position to keep down the price of Albertan crude than that from Venezuela or the Middle East. Suddenly, with United States prices soaring and the realization of Trudeau's motives, the independent producers weren't all that keen to put their oil into Montreal any more!

By this time, the government had started to rethink its policy on exports to the United States, although they were still running at over a million barrels a day. The crucial question was: just what price should be charged for the exports? Macdonald and his policy team decided that it had to be the "world market" price, as he pointed out to United States Energy Secretary Simon, since that was what Canada was having to pay for her imports.

The Alberta government would have had every reason to be delighted with this decision, indicating as it did significantly higher revenues, but for one thing. Donald Macdonald met Alberta Energy Minister Bill Dickie in Ottawa on September 13, 1973, and told him that the federal government would be taking the entire increase via an export levy of 40¢ a barrel.

The Gloves Come Off

When Dickie returned to Edmonton and told the Premier, Lougheed hit the roof. In a speech to the Calgary Chamber of

Commerce the following day, Lougheed called the export levy "the most discriminatory action ever taken by a federal government against a particular province in the entire history of confederation . . . Jobs, both existing and future, are in jeopardy in Alberta today . . . We have to try to protect the Alberta public interest — not from the Canadian public interest — but from Central and Eastern Canadian domination of the West."

Donald Macdonald dismissed the Lougheed comments as an "overreaction". The following Monday, Lougheed made a speech to the cheering natives of Taber, Alberta, telling them that he did not intend to "step back from any confrontation."

Going into that fateful December, the flak hadn't even started. On December 6, Pierre Trudeau got up in the House to announce a new oil policy. Bouyed by thunderous applause from his party and assaulted with derision from the opposition benches, Trudeau announced plans for the creation of a new national petroleum corporation — the very idea of which caused wood panelling to curl off the wall at the Petroleum Club — an oil pipeline to Montreal, the abolition of the Ottawa Valley Line, federal funds for oil sands research, and Ottawa's approval of the Mackenzie Valley pipeline to bring gas from Prudhoe Bay via the Mackenzie Delta, where it would pick up Canadian gas on the way.

Trudeau, however, also threw down the gauntlet to Lougheed, declaring: "We do not think it equitable or fair that surplus profits return solely to the provinces producing oil. In the government's opinion, the whole country should take benefit from any windfall profits."

Meanwhile, however, ominous bumper stickers were appearing in the West. "Let the Eastern Bastards Freeze in the Dark." They were, of course, disavowed by Lougheed, but nevertheless, they were a straw in the growing political wind.

In January, 1974 there was a meeting of federal and provincial energy representatives in Ottawa. Macdonald outlined a policy of longer term self-sufficiency within Canada; domestic prices tracking, but not necessarily catching up to, international levels; and a gas price moving up in line with oil. He suggested that oil prices could not move up more than $2, to about $6, over the following year without damaging the economy.

But the problem was, who would get the extra $2. Macdonald suggested a formula under which half the increase would go towards subsidizing imports and the remainder would be split between the provincial governments, the producing companies, and Ottawa.

But that was not the sort of arrangement Lougheed had in mind. It was Alberta's oil and Alberta should therefore take most of the increase. Failing to agree on the split, the meeting broke up and any increase was delayed for two months. On March 27, 1974, the First Ministers met and a domestic oil price increase of $2.40, to $6.50 a barrel, was announced.

For Ottawa, the fear of Alberta grabbing a large chunk of the increase was not inspired purely by feelings of federal equity and national unity. They were also deeply concerned about the impact on the "equalization" payments made to the have-not provinces to prevent too great a discrepancy between the provinces' economic status. If the producing provinces grabbed a major chunk of the oil price increase, their greater wealth would force Ottawa to give more to the have-nots in order to equalize their status. However, the very act by producing provinces of grabbing a larger royalty, since royalties were deductible from federal taxes, meant that Ottawa's taxing potential was reduced. Ottawa's obligation to the have-not provinces would far outweigh any extra taxes it might take from only marginally higher producing company incomes. A big grab by Alberta would thus be extremely costly to the federal government, but a big grab was just what Alberta made.

The province announced that it would cream off 65% of the increased domestic oil price, a royalty rate three times the existing level. Alberta's reasoning was that if the oil companies had been functioning with an oil price of $2.85 a barrel before world prices had gone berserk, they certainly didn't need a great deal more to make them happy now.

Ottawa, however, just couldn't bare to see that tax revenue disappear, especially if they had to make higher equalization payments. At first, Finance Minister John Turner attempted a little financial sleight-of-hand, suggesting that the amounts collected from higher royalties were in some way different from other provincial income and thus should be ignored for purposes of equalization. That however, didn't appear too plausible.

The oil companies, by this time, were understandably jittery, and they had every right to be. Like their American parents, around the end of February, 1974, they announced embarrassingly high profits for the final quarter of 1973. Those of Gulf Canada were up 89% vs the same quarter of 1972, those of Imperial up by 59%, Petrofina's up by 82%, Shell Canada's up by 87% and Texaco's up by 41%. There was little use in their pointing out that increases in, say, the pulp and paper industry were running much higher, or that their own return on equity was still relatively low. No, in the public mind, the major oil companies were all part of the great conspiracy.

On May 6, 1974, in the Federal Budget, John Turner dropped his bombshell. The new higher provincial royalties would be non-deductible for federal tax purposes. Ottawa was going to pretend that they didn't exist. Whereas companies would effectively receive 35¢ from each extra dollar of oil production after Lougheed had taken his 65%, the federal government was going to tax the company as if it had received the whole dollar.

The gloves were now really off between the federal and provincial governments, but they were demonstrating their punching power not on each other but on a hapless, though far from disin-

terested third party, the oil producer. The industry was not completely powerless, for it did have one, negative, form of action at its
disposal. It did what anyone else would have done in the situation.
It ran. Voting with its drilling rigs it headed, in the best western
fashion, for the border. In fact, the budget was not immediately
passed, for the NDP withdrew their support from the Liberals,
who then called a general election. Throughout the summer of
1974, however, the thought that the Liberals would reintroduce the
budget if re-elected hung like a cloud over the industry. On June 5,
1974, Trudeau found himself jeered at on a visit to Calgary.

The Liberals were re-elected on July 8 and on November 18, 1974
Turner brought out another budget, still containing the non-
deductibility provisions. However, by this time both the provincial
and the federal governments realized that there was little use in
fighting over something that was not there. Oil companies had
slashed their exploration budgets. Signs of a pull-back emerged on
both the federal and provincial sides. The easing-off went so far
that it was to herald the golden age of the Canadian oil industry.

The industry needed it. In the final nine months of 1974 stock
markets had witnessed a bloodbath. Western oil shares dipped by
a dismal 54%, while major oil companies' shares fell by 40%, helping to drag the whole index down 27%. The new Turner budget,
although it retained the non-deductibility provision, made a
number of significant concessions. Turner then deftly lobbed the
ball into the fuming Lougheed's court, saying: "We have done our
part. Now I appeal to the provinces, which have a responsibility to
these industries and the Canadian people, to do their part." That
night, Lougheed stared, square jawed, out of the province's television screens and declared the budget; "the biggest rip-off of any
province in Canada's history."

The war of words was reaching its peak. Don Getty, the tall,
handsome ex-football star Minister of Intergovernmental Relations — the Clint Eastwood of Western politics in both looks and
ideology — spoke of "outright battle . . . with every weapon at
our command."

Donald Macdonald called Lougheed "vicious" and Getty "drip-
ping with venom". However, Turner had done his public relations
job well. Opinion now said the time for concessions had come, and
on December 12, Lougheed produced a lavish birthday present to
producers in the shape of his "Alberta Petroleum Exploration
Plan." Although he still reasserted the province's jurisdiction over
setting prices, he announced a scheme to hand companies back
some of the funds taken because of the Federal Budget's non-
deductibility. He also gave every company a $1 million tax credit;
cut the marginal royalty rate on gas; increased drilling incentives;
and promised to bring down the marginal royalty rate on further
oil price increases from 65% to 50%.

Said Lougheed: "The aggregate effect of the Alberta Petroleum
Exploration Plan of December 1974, according to our assessment, is
approximately double the positive impact for the petroleum industry as compared with the changes made by the Federal Government in its November 18th Budget from its May 6th budget."

Anything you can do, Lougheed said to Ottawa, we can do better. The industry, so recently pounded from both provincial and
federal sides, now reeled under the gifts being showered upon it!

The temperature between Edmonton and Ottawa now returned
to a more normal level, although resentments had been ingrained
that would last throughout certain politicians' lives.

Almost immediately Alberta and the Federal government, along
with Ontario, had to act in concert to save the giant Syncrude tar
sands project when one of the partners, Atlantic Richfield, pulled
out because of lack of funds. Donald Macdonald described the
partners' relationship as "cordial" as they clubbed together to inject more than $600 million into the ailing project.

In February, 1975, Lougheed called a snap election and won a
landslide victory, which he regarded as a mandate to continue to
seek higher prices. However, by April it was Pierre Trudeau who
was indicating the need for higher domestic prices. In June, 1975
the Canadian oil price was hoisted from $6.50 to $8.00 a barrel,
while, perhaps more significantly, the gas price was raised to 97¢, a
quadruple increase over an eighteen months period.

"Our assessment", Lougheed told the Provincial Legislature, "is
that there has been very significant progress in the continuing negotiation between Ottawa and Alberta on energy matters. The petroleum industry at last has a sense of stability."

As far as the industry was concerned however, things looked a
good deal better than just "stable", and were to become better still.
By the middle of 1979, the price of gas had more than doubled once
again, the domestic price of oil had, with a small hiccup, reached
$13.75, an increase of 72%. Over those few years, the Canadian oil
industry had witnessed the greatest boom in its history. The stock
market had soared, profits had gone through the roof, takeover activity had reached unprecedented levels, and an almost incredible
number of multi-millionaires had been created overnight.

PART TWO

Petroleum and Corporate Power: Big Oil's Troubled Decade

"I don't have a whole lot of faith in what the oil companies say."
JAY ROCKEFELLER, GREAT GRANDSON OF
JOHN D. ROCKEFELLER

4 | Big Oil in Canada

Like the subtle climatic changes that signalled the end of the dinosaurs on earth, what happened in the first half of the 1970's marked a turning point for those large and previously self-confident creatures, the multi-national oil companies.

The names on the gas stations haven't changed. Canadian motorists from sea to shining sea still fill up beneath the symbols of Shell, Imperial/Esso, Texaco or Gulf. However, for the huge, foreign-controlled empires that extend like corporate icebergs beneath this "visible" part of the oil business, the 1970's was a decade of unprecedented turbulence.

In numerical terms, the "big four" still dominate the Canadian oil industry. They produce more than 40% of Canada's oil and gas, and control more than 60% of its refining capacity and retail outlets. They will likely continue to hold a commanding position for many years to come, and will direct the development of most of Canada's tar sands and heavy oil, resources that will be increasingly needed as Canada moves into the twenty-first century. How, then, has their position dramatically changed? The answer lies in their increasingly shaky political standing and in the increasing regulation of their activities.

Like the subtle climatic changes that signalled the end of the dinosaurs on earth, what happened in the first half of the 1970's marked a turning point for those large and previously self-confident creatures, the multi-national oil companies. Like the dinosaurs, the end will not be immediate, indeed there may not be an end at all. There will always be the chance to evolve. For those who do not wish to evolve, or cannot, then the alternative, rather than extinction, may be to sell out. One thing, however, is certain: the Canadian subsidiaries of the major oil companies are now operating in a more political environment than ever before.

Quite apart from political acceptability, the big oil companies have been buffeted in purely business terms over the past decade. On the one hand, the key element of their exploration strategy as they moved into the 1970's, searching for massive oil and gas reserves in the far north and off the east and west coasts of Canada, proved to be a disappointment. On the other, the impact of higher prices on demand led to a fight at the gas pumps and elsewhere in the market for refined products.

Suspicions Develop: How Much Oil and Gas?

Until the late 1960's, the foreign-owned companies, notably the big four, ruled the Canadian industry, both physically and psychologically. With a few notable exceptions, they found, and held, most of the oil; they refined and marketed virtually all of it. The independent, Canadian-owned companies scrambled in the shadows of the major oil companies' drilling rigs and came, cap-in-hand, to sell oil to the majors' refineries.

As well as producing most of the oil, and exporting a good deal of it south of the border, the majors also were responsible for procuring Canadian imports. They did this by buying cheap oil from their giant multi-national parents, who scoured the globe searching for low-cost sources of supply. Thus they inextricably linked Canada to the well organized world marketing system set up over the preceding fifty years by the multi-national oil companies. Eastern consumers liked cheap foreign oil and didn't care where it originated. In fact, few, if any, stopped to consider that it was foreign oil.

The engineers and geologists who had struggled up the hard promotional route to head the Toronto offices of the big four in Canadian oil looked at the world through businessmen's eyes. They spent their days concentrating on efficient administration of the huge corporate machines under their control, on eyeing their competitors' business strategies to make sure they did not increase their market share, and in planning for new sources of long-term crude oil supplies. Meanwhile, the head offices in New York, or Pittsburgh or London kept a constant watch on their budgets, their return on investment, and on management's performance to make sure that the Canadian companies fitted in with the parents' plans.

However, even before the OPEC crisis, forces were already at work that were to make it increasingly unacceptable to Canadians that the management of their most crucial energy source should be carried out by foreigners who saw Canadian oil only as a part of their global plan to maximize profits. Without realizing it, Canada's foreign-owned major oil companies were heading into choppy political waters for several years before OPEC made fully-fledged corporate villains of their parents.

Throughout the early 1970's, the feeling was growing in Canada
that the United States had been exploiting Canada's oil and gas resources with a bland disregard for Canada's welfare. The major
targets of the criticism were the subsidiaries of the Seven Sisters,
whose names were everywhere on the service stations and on the
tanker trucks: Imperial, Texaco and Gulf. Despite Shell's European
heritage, she too was lumped in with American interests.

Indeed, there was reason to be suspicious. At the beginning of
the decade, big oil was telling the government, and the government, in turn, was telling the Canadian people, that Canada had
virtually limitless reserves of oil and gas.

In June of 1971, in what rates as one of the most misinformed
statement ever to emerge from the lips of a Cabinet Minister, Energy Minister Joe Greene announced that "at 1970 rates of production, (Canada's) reserves represent 923 years' supply for oil and
392 years for gas."

In 1972, no less weighty a person than Bill Twaites, head of
mighty Imperial Oil, declared: "Canada is not in any way deficient
in energy resources. Our present reserves, using present technology, are sufficient for our requirements for several hundred
years."

Then, within a matter of just a few months, just as world supply
tightened, those reserve estimates were dramatically reduced.
Suddenly, it was not only the ardent economic nationalists who
were crying rape. At the same time, an awareness developed in
Canada, as it was developing throughout the world, that the
country relied on a relatively small number of giant oil companies
for its imported oil. They, in turn, depended on an equally small
but much more unpredictable group of foreign countries for their
supplies.

In the autumn and winter of 1973, the vulnerability of such a position became abundantly clear as the Organization of Petroleum
Exporting Countries cut back supplies, imposed an oil embargo on
the United States, and proceeded to quadruple the price of oil.

The embargo and the price increases were very conspicuous
signs that the majors no longer ruled world oil. That mantle had
passed to the oil producing countries.

However, within a short time it became apparent that, far from
being the losers in such a change of power, the multinational oil
companies seemed to be even better off than before. They turned
out to be richer as the servants of oil than as its masters. For the
OPEC countries, the majors were indispensible as middle men,
merchants who had a global distribution system that could ship the
oil out and the money in. Moreover, as the oil price soared in the
winter of 1973-74 so did the profits of the major oil companies. A
roar of public protest arose. On just whose side were the majors?

However, politics was only half the problem.

In business terms, the Canadian majors were in a different situation from their parents. Whereas Exxon, Shell, Gulf and Texaco seemed to shift with the utmost facility, and profit, from being the masters of OPEC oil to being its willing slaves, the outlook for their Canadian subsidiaries was quite different. Although Imperial, Gulf Canada, Shell Canada and Texaco Canada were major domestic producers, they were even more important as refiners and marketers of crude oil. Most of their capital was tied up in huge refineries and extensive sales networks, to which they devoted the bulk of their attention.

For most of the post-war period, the demand for key refined products, such as gasoline, grew at such a steady rate that the oil companies were lulled into a false sense of security. They based their refinery construction programmes and the growth of their marketing networks on the belief that those growth rates would continue for ever. To earn good profits from refining, since the capital investment is so large, it is always necessary to operate close to maximum capacity. Thus refinery capacity had to be matched closely to prospective demand. OPEC, however, threw a mighty spanner into those neat demand projections. And that was where one of the Canadian majors' principal problems arose in the five years after the OPEC crisis of 1973-1974.

In the late 1960's and early 1970's, the Canadian refiners had also seen opportunities for large exports of refined products to the eastern United States, where environmental problems had stalled the development of sufficient refining capacity. New refineries were built in eastern Canada with a view to grabbing a healthy and profitable share of this market.

Then, suddenly, OPEC came along and blew projections to the winds. Not only was there a decrease in projected rates of demand growth, but, much worse, the Canadian government erected a barrier to refined exports. The majors were horrified. With exports cut off, they had to devote all their attention to the domestic Canadian market, where demand was on the decline. The result was an unprecedented bout of marketing competition that chopped refining profits to the bone. In a desire to keep their highly expensive facilities running at maximum capacity, they slashed their prices in order to maintain or grab more market share.

But the whole strategy was delusive, because they were all doing it. The net effect was that they finished up with a market share very little different than if they had all left prices where they were. All they achieved was drastically reduced profits. In the first half of 1978, the return of capital in most of the refinery business slumped to less than 5%. In other words, the major oil companies would have been better off investing in saving bonds, where they could

have doubled their return and not had to bother about running the 53
refinery!

Due to the long lead times in refinery construction, the industry was also able to see, and dread, huge new capacity coming on stream towards the end of the 1970's. In particular, eastern Canada's refiners lived under the threat of two giant new refineries that started production in 1978, the huge government-backed PetroSar refinery at Sarnia, Ontario, and Texaco's $480 million plant at Nanticoke. Ironically, refiners south of the border were ogling the Texaco refinery in the summer of 1979 because of its huge capacity for producing unleaded gasoline, a product in increasingly short supply in the United States.

From the Canadian motorist's point of view, the need to trim corporate fat in refining and marketing demonstrated itself most clearly in the gradual disappearance of gas stations throughout the decade. In the 1950's and 1960's, filling stations had sprung up like dandelions, staring belligerently at rivals across busy intersections, offering all sorts of free gifts to entice motorists. But the party had gone too far and OPEC worsened the hangover. During the more sober 1970's, about 10,000 filling stations disappeared, leaving around 25,000. Moving into the 1980's, it seemed that rationalization in refining and marketing may have done its job. However, the events of the 1970's had sent a mighty shiver down the gas pumps of big oil.

For the majors, however, the problems were not restricted to the downstream end of the business. They had severe disappointments at the other end of their far-flung empires, in supply.

Exploration: But the Elephants Weren't There

Towards the end of the 1960's and at the beginning of the 1970's, while there was still a relative abundance of cheap foreign oil and the price of gas was languishing at very low levels, the majors all wondered where their longer term domestic Canadian supplies were to come from. Since prices were so low, and the companies were so big, it seemed inevitable that they would have to seek out "elephants", that is, huge deposits of oil or gas, in order to replace their dwindling reserves economically. The only place they thought they could find reserves of this size was Canada's frontier areas, the largely virgin territory offshore of the east and west coasts, in the Arctic Islands and in the MacKenzie Delta and Beaufort Sea.

The potential for the traditional exploration areas of the West, at then prevailing prices, was not great. So, to a greater or lesser extent, the major companies packed their bags and left Alberta to go elephant hunting offshore or in the frozen north.

Buoyed by optimism in the wake of the huge Prudhoe Bay discovery in Alaska in 1968, the majors believed it was only a matter of time before Canada's frontiers produced equally massive finds. But that assessement proved, or at least has proved to date, to be drastically wrong.

This is not, of course, to write off the frontiers for the future. It is just to say that the promised bonanza has not yet materialized. Again, significantly, as the 1970's drew to a close, the one Canadian frontier area that was continuing to generate huge stock market excitement, even if the industry remained a little more skeptical about it, was the Beaufort Sea. There the exploration effort was headed not by one of the majors, as such a massively expensive venture would have been in the past, but by Dome Petroleum. Dome had been greatly helped by selective exploration incentives from the federal government for which the majors could never dare have asked. Meanwhile, in the east coast and the Arctic Islands, it was federally-owned PetroCan that had taken over most exploration.

The failure of the frontiers to turn up the hoped-for massive reserves in the 1970's was a major disappointment to all the big oil companies, but in particular Imperial, which had not only spent $350 million on exploration in the MacKenzie Delta but had also, significantly, given up a great deal of its land in western Canada.

That was to prove to be a massive mistake.

Back Worshipping at King Peter's Throne

The majors' pull-out from Alberta at the end of the 1960's had brought home to Peter Lougheed the province's vulnerability to the corporate whims of big oil. The majors did not particularly like the noises that Lougheed made before he came to office, but then, they never thought that he would come to office. They had been perfectly happy with the Social Credit party, which had made a point, under Ernest Manning, of always consulting them before legislative changes were made.

Lougheed's arrival signalled a whole new approach to the affairs of the oil companies. He immediately set about imposing higher royalty payments. Then, when the OPEC crisis came along, he scrapped that whole new system and proceeded to impose much greater levies on new, higher, domestic prices. When the federal government disallowed the new royalties as deductions for federal income tax, the companies found themselves almost worse off than before the price increases. The federal and provincial governments eventually reached a compromise which subsequently allowed large inflows of cash to oil producers, but the oil companies had been given another fright.

Moreover, as the 1970's wore on, the big oil companies began to realize that the future of their Canadian oil supplies, in fact, still significantly lay within Peter Lougheed's backyard.

There were three reasons why the majors returned to Alberta: much higher wellhead prices for oil and gas, combined with an attractive set of exploration incentives; two major new finds in the province, at Elmworth and West Pembina; but finally, and most importantly, it was Alberta's tar sands and heavy oil deposits that lured them back.

For the majors, the tar sands always stood as "plan B" if the frontiers failed. They were the only potential source of major new domestic oil supplies, but there were also giant technological and financial risks attached to tar sands development.

As far as the great conventional Albertan oil and gas boom centred on West Pembina and Elmworth was concerned, most of the big four were conspicuous by their absence. Admittedly, it was one of the Seven Sisters' Canadian subsidiaries, the huge but low-profile Chevron, 100% owned by Standard Oil of California, that made the West Pembina discovery. But of the big four, only Texaco had a presence in both plays.

The majors' absence clearly demonstrated their similarity to the giant tankers that carry the international cargoes. Their enormous size enables them to weather the stormy economic seas that scuttle some of their smaller brethren, but when it comes to changing direction rapidly, they find themselves in trouble.

That is not to exaggerate their absence from Alberta. Texaco was in both areas of excitement, and Shell and Gulf had really never pulled out of Alberta to the degree that Imperial had. Imperial quickly started throwing money around to reassert its presence in the province, although many observers were aghast that it was prepared to commit $180 million, an amount large even by Imperial's standard, to earn an average of only 15% of the lands held by Canadian Hunter, the company built on a geological idea and some world-class salesmanship by John Masters and Jim Gray, that had discovered perhaps Canada's largest gas field.

It may be wrong to be too critical of the majors for missing out on the great Albertan oil and gas boom. Even if Imperial, Gulf, Shell and Texaco had managed jointly to keep the whole of West Pembina to themselves, the field would nowhere near solve their long term crude supply problems.

Nevertheless, their absence had a psychological significance. They had always been the industry's leaders, but the OPEC crisis had found them steaming in the wrong direction. Some of them, in particular Imperial, had been slow to react to the opportunities in Alberta.

But once they did realize that their futures lay within the borders of Alberta, they reacted with a vengeance. As the 1970's close, the gigantic new Calgary offices of Gulf and Shell, and the equally large structure taking shape on Fourth Avenue to house Imperial's new resource subsidiary, stand as massive monuments to the resurgence of western oil. Indeed, these giant, ultra-modern minarets to the religion of Albertan growth contrast sharply with the somewhat staid Toronto headquarters of the same companies. Imperial's impregnably solid head office on fashionable St. Clair Avenue; Shell's equally stolid headquarters on University Avenue and Gulf's nondescript offices on Bay Street all represent monuments to another era, an era when downstream activities, essentially, where the oil was going rather than where it came from, dominated the thoughts of these Torontocentric companies. Now the source of the oil and gas had assumed much greater importance. As the multinationals had become the slaves of OPEC, so the subsidiaries of big oil in Canada now made their obeisance to the political force in Canada that seemed to hold all the oil and gas cards and, just like OPEC, seemed intent to squeeze every financial advantage out of them: Peter Lougheed's Albertan government.

5 | Imperial Oil—
The Biggest Target

*Moreover, for an oil company to preach conserva-
tion is similar to a hooker espousing chastity.
They represent invitations to put both the company and the lady out of business.*

In a world where "big" has, in recent years, been increasingly
linked with "bad", the role of the very largest corporations has
been an increasingly uncomfortable one. In no industry is this
truer than in oil. To be big and foreign-controlled is to have two
strikes against you. To be not only by far the biggest oil company in
Canada, but also 70% owned by the largest oil company in the
world is, from a public relations point of view, a disaster.

Imperial is Canada's largest oil company. It ranked fourth in revenues among all Canadian industrial companies in 1978, with sales
of $5.7 billion dollars while its earnings of $314 million made it the
fifth biggest money earner.

During a period when open season has been declared on big oil,
Imperial Oil Ltd. has found itself the most hunted monster in the
Canadian corporate jungle. Even before the OPEC crisis, the very
name of Imperial was sufficient to rouse Canadian nationalists to
paroxysms of jingoistic fervor and cause those who didn't know
what "return on capital" meant to decry "huge profits". Since
OPEC, however, it is not only the most obviously left-leaning of
political figures who have considered the giant company's nationalization.

Imperial's reaction to all this has been one of corporate confusion. The hard working men who run the company were trained as
engineers, lawyers, geologists and accountants. Their struggle up
the corporate hierarchy was undertaken in order to run a big company, not fight an ideological war of words.

Imperial's problems in recent years reflect those of its huge
parent Exxon, whose shell-shocked senior executives have come
under an even greater barrage in the United States since the events
of 1973-1974.

More than any other company, it was Exxon, the chief heir of the dissolution in 1911 of John D. Rockefeller's serpentine Standard Oil, that was associated in the public mind with the global control over oil by a relatively few large companies.

Over the course of the 20th century, Exxon has played a leading role in shaping the world in which we live. But perhaps the astonishing thing is that Exxon's senior management seemed to pick up very little cosmopolitanism as they roamed the globe in search of the oil that would fuel the economic development of the western world.

As Anthony Sampson points out, despite the elegant and rarified atmosphere of Exxon's executive suite that looks down 51 floors on the vulgar bustle of Sixth Avenue in New York, "the directors themselves are something of an anticlimax. They are clearly not diplomats, or strategists, or statesmen; they are chemical engineers from Texas, preoccupied with what they call 'the Exxon incentive.' Their route to the top has been through the 'Texas Pipeline' up through the technical universities, the refineries and the tank farms."

Between Rockefeller's day and the OPEC crisis, the logic of being "big oil" had grown to absorb Exxon's executive suite. The corporate medium had become what little ideological message there was. Exxon existed to find oil in ever increasing quantities, refine it and market it, primarily to its fellow Americans. No thought as to any moral or political dimension in that activity crept into the boardroom. Of course, the American government had to be kept "onside", as did foreign governments, but politics was merely a sometimes bothersome variable to be fed into the great business equation.

Exxon's senior executives knew there was a vague feeling of mistrust out there among the general populace, but in their own Harvard-honed hearts they could take a certain paternalistic pride that they were doing a very significant amount for the greater good of mankind — that good being synonymous with rapid economic growth and two cars in the garage.

The OPEC crisis came as a profound shock to the men in the Exxon boardroom. Not only did Sheik Yamani and his colleagues seize the reins of oil control with remarkable facility, but oil consumers turned on Exxon with all the good feeling a reformed junkie would show to his former pusher.

Exxon had always portrayed itself as a bastion of free-enterprise and the American way. Now it appeared as if it had spent the entire 20th century leading the American people down a winding path only to deliver them to the infidel, in the shape of the Mephistophelean Sheik Yamani.

What seemed even worse, Exxon and its fellow majors not only found themselves administering the system for the genie petroleum's new masters, but they even *profited* from the change of control, earning huge windfall profits from the upward revaluation of their inventories in the wake of the fourfold OPEC price increase in the winter of 1973-1974.

For the American public, hit by supply shortages and forced to line up at gas stations, the sight of the Seven Sisters huge first quarter profits in 1974 was too much. A massive outcry against the "corporate rip-off" arose and was soon echoed by politicians. Perhaps the feeling towards Exxon was neatly embodied in the placard "Impeach Nixxon", that appeared at the time, which neatly killed two villainous birds with one slogan.

In 1979, America was treated to a reprise that made Exxon's corporate offices flinch once more. As gasoline shortages threatened to set off the short fuse of the American motoring public, Exxon announced a profits gain for the first quarter of 37.4% vs. the same quarter of 1978, to $955 million, by far the most impressive earnings performance in the company's history.

Where once that performance would have been a cause for executive chest-beating, after five years of the post-OPEC period, it led Exxon executives to get out their tin hats and head for a bunker.

The previously extroverted senior Sister of the world oil sorority has now been turned into a much more self-doubting creature, obsessed with its public image. Three quarters of Exxon's 1979 network television and magazine advertising budget was spent not on selling products but on trying to persuade a sceptical public that what Exxon was doing was essential in the nation's strategic interests.

Exxon's chairman, Jim Garvin, admitted to *Time* magazine in May of 1979: "I simply do not know of any operating decisions that now get made without lots of awareness of the political and public implications."

John D. Rockefeller would not have approved.

Why Does Nobody Love a Fat Oil Company?

Like its giant parent, Imperial has undergone a crisis of public image in the past decade. It has made massive, and highly expensive, efforts to make itself understood if not loved, but seems to have largely failed. Imperial has a public relations staff of more than 50 people, but the preponderance of marketing men among those who direct its operations is telling. It betrays a great deal about how Imperial views itself. Imperial perceives that its problem is not an inherent one, but rather one of faulty perception by the public. The answer, therefore, is to attempt to get across the right image. This has resulted, in the 1970's, in advertising campaigns that range from the self-congratulatory to the downright pious.

Hockey Night in Canada used to be interrupted by the message: "Each year Imperial spends hundreds of millions of dollars on the big, tough, expensive job of developing petroleum supply, and if the company is to be successful in helping Canada reduce its dependence on foreign sources, the company will have to put even more money to work."

A magazine ad in *Macleans* in 1976 asked, in bold type: "Like to guess how much profit Imperial Oil earns on each gallon of petroleum products it makes and markets? If you guess one or two cents a gallon, you're close. Actually, in 1975, the figure was less than one cent a gallon."

In 1979, Imperial was displaying itself as a model of the good corporate citizen, promoting selfless historical studies in Alberta and leading the way with conservation within its own organization. "At Imperial, we've discovered that the most resourceful barrel is the one we save."

Far from reducing public cynicism, such campaigns have, if anything, tended to increase it. Such image-mongery is not only obvious, it almost seems cynical. Talking about cents per gallon is no meaningful way of expressing profitability, and even if it were, should any corporation be boasting about how *low* its profits are?

Moreover, for an oil company to preach conservation is similar to a hooker espousing chastity. They represent invitations to put both the company and the lady out of business.

The slick superficiality of Imperial's attempts at image making is very much out of line with the nature of its executives, in particular that of the man who runs the company, Jack Armstrong. Armstrong, a big, solid figure, still indisputably stands at the pinnacle of Canada's corporate oil establishment, but his political ride through the 1970's has inevitably been a rough one. Like all Imperial men, he occasionally displays a quiet exasperation with the necessity to be "politicking" when he would rather be getting on with business.

Armstrong reportedly used to be the model of a two-fisted, hard-drinking exploration man until his second marriage brought him into Mormonism. It is rumoured that other executives try to avoid travelling on the corporate jet with him because he now eschews both smoking and drinking and frowns upon others who indulge in these vices.

Publically, Armstrong is nowhere near as outspoken as his predecessor, Bill Twaites. Facing the increasingly inevitable media, he seems uncomfortable, usually with good reason. In private, however, Armstrong is a powerful champion of the industry.

At the time when the oil companies were cast as the meat in the sandwich between the warring federal and provincial governments in the wake of the OPEC crisis, the exchanges between Armstrong and Federal Energy Minister Donald Macdonald at private meetings were sometimes reported as threatening to bring down the ceiling. But significantly, when Macdonald announced his retirement from politics, the man who went first and asked him to stay on because he thought the country needed him was Jack Armstrong.

Armstrong is one of Canada's highest paid corporate executives. His total income from Imperial in 1978 was $453,820. He can look forward at retirement in 1982 to a pension of $127,000 a year. However, in terms of the wealth of Calgary's petroleum entrepreneurs, he does not even come into the picture. In particular, the benefits of going the "entrepreneurial" route are exemplified by one of Armstrong's classmates at the University of Manitoba, Jack Gallagher. Gallagher made the decision to go it alone almost 30 years ago, and the company he has built from scratch, Dome Petroleum, is now more than half the size of Imperial, but the fruits of taking the risks have been considerably larger for Gallagher. In mid 1979, Armstrong's holdings in Imperial were worth about $400,000; those of Gallagher in Dome more than $50 million.

In fact, neither man is in any way ostentatious in the enjoyment of wealth, and Armstrong's income would be far more than sufficient to support *both* their lifestyles, but the differential of their wealth indicates the difference in the rewards between being at the pinnacle of corporate achievement and at the pinnacle of entrepreneurial achievement in Canadian oil.

Like Gallagher, Armstrong has a disarming and genuine personal modesty. "I really never expected to be here," he says, sitting back for a rare moment of relaxation in his huge office at Imperial's Toronto headquarters. And he means it. But Armstrong's route to the top has been a long and arduous one. After leaving the University of Manitoba, he went first into hardrock mining and worked with the Geological Survey of Canada. Then he went back to University, this time to Queen's, to take a degree in chemical engineering, working during the summer months with Imperial's exploration group, which was where he first developed his geophysical talents. In the early 1940's the pickings were slim for Imperial's explorationists, and in 1945, Armstrong was posted for the traditional period of overseas duty, in Ecuador. However, he was summoned back to Alberta when Leduc blew in and Imperial was repatriating every Canadian exploration man it could find. Armstrong stayed in Alberta until 1959, when he was called up for a stint at Exxon's New York headquarters, as assistant coordinator for Exxon's production group. Then he returned to Toronto as a man marked for the top. He joined Imperial's board in 1961. In April, 1973 he became chief executive officer. One year later he became chairman of the board, and in July, 1975 added the title of president.

Within the industry, there is enormous respect for Armstrong. The phrase "real professional" recurs again and again among those who have dealt with him. Armstrong also has enormous power in terms of getting to see people. He can probably get access to anyone in any Canadian government, provincial or federal, on any day. If the matter is felt to be important enough, that includes the Prime Minister. But although Armstrong may have unprecedented power in opening political doors, he is deeply aware of the narrowing parameters in which Imperial operates, the foreign-owned giant within an increasingly regulated and nationalistic industry. Government "tinkering" with energy policy for short-term political reasons is obviously a great cause of frustration to a mind that has been trained by years of experience in a purely business-oriented industry.

Imperial Knows Best. Doesn't It?

Armstrong's feelings are reflected throughout the executive suite at Imperial Oil. For men accustomed to the positive feedback received from addressing the converted at Rotary Clubs and trade associations, the hostility of the 1970's came as a profound shock. The shock was all the greater because Imperial had always been *the* Canadian oil company. It found, produced, refined and sold far more oil than any other company. It also provided a post-graduate training ground for many of the men who would go on to run other large companies or start their own businesses. Imperial's distinguished alumni include Armstrong's classmate Jack Gallagher, recognized today as the most dynamic oilman in Canada. It also includes an outstanding trio of young geologists: Bob Lamond, Roger Bethel and Uldis Upitis. These men all joined Imperial during its 1965 recruiting drive in the wake of the Rainbow oil discovery in northwest Alberta. They went on to work for other companies, and all now run their own companies as multi-millionaires. The list of Calgary's executives who have at one time worked for Imperial is a very long one.

Being a large and inevitably bureaucratic organization, many individuals with entrepreneurial drive, such as those mentioned above, found Imperial's hierarchic committee systems and strict channels of communication a little confining, but for the "company man" it was paradise.

Imperial's top management knew they were the best, and were prepared not to hide that fact. The archetypal Imperial man was Bill Twaites, the crusty and outspoken little firebrand who headed the company in the period before the OPEC crisis and retired during the furore. Twaites now operates as a consultant out of a small office on Bay Street in Toronto where the furnishings seem to belong to some indeterminate and tasteless period of the 1960's when Imperial was spiritual leader of the industry.

Twaites has a good deal of trouble coming to terms with the politicized environment of the post-OPEC era and still has a deep loyalty to Imperial that refuses to admit that the company made, or indeed was ever capable of making, any strategic errors. Twaites has managed to maintain his lack of self-doubt, and his faith in Imperial, despite all the events of the 1970's.

In a way, the outspoken championship of Imperial by Twaites is refreshingly different from the public relations-conscious non-commentary on contentious issues into which most major oil companies have now lapsed. Twaites still fumes about the decision on the gas pipeline from Prudhoe Bay, when the Arctic Gas group, headed by Imperial, was outmaneouvered by Bob Blair. He regards Blair as little more than a turncoat, and the National Energy Board's decision in his favour as the worst kind of political sell-out. Twaites had always been used to dealing with the federal government at the highest levels, but he was not a man with political antennae of the kind sprouted by Bob Blair. Indeed he obviously regards such appendages as somewhat obscene.

As for Justice Thomas Berger, the man whose report effectively mortally wounded the giant Arctic Gas group, Twaites feelings run even more strongly. "Why", he says, still reddening at the memory, "Berger took more notice of the Anglican Church than he did of Imperial Oil". Twaites obviously does not regard the Anglican Church as the most balanced authority to speak on energy development, and many would concur with him, but perhaps the most telling point is that Twaites feels perhaps that Imperial and the Anglican Church belong in the same category. For the oil industry, that may well have been the case during the 1950's and the 1960's, but the 1970's have brought new gods to the industry, companies like Alberta Gas Trunk Line, Dome Petroleum, PetroCanada and Alberta Energy Company.

Bill Twaites seems to feel a little like Moses looking down on the people cavorting about the golden calf. For him, deeply imbued with the twin philosophies that "straight" business is best, and nobody does straight business like Imperial, the people are worshipping false gods.

Does Sixth Avenue Call the Shots?

But what of the relationship with Exxon? Again, it is important to look at the fact that it was business that motivated the board of

Exxon. It led them to attempt to lobby politically at home, and meddle in political affairs abroad, but the principal objectives were always to keep the oil flowing into the markets and maintain a strong "bottom line".

In purely business terms, Exxon looked to Imperial to take oil from its foreign sources, supplying, in line with Canadian energy policy of the 1960's, eastern Canada with cheap overseas oil, and produce adequate financial results. Imperial paid Exxon for foreign oil and provided it with dividends out of its profits. Thus its Canadian subsidiary fitted neatly into Exxon's great scheme of things as a major customer within its huge sales network and a provider of profits to the corporate coffers.

Exxon's sales to Imperial are controlled by the massive computer system that operates out of the twenty-fourth floor of its New York headquarters. The system, named Logics (for Logistics Information and Communications Systems), records the movement of more than 500 ships between over 100 loading ports and almost 300 destinations throughout the world. As Anthony Sampson said: "From the peace of the twenty-fourth floor, it seems like playing God — a perfectly rational and omniscient god, surveying the world as a single market."

God looked at the performance of Imperial throughout the 1950's and 1960's and found it good. However, that computer was destined to cause a lot of trouble for Imperial after the OPEC crisis when it was discovered that, like God, the computer could giveth, but it could also taketh away.

Imperial's dependence for its imported oil upon its parent became a hot political issue early in 1979 in the wake of the political upheaval in Iran. For a time, key Iranian supplies were cut off to the majors. Exxon, via the great computer, decided to prorate oil to its overseas subsidiaries, cutting back supplies by 7% of each subsidiary's total sales. Such a move betrayed both high-handedness and unfairness when it came to Imperial, because the Canadian subsidiary received three quarters of its oil from domestic Canadian sources. Thus Exxon's cutback of 7% of total supplies meant that it was chopping Imperial's 119,000 barrels a day of imports by a quarter. Armstrong went and reportedly raised hell with New York, and Exxon soon reduced the shortfall to 7% of imports, or just 8,000 barrels a day. For Armstrong, however, Exxon's error meant that the tin hats had to be brought out once more at the Toronto headquarters.

Imperial winced as they realized the opportunity had been presented to Donald Macdonald's much more politically-inclined successor, Alastair Gillespie, to score some points in the run up to a national election in the spring of 1979. Conservative leader Joe Clark had been taking pot-shots at the Liberal creation, PetroCanada, so here was Gillespie's chance to belabour big, foreign-owned oil.

The obvious point seemed to be that Imperial was dependent for its imported oil upon the whim of its parent. Moreover, all of Imperial's imported oil was shipped from Venezuela, where there was no supply disruptions. Thus, was it not "unfair" that Imperial should be penalized?

"It's the principle I still object to," Gillespie told the *Financial Post*. "Imperial gets oil from Venezuela, which hasn't cut back at all. Why should Imperial suffer — why should Canada suffer — shortfalls when there's been no restriction from Venezuela?"

Gillespie began putting heavy pressure on Imperial to deal directly with Venezuela for its crude supplies. It was another attack on the global marketing system that companies like Exxon had erected so successfully in the pre-OPEC period. However, the question of dealing directly with Venezuela was neither a simple one, nor, in the long run, necessarily advantageous to Canada.

Armstrong, realizing that he was walking in a minefield, merely pointed out in a prepared statement: "It is true that Imperial does not receive any Iranian crude and that most of the supplies come from Venezuela. But supposing for a moment the shoe was on the other foot and that it was Venezuelan and not Iranian imports that were affected. If we were buying direct we'd be in real trouble. . . . Exxon gets its supplies from a large number of producing countries, which is safer than relying on a single source."

The point was a valid one. Despite the OPEC revolution, it was still the majors who ran the global supply system. Exxon's "playing God" perhaps was, after all, the most equitable way of administering shortages or disruptions from any one place, since they could spread the burden. However, it was precisely that sort of control that had been made politically unacceptable by the OPEC crisis.

Armstrong was once again put into the hot seat, caught between the desires of his American parent, the Canadian government, and Imperial's foreign-supply needs.

Canada, it seems, will continue to rely on a significant level of foreign imports in the years to come, so foreign-supply arrangements are obviously a matter for more than political point-gaining. The key issue, perhaps, is whether a company like federally-owned PetroCan, can, in a more nationalistic world oil environment, secure Canada's imported supply needs better than the multinationals. Since every other developed country seems to have a national oil company attempting to do exactly the same thing, the issue will not be an easy one to resolve. To the extent that any one country manages to obtain absolutely secure supplies, then supply cuts to other countries during any disruptions will be that much more severe. The transition period will not be easy.

For Imperial, the company whose size and parentage places it in perhaps the hottest political seat of all, the transition will be the most difficult.

Imperial is essentially in a no-win situation when it comes to talking about its relationship with Exxon — which is why it does so as little as possible. Announcing that it plays "tough ball' with its parent would be as counterproductive as boasting that it could outsmart the federal government. Imperial's executives might well, indeed almost certainly do, attempt to practice both strategies, but they would be very rash to talk about them.

There is, it seems, virtually no "meddling" by Exxon in the day-to-day operations of Imperial. The giant in New York obviously keeps a close eye on budgets and management strategy but it leaves Imperial to dictate its own business policies. However, Imperial has always meant more to Exxon than a submission in the great corporate budget and a demand factor in a global marketing programme. It also means people. Exxon has always recognized the importance of developing top executive talent, and outside the United States, Imperial Oil has always been a prime source of such talent.

In 1974 when Sampson was examining Exxon's rather disappointing — at least from a diplomatic point of view — array of top executives the man who headed the company was Ken Jamieson, a Canadian born in Medicine Hat, the son of a Mountie. Jamieson had succeeded Mike Haider, another ex-Imperial Oil man who had risen to the top spot at Exxon. Again, George Piercy, the man who had headed the team that, late in 1973, held the fateful negotiations with Sheik Yamani, whose breakdown was to provide the spark for the OPEC explosion, had been on the board of Imperial. Most recently, Don McIvor, a Canadian who, some believe, will eventually return to head Imperial, left to become head of worldwide exploration for Exxon, while Dick Bray, a fast-rising young Exxon executive was posted north of the border as senior vice president of Imperial's new Calgary-based subsidiary, Esso Resources. In all, it is estimated that there are between 60 and 80 Imperial people working directly for Exxon at any time, either destined to rise within Exxon's hierarchy, or return to Canada on a higher rung up Imperial's corporate ladder.

Nevertheless, the interchange of personnel has not always meant that the two companies have seen eye to eye on policy matters. In the industry, Imperial is generally regarded as having a large degree of autonomy, and potentially more so since the political change of OPEC. Just as Imperial can no longer afford to be seen to play the heavy in the Canadian oil scene, so Exxon has to tread a great deal more warily in the treatment of its Canadian subsidiary.

One recent, and outstanding, example of Imperial's autonomy was over the giant Syncrude tar sands plant. Exxon was deeply concerned about both the risks inherent in such a large venture and the volume of capital that Imperial would have to put up — more than $600 million for its 31¼ % of the $2 billion-plus project. However, Imperial decided to go ahead anyway and, with world prices escalating rapidly once more in the wake of Iranian disruptions in 1979, its gamble seems to have been a shrewd one.

However, all of Imperial's gambles in recent years have not paid off. The biggest, and to date most unsuccessful, gamble of all was in the company's strategic decision towards the end of the 1960's virtually to abandon exploration in the traditional areas of Canada and head for the frontiers. At the time the decision was made by the finely-tuned business brains that ran Imperial, it seemed like the quintessence of logic. Because of the massive oil finds in the Middle East, Libya and elsewhere throughout the 1950's and 1960's, world oil prices were low. These prices were reflected in low Canadian prices for oil and gas. At such low prices, the chances of Imperial finding large commercial fields in western Canada looked less than slim, so the company decided that it had to go looking for "elephants" in the Canadian frontiers, in the Mackenzie Delta and off the east coast. The geological prospects of these areas looked excellent. However, the east coast proved very disappointing. In the Mackenzie Delta, Imperial spent a massive $350 million to find 3.5 trillion cubic feet of reserves, a very significant amount, but then, when Arctic Gas was destroyed, so, it seemed, were the immediate prospects of bringing that gas to market.

Nobody could accuse Imperial of having been a slumbering giant. It had taken positively gargantuan financial steps in frontier exploration and in the development of Syncrude. But that was the problem. Imperial, it seemed had been too far sighted. While the giant was on its tip toes looking to a hydrocarbon future based on expensive frontier gas and costly non-conventional oil, it had missed out on the conventional oil and gas boom at its feet. However, one of the reasons it had missed out in the West was that it seemed to have become noticeably more Torontocentric as the move to the frontiers and non-conventional oil gathered momentum.

Since the West was effectively downgraded in importance for exploration purposes, decisions on any major expenditure had to go back to Toronto for approval. For those dealing with Imperial, the bureaucracy became decidedly bothersome. Worst of all, since Imperial really didn't think that there was anything more of significance to be found in the West, it allowed a great deal of its land to revert to the Crown. By the end of 1977, Imperial's 2.2 million net acres of exploration land in Alberta, Saskatchewan and British Columbia meant that it ranked only 15th among publically quoted oil companies in western landholdings.

Back to the West

It was time, it seemed, for a massive shift in strategy. Since the frontiers had not produced their promised bonanza, the importance of tar sands and heavy oil plants in assuring Imperial's longer term supplies became that much more important.

This, combined with brighter conventional oil and gas prospects in the West, meant that Toronto now had to recapture a position in an area it had more or less abandoned as far as conventional exploration was concerned.

The result was that in September 1978, Imperial set up Esso Resources Canada Ltd. and transferred all its oil, gas and other mineral activities to it.

The beefing up of operations in Calgary involved a massive new office block and the shifting of three very senior executives to Alberta. These were senior vice-president, Arden Haynes, as head of Esso Resources, senior vice-president, Dick Bray, as his number two, and Gordon Haight, Imperial's head of production. Imperial's move was a highly significant one, and a cause of considerable satisfaction to Peter Lougheed.

Tar sands and heavy oil plants promise to be a very significant source of supply for Canada as it moves into the 21st century. For the majors, led by Imperial, they have become a matter of top priority, and Imperial is likely to continue to play a leading role in their development. Indeed, Esso Resources is faced with potentially the largest project in Imperial's history, the development of a massive plant at Cold Lake to produce 1.25 billion barrels of oil from its heavy, viscous deposits over 25 years. The estimated cost of such a plant was, at the time of writing, a massive $6 billion, making it by far the most expensive project of its kind ever attempted anywhere in the world.

The plant is similar in size to Syncrude, but its technique is different, due both to the different type of oil produced and its location. Whereas Syncrude is an exercise in brute strength to produce oil from bitumen-soaked sands mined from the surface, Cold Lake's oil lies deeper and has to be cajoled to the surface by underground methods of heating. No underground reserves of such sluggish oil have ever been produced commercially before, so the plant depends on totally new production and drilling technology. Imperial is seeking partners to take 50% of the equity for the new project. In early 1979, the company anticipated that it could spend up to $10 billion on capital projects up to 1990.

Another major reason for the setting up of Esso Resources was the need for on-the-spot decision making in Alberta. Imperial was acutely aware that it has been made to look flat-footed by its absence from the Elmworth and West Pembina gas and oil finds. In 1978 it proceeded to adopt a typically "major" approach to the problem: it started to throw money at it. Compared with 1977, Imperial almost quadrupled its expenditure on western exploration to $131 million, paying huge amounts at provincial land sales in the Elmworth and West Pembina region to regain a piece of the action.

However, Imperial's management badly wanted a major presence in one of the areas. All of the big guns in the industry were, in the fall of 1977 and throughout 1978, pouring millions of dollars into the West Pembina area to buy land, and were utilizing every drilling rig on which they could lay their hands. What Imperial needed was to find a company with more land than it had the funds to explore. It was not going to find any such company in West Pembina. But Elmworth was a different matter.

There, the company with the biggest land position had a seemingly insatiable desire for money. So, one day in mid 1978, Cal Evans, Imperial's head of exploration, went to visit the man in whose mind Elmworth had first been found, John Masters, president of Canadian Hunter.

Canadian Hunter was the only company in Alberta with a powerful land position but insufficient funds to carry out a major drilling programme. Imperial had funds flowing out of its ears from its massive Albertan production. It still produced almost twice as much oil as anyone else in the province, but had a sore lack of drilling prospects. The companies seemed to fit very well. But then the dealing had to start.

Originally, Imperial wanted to spend $50 million under a complex scheme whereby they would earn interests in various geological zones. However, Masters and Gray decided that they wanted Imperial to take a piece of all their acreage. They also realized that they had the whip hand, since Imperial seemed almost desperate to reestablish itself in the West in a big way. Men to whom enormous amounts of money hold no mystery, Masters and Gray decided to "hit" Imperial for $100 million in return for an interest in all their acreage. They held a rapid series of negotiations with Evans and Dick Bray and, within a week, had sorted out the basis of the deal. Once Imperial's legal and land departments took over, the pace of things slowed down, somewhat to Masters' and Gray's frustration, but in the end a deal was signed in October, 1978, whereby Imperial committed to spend a total of $150 million over 30 months in return for 17.5% of Hunter's Elmworth acreage and 12.5% of its other western Canadian acreage. The giant also committed to spend another $29 million depending on further expenditure by Canadian Hunter.

At the end of a turbulent decade, Imperial had staged a major about face in its strategy. But the principal change in the view from the company's executive offices on St. Clair Avenue — whose monumental architecture and outmoded furnishings, like those further downtown of Bill Twaites, seem faintly redolent of a previous age — was of a much more politically-charged atmosphere.

6 | Imperial's Sisters: The Bumpy Road to the Tar Sands

However, when the Ayatollah Khomeini swept to power in Iran, early in 1979, chopping back exports and proving the excuse for further massive OPEC price increases, nobody was more pleased than big oil in Canada.

For Gulf Canada, the political and business problems brought by the OPEC crisis were compounded by scandals that rocked the pyramid-topped tower of its mighty parent in Pittsburg, and by muffled wrangles from behind its own Toronto boardroom door.

The concerns of refinery overcapacity and longer term supply sources were, in Gulf Canada's case, added to by a prolonged dispute over management succession in the wake of the departure of one of its ablest chief executives, Jerry McAfee. Under McAfee's direction, Gulf Canada produced the outstanding performance among the Canadian majors during the first half of the 1970's. Between 1970 and 1974, the company quadrupled its earnings to $176 million and raised its return on capital, the key measure of business success, from being the lowest to the highest among the big four.

But while McAfee — a brilliant manager with "the common touch" who had adopted the role of industry spokesman when Imperial's Bill Twaites retired — was riding the crest of the wave, his counterpart at Gulf's Pittsburgh headquarters, Bob Dorsey, was suffering a much bumpier ride. Gulf Corp. was not only implicated in "slush funds" related to the Watergate scandal, but it was also in the middle of a furore over an international uranium cartel that was being accused of attempting to fix world prices.*

---

* An illegal slush fund for making political payments was first set up in 1958 by William Whiteford, the man who presided over Gulf Corporation's major move into Canada by taking over British American Oil. Money was delivered by hand to Bahamian subsidiary, Bahamas Exploration, whence it returned in discreet sealed envelopes to the Washington offices of senators and congressmen from both parties. Most of the donations were presided over by Claude C. Wild Jr., Gulf's vice-president for government relations. The Securities and Exchange Commission later charged Gulf with falsifying financial records so as to conceal $10 million that

There had, in fact, always been a rivalry between Dorsey and
McAfee within the Gulf hierarchy. Both had come from Port Arthur, Texas, home of Gulf's largest refinery, but Dorsey's origins were more humble than McAfee's, and his corporate tactics indisputably rougher.

It was generally considered that while Dorsey held the reins, McAfee's route to one of the top positions in Pittsburg would be blocked.

However, after the Watergate scandal and uranium cartel problems, the star of Dorsey's uncompromising corporate style, a throwback to less politically sensitive days, rapidly declined. Looking around for a successor, the board picked up Jerry McAfee. The nuance of his selection was not lost on his colleagues at the Bay Street headquarters of Gulf Canada. When he left, they gave him a tee-shirt emblazoned with the title "Mr. Clean". In a further attempt to produce a rather more saintly image on its main board, Gulf then went to the unprecedented length of appointing a nun, Sister Jane Scully, as director. However, despite the presence of Mr. Clean and Sister Jane of Pittsburg on the board — a combination that sounded as if it had been dreamed up by a writer of television corporate sitcoms — the oil giant of Pittsburg still had some sweating out to do in the following couple of years.

For Gulf Canada, McAfee's departure created major succession problems, since there was nobody obviously capable of filling his shoes. John Stoik who had returned to Gulf Canada after heading Gulf Oil Corp.'s Korean operations, was clearly being groomed for a top job, but he was still felt to be some way short of taking over from McAfee. A big, heavy-set bespectacled man, he was made president of the company, but really only given half McAfee's job, receiving the title of chief operating officer, while the title of chief executive officer was given to Clarence Shepard, the tall, balding, avuncular lawyer who was the company's chairman. Stoik was obviously being told that he was not a shoo-in for the top spot. Indeed, it was rumoured that the presidency had first been offered to Lorenz Blaser, the blunt executive vice-president of refining and marketing, but that Blaser had turned it down on the grounds he was too close to retirement.

Then, in late 1977, the cat was really thrown among the corporate pigeons when Bill Wilder, former head of the Arctic Gas group, the consortium that had lost out in the bid to build the gas pipeline from Prudhoe Bay, was elevated straight into the upper

passed through the Bahamas between 1960 and 1974. In August, 1973, during the unveiling of Watergate, it was revealed that Gulf had been a major illegal contributor to President Nixon's re-election fund, the Campaign to Re-elect the President (known unaffectionately as "Creep"). Between 1966 and 1972, $5 million was paid to foreign politicians and parties, including $4 million to President Park in South Korea. Dorsey said he was "basically ashamed of what was going on", but claimed that Gulf's management thought it had "no choice."

echelons of Gulf Canada as an executive vice-president. McAfee, although still embroiled with hearings on the uranium scandal, was obviously worried about the senior management of the Canadian subsidiary. He had worked closely with Wilder — a pillar of Toronto's Bay Street financial community, during the Arctic Gas days. When the consortium crumbled, McAfee snapped him up as a potential heavyweight to fill the chairmanship when Shepard retired. The move, perhaps understandably, was less than popular with the solid but uncharismatic Stoik, who now was set on gaining complete control of the company and had no desire to share his job with a new, powerful chairman. Wilder's appointment obviously came straight from McAfee and thus he would hold enormous clout within the Canadian organization.

How the relationship between Stoik and Wilder developed within Gulf's boardroom will probably never be known. It was almost certainly a testy one. However, within a little more than a year, Wilder had departed once more to become head of Consumers' Gas, the giant Ontario utility that controlled Home Oil Co. Somehow, it seemed, he had dropped, or been dropped, out of the running for the chairmanship.

In the meantime, the uncertainty in Gulf's boardroom had spread throughout the company. Stan Pearson, Gulf's widely respected head of exploration and production, had been moved to Toronto from Calgary in the management reshuffle that had seen Wilder brought into the company. Then, within six months, he had taken early retirement and the exploration and production functions had not only been moved back to Calgary but considerably beefed-up. Following the lead of both Shell and Imperial, Gulf set up a Calgary-based resource subsidiary. Gulf was also faced with a spate of departures at the senior management level from its Calgary office.

At the Toronto head office, it was rumoured, bureaucratization had set in. Gulf's organization structure was shown to a management consultant without telling him the function of the company involved. After analyzing it carefully, he declared that it had to be either a hospital or a university, because no business organization could function with that many committees!

It is important to remember that huge corporations like Gulf have such business momentum that management problems can rarely create much more than a wrinkle. However, absence of strong management direction for any extended period of time can obviously have a harmful effect.

To this extent, the existence of the higher authority down in Pittsburgh provides a check on management performance, although it would again be wrong to suggest that Pittsburgh controls Toronto. Indeed, for most of the past decade, Pittsburgh has had enough trouble keeping control of its own affairs.

Nevertheless, as 1979 drew to a close, the final resolution of management uncertainties, plus a little luck in exploration, seemed to place Gulf on a much firmer footing as it entered the new decade.

In mid 1979, Gulf Canada opened its squat but massive new Calgary headquarters, the "biggest building in the West", as the new focus for its exploration, production and non-conventional oil development. Some consider the building's profile on Ninth Avenue to reflect that of Gulf Canada during the turbulent decade of the 1970's — huge but not outstanding. However, there were clear signs that what appeared like the conservative management strategies of the latter half of the decade were beginning to pay off.

By the end of the 1970's Gulf had not really developed a leading role in any key area of the industry, pursuing the quintessential "shotgun" approach and taking a piece of the action in most key areas, thus spreading its risks.

Gulf has a 16-2/3% interest in Syncrude, is set to take a 10% share in the Alsands project led by Shell and is also interested in heavy oil development. The company considered making a takeover bid itself for Husky Oil early in 1978 before perhaps being "warned off" by its prospective joint venture partner, PetroCanada.

Late in 1979, Gulf's shotgun approach seemed to be paying off in spades. Within a couple of weeks of each other, two offshore exploration wells in which the company had an interest of 25%, one in the Beaufort Sea and one off Canada's East Coast, showed significant flows of oil. The result was a doubling of Gulf Canada's share price, to $100, in less than a month. That sort of performance seemed just the sort of fillip that Gulf's newly reorganized management needed.

At the company's 1979 annual meeting, the problem of management succession was finally solved. John Stoik emerged as king of the corporate castle, assuming the title of chief executive officer, while it was announced that senior vice-president J. C. Phillips would take over the chairmanship. Gulf's employees all hoped that, with the management issue settled, the company's top echelons would settle down to finding their corporate compass once more in the 1980's.

Texaco — The "Ugly Sister"

Kind words about either Texaco Canada Inc. or its American parent are rare commodities in the Calgary oil community.

In the city's wheeler-dealer environment, where rivals can become partners overnight, and at some stage everybody has to do a deal with everybody else, Texaco is renowned for its corporate anti-sociability. The people who work for the company are not necessarily any less personable than anybody else in the industry, but they seem to be constantly looking over their shoulders to the tight-wad centralization that reigns from the company's world headquarters, now in the tranquil setting of Harrison, New York. A pervasive meanness and secrecy rules over the company's operations. The curtains in the executive offices in Calgary are drawn even on the sunniest days.

And yet Texaco's Canadian companies, Texaco Canada and Texaco Exploration Canada, that were merged in mid 1978 to form Texaco Canada Inc. have, in the past few years had that one crucial commodity: luck. Of course, it was not pure luck that they found themselves with land close to the centre both of the Elmworth gas exploration play and to the West Pembina oil find. That comes under the category of keeping a balanced exposure, which always puts the odds a little in your favour.

However, almost everyone in the Calgary community who has dealt with Texaco is reluctant to give the company any praise. Here is a selection of comments from leading Calgary oilmen:

"I have little more than contempt for the Texas Company, except that somewhere in that building they have a genius locked up who tells them where to buy land. They are arbitrary, stubborn, prejudiced and short-sighted."

"Texaco are the dumbest guys I ever saw, the worst kind of bureaucrats, and yet they are always in the big fields."

"Texaco men are big, tough, cigar-smoking, blue-jowelled loners. Texaco has a word. It is a flat, cold "NO".

"Every company has a mould. If you want to be a civil servant, go and work for Texaco."

Hardly a flattering bunch of assessments. Nevertheless, this cross-section excludes some of the less charitable, and unprintable, comments on the "Ugly Sister".

And yet, despite all the vituperation, Texaco was the company that found itself best represented in the most exciting areas of exploration activity found in the West for more than ten years. Indeed, it was on a farm-out from Texaco that Canadian Hunter made the original discovery at Elmworth. But, although Texaco had access to Canadian Hunter's information, the company seemed particularly uninterested in using it, and although they had the opportunity to bid along with Canadian Hunter when the little company was snapping up land for all it was worth, Texaco took only 15% overall.

Again, in West Pembina, the company found itself in partnership with Pacific and Amoco on a good deal of potential land, but when it came to the run up to the land sale at which the group of three companies paid an all-time record of more than $26,000 an acre, Texaco wanted to pay little more than $8,000 and is reported to still grumble at the thought that it may have left too much "on the table".

Texaco just doesn't seem interested in winning popularity polls, and the origin of that attitude seems to stretch back to the very beginnings of the company.

The Texas Company, like Gulf, had its origins at the wondrous Spindletop gusher.* The founding forces behind the company were "Buckskin Joe" Cullinan and Arnold Schlaet, a German-born merchant. Schlaet and former Texas governor, James Hogg, put up the financing and Cullinan put up the expertise in production he had acquired over twenty years working for Standard Oil. The Texas Company survived the rapid exhaustion of Spindletop and found more oil in the state. Schlaet set about building up a nation-wide marketing organization and by 1913, Texaco had an imposing 13-storey headquarters in Houston. However, that same year an irreperable rift opened between Cullinan and Schlaet over corporate policy, and the men from New York headed south in a special railroad car to vote Cullinan out of the company. Cullinan went on to run another oil company and emerged as a notable Texas eccentric, flying the Skull and Crossbones over Houston's Petroleum Building. It was that act of flag-waving that was to set Texaco's corporate style throughout the 20th century.

In the post-war years, the hard-faced image of Texaco was set by Gus Long, a salesman from Florida and the original "no" man, who dominated the company for twenty years.

Stories about Long's sometimes mindless penny-pinching are recounted with relish by former Texaco employees. Walking unexpectedly one day into a subordinate's office, he asked the seemingly ridiculous question of why the man had so many buttons beneath his telephone. Dumbfounded, the man couldn't think of an immediate reply. "Right," shouted Long, "get rid of them. From now on its just one button."

Although Texaco may be the least popular company within the oil fraternity, as far as the public is concerned, it has made a deliberate and successful effort to keep its head down. Its public relations staff is only one tenth the size of that of Imperial. Its strategy was summed up by one of its executives: "I was in the infantry," he said, "if you kept your head down you survived a long time. If you put it up, you were gone pretty quickly."

Texaco has never had any confusion about its purpose in life. It is there to find oil and make money. Some of its executives look with almost undisguised glee on Imperial's public image problems.

Nevertheless, in the modern era of public relations consciousness, even Texaco, despite its anti-social leanings, has to put on

---

* The discovery of oil at Spindletop near Beaumont, Texas, in 1901, caused the first great oil-rush of the 20th century. Within a year, there were 200 wells. By 1904, overproduction had reduced the gushers to a mere trickle.

some sort of a display of good corporate citizenship. Texaco Canada's most prominent piece of public service lies in its sponsorship of the opera. But that patronage, in which it follows the lead of its parent, has somewhat bizarre origins in the early years of the Second World War. It seems that support for the opera started when the Texas Company's image throughout the world reached an all-time low because of its patronage of a less artistic organization, the Nazi party.

In 1940, the Texas Company had a buccaneering and romantic figure as its president, a former Norwegian seafarer, Torkild "Cap" Rieber.

Rieber had organized Texaco's tanker fleet and become a prominent figure in Houston. Rising to the top in Texaco, he had displayed a swash-buckling internationalism, pushing pipelines across the forbidding terrain of the Andes and joining Socal in grabbing control of Saudi oil. But Rieber also displayed the essential international amorality that marked many of his oil colleagues.

He aroused the ire of President Roosevelt by supplying vast amounts of oil to General Franco during the Spanish Civil War, and then began to supply oil to the Nazis after the outbreak of the Second World War, dodging the British embargo by sending his ships into neutral ports.

In return for the oil, Rieber, who could not get money out of Nazi Germany, agreed to a barter deal with the Nazis for three ships. More than that, however, he made the gross error of becoming involved politically, by meeting Goering in Berlin and agreeing to put a peace plan to Roosevelt that ensured Britain's surrender. The American President rejected the plan out of hand.

Then, however, he became much more deeply involved with the Nazis. He offered Texaco's hospitality to Dr. Gerhardt Westrick, the German lawyer who, disguised as a commercial counsellor, arrived in New York in 1940 with the express purpose of undermining support for Britain. Texaco paid Westrick's salary, provided him with an office at Texaco's headquarters in the Chrysler building and furnished him with a large house in Scarsdale.

In the end, however, the man who exposed Westrick was the Canadian millionaire head of British intelligence, William Stephenson, alias "Intrepid". Stephenson managed to have Westrick's purpose "leaked" through the New York Herald Tribune. Westrick was thrown out of the country, Rieber was discredited and, at around the same time and with perhaps a rare desire to improve its corporate image, Texaco started sponsoring weekly radio broadcasts of the Metropolitan Opera, as did its Canadian subsidiary. The tradition continues to this day.

Again typically, there was nothing friendly about the way Texaco muscled its way into Canadian oil. In 1938, the men from the

Texas Corporation showed up at the annual meeting of a company
called McColl-Frontenac, a Montreal-based refining and marketing
company, and announced that they had, in the previous two
years, been secretly picking up its shares in the market. They had
also sidled up to a sufficient number of the company's other shareholders to be able to throw out the slate of directors nominated by
the company management. They then nominated and elected their
own board.*

For McColl-Frontenac it was the story of yet another burgeoning
Canadian oil company swallowed by the gaping maw of one of the
Seven Sisters. The company had its origins at the beginning of
Canada's oil history, in the Ontario oilfields of Oil Springs and Pe-
trolia, where it started as McColl and Anderson in 1873. By the end
of World War I it had become McColl Brothers, with headquarters
in Toronto. In 1927, under the aegis of leading Montreal-based brokerage house Nesbitt, Thomson & Co., it was merged with Fron-
tenac Oil Refineries Ltd. of Montreal to become McColl-Frontenac
Oil Co. Supplied with oil from a Trinidadian subsidiary, Antilles
Petroleum Co., the company performed strongly. In 1930, its earnings were, for the time, a sizable $1.4 million.

However, then came the Depression, crippling competition in
the Quebec refining business from British American and Shell, and
the perennial shortage of capital. The predatory Texas Company
sniffed an opportunity and began buying McColl shares for as little
as $8.50, compared with a high of $45 in 1929. Then, in 1938, the
blue-jowelled, cigar-smoking men from New York moved in and
muscled out the board. After World War II, McColl-Frontenac
moved into the West, although most of its activities were eventually taken over by the Texas Company's directly owned subsidiary.
In 1959, the name of McColl-Frontenac was changed to Texaco
Canada. Over the ensuing years, Texaco Canada concentrated
overwhelmingly on the refining and marketing end of the business
while the Texas Company's wholly owned Canadian subsidiary
Texaco Exploration Canada Ltd., continued to build up a major position as a Western explorer and producer.

Then, early in 1978, the two companies were merged to form a
new Canadian super-company, Texaco Canada Inc. of which the
New York parent now holds almost 90%.

For Texaco Canada, the amalgamation was a timely one, for the
company had been almost drained financially dry by the building

---

* According to the official company history: "The high rate of growth in the mid to
late 1930's placed severe strains on the capital available to McColl-Frontenac.
Being committed to continued growth, the company Directors felt it was time for
McColl-Frontenac to become part of a larger, world-wide organization which
would have access to the capital needed for such expansion. Consequently, the investment by the Texas Company in McColl-Frontenac shares was encouraged."

of perhaps the most sophisticated and expensive refinery ever seen in Canada, at Nanticoke on Lake Erie, Ontario. The refinery, which cost $480 million, was a classic example of how the Canadian refiners were caught out by the stagnation of the domestic retail market in the wake of the OPEC price increases and the cutting off of exports to the United States.

The good news for Texaco is that this "Cadillac" of refineries produces a very large proportion of unleaded gasoline, for which market demand is growing very rapidly. Nevertheless, in its construction phase, financing the project led Texaco Canada to cut its exploration expenditure virtually to zero. The merger with the powerful production and exploration Canadian arm of Texaco makes a combined company of impressive proportions, close in size to Gulf Canada and Shell Canada.

In 1978, Texaco Canada Inc. had revenues of $1.9 billion and net income of $147.9 million. Its long-term problem, however, remained the common one of replacing its fast-dwindling reserves. Taking the two components of the new company together, they had managed to retain gas reserves between 1974 and 1978. However, oil reserves had dipped by almost 30% over the period to 539 million barrels. West Pembina will provide a boost. But Texaco still has to decide where her longer-term supplies will come from. As yet, Texaco stands out among the big four as having no significant commitment to heavy oil or tar sand development. However, the ugly sister cannot sit on the sidelines for ever.

Shell: Avoiding the Flak and Heading for the Tar Sands

Shell worldwide has always been renowned as a much more politically-aware company than its major rival, Exxon. For aspiring young graduates from Oxford and Cambridge, Shell's London headquarters, on the banks of the Thames opposite the Houses of Parliament, have always seemed like a close alternative to entering the diplomatic service. The monumental graystone architecture of those offices is reflected in the Canadian subsidiary's Toronto head office, although the men inside are indisputably North American in their orientation. Just as Jerry McAfee succeeded Imperial's Bill Twaites as unofficial spokesman for the industry, that mantle seems now to have fallen on the shoulders of Bill Daniel, Shell Canada's chief executive. Somehow, Shell seems to have largely avoided the flak that has come the way of their rival, Imperial, and has also taken a more aggressive role in defending the system.

Shell Canada's parent has always placed emphasis on "regionalization" of its companies, stressing their local autonomy, and indeed, it is true that Shell Canada has negotiated its own import contracts with Venezuela rather than operating through Royal

Dutch, unlike the close, and controversial, relationship between
Imperial and Exxon.

Shell started operating in Canada in 1911 and gradually built up a significant presence in refining and marketing. However, it did not start exploring until 1939, under the direction of Shell's American subsidiary, Shell Oil Co. With a piece of classic bad luck, the company decided in 1946, after ten years without a major oil find by anyone in Canada, to abandon all its Canadian acreage and, as part of a worldwide retrenchment of the company, concentrate on Venezuela. The following year, Imperial discovered Leduc, and, shortly afterwards, the Redwater field on land that Shell had abandoned two years before! Shell had to struggle to re-establish itself during the 1950's and the early 1960's and did this most significantly through the, by then, well-worn route of buying out Canadian companies. The chief of these was Canadian Oil Companies Ltd., the last of the Canadian integrated oil companies, which Shell bought out in a hotly contested bid of $152 million in 1962.

Shell is gas rich and oil poor, so longer-term oil supplies are of critical importance. The company was obviously deeply disappointed by its lack of success in exploring Canada's frontiers. Now, like Imperial and Gulf, it has turned to the tar sands of western Canada for its future supplies.

In the terms of corporate strategy, Shell has always been inclined to zero in on major targets with its full resources, and, if unsuccessful, pull out again as quickly.

Shell is gas-rich and oil poor, so longer-term oil supplies are of critical importance. The company was obviously deeply disappointed by its lack of success in exploring Canada's frontiers. Now, like Imperial and Gulf, it has turned to the tar sands of western Canada for its future supplies.

Starting in 1963, Shell Canada spent more than $30 million over six years off the coast of British Columbia to drill 14 dry holes. It then drilled 40 dry holes off the east coast. It has not become involved in the Beaufort Sea at all. However, Shell's saving grace was that while some of its competitors were abandoning the West completely, it continued to explore. It was the first of the majors to realize the attractions of the exploration incentives introduced by Peter Lougheed at the end of 1974. The same year, Shell decided to abandon the frontiers, although it still has considerable east coast landholdings that it is prepared to farm out.

Now, with typical thoroughness, the corporate attentions of Shell Canada seem to be focused completely on by far the biggest project in its history, leading the Alsands consortium that plans to build the next giant tar sands plant. Shell, with a 25% interest, in the $5 billion-plus project is project manager for the group, the other members of which are: Shell Explorer, part of Shell's American arm; Amoco, Chevron, Dome, Gulf, Hudson's Bay Oil and Gas Co., Pacific Petroleums and Petrofina.

The Tar Sands — Big Oil's Last Waltz?

The impact of the OPEC crisis of 1973-1974 was, on balance, a negative one for the Canadian oil majors, since the corporate benefits of higher oil and gas prices were offset by lower demand at the refining and marketing end of the business. However, when the Ayatollah Khomeini swept to power in Iran early in 1979, chopping back exports and providing the excuse for further massive OPEC price increases, nobody was more pleased than big oil in Canada. Of course, neither Jack Armstrong nor Bill Daniel nor John Stoik fought his way onto the television screens or sent out press releases announcing "This is the best thing that has happened to big oil in the past five years!" But the truth of the matter is, that it is. A little later than their parents, admittedly, but no less powerfully, all of the big four in Canada have now firmly aligned themselves with the cause of high and rising oil prices. The reason is that big oil needs big oil finds. Chevron's find had become the exception rather than the rule, so, in the absence of large discoveries of conventional oil, the majors have been forced to turn to "non-conventional" oil — the technologically, financially and literally sticky tar sands and heavy oil deposits of Alberta and Saskatchewan.

Canadian energy development in the 1980s may well be dominated by Alberta's non-conventional oils. Lying as molasses-like bitumen in tar sands, and as equally gooey heavy oil in deeper reservoirs, what makes them non-conventional is that they do not show the tendency of light oils to rush gratefully up the drill-hole and soak their equally grateful finder. Their inclination is to just sit where they are. To wrestle them from the ground, they have to be dug or burned out, then treated through expensive processes until they are transformed into "synthetic" or "upgraded" oil suitable for use in conventional refineries. For many years, they have sat as the plump, unattractive wallflowers of Canadian oil. A company called Great Canadian Oil Sands asked one of them to dance in 1967, and had its financial toes trodden on for seven years. But their outlook has changed dramatically in the course of the 1970's. Previously the "Cinderella resource", fairy godmother OPEC's magic economic wand has enhanced their attractions enormously. What is more, midnight is approaching at the great energy dance and the supply of partners is fast running out.

For big oil in Canada, restricted in its contacts with its dusky foreign oil mistresses by the federal government's desire for self-sufficiency, and given the cold shoulder after its flirtations in frontiers, it appears that "last waltz" may well be with Canada's non-conventional oils.

The magnitude of the tar sands potential has been known for many years. Most recent estimates put the tar sands bitumen (thick tar-like oil) deposits of Alberta at 800 billions barrels in place. For reference, the *entire world's conventional oil reserves are less than 600 billion barrels.* However, the problems of the tar sands have always been the related ones of technology and economics. How can you get the oil out, and at what cost? The technology may still need considerable refinement, but the economics have never looked better.

There are now two giant plants extracting synthetic oil from the Athabasca tar sands of northeast Alberta, Canada's foremost tar sand deposit. The first, opened in 1967, is Great Canadian Oil Sands, a company owned by Sun Oil. The second, opened at the end of 1978, is the far larger Syncrude, owned by a consortium now consisting of four companies: Imperial, Gulf Canada, Cities Service, and Pan Canadian Petroleum, and the federal and Albertan governments.

The assumption on which the economics of Syncrude were based was that world oil prices would, over the life of the plant, increase by 5% per annum. Within nine months of Syncrude's official opening, OPEC prices had increased in a range between 42% and 85%!

Even before the additional boost to non-conventional oil's attractions given by the second major OPEC crisis within a decade, the 1980's were already set to witness a level of tar sand and heavy oil development in Alberta unsurpassed by anything similar in the world. The Alsands group, led by Shell Canada, plans to build another tar sands plant similar in size to Syncrude, with a price tag of $5 billion. Imperial plans to build a $6 billion recovery system and upgrading plant at Cold Lake, Alberta. Meanwhile, other Canadian consortia, one of which might easily be led by the ubiquitous Bob Blair, have plans for heavy oil upgrading plants.

These ventures are significant because they mean that big oil in Canada will increasingly slip into giant, long-term, government-regulated projects for its oil supplies. Although it remains true that the majors still have some control over the pace of development, once funds are committed the companies are significantly locked into such projects. Three of the big four, Imperial, Gulf and Shell, are making, or have made, the biggest expenditures in their history on tar sand and heavy oil development. Only Texaco, with perhaps typical reluctance, is holding back. What, wonder the others, does it have up its sleeve? They ask this question because for them there is no alternative to non-conventional oil if they are to stay in business as oil producing companies. Perhaps the simple and most likely answer is that Texaco has not been able to afford to get into non-conventional oil. In the longer term, the question will likely turn on its head. How long can the "ugly sister" afford to stay out?

The beneficial impact of Syncrude participation is more than apparent in the hefty boost to the reserve figures of participants given by inclusion of the plant's projected output. Imperial's gross proved reserves at the end of 1978 jumped 32% to 1.37 billion barrels, while Gulf's reserves increased almost 50%, to 576 million barrels as a result of Syncrude.

The higher goes the world price of oil, and the more uncertain become foreign supplies, the more desirable a resource Canada's non-conventional oils become. The Japanese have for some time looked longingly at this enormous potential. They are involved in a joint venture with PetroCan, Esso Resources, and Canada Cities Service in developing a technology that PetroCan inherited from Atlantic Richfield Canada, which it took over in 1976.

But it is, of course, the Americans who have most frequently cast their petroleum-lusting eyes to the wealth of the tar sands. Perhaps the most bizarre proposal to exploit the sands came from Herman Kahn of the Hudson Institute, the United States' best-known "Think Tank". In November of 1973, after the Arab embargo and the announcement of rapid escalation of OPEC oil prices, the mountainous Kahn, once described as a "huge man who thinks on a huge scale", paid one of his frequent visits to Ottawa. The *Financial Times of Canada* revealed that Kahn's visit was to none other than the very highest echelons of the government, Pierre Trudeau, Donald Macdonald and senior members of Macdonald's staff. Kahn's modest proposal was to initiate a gigantic, internationally-financed effort to develop 20 tar sands plants by the end of the 1970's. To build the plants, 30,000 to 40,000 south Koreans would be imported and then shipped out once more when the work was completed. Larry Pratt, a University of Alberta political scientist, in his book *The Tar Sands, Syncrude and the Politics of Oil*, maintains that Kahn was "an informal envoy for the American government", but whether this was true or not, his mammoth ideas didn't receive much support from Ottawa.

Kahn's failure to understand why Canada shouldn't want to lay waste to the Albertan landscape in order to keep the United States supplied with oil seemed typical to those becoming increasingly skeptical about the attitude of the United States toward Canada. Their suspicions were to be further fed by the Syncrude crisis, which followed exactly one year after the original OPEC crisis.

In the wake of the federal-provincial wrangle over the spoils of increased domestic oil prices in 1974, Syncrude provided a much-needed opportunity for the two levels of government to prove that they could work together. The circumstances, however, were not entirely welcome. The problems started one night in early December, 1974, when Frank Spragins, the avuncular driving force behind the project, received a telephone call from one of the group's four participants, Atlantic Richfield, announcing that it was withdrawing immediately. Arco had been a 30% participant, so it meant that the other three companies involved, Imperial, Gulf and Cities Service Canada, were going to have to find someone to put up 30¢ of every additional dollar they spent. After the Alberta government was shown a copy of the telex giving Arco's official notification of withdrawal, Bill Dickie, Energy Minister of the province, sent letters to a number of potential participants. These included Ontario and Quebec, as the major oil consuming provinces, and Shell Canada, the other major company known to be committed to tar sands development. However, the "saviours" came down to Alberta itself, Ontario and the federal government. Alberta was not keen on having Ottawa involved in the tar sands, and told them so in no uncertain fashion. Lougheed told them that if the federal government "came in" it would have to be like any corporate participant. However, Alberta was keen to have Ontario's involvement to balance the federal presence. The final package that was to save Syncrude was hammered out in a single day at a meeting in a Winnipeg motel on February 3, 1975. The revised shares in Syncrude were: Imperial, 31.25%; Cities Service, 22%; Gulf, 16.75%; the federal government, 15%; Alberta 10%, and Ontario 5%. (In December, 1978, Ontario announced that it was selling its share, which cost $100 million, to PanCanadian Petroleum for $160 million.)

The Winnipeg agreement caused an uproar from left-wing nationalists. In particular Larry Pratt's book accused both sets of governments of being duped by multinational oil. The fact was, however, that the left wing was once again attributing far more Machiavellian intelligence to the big oil companies than they really deserved. Of course big oil was going to try to squeeze as many concessions out of government as it possibly could. To suggest otherwise would be naive. But having governments as partners also made the majors a little uneasy.

Pratt's assertion that Lougheed was acting in concert with the oil companies was perhaps the one that was widest of the mark. Lougheed and his closest advisers couldn't have played it any tougher with Syncrude. Lougheed and Don Getty at one stage sensed that the Syncrude participants were growing overconfident because they thought that the province wanted the development at all costs. They decided to make it clear that the province didn't. The Syncrude group presented a set of demands that they indicated were their "final" position. Getty went to the meeting at which the demands were to be discussed and asked: "Is that your final position?". The companies said yes, whereupon Getty, to their astonishment, closed his books and got up to walk out. All of a sudden, panic seemed to break out among the company men. Brent Scott, a Gulf man destined to take over the presidency of Syncrude, grabbed Getty by the arm. Both are big men. There was a moment of tension. But then Scott let go and Getty left. "The whole climate of negotiations changed after that meeting," Getty told the author.

(The CDC subsequently produced a "docu-drama" based on the

Syncrude crisis. Lougheed subsequently sued the CBC for a total of $2.75 million.)

Far from being duped, Alberta seems to have emerged as the big winner from Syncrude. Not only did it receive the direct economic benefits of the plant's construction in the province, but, under a unique royalty arrangement, it receives half of the plant's net profits. (The province has an option to convert this royalty to a more conventional 7½ % gross royalty.) It also has an option to take up to an additional 20% interest in the plant through provincial vehicle Alberta Energy Company.* AEC also receives income from running Syncrude's power plant and the pipeline from Syncrude to Edmonton. The province also has the opportunity to take further equity interest in the project through convertible debentures it holds with Gulf and Cities Service.

Everything but the Kitchen Sink

Tar sands have never made any effort to hide themselves from oil searchers. While conventional exploration represents a more and more sophisticated game of hide-and-seek, with the volatile and deeply-buried deposits whispering "Catch me if you can", tar sands have always said, "Here I am. Come and get me."

The first historical mention of the tar sands came in 1788, when explorer Peter Pond noted the sticky black mass along the banks of the Athabasca River. The following year, another noted explorer, Alexander MacKenzie wrote of "Some bituminous fountains in which a pole 20 feet long may be inserted without the least resistance." However, apart from providing caulking material for native canoes, the tar sands provided little more concerted interest until the birth of the oil era. Between the great wars, tar sands were used as paving material, but the great mystery remained: how could precious liquid petroleum be separated from all that sand and clay? Early on, one adventurer hit on the idea of heating the sands and thus causing the oil to flow more easily. Another had the more science fiction notion of introducing micro-organisms that would feed on the sands and, in the process, extract the bitumen. Neither scheme worked. Calgary inventor Gordon Coulson, with that great leap of lateral thinking common to all great scientific advance, used his wife's washing machine both as the inspiration and the tool for a scheme based on centrifugal force. At one time, Royalite Oil Co. was going to spend $50 million on developing a commercial scheme based on Coulson's ideas, but in the end

---

* In the latter half of 1979, AEC was reported to be inundated by requests from oil companies to buy its Syncrude option.

abandoned the project. Nevertheless, Great Canadian Oil Sands
still uses centrifuges as one part of its process.

What, in the wake of the renewed furore over nuclear development in the late 1970's, seems like the most unattractive technology for unlocking the tar sands was inspired by a Saudi Arabian sunset in the late 1950's. M. L. Natland, a senior geologist with the Richfield Corp. of Los Angeles, was watching the spectacular sight from a small hill overlooking the desert. As he saw the giant fireball sink beheath the sand, it suddenly occurred to him that a similar thermo-nuclear reaction might be sunk beneath less attractive sands of Alberta on the other side of the globe. Eureka! Henceforth, a scheme was launched to explode a "small bomb", a nine kiloton nuclear device, 1,200 feet underground. In fact, the scheme received both provincial and federal approval towards the end of the 1950's, but was effectively killed by the spirit of nuclear disarmament. The idea was raised once more im 1974, but seems to have now slipped once more, perhaps gratefully, into oblivion.

The technology of the tar sands that has evolved is inevitably one of size and brute strength rather than scientific complexity. For great Canadian Oil Sands, pioneering the technology of commercial production proved to be a nightmare.

Great Canadian Oil Sands was built as an act of faith by the chairman of Sun Oil Co., John Howard Pew, patriarch of the family that controlled the Philadelpia-based company. GCOS was in fact the smallest of three competing proposals to build tar sands plants that came before the Alberta Oil & Gas Conservation Board in the early 1960's. It won, it seems, because it was the smallest of the three. At that time, the fear was that tar sands production would disrupt the uncertain market for conventional oil. "Tar sands miners" were not popular in Calgary and their presence was not welcomed in the Petroleum Club. However, Alberta wanted to make a start on developing the sands, so the least controversial approval seemed to be to the smallest of the three proposals. Groups led by Imperial and Shell (the forerunners, respectively, of Syncrude and Alsands) each wanted plants producing 100,000 barrels of synthetic oil a day, but GCOS's project was for a more modest 31,500 (this was later raised to 45,000). The original cost estimate for GCOS in 1960 was $110 million. By 1967 its final price tag had escalated to $250 million. On September 25, 1967, the simian, bespectacled J. Howard Pew told those at the plant's opening: "It is the considered opinion of our group that if the North American continent is to produce the oil to meet its requirements in the years ahead, oil from the Athabasca area must of necessity play an important role."

Pew's words were prescient, but he surely did not realize the sacrifices that Sun was going to make in the cause of the advance of science. GCOS was plagued for years after start-up with unforeseen technical problems that caused it to grind to a halt time and time again. The plant did not achieve its target output of 45,000 barrels a day until 1972, by which time it had an accumulated financial deficit of $90 million. The fight to dig out and convey the bitumen-laden sands produced a battle in which the machinery often came second. The huge bucket wheels that dig out the sand aged visibly. Soon, like old men, their teeth broke and they sputtered to a halt. The conveyor belts that carried the reluctant tar sand to the processing plant were constantly clogged up. Each solution created a new problem. To free the sands from the conveyor belt, water was used. But then in winter it froze, making the problem worse. Additives were dissolved in the water, but they froze too. Finally, the sands were successfully loosened by using kerosene. That caused the whole conveyor belt to disintegrate!

Syncrude has been able to learn something from many of GCOS's mistakes. The plant is much bigger but the technology is broadly similar. At Syncrude, huge, crane-like drag lines scrape up the tar sand with gigantic buckets. Each of these 6,500 ton monsters is built to handle 23 million tons of material a year. The sand is then moved onto conveyors by bucketwheels and transported to the processing plant. There, it is mixed with hot water, steam and chemicals to separate the bitumen from the sand. The bitumen is subsequently treated by heating or "cracking" it into its various constituents — coke gas, naptha and gas oil. The coke gas is treated and is then usable as a fuel, while the naptha and gas oil have the nitrogen and sulphur removed and are eventually blended once more to form high quality synthetic crude oil.

Apart from the tar sands, the heavy oils of Lloydminster, an area straddling the Alberta Saskatchewan border, and Cold Lake, Alberta, also offer great potential for development during the 1980's.

Heavy oils are drilled for, but dribble to the surface in very small amounts, providing just a glimpse of the potential beneath. They lie halfway in consistency and economic attractiveness between conventional oil and the tar sands. Conventional drilling enables perhaps 5% of heavy oil to flow sluggishly to the surface, but greater levels of recovery require underground stimulation. At the moment, there are a large number of *in situ* (that is, underground) experimental projects underway in Alberta seeking to find an economical way to recover more of this oil. Often part funded by another of the Lougheed government's creations, the Alberta Oil Sands Technology and Research Authority, these schemes utilize some method of underground heating to enable the oil to flow more freely. Once produced, heavy oil needs upgrading to become a normal refinery feedstock. The reason is that it is not only thick and sticky, but also has a high sulphur and asphalt content. Canada's major heavy oil producer is Husky Oil, so it is almost inevitable that Bob Blair, now that he controls Husky, will play a key role in the development of this resource. To the north of Lloydminster lie the Cold Lake deposits that Imperial plans to develop. Cold Lake oil lies halfway in consistency between Lloydminster heavy oil and the tar sands. Imperial plans to use *in situ* methods of heat stimulation to make the oil flow to the surface where it will be upgraded to a refinable product. Imperial estimates that the plant could be on-stream by 1986 and that it would produce about 1.25 billion barrels of oil, almost one-fifth of Canada's present conventional oil reserves, over its 25 year life.

It seems reasonable to assume that the technology of Syncrude, and subsequent plants, will be improved to make that end of the non-conventional oil business less uncertain. However, the principal uncertainty remains that of the price fetched for the oil. Or at least, that seemed to be the principal uncertainty until the downfall of the Shah of Iran led to a further major escalation in world oil prices during 1979. At a meeting of OPEC nations in Geneva in May of that year it was decided to adopt a "two-tier" approach to oil pricing. The Saudis, the most moderate group within OPEC, decided on an increase to $18 US a barrel, while the more militant nations, such as Algeria and Libya, imposed prices of $23.50 US. In the first half of 1979, spot prices had been as high as $38 US a barrel.

This disruption meant a truly dramatic change in the economics of the Syncrude operation. One of the stipulations demanded by Syncrude's corporate participants was that the output of the plant should receive world price. The argument was that it was better to pay world prices to domestic producers to increase oil supplies rather than pay the same amount of money for imports, because the money paid domestically would be ploughed, at least partly, back into Canada. When Syncrude opened in September, 1978, the world price was $12.70 US a barrel. The decline of the Canadian dollar against its U.S. counterpart had already provided a boost of about 15% in Canadian dollar terms, but the boost from the Iranian disruptions was enormous. Taking $20 US as the prevailing world price by mid 1979, Syncrude's participants were looking at additional gross profits of more than $1 million a day at full capacity, vs profits based on September, 1978 world prices.

The last waltz partner was beginning to look very attractive indeed.

7 | The "Invisible" Oil Companies: Brickbats for Mobil and Bouquets for Chevron

The whole affair read like a tendentious script written by a far-left Canadian Nationalist to dramatize manipulation of Canadian oil companies by their U.S. parents.

Their arms are in Calgary, but their hearts and minds are quite obviously elsewhere. This may explain why they take just that little bit longer to do everything than their industry counterparts — to take farm-ins, to bid at land sales, and generally participate in the wheeling and dealing that makes Calgary one of the world's most exciting oil cities.

Their big decisions come by telex or telephone out of New York, San Francisco and Chicago. Their chief executives, like nerve impulses travelling along a corporate spinal chord, spend much of their time shuttling between Calgary and "head office" as the messengers of "approved" action.

They are Mobil Canada, Chevron Standard and Amoco Canada, Canada's "invisible" big oil companies.

Mobil Canada and Chevron Standard are the Canadian arms of the second and third largest (after Exxon) of the Standard Sisters, Mobil Oil Corp. of New York and San Francisco-based Standard Oil of California (Socal). Amoco is the arm of another Rockefeller offshoot, Standard Oil of Indiana, based in Chicago, that really ranks as the eighth sister.

Of the three, Amoco could be considered the most open and traditionally the most active explorer. Early in 1979, the company went through the unprecedented step of raising $100 million of debentures in the Canadian market, thus it had to make extensive revelations in the form of a prospectus. The prospectus showed that Amoco has a land position in western Canada second only to PanCanadian Petroleum and that in 1978 it participated in 10% of all the wells drilled in Alberta. It also showed that Amoco's parent is clearly keen on taking some profits out of Canada after plowing back earnings for many years. Indeed, between 1976 and the end of 1978, Standard of Indiana took more than $277 million out of Canada, although this seems to have in no way dented the powerful upward trend in the company's Canadian exploration expenditures.

Chevron is a much more shadowy company, although it leaped into the limelight in 1977 with the discovery of the West Pembina field. The find has done nothing to remove Chevron's mystique. Indeed, now the word is going around the industry that Chevron has some kind of "Black Box" — the geologists equivalent of the alchemists' touchstone — that enables it unerringly to spot oil-bearing anomalies two miles below the surface.

Finally, comes Mobil Canada, a company that perhaps wishes it had stayed in the shadows. Until 1978, Mobil seemed to be going its own quiet way, indeed, a little quieter than most since it seemed to be doing very little exploration in the West. It had been a leading explorer off the Nova Scotian shelf, but the results had been disappointing. Then, suddenly, the usually unwanted glare of publicity fell on Mobil Canada, and the picture that it illuminated was not a pretty one.

Mobil: Malice in Blunderland

The whole affair read like a tendentious script written by a far-left Canadian Nationalist. The clear objective would have been to dramatize manipulation of Canadian oil companies by their United States parents. It had everything: a head office in New York where an insensitive businessman called the shots for Canada with complete disregard for local employees and a local Canadian hero fighting impersonal, and inefficient, central control. The hero was being put under intense personal pressure and, in the end, felt forced to leave. Then, finally, with what looked like a classic display of corporate malice, head office sued the departing Canadian executive in an almost surreal attempt to keep control of the contents of nothing less than his head!

It could have been subtitled Malice in Blunderland. But the really amazing part was that it was all true. As a piece of corporate public relations, the picking of mighty Mobil Oil Corp. on the departing head of its Canadian operation, Arne Nielsen, might not rank with Texaco's support for the Nazi party during World War II, but it stands up as one of the greatest blunders seen in the oilpatch for many years.

Not only did Mobil lose its case against Nielsen, but, in the course of the five day trial, in January, 1979, the world's third largest oil company had all sorts of dirty linen washed in public.

Mobil Canada's parent was long regarded as "Exxon's little sister" but with 1978 worldwide sales of $34.7 billion, Mobil Oil Corp. hardly rates as small. It had its origins in the breaking-up of the

Standard Trust and, over the years, had developed a reputation as not only one of the most aggressive but also perhaps one of the more enlightened of the Seven Sisters. Indeed, its reputation in Canada had not been bad until 1977, when Nielsen left the company to take over as senior executive of Canadian Superior.

At first, it seemed that Mobil saw Nielsen's departure as part of a greater drama being played out in the American courts between Mobil Oil Corp. and Canadian Superior's parent, Houston-based Superior Oil Corp. More than 30 of Mobil's employees had moved to Superior within a relatively short time and Mobil was accusing Superior of unfairly enticing them away. Thus, when Nielsen departed, Mobil saw it as part of the same "plot", with the result that they cried "conspiracy" and, sued both Nielsen and Canadian Superior. However, as the case unfolded in court, it emerged that Nielsen's reasons for departure were very significantly due to the deteriorating relations between himself and New York. They were also based on the head office's insensitive treatment of its Canadian subsidiary's employees and the downgrading of its activities.

Of course, with 100% ownership of Mobil Canada, Mobil Oil Corp. might well maintain that it had every right to do just what it liked with its Canadian subsidiary. However, in the politically-sensitive environment of the 1970's, expounding such a view is more than unwise, particularly when central control had obviously been a strategic mistake.

Arne Nielsen, moreover, proved almost perfect for the part of David against Mobil's Goliath. One of the most popular and widely respected figures in the Calgary oil community, Nielsen typified all that was considered best in the Canadian oil business. Born on a farm near Standard, Alberta, to Danish immigrant parents, his original move into the study of geology shortly after the end of the Second World War had truly romantic origins. He and his father Aksel had gathered from their farm a collection of fossils and sea shells, remnants of the sea that had washed the prairies more than 30,000 years before as the last ice age retreated over North America. It was these reminders of the changing earth that led Nielsen into the study of geology at the University of Alberta in 1946, the year before Imperial's find at Leduc was to revolutionize the Canadian oil industry.

When he graduated he immediately joined Mobil's Canadian subsidiary and, three years later, was responsible for the discovery of the Pembina field, which lies half as deep and almost directly above the West Pembina field that Chevron was to discover 24 years later. Covering 1,000 square miles, Pembina proved to be the largest oil field, in areal extent, in North America, and Canada's largest producing field. Thus Nielsen helped Mobil Canada to its permanent niche in Canadian oil history. In 1967, at the age of 41, Nielsen achieved full local-hero status as the first Canadian to become president of Mobil Canada.

Nielsen moved on to become a pillar of the Canadian oil community, serving as head of the Canadian Petroleum Association and as a member of the key industry group, the National Advisory Committee on Petroleum, set up under Liberal Energy Minister Joe Greene in the early 1970's to give advice to the government on energy policy matters.

Over the years, Mobil Canada built a solid position in Canadian oil. By the mid-seventies, it was the top producer among the three wholly American-owned majors, ranking sixth in overall production in Canada. But although it continued to produce from its past discoveries, what was not apparent to the public at large was that its exploration activity had virtually ground to a halt. A massive internal reorganization had taken place within the company's New York head office that had stripped the Calgary-based subsidiary of what little autonomy it had, and made it impossible for Nielsen to have any significant input into corporate decision making.

More than that, Mobil Oil Corp., desperately short of cash to carry out immensely expensive development projects in the North Sea and the Far East, was busily milking Mobil Canada for all the funds it could get. It desperately wanted to get its hands on the $100 million or so annual earnings of Mobil Canada. However straight dividends were subject to a 15% Canadian withholding tax, so the way that New York dreamed up of getting around that immediate problem was to take as much of Mobil Canada's oil exports as it could to its refineries at Jolyet and Buffalo, but not pay for them at once. By simply "owing" Mobil Canada the money, Mobil Oil Corp. managed to get its hands on hundreds of millions of dollars. New York also considered the possibility of Mobil Canada being forced to lend money directly to its Norwegian North Sea operations.

Mobil couldn't get away with that sort of thing for long because of the Canadian Government's Petroleum Industry Monitoring provisions, under which Ottawa took a very close look at how much of oil companies' income was being reinvested. Although only the overall reinvestment figures were released to the public by the government, and those figures demonstrated that the industry was pouring virtually all its income back into new ventures, Mobil's performance was abysmal and there was concern in the company's Calgary office that the government might at any time "expose" them, as the monitoring act enabled them to do.

The source of Mobil Canada's problems lay not only in New York's need for cash but also in the post-OPEC Federal-Provincial dispute in Canada, and a global corporate reorganization undertaken by Mobil with effect from the beginning of 1976. In 1974, when Peter Lougheed's Albertan Conservatives and the federal Liberal government of Pierre Trudeau had been locked in battle over the spoils of higher oil prices, most larger companies had cut back on exploration expenditure. In some cases, and, it seemed, with more than a little justification, the companies had stopped spending completely. Mobil, with Nielsen's hearty support, was one of these.

New York then developed a "down" on Canada that prevented it from seeing the opportunities that subsequently appeared as the political dispute was cleared up and considerable incentives were introduced. Throughout 1975, it gradually appeared that the situation might be improving, but then in 1976 the reorganization within Mobil Oil Corp. took place that was to cut off Canada from access to the ear of the company's executive committee. The reorganization de-emphasized geography and re-emphasized functional responsibility. At a time when nationalist sensitivities to the moves of major oil companies had never been greater, it seemed that Mobil Oil Corp. was erecting a corporate structure that went out of its way to ignore these potent forces. One of the brains behind this scheme, and a man who fits neatly into the unattractive role of the U.S. corporate "heavy", was Mobil's head of worldwide exploration, Alex Massad.

Massad's view of the corporate world seemed particularly out of phase with the majors new "awareness" of the growing hostility to big oil. He still regarded Mobil's worldwide strategy as being a glorified and impersonal chess game, in which managers were pawns, and there was little regard for personal feelings or nationalities.

For Nielsen, Massad emerged as his personal bête noir. Under the corporate reorganization, Nielsen now found himself four steps removed from the top layer of Mobil's executive as opposed to the previous two steps. Whereas before he had been able to put his view personally before the company's executive committee, after 1976 he was never permitted to approach them. Moreover, the new emphasis on functional responsibility meant that a number of Nielsen's theoretical subordinates in Calgary in fact reported straight to New York. Everywhere, Nielsen found his personal authority being undermined.

The already short rein on expenditure tightened into a stranglehold and Nielsen had to go to New York for approval on almost everything. He had no authority to spend anything that was not included in the budget the company presented at the giant's annual financial get-together in Phoenix, Arizona. Moreover, if the cost of any approved item increased, he had to go once more to New York. The financial pickiness extended to the lowest levels. All contributions to charities such as the United Way had to go to New York and only five corporate memberships of the Petroleum Club were permitted. When Nielsen tried to "sneak" an extra membership, Massad personally crossed out the authorization. Nielsen, concerned about the status of his employees within the local community, told another Mobil employee to put Petroleum auditors winkled it out and disallowed it.

However, the move that Nielsen realized could be political dynamite was New York's decision to put control of exploration in Canada's Arctic Islands and off its east coast in the hands of a Mobil subsidiary based in Dallas. Nielsen managed to persuade Massad of the potential political problems of such a move, but Massad did not reverse the decision, he merely told Nielsen the company would leave the organization chart looking the same but that effective control would still shift to Dallas.

Meanwhile, Nielsen's opposition to these moves was regarded by Massad as being obstructive. Mobil Canada's head already had one black mark against him for rejecting a call to Mobil's New York head office in 1974 because of family circumstances. He had originally agreed to move but then his wife had been discovered to be ill. Nielsen also had a paraplegic teenage son who needed constant attention. Nielsen's wife died six months after he turned down the move. As a sign of the diminishing importance of Canada and of Mobil's personal displeasure with Nielsen, his job was downgraded within the great Mobil hierarchy and, what hurt most of all, in two consecutive annual assessments of his management performance, he was judged to have produced a poor show.

By now Nielsen was becoming clearly disillusioned with Mobil's impersonal approach and concerned about the morale of his staff. In line with Mobil's "pawn" approach, he had been told in January of 1976 that Mobil Canada had 35 too many geologists and geophysicists and that these should now be transferred to Dallas. For big companies, which demand their employees scuttle around the globe in pursuit of the great God profit, the move was not unusual. But, by mid 1977, Arne Nielsen had had enough.

For a man of Nielsen's qualifications, job offers were plentiful, particularly when it was discovered that he was growing increasingly discontented at Mobil.

In the late 1960's he had been offered the chief executive post at Panarctic Oils, the consortium set up to explore the Arctic Islands. He had been offered the presidency of CDC Oil & Gas and, on two occasions, in the summer of 1975 and the spring of 1977, he had been considered for the top job at federally-owned PetroCanada.

In June 1976, he had also been approached by Superior Oil to head up their 53% Canadian-owned subsidiary Canadian Superior, whose taciturn head, Art Feldmeyer, was soon to retire. They offered Nielsen $125,000 a year, plus a $30,000 bonus, similar to the one he was getting at Mobil. However, in the end, he decided not to accept the job. But then, late in 1977, when Nielsen had become much more keen to move, the negotiations were reopened. This time, the salary had been considerably sweetened, and Nielsen was offered $225,000 a year, plus a one time bonus of $30,000, a

Lincoln, and, for good measure, membership in the Petroleum Club.

Nielsen decided to accept and, on November 22, travelled to New York to deliver his letter of resignation. (Maintaining its tight wad image to the end, Mobil suggested that Nielsen should have paid his own fare to New York!).

Upon Nielsen's departure, Mobil, already legally at war with Superior in the United States, decided to sue. They accused him of not giving reasonable notice and of carrying trade secrets and confidential information with him that could be damaging to Mobil. They accused Canadian Superior of seducing Nielsen away by the devilishly clever and devious tactic of offering him large amounts of money, and finally they accused Canadian Superior and its American parent of being in league to rob Mobil of the flower of its corporate talent.

By the time the case reached the Calgary courthouse in January of 1979, even the insensitive Mobil realized that they had made a big mistake. They were desperately trying to settle out of court. However, the case went on and in five days of testimony, the full, and somewhat sordid, story of Mobil's treatment of its Canadian subsidiary and of Arne Nielsen unfolded. Nielsen, if anything, emerged as a more of a hero than he had been before. By contrast, Mobil's counsel could only limp away to await the seemingly inevitable judgment that came down against the company in May of 1979.

Due to Nielsen's inability to get the message through to New York that the situation in Canada had changed completely by the beginning of 1977, Mobil Canada missed out both on the West Pembina and Elmworth exploration plays. The fact that the company did not go into West Pembina, throwing huge amounts of money around, as some companies did, on the scantest information, may have been to its advantage. However, Nielsen and his exploration team had desperately tried to interest New York in Elmworth, asking them to bid for the last big acreage reservations that came up for sale in northeast British Columbia in the spring of 1977.

But the Mobil Canada team were going significantly on a hunch, because details of Canadian Hunter's discoveries had not been published. The "system" down in New York demanded a complete prognosis of the exploration play. Mobil Canada could not give one and so the last cheap acreage in Elmworth was allowed to pass into other hands.

The Nielsen case does at least seem to have awakened Mobil in New York to the potential of Canada once more. The Arctic Islands and east coast lands have now been put once more under the jurisdiction of Mobil Canada, while the company seems now to be spending money once more at land sales. However, Mobil's insensitive treatment of Arne Nielsen has probably damaged its Canadian image for years to come, and certainly did nothing for the more general cause of "big oil" in Canada.

Chevron and West Pembina: The Benefits of Keeping your Head Down

Mobil, like Imperial, learned a valuable lesson from the Arne Nielsen case. Since OPEC, it is a bad idea for big oil to stick its head out of the bunker. By distinct contrast, however, another of the invisible companies, Chevron, kept its head down and was responsible for Canada's largest conventional oil find in ten years. Chevron's find re-established that nobody is as good at finding big oil as big oil. However, for most of the other large oil companies, whose exploration departments were steeped in the conventional geological wisdom that there were no more major oil pools in western Canada, it led to a mad and often ill-judged scramble for land at enormous prices. Evidence of some sort of presence in the West Pembina area became a must for 1977 annual reports as managements attempted to demonstrate to their shareholders, and each other, that they were where the action was. Nobody wanted to appear to have missed out on the "big play". All time record prices were paid for land and Alberta's already bulging coffers received a further massive boost. When many of the eager companies drilled on their prized acreage they discovered they had paid many millions of dollars to be where the action wasn't.

For investors, the find sparked a stock market surge the likes of which had not been seen since the early 1970's. Not only did the professionals make millions, but for many stock market dabblers, West Pembina revived belief in the stock market "killing" and provided a key element of the longest-lasting and greatest stock market boom in Canadian history.

Small companies in the middle of the activity, usually completely by chance, found their share prices doubling, trebling or even quadrupling as more and more investors got hooked on West Pembina fever. A company called Amalgamated Bonanza had whetted investors' appetites by increasing from $7 to $50 in the course of 1977. Now here was a chance for everyone to get a piece of the action.

In strategic terms, the discovery and exploitation of West Pembina by Chevron Standard Ltd. was a masterpiece following a classic pattern. Seismic examination produced the ghost of a genie; a land position was carefully built up, both by taking farm-ins from other companies and by buying from the Crown, wells were drilled, and, most important, oil was struck.

Chevron first knew it was onto something in the autumn of 1974. Then, when the dispute between the federal and provincial governments over the spoils of higher, OPEC-induced, domestic oil prices was at its height, the company shot a 300-mile long seismic line right across the province, from the Saskatchewan border to the Foothills, passing close to Edmonton.

Chevron's exploration team, headed by the tall, professorial Gerry Henderson — who, with an educational background embracing Trinity College Dublin, Oxford, McGill and Princeton must count himself one of the more comprehensively educated of the Calgary oil community — spotted a couple of geological anomalies, ghosts that looked as if they could be oil traps, just west of the main Pembina field, but at about twice the depth. The anomalies, which showed up after extensive computer massaging of the seismographic readings, looked like reef formations, those pointed hummocks far below the earth's surface that often contain hydrocarbons.

According to conventional geological theory, such reefs should not have been there. The reefs at Leduc, where Imperial Oil had started Alberta's postwar boom with its discovery in 1947, were only found built on an underlying base known as the "Cooking Lake" formation. If there was no Cooking Lake formation, as there was not in the Pembina area, then there could be no reefs. So, at least, said geological theory. But Chevron's computer programmes, working over the mystical squiggles of the seismic readings, said that whatever the theory, there was something there.

The next logical step might appear to be to drill and find out. But that was exactly what Chevron could not afford to do because they had no land in the area. Not only did they not own land in the area, but most of the acreage was already held by other companies. Indeed, the general area had been heavily explored because one of Canada's largest oil fields, the Pembina field, discovered in 1954, was within geological spitting distance. What Chevron thought they had discovered was, at about 11,000 feet, twice the depth of the Pembina field. Other companies might be blissfully unaware of its existence, but they still held the key land. Chevron felt like a visitor to the zoo who spots that the lion's bed is made of gold. The prize was valuable, but achieving it could prove perilous!

As a large company, and one that had already been doing extensive seismic work in the area, it was out of the question for Chevron to go about accumulating land in its own name, since that would have immediately given the game away. So, for the two years after its first "sighting", throughout 1975 and 1976 it went about stealthily building up a land position through third parties.

Inevitably, the companies who actually gave up land, or a share of their lands, were a little sheepish when they discovered what they had done. But they also had reason to be grateful, since in most cases they finished up with interests in a major new oil field.

The two "lions" who seemed to willingly move over and share the most valuable beds were among Canada's most prominent western exploration companies, Pacific Petroleums Ltd., later to fall into government hands when taken over by PetroCan, and Norcen Energy Resources Ltd.

Pacific gave away 13 sections (8,320 acres) in the middle of the play in return for a measly 10% override on production, while Norcen gave away half the production from 42,000 acres of land in return for Chevron drilling two wells. However, both companies finished up much richer in the process.

Chevron approached Pacific through its main agent, Nairb Petroleums Ltd. Nairb, in the shape of its president, Joe Johns, sidled up to Pacific's chief landman, a canny Scot named Ken Smith, in early 1976, and said it would like to take a farm-in on certain of Pacific's acreage in return for drilling a well. The land in question was due to return to the Crown in March 1977 when the lease ran out, and Pacific had no intention of drilling on it, so Smith, after consultation with Pacific's head of exploration Syd Smith said "Why not?"

In normal circumstances they would have taken a 50% share of both the exploration and whatever production resulted. Pacific had never had dealings with this little company, and it knew that a number of larger oil companies had had problems getting involved with small, inexperienced oil concerns that had let wells get out of control. So Pacific decided to avoid the potential hassles of co-operation and go for the 10% override, i.e. taking the top tenth of any production but avoiding participation in the exploration, thus limiting their liability in the event of problems. But what made the matter vastly worse for Pacific was that somehow, when a young landman was drawing up the agreement, he left out the normal provision under which the company would obtain all information on the well drilled. Not only was Pacific giving its land away for next to nothing, but it was missing out on the opportunity to at least find out quickly how much it had abandoned. Chevron couldn't believe its luck. Nevertheless, Pacific was neither slow to admit its error nor to pick up the scent when the faint whiff of a major oil find found its way into the fields and muskeg west of Edmonton.

As for Norcen, they did not give up such an enormous interest but the tract of land involved was much larger, and Chevron were bold enough to do a deal with them face to face. If the executives at the Norcen Tower in Calgary need comforting, however, they can reflect that the 42,000 acres of which they gave up a 50% share to Chevron had been obtained in the late 1960's for the sum of $5.71 an acre! Chevron's drilling made some of that land worth several thousand dollars an acre. Norcen had bought the land on the basis of testing a particular zone, the unattractively named Belly River.

They had drilled a well, found nothing, and the land had been left to nature. Eventually, another spot of exploration activity developed to the southwest which seemed to tend towards Norcen's acreage, although the company thought it was probably on the fringe of it.

It was at this stage that Chevron appeared on the scene, like the antique dealer turning up at a country farmhouse and eagerly praising all the farmer's possessions with the exception of the Rembrandt hanging over the hearth. Chevron offered to drill a well to test the zone where the gas from the southwestern play might crop up.

After months of what they presumably considered hard bargaining, Norcen finally got Chevron to agree to drill that test well and take no interest whatsoever in any discovery. However, the quid pro quo was that Chevron wanted the option to drill a deeper test. Norcen knew that Chevron had been doing lots of seismic work in the area, and were after something in particular. However, they had no idea what it was. Like Pacific, Norcen knew that their tenure of the land ran out, in the latter case, November of 1978, unless some drilling was done. They had no geological theory on which to drill, so, after months of negotiation, they finally gave Chevron a farm-in. Chevron meanwhile had also been asking for "unoccupied" lands to be posted for sale, and had snapped them up through agents. So, after two years of stealthy buying, without arousing too much interest or pushing land prices too high, Chevron had what it needed, the acreage from which it could find out what was really down there more than two miles below the surface. By this time Chevron had done a great deal more seismic work and knew where all the most likely drilling locations were. Of course, they could still not be sure that they had anything, but towards the end of 1976, they at least were in a position to find out.

On December 1, 1976, their chief "secret agent", Nairb, which itself did not know what it was seeking, started drilling. After ten days, the well lost part of its surface casing, and the drilling rig had to be moved about 15 feet. On December 15, a second start was made. Over Christmas and into the New Year the drill bit ground, yard by yard, into the earth's crust until, on January 14, 1977 the rig supervisor told Henderson that the well was "speaking to them", literally making rumbling noises that often indicate something powerful has been penetrated far below the surface. Nairb, under instructions, then set about finding just how powerful a genie they might have disturbed 11,000 feet below ground. As concerned as ever about keeping their find, if it was a find, to themselves, the Chevron team instructed Nairb to carry out a "tight hole test". Great gushers of oil shooting into the air were the last thing Chevron wanted, for all major companies employ scouts — more

precisely spies   to check up on the activity at competitors' wells.
The fact that it was "only" Nairb drilling the well inevitably aroused less interest in the scouts than if a major company had been drilling. Nevertheless, Chevron didn't want to take any chances. The idea behind tight hole testing is that lots of pressure is forced down the hole. If anything is found, it appears as a discrete little flare beside the rig: nothing conspicuous for prying eyes to behold.

However, the plan went slightly awry when the enormous pressure from the Devonian reef, released after sitting there hunched up for many millions of years, blew the testing equipment clean out of the hole and sprayed oil all over surrounding trees. It was a gusher that would not be denied its temporary place in the Albertan sun. It took several days to bring the well under control. Not only that, but the drilling crew actually saw the head of one of the dreaded scouts appear, and then rapidly disappear, behind a tree. The scout presumably went back to report to his master, but his master, blinded by what geological science said about the area's potential, took no notice.

The Nairb A 11-22-49-12W5 discovery well — as it will pass somewhat unromantically into the history of Canadian oil — was also being used to "drill into" a land sale, that is, the results of the test would be critical to the price Chevron's agent was instructed to pay in a sale of nearby land. The results being excellent, Chevron badly wanted that land. There was still little reason that anyone else should bid high prices at the sale, but just in case, Chevron's agent bid $1,000 an acre for the posted land, which created more than a ripple of interest. The word went around that Nairb had discovered a deep oil formation.

One company dispatched a scout to the Nairb drilling site three days after the sale to look for telltale signs of a discovery. Ironically, the scout met one of Chevron's own scouts and invited him along. The two scouts saw oil scum at the site, from which the rig had now been removed, and also that the trees around the site had been burned. The Chevron scout, himself blissfully unaware of what was going on, dutifully reported back to Chevron what he had seen. They thanked him very much.

Rumours were definitely starting to buzz around Nairb's activity, but, as chance and a little bit of strategy would have it, the most effective of dampers was applied to the many-tongued deity. Nairb's next two wells were dry!

One of these Chevron deliberately had drilled off target because the company wanted to check out one of its leases that was due to expire. However, the other well simply missed its objective. There were, in this latter case, problems with reaching the potential drilling site dead on the geological bullseye because of muskeg, so it was drilled off to one side and angled towards where it was supposed to make a strike. It didn't. But Chevron had not only drilled a dry hole, it had killed outside interest once again, at least temporarily. Ironically, those two dry holes were virtually the only dry holes drilled by Chevron or its agents for the remainder of 1977. In April, the strain of keeping the secret finally seemed to be too much for Chevron. It actually made an announcement of a "significant" oil discovery. The strategem could not have been smarter. Those who even took any notice of the announcement merely asked: "What the hell is Chevron up to? Who are they trying to bluff?"

However, one company that was becoming a little restive was Pacific, the large independent that had sold a good part of its estate for the proverbial mess of pottage.

Pacific, and its partners, Amoco and Texaco, held extensive lands to the south of where Nairb was drilling. The lands were due soon to revert to the Crown unless drilling was carried out on them, so one day Pacific's Syd Smith sat down with his opposite number at Amoco, Dave Martin, and began discussing, with half an eye on Nairb's activities, what a shame it would be for those lands to go back to the government. So they said, why don't we drill a well? Indeed, why not two? Texaco had been the operator responsible for drilling in the area but had bailed out of this particular venture. So it was left to Amoco and Pacific to drill one well each at either end of the property. To see which would drill which, they tossed a coin. Amoco's well was dry but Pacific's produced an astonishing and quite unexpected result. The well had reached the Mississippian formation, at which stage the company might well have stopped drilling. However, having heard the rumours about Nairb's find deeper in the Devonian, and also taking into account that Alberta's drilling incentive programme made it cheaper to drill deeper horizons, they drilled on.

Admittedly they were going to have to spend another $500,000 to get to the Devonian formation, but the Alberta government would be putting up half the cost in allowances against tax. In midsummer, Pacific hit its motherload, when the Devonian reef it penetrated blew out of control. It was another gusher, subsequently tested at 3,800 barrels a day of high quality oil through a choke smaller than your little finger. Pacific, Amoco and Texaco, partners in the area, were now more than aware that there was a secret. But although they had abundant proof of something big down below, they still lacked the comprehensive geological theory that Chevron had pieced together. Pacific's discovery well threw the venerable Wallace Pratt upside down. Oil had been discovered, abundantly, in the ground. Now it had to be discovered in the minds of the men who had found it in order that they could piece together the puzzle of where the rest of the field lay.

Towards the close of the Summer of 1977, two groups were involved in the West Pembina field, but Chevron was still way out in front. Pacific and its partners knew there was definitely something big down there, but Chevron now knew exactly what. And where.

However, the word, at long last, was about to get out. Ironically, but perhaps appropriately after so many blatant clues, what sparked the subsequent stock market boom and high-priced land grab was not a direct statement about West Pembina, and it came from someone who was not directly involved in it. Donald Getty, Alberta's widely-respected Energy Minister and pin-up of the Lougheed cabinet, was appearing late in September, 1977, before a legislative committee in Edmonton, talking about energy prospects for the province. Getty was asked if the tar sands and heavy oils were not now Alberta's only remaining sources for oil. Knowing of the Chevron and Pacific finds and feeling himself bound to answer as truthfully as possible without giving away any confidences, he said that was not true. He said there was still tremendous potential in conventional oil and gas. Indeed, he want on to say they would soon hear of some, and he was hopeful of a "very significant discovery in the conventional reservoirs." The magic words, West Pembina, were never mentioned, but somehow, within the following few days, Getty's remarks came to be associated with Chevron's find earlier in the year. Chevron were alarmed and Getty even phoned the company to assure them that he had not mentioned their name. But the word somehow found its way into the press and then to its most fertile ground, the stock market.

As with oil, stock market booms are found in the minds of men, and the biggest financial gushers are often predicated on the most scant information. Getty's rather vague remark was the tiny seed out of which the subsequent surge in both share and land prices grew. The belief that he had "given the game away" caused him considerable embarrassment. For many months afterwards, stockbrokers would edge up to him at cocktail parties with sly smiles on their faces and say: "Thanks a lot for the business. You certainly got those land sales going too, eh?"

For the stock market, which thrives on rumour, the situation was ideal. All the wells drilled in the West Pembina region were "tight holes", that is, no information about them was released. Under provincial regulations, the results of successful wells had to be released after a year. But that meant that investors had a full four months to revel in blissful ignorance before Chevron had to reveal what it had found in that first well. And investors certainly made the most of it.

At times, trading in the final three months of 1977 reached fever pitch. The Toronto Stock Exchange oil and gas index doubled from its year's low, and the mood infected the whole market. In the first full week in December, the Toronto Stock Exchange saw a total of 28.6 million shares change hands for $209.7 million, a level of trading it had not seen for eight years. What was more, one out of every three of those 28.6 million shares was an oil share, and most of the oil shares were being traded on the basis of their holdings in West Pembina.

As soon as the word had circulated that there was something big beneath West Pembina, everyone in the industry reached for their land maps. Who held land in the area? Investors could not buy Chevron, but they soon spotted that the other key players were Pacific and Norcen, whose share prices immediately surged. Home also had a strong land position, so it too found itself buoyed along on the crest of the wave. But it was Norcen's 50% share in those 42,000 acres right in the middle of the exploration play that made it the bellwether stock for the market. Towards the end of the year, its price had risen more than 80% from its 1977 low to $19 and the total dollar value of its shares traded on the Toronto Stock Exchange, for 1977, at a massive $149 million, placed it second only to old Ma Bell herself, Bell Canada, the greatest of widows' and orphans' stocks. A number of other, much smaller, companies found themselves in the eye of the hurricane. Typical was Oakwood Petroleums Ltd., whose head, Dallas Hawkins III had taken a farm-in from Amoco of 6,560 acres in the target area in the hope of finding something in the Cardium sands, where the original Pembina field had been discovered at between 5,000 and 6,000 feet. Then suddenly there was the geological equivalent of a ruckus in the basement, another 4,000 feet or so down, and the shares of Oakwood shot from less than $1.50 to almost $6.

Dallas Hawkins III suddenly found himself personally $6 million richer, but perhaps the greater impact was on the small investor, the share dabbler. For him, the dream of oil gushers revived the eternal hope of the quick killing. Meanwhile, his stockbrokers could point out examples even more spectacular than Oakwood. There was American Eagle, which Oakwood controlled, that had shot up from 37¢ to $4, Conventures Ltd., up from $2 to $8, and a whole hoard of others.

The flames of speculative enthusiasm were fanned not only by the rumour mill surrounding the "tight holes" in West Pembina, but also by rocketing prices for land in the area. On November 29, Home paid a record single bid of $18.2 million for a licence, and early in December, Chevron paid a record price per acre of $20,556.93 for a 640 acre section of land. The four sales that took place in November hauled in a mind-boggling $133.6 million, which compared with a previous annual record for Alberta of $160.1 million, set in 1976.

However, in early December, 1977, a little too much haste in drilling into a land sale, that is, attempting to take a well to its target depth and test it in order to assess the value of an adjoining block of land, caused the sweet smell of success temporarily to turn sour; literally.

On the afternoon of December 6, the workers on the rig at Amoco Pacific Brazeau 7-10, 80 miles southwest of Edmonton, were in the process of bringing the pipe out of the hole in order to change the drilling bit. The weather was bitterly cold, the men were working to a deadline, and they had only a few hundred feet to go to reach their target depth. They had changed the bit several times without problems, and since they were in a hurry they had not bothered to hook up a measuring system that would have told them how much "mud", the drilling fluid made up either of water or oil mixed with clay or chemicals, was moving into the hole as the pipe was pulled out. Apart from performing a lubricating function for the drilling bit and the rotating pipe, mud also serves to hold down the pressure from below if petroleum is struck. If that measuring device had been used, then the drillers would have noticed that something was creeping up the wellbore despite the enormous pressure from the two mile column of mud sitting above it. A genie had been released and was about to revel in its freedom. Eventually, the drilling crew noticed that mud was being forced out of the hole. There is an emergency tool, called a "stabbing valve", that can be used to shut down the flow, but when the crew tried to grab it, they found that it was frozen to the floor and couldn't be moved. All the other equipment designed to prevent blowouts was frozen in the minus 40 Centigrade temperatures, so at 4.45 p.m. on the afternoon of December 2, 1977, with a roar like a steam train, Amoco Pacific Brazeau 7-10 blew out. Originally, there was considered to be no great cause for concern, but then it was realized that the gas that was shooting from the hole into the rig at a rate of 30 million cubic feet a day and then billowing away into the atmosphere was "sour", that is, contained a large proportion of highly toxic hydrogen sulphide. In very small concentrations the gas smells like rotten eggs, but at concentrations of more than 100 parts in a million it can be lethal.

It seemed there was only one thing to do. Call Red Adair. Adair, over 60 years-old when called in by Amoco, is a figure held in almost religious awe by that tough breed of men who drill oilwells. Mementos of the man — a pin, a badge or a hat sticker — pass among the oil drilling fraternity like pieces of the Holy Shroud. John Wayne starred in a film, "The Hellfighters", based on his exploits. Adair has made a highly lucrative career from the dangerous business of capping wild wells and has brought more than 1,000 under control in his time. His charges are high, a phonecall to him can cost $5,000 and his fee for capping the wild well in the North Sea Ekofisk field earlier in 1977 had been $6.6 million — but he is quite simply the best in the business.

The Amoco wild well was to present Adair with one of his greatest challenges and it was to take him almost a month to finally bring the raging monster under control. By the time it had at last been capped, the smell of rotten eggs had found its way not only into every nook and cranny of the little village of Lodgepole, 14 miles away, but also into the streets of Edmonton, 80 miles to the east, and Calgary, almost 200 miles to the south. The smell was even recorded below the border in northern Montana!

30 miles northwest, at Drayton Valley, the word somehow filtered into the local tavern that a couple of moose had been found gassed. By the end of the evening beer and vivid imaginations had taken the moose toll to 17! But there were in fact no fatalities reported among either moose or men.

Nevertheless, between December 6 and January 2, the situation was more than tense. Bulldozers and workmen clad in oxygen masks and yellow protective suits circled the monster tentatively while it rained condensate, a natural form of gasoline, on them, leaving huge yellow puddles all around the well. Just one spark could have set the whole area ablaze. And eventually one spark did.

Shortly after the arrival of the short, chubby Adair at the site, he decided to attempt to force heavy drilling mud down the hole to counter the gas flow. Meanwhile special pipe cutting equipment was ordered up from Houston. However, it seemed that mother nature was conspiring to let the wild well have its day. At first, operations were crippled by temperatures down to minus 46 C. Then, when the temperature rose, mild winds left the deadly hydrogen sulphide hanging like a lethal pall over the site.

For four days, Adair and his team attempted to close the hydraulic devices known as blind rams that would have shut off the well, but the cold and malfunctioning equipment eventually forced them to abandon that idea. Preparations were made to remove the rig and to drill in a diagonal relief well.

Then, on the morning of Christmas eve, the column of gas suddenly caught fire, sending a towering column of flame 300 feet into the air. Adair arrived on the scene shortly after the ignition and, in an act that further served to enhance his already heroic reputation, leaped into a bulldozer and pulled the black and buckling rig clear of the well, thus risking his life to make sure that it did not melt into the well. John Wayne couldn't have done it better himself. The pools of condensate around the rig eventually caught fire, as did the surrounding forest, turning the scene into a blazing inferno. But at least it solved the problem of the hydrogen sulphide.

Eventually, on January 1, 1978, a modified bulldozer dropped 350 pounds of explosive at the top of the well, and an enormous explosion snuffed out the flame. At 2 p.m. on Monday, January 2, Red Adair finally put the cap on the wild well. The blowout had impressed the mighty Red Adair further into the hearts and minds of the oil community. But it had also left a lingering smell of West Pembina in the noses of an estimated one million Albertans.

8 | Blair and Bloody Noses

It could be that his mind is revolving some multi-million dollar energy scheme; or it could be that he looks neither right nor left in case he is caught in some undesired social encounter. For the rapid expansion of Blair's corporate personality in the past few years seems to have been counterbalanced by an increasing introversion about his private life.

For the rising West, Bob Blair has emerged during the 1970's as a dour, aggressive and skillful corporate champion. While Premier Lougheed was showing an uncompromising political face to Ottawa in the wake of the 1973-1974 OPEC crisis, Blair was squaring up to bloody some of the eastern Establishment's most prominent noses including those of the major oil companies. In just a few years, Blair leaped from provincial obscurity to national prominence. Pulling off a startling corporate "double", he won regulatory approval to construct the world's "most expensive privately-financed capital project", the Alaska Highway pipeline, and he snatched control of Husky Oil Ltd. away from PetroCanada and giant Los Angeles-based Occidental Petroleum in what was, at the time, the country's largest takeover struggle.

Blair has become a focal point not only for burgeoning Alberta corporate power but also for wresting back control of the Canadian energy industry from American domination. Just a few years ago, those who controlled Canada's major, foreign-owned oil companies regarded Blair as merely another example of the nationalist cry that bounced from time to time harmlessly off the towers of their corporate strength. By the end of the 1970's they had learned to take Bob Blair very seriously. The corporate terrier snapping at their heels in the early 1970's had grown into a much larger and more threatening animal.

Blair's power is not money power (he held 180,000 shares of Alberta Gas Trunk Line — valued at $4.5 million in mid 1979 "with corresponding bank debt", he hastens to add — but that would probably not put him in the oil industry's top 100 wealthy men). Nor is his power subtle behind-the-scenes power of the sort wielded in eastern boardrooms. Rather it is a politically-sensitive fighting power, and ability both to read the minds of governments and to take on big opponents and floor them.

"Blairology" has become a consuming pastime for Blair's fellow businessmen, who have seen him grow apart from them in recent years. Until relatively recently, the barbecues that Blair and his wife held at their ranch north of Calgary were one of the events of the province's social calendar, one of the largest gatherings outside the Stampede itself. But those stopped after his pipeline victory and his separation from his wife. He avoids Calgary's cocktail circuit and is infrequently seen at the Petroleum Club.

Frustrated by personal observation, Blairologists inevitably turn to his background for some clue to his uncompromising character. However, the only exotic detail of an otherwise conventional, but certainly well-heeled, upbringing was his place of birth, Trinidad, where his father Sid managed a refinery. Sid was born in Parry Sound, Ontario but moved to Edmonton just after the turn of the century. A well-known engineer, he went on to become president of giant engineering contractor Canadian Bechtel Ltd. and was credited with much of the research into developing the economic feasibility of the tar sands.

Blair, at the age of nine, two years ahead of most of his classmates, was sent to the exclusive Choate school in Connecticut, where young Rockefellers and Mellons spent their formative years.

Blair's precocity continued when he went to Queen's University at Kingston when he was only 16, emerging with a degree in chemical engineering. He worked for a number of years on pipeline construction in Alberta before joining Alberta & Southern Gas in 1959 and AGTL in 1969. He has thus spent virtually all his working life in Alberta. However, in recent years he has seemed less and less at home in Calgary's gregarious wheeler dealer environment. At times, Blair, who is by nature a shy man, looks like the improbable combination of a gladiator and an absent-minded professor. Grim, stocky — almost threatening — he can be seen walking amid the bustle of downtown Calgary, staring fixedly at some indeterminate spot on the sidewalk in front of him. It could be that his mind is revolving some multi-million dollar energy scheme; or it could be that he looks neither right nor left in case he is caught in some undesired social encounter. For the rapid expansion of Blair's corporate personality in the past few years seems to have been counterbalanced by an increasing introversion about his private life.

Although his profile as president of AGTL is high, giving speeches, addressing analysts, making stinging verbal assaults on opponents and critics, the search for a completely separate persona behind the corporate image produces little. Bob Blair seems to be almost totally taken up with his corporate life. The association between the man, the company and his consuming vision of national interest are producing, indeed may have already produced, a single entity. Blair's ego, AGTL's corporate objectives and the best interests of Canada — as perceived by Bob Blair — have become rolled into one. This metamorphosis, in which Blair seems to have assumed an almost Messianic mantle, is somewhat disturbing to other executives. At times, Blair has condemned rivals for acting in "self-interest", implying that his own purpose is a much higher one. Blair's obsessive nationalism thus often relegates his business opponents to the position of heretics.

One of Blair's distinguished board members, Daryl K. "Doc" Seaman, chairman and chief executive of fast-growing Bow Valley Industries, says: "Blair has a genuine altruism. He firmly believes that corporations should take a national stance and lead in situations even when they don't make money. But," Seaman hastens to add, "that is certainly something we don't do here at Bow Valley."

Blair's espousal of non-corporate objectives is not understood by many of his counterparts, particularly within the singularly muscular free-enterprise climate of Calgary, and a number of them regard his nationalism as no more than a convenient stance. However, such an easy assessment does an injustice to Blair.

Countering the condemnation of opponent's "self-interest", Blair told the author in mid 1979: "That phrase has been played up as if I was using it piously. The truth is that we feel that our role in the Alaska Highway project has become more of a kind of stewardship. To carry out that role, we do feel that we have to subordinate our self-interest."

Those who have looked for a personality that matches Blair's dazzling corporate tactics have been gravely disappointed. Talking to individuals he often mumbles, addressing groups he tends to drone. There is a certain self-conscious trendiness in his dress and appearance that one does not associate with 50 year-old corporate executives. During the period of the great pipeline debate, he developed a long droopy moustache and wore his hair far too long for regulation Petroleum Club standards. Perhaps it was a capillary obeisance to the ecologists and environmentalists that Blair knew would kill the opposition. Perhaps he was physically setting himself apart from the hoards of company men he knew he could outsmart.

But although he may not be silver-tongued or physically prepossessing he has a business mind that transcends that of most of his rivals. His political awareness in the pipeline debate proved to be the key to victory. His tactics in the takeover of Husky were to be almost an example of lateral thinking.

Blair is frequently painted not as the corporate counterpart of Premier Lougheed but as Lougheed's corporate right-hand man.

However, to regard Blair as in any way a puppet of Lougheed would be a very grave mistake, particularly if you made the error of suggesting it to any of AGTL's fiercely loyal staff. They work, and they work long and hard, for Bob Blair.

The fact remains that AGTL is firmly rooted in the province by virtue of its monopoly to collect gas, the purpose for which the company was created by the Social Credit administration in 1954.

The undoubtedly powerful link between Blair and Lougheed is not one of government-corporate conspiracy, it is one of mutual interest. Blair has been referred to as the "Deputy Prime Minister of Alberta", and there are frequent insinuations that Blair has the $5 billion Heritage Fund as a phantom footnote to the assets on his balance sheet, thus providing a massive base for expansion and a very large safety net against failure. However, the connection between the two is far more subtle. Lougheed wants a more powerful and diversified corporate base in the province, big companies that can hold their own both in Canada and abroad. Blair stresses nationalism and the building of Canadian expertise, and AGTL is the fast-expanding corporate base he needs for his ambitions.

Alberta Gas Trunk is the key player in the billion dollar petrochemical construction programme that Lougheed sees as a major step towards upgrading the province's gas and thus keeping both jobs and money within Alberta rather than shipping them east down the pipeline. The Alaskan Highway pipeline, if and when it comes, will provide many thousands of jobs for the provincial economy. Anybody instigating or willing to play the leading role in such projects is bound to have Lougheed's support, and his ear.

There is little doubt that the perception of a "preferred position" in the province for Blair increases his financial standing with the Canadian banking community, making him, like some Homeric character touched by the hand of a god, something more than a mere corporate mortal.

The Great Pipeline Debate

If one had to choose any one achievement for which Blair will go down in the great corporate history books, it would be his victory in the great northern pipeline debate. It was during that debate, to build the world's most expensive pipeline, that Blair established his skill at "Ottawa poker."

The debate was ostensibly over alternative routes by which United States gas from the giant Prudhoe Bay field could be brought to increasingly hungry markets in the "lower 48" United States. About half of American homes and 40% of its factories depend on natural gas. When Prudhoe Bay was discovered, top priority had been to get the field's oil to American markets. That priority became much more urgent when the OPEC crisis struck in the winter of 1973. In November, President Richard Nixon certified a trans-Alaska oil line that would carry the oil through an 800 mile pipeline across the state to the port of Valdez in the south, where it would be shipped south by tanker. Gas, as usual, had been very much an afterthought. But then, in the severe winter of 1976-1977 the northern parts of the United States received frightening intimations of the mortality of its gas supplies. Factories, schools and businesses were closed in 20 states as more than 2 million workers were laid off. *Newsweek* reported that the United States had been brought to "a natural gas crisis every bit as serious as the 1973 Arab oil embargo." Suddenly the gas from Prudhoe Bay, with the potential to supply about 5% of total U.S. demand, became an even greater public issue.

By that winter, however, a complex battle for control of a northern gas pipeline had been in progress for six years. There were three contestants, the mighty Arctic Gas consortium, that planned to bring Prudhoe Bay gas via Canada's Mackenzie Delta ("piggybacking" Canadian gas that had been found there) down the Mackenzie Valley; the Foothills Group, headed by Blair, that planned a route following the Alaska Highway, with a linking lateral line to the Mackenzie Delta along the Dempster Highway; and the El Paso group, planning to pipe Prudhoe gas along the same route as the trans-Alaska oil line and then liquefy it before sending it to southern markets by ship.

The Liberal Party had previously expressed their strong support for an "energy corridor" down the Mackenzie Valley. In 1972, Pierre Trudeau had referred to a Mackenzie Pipeline as part of a "northern vision", and the Cabinet seemed to firmly support pipeline corridors through Canada from Alaska to the lower 48. The then head of the Treasury Board, C. M. "Bud" Drury, declared: "The Canadian government would welcome applications to build oil or gas pipelines from Alaska through Canada in a "land bridge" to the Continental United States." Jean Chretien, then Minister for Indian Affairs and Northern Development, ringingly declared: "We are in the midst of an adventure of social and economic impact rivalling the construction of the Canadian Pacific Railway." The government line was that a pipeline could be a chance for economic independence for the northern native peoples.

However, in the following two years, relationships between Canada and the United States deteriorated as the OPEC crisis unfolded. Uncle Sam perceived the blue-eyed Arab coming out in his northern neighbour, while Canadian nationalists began to declare that Canada had been ripped-off by the United States over energy for years. Cosy co-operation on pipelines suddenly became a much more sensitive area.

Perhaps more important, there was an upsurge in activism by increasingly well-organized environmental groups. This, in turn, led to a growing awareness among the general public of ecological and social issues. These environmental groups had already cut their teeth on the northern energy development issue by successfully holding up the certification of the TransAlaska oil pipeline for more than three years. The delays they managed to impose on the TransAlaska line contributed to the transportation system's most horrifying statistic, its cost. In 1968, it had been estimated that the line would cost $900 million. The first official cost estimate, in 1972, was for $3 billion. By early 1974, the figure had risen to $4 billion, and, by the end of the same year, $6 billion. When oil finally started flowing from Prudhoe Bay in June, 1977, the pipeline that carried it had cost a grand total of $9.3 billion, more than 10 times the original estimates.

Those seeking regulatory approval for a northern gas pipeline from both the United States and Canadian governments were thus more than aware of the power of the environmentalists. However, it was the interplay of both nationalistic and environmental concerns that made the gas pipeline debate uniquely complex. Bob Blair emerged as the only participant adapted to such a heavily politicized environment.

Since the Arctic Gas consortium was composed chiefly of American controlled companies,* it obviously became the focus for nationalist resentments. If Arctic Gas could also be excluded on environmental grounds, then two political birds could be killed with one stone. The man who more than anyone else carried out that lethal function was not so much a stone-thrower as a human time bomb. He had been left as a legacy of the New Democratic Party when they lost their status as holders of the balance of federal power in 1974.

The name of the explosive device in question was Justice Thomas Berger. When he finally went off in May, 1977, he blasted into small pieces the greatest consortium of energy companies ever seen in Canada.

Berger, a member of the Supreme Court of British Columbia, was chosen by the Liberals early in 1974, undoubtedly as a sop to the NDP, to head an inquiry into the environmental and social impact of a Mackenzie Valley pipeline. There could have been no doubt about his political leanings. Born in Victoria, B.C. during the

---

* In 1977, there were fifteen members of Arctic Gas: Alberta Natural Gas Co.; Columbia Gas Transmission Corp.; Consumers' Gas Co.; Gulf Oil Canada Ltd.; Imperial Oil Ltd.; Michigan Wisconsin Pipe Line Co.; Natural Gas Pipeline Co. of America; Northern and Central Gas Corp.; Northern Natural Gas Co.; Pacific Lighting Gas Development Co.; Panhandle Eastern PipeLine Co.; Shell Canada Ltd.; Texas Eastern Transmission Corp.; TransCanada PipeLines Ltd.; Union Gas Ltd.

depression, the son of an RCMP sergeant, Berger was known to be an ardent humanist and socialist. As a young lawyer, he had always fought for the underdog and against the "Establishment" on behalf of Indian minorities and victims of pollution. He joined the New Democrats in B.C., became an MP in the early 1960's and at the end of the decade briefly headed the provincial NDP party before they were roundly defeated by W.A.C. Bennett's Social Creditors. In 1971, Berger moved onto the B.C. Supreme Court, where he remained until the minority Liberal party gave him the call in 1974.

It will perhaps never be known whether the Liberals planted Berger deliberately, knowing what his conclusions would be; or whether they simply didn't see the long-term implications of their short-term political expediency. But from day one of the Berger inquiry one thing was very clear, Mr. Justic Thomas Berger took his mandate very seriously.

Until Berger came along, Canadian Arctic Gas had been the front runner to build an enormous gas pipeline carrying 4.5 billion cubic feet a day from Prudhoe Bay. It was to be the world's biggest and most ambitious pipeline project, pumping gas in a 48 inch diameter pipe more than 2,500 miles south to the homes and factories of the lower 48 states. On the way it was to take a detour to the east to pick up Canadian gas from the Mackenzie Delta. Some of this gas would initially be exported to the United States, but in the longer term, Delta gas would be transferred to Canadian domestic use as demand increased.

It was a masterpiece of corporate logic, hatched by a Who's Who of Canadian energy companies. The three largest oil companies in Canada were there, Imperial, Gulf and Shell; Canada's largest domestic gas artery, TransCanada PipeLines; the country's three largest gas utilities, Consumers' Gas, Northern and Central Gas and Union Gas (all Ontario based); along with Alberta Natural Gas. And for balance, there were also seven American transmission companies lining up to make sure the gas had customers. They were fifteen companies with an admittedly eastern Canadian and American bias, but with spotlessly clean, and large, balance sheets.

The Reluctant Partner

Blair had, in fact, been a reluctant member of the Arctic Gas consortium for two years. In 1972, the group of which he was head, Gas Arctic Systems Study Group, had been shotgunned together with the rival group, NorthWest Project Study Group, headed by Trans-Canada PipeLines, to form Arctic Gas. But the marriage had never been a happy one.

Blair had joined AGTL as executive vice-president in December

1969 and became president only seven months later. He came to the company after 10 years with Alberta & Southern Gas, transmission subsidiary of U.S. Pacific Gas & Lighting, where he spent his final three years as president. Blair was well known around Calgary as an amiable executive, but he was by no means considered a corporate "heavyweight". Moreover, the company he was joining, AGTL, had a far from dynamic profile. Set up in 1954 "to gather and transmit gas within the province", AGTL was essentially seen as a collection system that would deliver Albertan gas to the two pipeline systems that carried the gas west and east from the province, Westcoast Transmission and TransCanada PipeLines. However, AGTL also had a political purpose, summed up by Earle Gray in *Super Pipe*. Said Gray: "There was only one purpose in mind when Trunk Line was established under the auspices of the Alberta government in 1954. That purpose was to prevent the federal government from exercising legislative and regulatory control over the production, marketing and pricing of Alberta gas."

Nevertheless, despite that political origin, since it basis, Alberta's gas, was a depleting resource, AGTL was a corporate creature that could look forward only to decline. When Bob Blair joined the company, he decided that that would not happen. Pursuing two parallel strategies, revitalizing AGTL's transmission function by directing northern gas through the province and diversifying into other corporate areas, Blair has transformed Alberta Gas Trunk Line into one of the two most dynamic companies in the country.

Under Bob Blair, AGTL has not only been revitalized as a force within Alberta, spearheading the province's drive for diversification into petrochemicals, but has blossomed as a leader in national energy ventures. Under Blair's stewardship, AGTL's profits have increased almost tenfold. In 1978, AGTL had net income of $85.6 million on operating revenues of $464 million. If Husky Oil, the company it finally absorbed in 1979, had been included, combined revenues of $1.167 billion and net income of $141 million would have ranked it 28th by sales and 12th by profits among all Canadian industrial companies in 1978.

In 1970, Blair saw that bringing Prudhoe Bay gas, and gas for the western Canadian Arctic, through an expanded Albertan transmission system would not only maintain AGTL's original function, it would greatly expand it. That was the corporate rationale behind his bid for a central role in the northern gas pipeline.

As head of Alberta Gas Trunk Line, Blair already presides over the country's second largest gas transmission company, whose 6,500 miles of underground steel pipe collect all the gas produced in the province for shipment to other Canadian provinces and the United States. His aggressive temperament is well suited to the cut and thrust of the transmission industry.

Whereas the exploration business lends itself, almost uniquely, to cooperation between companies, the gas transmission business seems like a natural battleground. Whereas, in exploration, companies will leap in and out of bed with each other at a dazzling rate — in a display of corporate promiscuity that, perhaps surprisingly, leaves very few ill feelings — transmission companies seem to spend their lives in adversity. If they are planning new schemes, then attacking rival applications is a key part of the game. When it comes to justifying the rates for their services, those for whom they transport oil or gas inevitably claim they are being charged too much. Running an oil or gas pipe line is not a good career for someone whose highest priority is being loved.

The additional, heavy political, overtones of the business in the period since 1974 have increased the need for political awareness and Machiavellian deviousness to achieve success. These are characteristics with which Bob Blair has proven to be abundantly endowed.

The Social Credit government in Alberta that ruled when Blair ascended to the AGTL presidency in 1970 was a little sceptical about his grandiose plans to bring Prudhoe Bay gas through the province. But they were also a little scared that transporting gas from outside Alberta might lead the federal government to attempt to gain jurisdiction over AGTL and hence the province's gas resources. Nevertheless, Blair eventually won them round. In 1970, shortly before his appointment as president of AGTL, Blair had attempted to negotiate his way into the Northwest Project Study Group headed by TransCanada. However, they would not have him. He never forgot the slight. Nevertheless, there were at least two fundamental disagreements between the TransCanada group and Blair over control and ownership of the line. Blair was firmly in favour of Canadian control for the Canadian portions of the line. However the TransCanada-led Northwest group balked at the idea. For two years, Blair's group and the Northwest group went their separate ways until, in 1972, Energy Minister Donald Macdonald forced them to come together to formulate a pipeline proposal "Which combines the best features of all the projects now being prepared."

Blair, however, was far from happy with membership of Northwest, a group he essentially saw as being dominated by the three American giants that had discovered Prudhoe Bay — Exxon, Atlantic Richfield and Standard Oil of Ohio (Sohio). It could be considered as something less than Machiavellian that these three companies, as the main owners of Prudhoe Bay gas, should be concerned that their reserves reached market in the cheapest and most efficient way. They saw financing such a huge project as one of the main problems, particularly after their traumatic experiences with the TransAlaska oil line, and they knew that financiers liked to lend money on the basis of the size of the borrower and the financial viability of his project, not, as in Blair's case, on the basis of corporate aspirations and nationalistic sentiments.

In line with the perception that finance would be the main problem of the line the man chosen to head Arctic Gas was William Wilder, a brilliant and personable financier who, in his 26 years with Wood Gundy, Canada's premier investment house, had risen to be president and chief executive. The pipeline was an unprecedently huge project, whose final cost estimates rose to a mind-boggling $10 billion, so Wilder's knowledge of financial markets and his experience with the Churchill Falls project were considered essential. To take care of the technical side, Verne Horte, former president of TransCanada PipeLines took over as Wilder's second-in-command.* Beneath them, at their headquarters on Wellington Street in Toronto (previously occupied, somewhat ironically, by Walter Gordon, patron saint of economic nationalism) they assembled a dazzling array of talent.

Blair, however, regarded Wilder's appointment as a "railroad job" and objected to it because, as he later said, "I thought we needed a real lion of a man for this new job — not a technician." Blair's own actions were to prove his assessment correct. Wilder may have been a brilliant financier, but his 26 years within the cloistered portals of Wood Gundy were not the ideal training ground to develop the speed and political adaptability that were needed to win the debate.†

Playing the Environmental Game

That is not to say that Arctic Gas was ignorant of the potential problems facing them from ecologists. They had seen the Trans-Alaska pipeline's problems with environmentalists and native groups and they knew that they were in for a similarly rough time. They were well aware that the array of regulatory agencies and courts they would have to brave to obtain final approval repre-

---

* Blair and Horte, when Horte had worked as chief gas engineer for TransCanada in Alberta before moving to Toronto as president of the company, had been good friends. They had even had neighbouring cottages at Bragg Creek just outside Calgary. The pipeline affair was to make them bitter opponents.

† When Arctic Gas was defeated, Wilder became a senior vice-president of Gulf Canada and was touted for the job of chairman when present chairman John Shepard retired. However, Wilder left Gulf after little more than a year — amid rumours of boardroom turmoil — to become president of Consumers' Gas. The man fired from the Consumers' presidency, Ted Creber, had been general counsel for Arctic Gas. The reason for Creber's prompt dismissal in December, 1978, has never been officially announced.

sented battlefields almost ideally suited to guerilla tactics. There, the most seemingly ill-equipped could keep vast armies bogged down for months and even years.

Blair, however, was much more acutely aware, and perhaps also more genuinely sensitive, regarding the native rights and environmental issues. In 1970, shortly after unveiling his scheme for piping Prudhoe Bay gas, Blair had come up with the concept of "participatory planning". In October of that year a seven-man Trunk Line road show had headed north to consult with the natives over the pipeline. People from local communities were flown over the proposed routes and asked to point out traditional hunting and fishing lands. The rather bemused natives were also asked whether a pipeline would interfere with any of their traditional pursuits.

It was only after they had returned from their trip that Northwest Territories Commissioner Stuart Hodgson pointed out rather tentatively to AGTL representatives that the natives had absolutely no idea what natural gas was. He suggested a somewhat crude, but certainly comprehensible, analogy that the native people might appreciate. Natural gas was just like broken wind, "you could hear it, you could smell it, you might even be able to feel it pass, but you could not see it." After that explanation, the native people might well have wondered even more what all the fuss was about! (That same autumn, AGTL brought some natives from the picturesque village of Old Crow in the Yukon down to Alberta to show them a working model of a pipeline. It exploded!)

The response of the Canadian Arctic Gas to the environmental "threat" was perhaps typically big business. They would simply throw money at the problem. They would produce an iron-clad case for their pipeline by presenting the most detailed submissions to regulatory bodies the world had ever seen. But their tactics proved badly mistaken.

When, in March, 1974, they filed applications in Ottawa and Washington, each application was accompanied by 100 pounds of supporting documents! Perhaps the environmentalists first line of attack might well have been the deforestation implied by such a deluge of paper. Moreover, those documents merely covered environment, engineering, land use and the regional socio-economic impact of the line. What, at the time, were considered the "more sensitive" documents, relating to financial and economic matters, had yet to be filed.

But Arctic Gas thought it had things down pat. It virtually knew every northern muskrat by name and had expressed due regard for the breeding habits of the peregrine falcon and the whooping crane. For what more could any environmentalist ask?

But the answer proved to be that not more, but *less* was what was required. The massive volumes of submissions by Arctic gas merely served to anchor the participants down as sitting targets for the mounting nationalist sentiments the issue was arousing.

Meanwhile, Berger had also appeared as a small ticking dot on the map of the north, travelling at a leisurely pace between communities, listening patiently to evidence from natives that proved all the more forceful for being only semi-literate.

Blair sensed that the environmental and sociological concerns of Berger might well work to his advantage, as might the upsurge in nationalism over American control of Canadian energy. He also perceived that with the federal provincial dispute over oil prices in full swing, his special position in the province could also be used to advantage.

During 1974, Blair and his corporate team at Trunk Line hatched a scheme that would concentrate on bringing Canadian frontier gas to market. Effectively, it followed the Arctic gas route down the Mackenzie Valley, but, since it did not link up the Mackenzie Delta with Prudhoe Bay, it was a smaller line. Blair remained a member of Arctic Gas for the moment, explaining that the all-Canadian Mackenzie Valley line was a "contingency plan". But he was becoming increasingly discontented within the ranks of Arctic Gas. Other members remember him sitting glumly through meetings taking copious notes. Bob Blair was getting ready to jump off what he considered a doomed ship.

Blair's thinking is neatly summed up in a letter he had written to Alberta Energy Minister, Bill Dickie, in April of 1974*:

"In our company, we are distressed that the trend of events connected with the filing of the Arctic Gas pipeline application by Canadian Arctic Gas Pipeline Limited. Our distress is in two directions. First, we do not believe that the application as filed, by majority vote of the twenty-seven members, is sufficiently tailored *to meet the future commercial involvement of our own company or of gas services in and for the province as reflected through our operations.* Second, we judge that the project applied for may not be a practical proposal when assessed in the whole range of considerations covering ownership, financing, service to Canadian markets and *political acceptability in Canada."* (my italics)

But Blair still lacked partners for his venture. In the summer of 1974, he found not only a partner but a kindred spirit, Kelly Gibson, head of Westcoast Transmission. Westcoast had originally hatched its own plans for a pipeline out of the north, but these had been abandoned. The company had been invited to join Arctic Gas but had repeatedly turned down offers.

Gibson was an old time oilman who had witnessed virtually the

---

* Donald Peacock, *People, Peregrines and Arctic Pipelines* (Vancouver, J. J. Douglas, 1977).

whole growth of the Canadian oil industry, and had risen through its ranks to head one of its most-respected companies, Pacific Petroleums (which owned 33% of Westcoast Transmission). When he approached Blair he had retired from Pacific, but he still had his finger firmly on the pulse of the industry. Gibson told Blair that if he pulled out of Arctic Gas, then Westcoast would support him in the Mackenzie Valley project. On September 13, 1974, Blair withdrew what was left of his support for Arctic Gas and on March 27, 1975, AGTL and Westcoast filed the "Maple Leaf" project to carry Mackenzie Delta gas down the river valley to market. There might have to be some initial exports to the United States, but the message was in the name. The nationalism might have been a little heavy-handed, but it seemed like the line for the times.

That still left the question of the route for Prudhoe Bay gas. Within a year, Blair and Gibson came together with a two-fisted ex-Texas oilman, John McMillian, who had recently gained control of Salt Lake City-based Northwest Energy Corp., and the three became joint sponsors of a Prudhoe Bay gas pipeline that would follow the route of the Alaska Highway. The Alcan project was born. To cover the possibility of the all-Canadian Mackenzie Valley line running into regulatory approval problems the Alcan sponsors added a branch line along the Dempster highway to link up the delta gas with the Alcan line.

For the Arctic gas sponsors, who had picked the "best" route and then gone about the exhaustive business of establishing its viability, Blair's "alternatives" were initially more a source of irritation than genuine concern. Arctic Gas lived in a world where projects had to be anchored down as quickly as possible. But Bob Blair seemed to be floating with the political winds. Annoyed that he should even be considered a serious rival, they tried to get the NEB to reject the Alcan submission, but the board both accepted the submission and gave Blair's group time to develop its plans.

Nevertheless, it seemed inconceivable that AGTL, Westcoast and Northwest, with their hastily drawn lines on the map, could be really considered serious contenders. On February 1, 1977, Judge Nahum Litt revealed an advisory report to the Federal Power Commission, which had to make a recommendation to the President in Washington, discounting the El Paso project entirely on economic grounds and recommending Arctic Gas as being "vastly superior" to Alcan.

However, the first clear sign that politics might prevail came with the FPC's recommendations on May 2, 1977. Despite Judge Litt's clearly pro-Arctic Gas advisory report, the commission's four members split two and two between Arctic Gas and Blair's Alcan route. What the FPC seemed effectively to be doing was leaving the decision up to Canada. As long as the United States gets the Prudhoe Bay gas, the FPC appeared to be saying, we don't care how it comes.

Then, in May of 1977 Berger finally exploded. In a finely-presented, 213-page report, written in the first person, Berger dealt not one but two ultimately crushing blows to Arctic Gas. On the one hand, he suggested a 10 year delay in any development of the Mackenzie Valley, and on the other he condemned altogether a pipeline across the Arctic National Wildlife Refuge, which was on the route from Prudhoe Bay to the Mackenzie Delta. Arctic Gas wasn't dead, but it looked desperately wounded. It was left to the National Energy Board to deal the final blow with its recommendations two months later.

The board, which had to make a recommendation to the Canadian Cabinet, had completed its 211 days of public hearings on May 12, 1977. The transcripts of the hearings filled more than 37,000 pages. Eight weeks later, on July 4, 1977, the applicants assembled at the NEB's headquarters in the Trebla building (that's Albert spelled backwards) in Ottawa to hear the final decisions. The three NEB panel members, chairman Jack Stabback, Ralph Brooks and Geoff Edge, took it in turns to read portions of their conclusions. At the end of an hour, when Stabback had read the final portion "John McMillian was grinning like a schoolboy; Bob Blair had lost his constant stern expression; Wilder, Horte and the other Arctic Gas representatives were stunned and grim."[*]

What the NEB did was to reject Arctic Gas and the Maple Leaf Line (which Foothills had by that time withdrawn in any case) and recommend the Alaskan Highway Alcan alternative with a number of route variations that would take the line closer to the Mackenzie Delta and thus theoretically aid the linking up of delta gas. (The route alterations were eventually rejected by both the United States and Canadian governments in favour of a return to the original Alcan line. Instead of shifting the whole line, the Americans agreed to subsidize the Dempster spur that would link up Delta gas with the main line. The degree of the subsidy would depend on the success of Foothills in keeping down cost overruns.)

Arctic Gas, which had spent five years and $140 million producing the impregnable case, had been destroyed by nationalist sentiment and the NDP's "revenge", Justice Thomas Berger. The man left as the conqueror, much to the disgust of his former colleagues in Arctic Gas, was Bob Blair.

Bill Twaites, the crusty and outspoken former chief executive of Imperial Oil, sat down after the NEB decision and wrote three letters to Jack Stabback, but, perhaps wisely, tore each one up. In the spring of 1979, two years after the decision, Twaites' craggy face still reddens with indignation at the thought of the NEB judgment. "Just read the decision," he says, "all the way through it speaks of the superiority of the Arctic Gas proposal, and then right at the end stands on its head."

[*] Earle Gray, Super Pipe, (Toronto, Griffin House, 1979)

Blair was subsequently quoted in *Maclean's* magazine as saying: "The decision has wrenched power away from some people who have become accustomed to having power. The big oil companies, for example, and certain parts of the Toronto financial establishment."

Vancouver columnist Allan Fotheringham, writing in the same publication, said: ". . . half of Toronto is going to collapse in a psychic faint when it realizes what the decision to give the Alaska Highway pipeline route to the Foothills group of Calgary is going to mean to the traditional power base of Canada."

Nevertheless, perhaps the dancing in the streets of the West was coming a little too soon. Blair had proved that he could play Ottawa poker, but that had only brought him regulatory approval to build a line.

Financing: Big Oil's Revenge?

A crucial part of Arctic Gas's submission had been the claim that the line could not be financed without some form of guarantee from one or both governments involved. For the big banks and, more important, insurance companies who would be asked to put up most of the money for the line, the collective nightmare was that the project would be half built; that $5 billion of their money would be left sitting there idly in the northern wilderness, costing them $2 million or more in interest alone for every day that nothing happened. For any financier, the idea of money lying idle is acutely painful. They couldn't rely on the participating companies to guarantee the loan, because they simply did not have the financial size, or inclination, to do it. A protracted delay in the middle of construction could force even the biggest participants to the balance-sheet bread line in pretty short order.

With the example of the Trans Alaska Pipeline in front of them, a project which had escalated in cost from under $1 billion to almost $9 billion, not even governments were willing to provide guarantees.

So Blair, as ever riding the crest of political opportunism, had declared that the Alaskan Highway line simply wouldn't need government guarantees. But although Blair might have been floating with the political winds during the regulatory debate, he was now flying in the face of the financial community and big business. The three giant oil companies that had financed the Trans Alaska oil line, British Petroleum, Exxon and Standard Oil of Ohio (Sohio), vowed, after that costly experience, that they would never undertake such a project again. It had almost bankrupted Sohio.

Arctic Gas had produced the voices of Canada's largest bank, the

Royal, its largest investment house, Wood Gundy, and huge Wall Street investment bank, Morgan Stanley, all claiming that guarantees would be needed.

Yet in June, 1978 Blair was telling skeptical Toronto audiences: "In retrospect, I think we'll look back on the financing as one of the simpler and less troublesome aspects". But Blair was not talking now to men who were interested in public relations exercises, no matter how successful. They were the men who managed the largest pools of money in North America, cold eyed financiers with minds like steel traps, experienced in squeezing the last sixteenth of a percentage point out of a deal. The governments of Canada and the United States might have been prepared to accept the somewhat scantily presented Alaskan Highway proposal, but financiers are men who like to have things tied down. They didn't like the idea of men floating in ideological balloons.

That was not to say, of course, that they weren't interested in the Alaskan Highway project. With a projected cost at the time of approval of over $10 billion*, it would represent the largest private financing ever undertaken, a prospect to make every major banker in the western world want a piece of the action. However, the essential thing for bankers is when, and at what terms, they are going to get their money back. The word "whether" is something they prefer not to countenance. And it was that key word that made them very wary about the Alaska Highway line.

Blair and his co-sponsors may have said that they would not need government guarantees, but for the key financiers that opened the frightening possibility of the pipeline becoming a very large risk.

But, of course, the last act of the drama has yet to be played out. In the renewed crisis atmosphere of 1979, the American people were clamouring for solutions to fuel shortages and the government was struggling to find them. There was absolutely no reason why the Canadian government should provide any financial backstopping, but the hard-pressed government of Jimmy Carter was in a quite different position. Of course, if the United States government *did* finally come up with financial guarantees for the line, then Blair's tactical victory would appear all the greater. He had won the battle with Arctic Gas partly through his claim that he could walk the tightrope of pipeline financing without a safety net. If the United States government now provided him with one, his risks would be obliterated. In March of 1979, Premier Trudeau had flown to Washington to meet with President Carter amid a flurry of speculation that guarantees might ensue. However, nothing emerged, at least publicly.

Moving into the summer of 1979, financing seemed to remain

---

* And over $15 billion towards the end of 1979.

the major potential stumbling block. However, in July, what Blair, Gibson and McMillian had been hoping for happened. Jimmy Carter, facing a major crisis of confidence in the presidency, particularly over his lack of firm policy on energy, announced that he would "insist personally" that the pipeline be built.

Speaking in Kansas City on July 16, 1979, Carter scolded the major oil companies involved in Prudhoe Bay for having "dragged their feet in helping to finance the pipeline needed to bring Alaskan gas to market . . . I have instructed the Secretary of Energy to call them in and get them going. And I will insist personally that this gas pipeline be built."

The commitment was somewhat vague, and it was far from clear how the President was going to sway big oil's corporate policies with his "personal insistence". Nevertheless, most observers took it as a positive sign, and many believed that Carter's statement foreshadowed the provision of the guarantees that the President previously had declared he would not provide. However, going into the fall of 1979, a number of significant political forces, including Senator Edward Kennedy, were still speaking out against highly expensive gas from the North Slope. The issue remained, perhaps fittingly, floating in the political winds.

9 | Shoot Out at the Cody Corral

With the mammoth task of the Alaska Highway pipeline before him, Blair was considered in most quarters to have neither the financial backing, the management depth nor the inclination to go after Husky.

On the morning of Thursday, June 8, 1978, the whisper that someone was going to take a run at Husky Oil Ltd. turned into a roar. In the first hectic twenty minutes of trading on the Toronto Stock Exchange, Husky's share price rose $4.75 to $35.75. Such a surge was like a flare soaring above the trenches. It meant a battle was in the offing. And what a battle it turned out to be.

Over the following three weeks, the action in one of the biggest corporate fights in Canadian history was to swing from Husky's headquarters in the one-horse town of Cody, Wyoming, through Calgary, Edmonton, Ottawa, Los Angeles, Toronto and New York. While the war of highly-political words and competing financial offers raged, and New York's shrewdest wheeler-dealers were laying enormous bets on the outcome, Bob Blair was preparing a tactical masterstroke.

On that first morning, when the TSE telephoned Jim Nielson, Husky's slight, bespectacled president, to ask for an explanation for the share movement he could offer none. He told the exchange that he knew PetroCanada, the national oil company set up in 1976 amidst a barrage of industry and political abuse, was very interested in Husky, but that no approaches had been made to him.

That soon changed. Later that day, Nielson received a call from Toronto stockbroker Ted Medland, a senior partner in the giant investment house Wood Gundy, announcing that Gundy and another large Toronto brokerage house, Pitfield, Mackay, Ross, were acting on behalf of a "reputable Canadian principal interested in visiting with Husky".

The rather quaint phraseology was reminiscent of turn-of-the-century courtship procedure, but as far as Husky was concerned, what was about to happen was attempted rape. Moreover, the Nielsons, Jim and his father Glenn, Husky's chairmen, were more than a little disheartened at the source of the news that they were under attack. Gundy and Pitfield were their own investment bankers. Worst of all, Pitfield's head, Ward Pitfield, was on the Husky board.

Husky, a large producer and refiner with activities split between the United States and Canada, had been considered a potential takeover candidate for a long time. In the post-OPEC era of high oil prices and obsession with national security, its chief attraction lay in the 1.6 million acres of heavy oil lands it held in Saskatchewan. Heavy oil, like thick, sluggish molasses, is reluctant oil. Whereas conventional oil gushes, heavy oil oozes. It doesn't show any great enthusiasm to see the light of day. Only a relatively small portion of a reservoir, perhaps 5% of the oil-in-place, will flow to the surface unassisted. Any part of the remaining 95% has to be part cajoled, part forced out by the injection of fluids or by heating the oil underground.

Moreover, the problems do not end once the oil has reached the surface. Heavy oil is low quality oil and needs "upgrading" before it can be sent to refineries to be transformed into gasoline and other products. Without upgrading, the markets for heavy oil are severely limited.

Before the OPEC crisis, heavy oil had been as economically marginal as it was technologically trying. But Sheik Yamani's magic economic wand changed all that, lending it new, Cinderella-like charms. The West had large heavy oil resources and the federal government suddenly realized they could play a significant part in Canada's energy future.

Wishing to assert itself quickly after its creation, PetroCan had approached Husky in June, 1976 about farming-in to Husky's lands, that is, committing to spend money in order to gain a share of production. Gulf Canada, too, had been interested in a similar arrangement, and had joined in three-way negotiations. But the talks had dragged on, bogged down over acceptable terms. Jim Nielson balked at the scale of development desired by PetroCan and Gulf, realizing that Husky could easily be dragged out of its financial depth.

In 1978 Gulf Canada had looked at the possibility of acquiring Husky, but was dissuaded by the lack of enthusiam of its American parent and by the prospect of a run-in with the Foreign Investment Review Agency — Ottawa's belated bolt to the stable door of United States control of Canadian business.

But now, with the stock market leak, it was obvious that somebody was about to break the impasse. Medland asked for a meeting in Cody the following Saturday morning, June 10. One compelling reason why Medland couldn't say who his "principal" was — and

it was indeed PetroCan — was that although the Crown Corporation had been planning to take over Husky, the stock market leak
had forced its hand. It had federal Cabinet approval for the deal,
but had not yet obtained approval from its own board, so a hasty
meeting had to be organized in Ottawa for the Saturday morning
before the meeting with Husky.

Once Wilbert Hopper, PetroCan's president, received board approval, he immediately called Glenn Nielson, Husky's 76 year old
founder, in Cody, apologising for not being able to reveal himself
before, and said he was just about to board the PetroCan jet. However, they agreed that the meeting be switched to Husky's Calgary
office. The Wood Gundy jet, already heading for Cody with Medland and Pitfield aboard, had to change course in mid-air.

As soon as the two sides got together on the afternoon of Saturday, June 10, Hopper said the national oil company was planning
to offer $45 a share for Husky, a $9 premium over its price when
suspended the previous Thursday. With 10.9 million shares outstanding, that valued Husky at $490 million, and made the 18% of
the company held by the Nielson family worth close to $90 million.
But the offer found very little favour with the Nielsons.

After Hopper had delivered his set speech, pointing out that $45
a share in cash was an attractive offer, Dick Matthews, a prominent
Calgary lawyer and a Husky board member, turned to him and
said: "You must have a commission from the U.S. government."
Hopper looked puzzled. "Why?" he asked. "Because", said
Matthews, "how much tax do you think the Nielsons will have to
pay on that offer?" Hopper reddened. That, apparently, was just
one of the features of the deal that had not been considered. Glenn
Nielson had built the company over 40 years from one refinery and
19 employees to an integrated company with revenues of more
than $600 million. The thought of selling out at all was a painful
one to him. The thought of the U.S. government taking one-third
of the reward for a life's work was more than he could counte-
nance.

Glenn Nielson is a figure held in enourmous respect in the Albertan oil community. A deeply, although far from obviously, religious man, he is a pillar of the Mormon Church, for whom he
worked five years full time in the early 1970's. Despite his profound convictions, however, there is no odour of sanctity about
Nielson. The only indication of his beliefs — and perhaps also his
dry sense of humour — is the plaque behind his desk in the wood-
panelled corner office of Husky's single story Cody headquarters.
It bears the legend: "Lord Make Our Blunders Wise."

Unfortunately, in some quarters that divine imprecation was
also seen as embodying Husky's management style. Many felt that
the company had become too complex and unwieldy and that its
management was weak.

One of the most frequent, and compelling, criticisms surrounded Nielson's steadfast refusal to move the company's headquarters from Cody, Wyoming, the little town to which he was absolutely devoted.

Set 50 miles from the main gates of Yellowstone National Park, Cody sits in the middle of real cowboy badlands. Hopping over the hills from Casper, Wyoming, in a single-engine Cessna you pass over the red bluffs where the "Hole in the Wall" gang — including Butch Cassidy and the Sundance Kid — had their hideout. Beyond the hills to the right, as you cross the Big Horn River, lies the site of Custer's last stand. Ironically, perhaps the only thing that spoils the town's picturesque nature is its most prominent landmark, the Husky refinery. Next to the refinery — indeed, a little too close for comfort on hot days with the wind in the wrong direction — sat Husky's less-than-grandiose headquarters, a converted single story railway hotel. On the other side of town, surrounded by a neat circle of trees, lies Glenn Nielson's house, fittingly, "the biggest house in town". The little town does a thriving tourist business and is an agricultural centre, but first and foremost, as the billboards proclaim, it is the "Home of Husky Oil".

It was the financial support of the townspeople that helped Nielson when he was struggling to get Husky started 40 years before, and he consistently refused to abandon the town. Ironically, when the news of the bid came, a new landmark was taking shape in the middle of town, a huge half-finished building that was to be Husky's new headquarters. As news of the bid filtered through the town, the shell of the structure became symbolic as a huge question mark over the Cody's future.

In the terminology of the investment business, PetroCan's bid was seen as a "Saturday Night Special", the launching of a full-scale assault over a weekend in the hope of gaining complete victory before the target can muster its defences. Ideally, the aggressor hopes to be able to come out with a nice, clean announcement when stockmarkets open on the Monday morning. PetroCan certainly seemed to have the cards stacked in its favour. Nielson's seventy-six-year-old face, as lined and craggy as the countryside around Cody, is a face that can look very sad. It looked very sad as the meeting with PetroCan started that Saturday afternoon. But underneath there was also anger.

For Nielson, the fact that Ward Pitfield turned up on the other side of the table amounted to betrayal. The aristocratic Pitfield, whose brother Michael was one of Pierre Trudeau's key advisors, had effectively gone behind the back of the Husky board, on which he sat, in acting for PetroCan. It was not only in the minds of the Nielsons that that represented treachery of the worst kind.

heavy oils, and that the United States side of the business would
be disposed of in some way. He said that he would like to have
Husky's approval the following day so that an announcement
could be made on Monday morning. During the meeting, Glenn
Nielson tried to suggest alternatives to an outright takeover. Why
didn't PetroCan put the enormous cost of buying Husky — two-
thirds of which would disappear from the country to U.S. shareholders — directly into Lloydminster? But PetroCan obviously had
its mind set on a takeover.

As a last resort, Glenn asked Hopper if he would consider sep-
arating the company into its American and Canadian parts, so that
the family might be left with control of the American interests, and
no massive tax bill.

The national oil company's officials left the room to consider this
but eventually decided that the process would be too complex and
take too long. They returned to say that they wanted the whole
thing.

The rationale put forward by PetroCan for the assault on Husky
was that it would speed development of Canada's heavy oils. But
that was only part of the reason. Wilbert Hopper knew that there
would be a federal election within a year, and that the Conservative opposition had been making some very belligerent noises
about winding up his company. One defence against that might be
to make the company such a size that disbanding it would be too
big a job.

Glenn Nielson told Hopper at the end of the meeting that he
could not make any decision without his board and that he could
not get the board together until Monday. As he left the meeting,
the infinitely sad look of Glenn Nielson might have been mistaken
for helplessness. "I felt," he told the author, "that I had a gun at
my head and a gun at my back."

Doc Hammer to the Rescue

But Nielson, true to his western grit, had no intention of going
down without a fight. But to fight he needed a counter offer.
Where would he get one? The answer lay with a frail little eighty-
year-old man who operated out of a modest office in the Los Angeles suburb of Westwood, in a building that did not even bear his
company's name. The man was Dr. Armand Hammer, and the
company was Occidental Petroleum Corp.

Hammer is a man with a career that qualifies as stranger than fiction. Behind the desk of his office stands a table covered with personally dedicated pictures of prime ministers, presidents and other

heads of state, but one immediately catches your attention. It is a photograph of a bald man with a mephistophelean beard, a stern look and penetrating eyes. The inscription reads: "To comrade Armand Hammer, from VI Iulanoff (Lenin)". It is immediately clear that Hammer is no ordinary businessman.

Hammer's father had himself been an extraordinary man. A Russian immigrant who started as a laborer, he put himself through medical school in his spare time and finished up owning a pharmaceutical business. His son, Armand, had to take over the ailing business while he was still at medical school, and he ran it so successfully that he became a millionaire before he became a doctor. In the early 1920's, he went to Russia, a country torn apart and exhausted by years of war and revolution, became friends with Lenin and pulled off a number of major trade deals providing grain for starving Russians while winning the concessions from major American companies such as Ford Motor to sell their products in the U.S.S.R. Moving into manufacturing, he established in Russia the world's largest pencil factory, while he accumulated a vast collection of Russian art treasures.

He returned to the United States at the end of the 1920's to pursue not one but a whole range of dazzling careers. He became one of the country's largest whiskey distillers, revolutionised the business of selling art, and was at one time the nation's foremost breeder of Aberdeen Angus bulls.

Unknown to PetroCan, Hammer had been interested in Husky for a number of years. He knew Glen Nielson originally not through oil but through their interests in art. Hammer had negotiated with Nielson for the loan of paintings from Cody's famous Buffalo Bill Museum, of which Nielson was a trustee, several years before. Hammer took the paintings to Russia as part of a cultural exchange, and they proved to be the hit of the tour. (Leonid Brezhnev, perhaps somewhat unexpectedly, heads a large group of cowboy and indian enthusiasts within the Kremlin.)

At Husky's request, in fact, Occidental had for some months been looking at a "joint venture", a polite phrase often used in the exploratory phase of a merger.

Some of Hammer's deals had skated perilously close to United States investment regulations, and his corporate style was a long way from Glenn Nielson's, but Nielson now clearly saw that Hammer was his only line of defence. So, after the meeting with Petro-Can, the septuagenarian Nielson gave the octagenarian Hammer a call, explaining what had happened. "Have you got a plane?" asked Hammer, "why don't you come on down."

Hammer immediately put a call in to Occidental's aggressive ex-banker president Joe Baird, who was just about to go to a wedding in Boston, telling him to return to Los Angeles as quickly as possible. Stopping in New York to pick up Raymond Raff, financial

wizard with investment house Kidder, Peabody, Baird headed
west.

The Nielsons meanwhile were shepherding key board members David Kennedy (ex U.S. Secretary to the Treasury and one of only three men ever made U.S. "Ambassador at Large"), George Eccles, chairman of First Security Corp., legal brain Dick Matthews, and tax expert J. Waddy Bullion, to Los Angeles for the meeting.

By the time the Husky directors reached Hammer's house for the meeting, which started at 4:30 on the afternoon of Sunday, June 11, Baird had organized three teams of lawyers and accountants, many of whom had worked through the night, beavering away at the technical aspects of the deal. By 11:30 that night, a complex share-swap deal had been worked out that the Nielsons felt was superior to PetroCan's cash offer — and would also avoid the horrors of a multi-million tax bill for Husky shareholders, and particularly the Nielson family.

Under the arrangement, Husky investors would receive Occidental preferred shares in exchange for their Husky stock. Of the Oxy preferred, 90% would carry a 10% dividend but have no conversion rights into Oxy common shares. The remaining 10% of Oxy preferred, carrying a dividend of 7.5%, would be convertible into Oxy common shares. Husky shareholders would receive 0.402 of a $100 Oxy non-convertible preferred share and 0.045 of a $100 Oxy convertible for each Husky share they offered. The value of the offer at the time was about C$49, $4 higher than PetroCan's cash offer, but the key attraction was that the Husky shares would be "rolled-over" into Occidental shares without the payment of any tax.

Originally, the meeting at which Glenn Nielson was to give his board's response to PetroCan's bid was to be in Calgary early the following day, Monday June 12. However, the city, as usual, was packed with businessmen and conference delegates and the Husky board simply could not get hotel rooms, so the meeting was switched to Edmonton. The Husky team had problems with their aircraft, so the two sides did not get together until after 11 pm on the Monday night.

That morning, PetroCan had announced its $45-a-share offer. There had been intense speculation since Husky's suspension four days earlier and PetroCan had emerged in the press as the likely candidate. However, news of the bid brought a predictable wave of indignation throughout Calgary. The Petroleum Club resounded with ringing condemnations of the national oil company's move.

But that night it was Nielson's turn to drop the bombshell.

When Rob Jennings, a bright young financier with Toronto investment house McLeod Young Weir, heard that Ward Pitfield had "gone over to the other side", he phoned his Toronto office and suggested they offer their services, which the Nielsons accepted, so a McLeod team consisting of Jennings, Bryce Farrell and Ivan deSouza were among the first in Calgary to know of the Oxy counteroffer.

At 11:30, the two sides sat down in the Edmonton Plaza hotel. Pitfield's action was still eating away at Glenn Nielson, and the first thing the Husky chairman said when the meeting started, staring straight at the Toronto investment dealer, was that he was very disappointed to see old friends on the other side of the table. Pitfield went white.

Then Nielson turned to Hopper and said that Husky had received an alternative offer from Occidental that the board planned to accept. PetroCan had not expected Nielson to be able to muster a defence and Hopper was flabbergasted. But he soon recovered. Indeed, he felt far from dismayed because he knew that Oxy's offer would have to get approval from the Foreign Investment Review Agency. Hopper expressed his disappointment, but then said that he would need time to consider the change in events. Nielson, perhaps in a show of strength and to prove that he wasn't bluffing, pointed out that Joe Baird and a team from Oxy were in the hotel. Would Hopper like to meet with them? Hopper declined.

Before dawn the following morning, Husky and Occidental made a joint announcement of the offer. When trading in Husky shares was resumed at lunchtime on Tuesday, June 13, they leaped $11.50 to close the day at $47.25 as almost a million shares changed hands.

In a gesture designed to look generous but which must have rubbed salt into PetroCanada's wounds, Husky and Oxy later the same day issued another joint statement offering one-third of a heavy oil development programme to PetroCanada. The Crown corporation did not respond. It had not expected to find itself in the middle of a battle, but now it was, so it had to think up a new strategy.

One possible alternative was simply to wait for FIRA to turn down Oxy, which it seemed certain it would. However, then PetroCan would come under a renewed barrage of abuse for hiding behind the government's apron strings. So, at the end of long and at times contentious meetings in the Constellation Hotel at Toronto's airport strip on Wednesday, June 14, PetroCan decided to up its offer. On Thursday morning, PetroCan announced a revised offer of $52 a share for Husky, thus upping its valuation of the company by a cool $76 million.

Occidental responded with lightning speed with a new share swap worth about $54.

Sitting in front of the table of photographs in his office in Los Angeles that Thursday, Hammer sat smiling like a benign hawk. His secretary was reading him an item on the Dow Jones newswire; "Canadian Energy Mines and Resources Minister Alastair Gillespie indicated that Occidental Petroleum Corp.'s bid for Husky Oil Ltd. could be acceptable to the Canadian government if Occidental's offer meant the development of Canada's heavy oil were to be 'guaranteed in every way' and in accord with Canadian objectives."

That bit about guarantees could be a problem, but the doctor took the message as a clear sign that he was still very much in the fight.

For one particularly sharp group of high-stake wheeler dealers, the New York arbitrageurs, this fiercely contested bidding war represented an ideal opportunity to do what they enjoy most — making money. Arbitrageurs, who work for giant Wall Street investment houses like Morgan Stanley, Bear Stearns and L. F. Rothschild, specialize in gambling millions of dollars on investment situations, usually takeovers.

When takeovers are announced, the share price of the prey usually stays some way below the offer price, reflecting the degree of risk that the deal will not go through. It is these risks that the arbitrageurs bet on. When there is more than one suitor for a company there is also the possibility of a bidding war, forcing share prices higher and higher. For the arbitrageurs, the struggle for Husky was ideal. When Husky stock had recommenced trading on the Tuesday, a large portion of the shares had been snapped up by the arbitrageurs in anticipation of what indeed happened two days later — both rivals upped their bids. Now, with the possibility of yet further counteroffers, and even a new contestant for Husky, they licked their lips and carried on picking up Husky stock, sometimes in multi-million dollar lumps.

But the action of the arbitrageurs, by concentrating large blocks of Husky stock in New York, was to play a critical part in what was to be a truly astonishing finale to the battle for Husky.

Enter the Fastest Gun in the West

By the end of the first week of the battle, with bids and counterbids in, observers settled back to speculate on the relative merits of the two offers and the role that FIRA was likely to play. Across Canada's press, editorial comment ranged from knee-jerk left to knee-jerk right, from stop-the-damned-Americans to stop-the-damned-government. Predictable words of condemnation of PetroCan's action came from the federal opposition. There were rumours of a further suitor, or group of suitors, planning to enter the fray, but nobody foresaw what was about to happen.

Bob Blair was about to do it again.

Unknown to Husky, AGTL had been picking up its shares in the market since the previous January. The stock had been bought in relatively small lots on the American Stock Exchange through a Boston-based company called Energy Ventures Inc., a small vehicle with a lot of financial clout behind it. Also involved in the company were John McMillian's Northwest Energy Corp. (Blair's partner in the Alaskan Highway pipeline project), New York investment house Loeb Rhoades, and Marshall Crowe, former chairman of the Canadian National Energy Board.

By coincidence, when Husky shares were suspended on June 8, AGTL was approaching the 5% level of ownership of Husky at which it would have to declare its position to the United States Securities and Exchange Commission, watchdog of the American investment community.

AGTL's long term intentions towards Husky, whether they looked on the company merely as a good investment or whether they had longer term acquisition in mind, was not clear. However, PetroCan's assault on Husky apparently came as much as a surprise to Blair as it did to the Nielsons.

When Blair had heard of the suspension on June 8, he had telephoned Jim Nielson in Cody and revealed "as a matter of courtesy" that he had been picking up Husky shares. He told Nielson that the purchases had been as an investment and assured him that he was not involved in the present assault on the Company.

When AGTL's position became known, a number of other companies approached Blair during the week beginning June 12 to see if he was interested in selling out or leading a consortium. However, with the mammoth task of the Aslaska Highway pipeline before him, Blair was considered in most quarters to have neither the financial backing, the management depth nor the inclination to go after Husky.

Most quarters proved to be very wrong.

Nevertheless, Blair had almost certainly not worked out his strategy at the end of the battle's first week. He obviously did not want to make any precipitous decisions until he had checked out the lie of the battlefield, the forces at his disposal, and the possible consequences of victory.

His choice seemed either to sell out, probably to PetroCan, turning a very nice profit in the process, or to put together a takeover himself.

In the event, Blair typically transcended the conventional alternatives and finished up gaining control of Husky without taking it over, by the totally unexpected but devastatingly simple tactic of buying minority control in the open market.

In the week beginning Monday June 19, Blair had to make the decision on whether to go for Husky, and if so, how. It was obvious that the federal government would be concerned at Blair possi-

bly taking on Husky while also having the pipeline in front of him.
He had in any case to visit Ottawa that week for a meeting of the
Economic Council of Canada, on which he sat, so on Monday and
Tuesday, June 19 and 20, he made a number of key political visits.
First on the list was Allen MacEachen, Deputy Prime Minister and
Minister for the pipeline. Then Mitchell Sharp, Northern Pipeline
Commissioner, and then Jack Stabback, head of the National En-
ergy Board. He reassured them all that if AGTL did make a move
on Husky, the pipeline remained the company's top priority.

He also checked out the positions of the three political parties
and kept in constant telephone contact with Premiers Peter Lougheed and Allan Blakeney of Saskatchewan. Also he spoke with another of his keen supporters, Albertan Energy Minister Donald
Getty.

One thing emerges by implication as absolutely certain, that
Alastair Gillespie, Federal Energy Minister, and responsible for PetroCan, did not tell Blair to keep his hands off Husky. Some of PetroCan's executives still believe that Gillespie should have told
Blair that.

Alberta Gas Trunk seemed to have a number of things going for
it. From the government's point of view, it was preferable to Occidental because it was Canadian. From a business perspective, particularly in the West, anything was better than PetroCanada.

The possibilities of furling himself in the twin flags of Canadian
nationalism and free enterprise were not lost on Blair. On the one
hand he appeared to be fighting off the predatory eagle of United
States economic imperialism; on the other, he was battling the
ever-reaching tentacles of federal government control. How could
he emerge as anything but a hero?

But that still left the all-important question of the economics of
involvement in heavy oil and of financial strategy. So, on Wednesday, June 21, Blair and three of his four AGTL "Inner Cabinet" —
senior vice-presidents Robin Abercrombie, William Rankin and
Dianne Narvik — headed for New York.

One of the key figures they turned to in New York was Mark
Millard, who had played a leading part in the original investment
in Husky through Energy Ventures. Millard, the very epitome of a
Wall Street Financier and one of the leading lights at Loeb
Rhoades, has already played a leading financial role for the Foot-
hills Group during the great pipeline debate.

His connections had originally been with the American partner
in the group, Northwest Energy Corp., but he had become well ac-
quainted with Blair during the battle.

Millard's impeccable nose for investment opportunity had already picked out Husky as an attractive proposition some time before, and he had teamed up with AGTL as an amenable partner.
One of the group's problems, however, was its limited knowledge

of heavy oil which, after all, was considered Husky's main attraction. How could they take a crash course without arousing too many suspicions?

The essence of the low-key power of men like Millard, whose mid-European accent and impeccable manners somehow remind one of a perhaps more benign version of Count Dracula, is their enormous circle of contacts. *Eminences grises* achieve their status by their ability to pull strings. Millard was about to pull strings.

A couple of years before, he had been in Calgary at a dinner party given by Bob Wisener, a leading figure in the brokerage community and head of Walwyn Stodgell's Calgary operations. At that party Millard had been introduced to John Masters, president of Canadian Hunter, the company that was to spark off the enormous bout of exploration activity at Elmworth in northwest Alberta. Millard was as impressed by Masters as Toronto-based mining giant Noranda had been, and Imperial Oil was to be (between them, the two companies backed up Master's geological theories with more than $200 million). As a result of the meeting, Millard gave Masters a good deal of business advice. Masters asked him how they could compensate him for his time and trouble. Millard pointed out that it was a long time since he, a multi-millionaire, had given advice for money. But one day, he told Masters, perhaps Canadian Hunter would be able to "return the favour".

That week in New York, the time had come to return the favour. Millard knew that one of the key personnel that Masters had hired for his fast growing company was Jay Christiensen, who, it just so happened, had been head of oil development at none other than Husky Oil!

So Millard put through a call to Masters. "John," he said, "you told me that you would make any of your people available to us. I wonder if you would send Jay Christiensen down to New York for a couple of days." Millard apologised that he could not reveal why he wanted him.

When Christiensen walked into Millard's office, he was stunned to see the team from AGTL, which swore him to secrecy and then proceeded to quiz him. They found out enough to realize that heavy oil could be a good investment, but the other problem was still that of financial tactics. Blair, his directors and their financial advisers at Loeb Rhoades and Dominion Securities in Toronto finally decided that the way to victory lay in going for minority control through the market, an alternative that virtually no one else had considered.

What made this viable was that huge blocks of shares had now moved into the hands of the arbitrageurs and other New York investors. At the end of 1977, about 65% of Husky shares had been held in Canada. By the start of the Husky takeover, there had been a 30% swing and 65% were held in the States. After two weeks of intensive buying by the arbitrageurs from willing Canadian sellers, the proportion of United States ownership had risen to 90%, and that 90% was held in large blocks. Under normal circumstances, buying massively on the market runs into the problem of availability of stock for sale. Now, however, AGTL knew that it could buy a very large position very quickly.

The Shoot Out Becomes a Massacre

Blair, it seems, still had doubts about the magnitude of what they were planning to do, but a decision had to be made because Blair and Narvik had to return to Calgary for a meeting with the Pension Investment Management Association, a body of key significance for pipeline financing, the next day.

Momentous events are sometimes decided upon in less than spectacular surroundings. The decision to go for Husky was made by Blair the afternoon of Thursday, June 22, while eating fish and chips with his colleagues at a restaurant on Manhattan's Seventh Avenue. Blair admits that some of his senior executives were more enthusiastic than he was about the purchase. In the end, swayed by their judgment, AGTL's President looked from under his bee-tling brows and said: "Alright, lets go after this." Bill Rankin, the relatively new finance brain brought from the Eaton's group, was left to take care of the purchases.

Just before the close of trading on Thursday, heavy buying appeared in the Toronto and New York markets. It continued throughout Friday, pushing Husky's share price above $50. By the end of trading on Friday night, AGTL had pushed its holdings in Husky to 10% and the price was hovering around PetroCan's offer of $52. PetroCan, meanwhile, wondered what was going on. They had been working feverishly for the past week to get an offer document together and were planning to mail it over the weekend. But the action in the market was threatening to push Husky's price above PetroCan's offer thus making it look ridiculous. Over the weekend, Hartland McDougall from the Bank of Montreal and Ced Ritchie from Bank of Nova Scotia flew to Calgary and lent Blair the financing he needed to complete the coup.

The Nielsons also visited Blair at AGTL's Calgary office, but he obviously didn't let on to them what he was doing. On Monday, the unprecedented buying spree continued. It began to dawn on most of the arbitrageurs what was happening and they proved, in most cases, willing to unload. By the close of trading on Monday, June 26, Blair had 23% of Husky. Perhaps the irony was that some observers thought Blair might be buying with a view to going into partnership with PetroCan. Perhaps he was even buying *for* Petro-Can. After all, the two companies were already involved in a number of joint ventures, including the Q&M pipeline to take gas east beyond Montreal, and an almost science-fiction scheme to haul liquefied natural gas out of the Arctic Islands. But PetroCan was as mystified as to what was going on as everyone else.

The following day the binge continued. By the close of trading on Tuesday, June 27, after spending something over $160 million on the stock market in three trading days, AGTL's total holding of Husky shares reached 35%.

Then, to the horror of those who had hung on to their Husky shares, Blair, like the Lord on the Seventh Day, stopped. On the Wednesday and Thursday, Husky shares were suspended pending announcements, but Blair really had no announcement to make. It was as simple as it looked. He had just bought 35% of Husky's shares.

When trading in the shares reopened on Friday, June 30, the battle for Husky ended as it had started three weeks before, with a flurry on the Stock exchanges. Only this time, the shares were plummeting. It was black Friday for Husky shareholders — the stock dipped $9⅞ on the TSE to $38⅝ and U.S. $8⅞ on the American Exchange to U.S. $34⅜.

What had been billed as the fight of the century was over in a somewhat anticlimactic fashion. For although the battle had a very clear victor, in the shape of AGTL, and two obvious losers, Petro-Can and Occidental (three if you include Husky), it lacked one feature usual in such circumstances: a takeover.

Those left holding Husky shares weren't the only unhappy ones. Stock exchanges and securities commissions both in Canada and the United States blinked in disbelief. Could Blair do what he had just done? Didn't he need their permission? What about all those shareholders left holding the baby?

Believing that they were on relatively strong ground on the last point, since it always looks good to be seen to champion the small shareholder, both the Ontario Securities Commission and the Toronto Stock Exchange were rash enough to express the opinion that Blair's action had left the minority shareholders out in the cold by not making a bid for the whole company.

Blair turned on them like a lion cornered by small rodents. With visible indignation that anyone should suggest that his actions had been in someway against the rules, he pointed out that he had not done any underhand deals with large block holders, which is the usual way for small shareholders to be left shivering on the outside during takeovers. Indeed the people left out in the cold were all very large and sophisticated American shareholders, who should presumably be able to look after themselves.

These included the Nielsons themselves and some of the arbitrageurs who had not been smart, or quick, enough to pull out before trading closed that fateful Tuesday. Unaccustomed to anyone roaring back at them quite so strongly, the OSC and the TSE fled chastened back into their holes.

Once again, by brilliant tactical maneouvering, Blair had blasted the opposition "big guns" out of the water. PetroCan and Husky were left to shuffle away as quietly as possible. Hopper immediately withdrew his bid, while Occidental hung in for a little while but then withdrew its offer as it became obvious that Blair was not interested in doing a deal with them.

For PetroCan, the blow was a bitter one. Blair had made them look more than lead-footed. But in many ways they had only themselves to blame. Some of PetroCan's advisers, notably Salomon Brothers, the leading New York investment house, had urged them to put their bid "out on the streets" as soon as possible. But perhaps because of the Foreign Investment Review Agency, they felt overconfident. Now they not only had opprobrium heaped on them for assaulting the private sector, but they had derision heaped on them for having failed. PetroCan had been naive, although a goodly share of the blame had to fall on their investment advisers, Pitfield Mackay Ross and Wood Gundy. For Ward Pitfield, a position that had originally looked untenable turned into a fully-fledged disaster. Acknowledging a conflict after the uproar at his changing sides, he stopped acting for PetroCan. Then, inevitably, he was forced to resign from the Husky board.

The final irony was that Pitfield Mackay Ross was also one of AGTL's leading investment houses, but, due to Ward Pitfield's earlier involvement in the battle for Husky, they missed out on the commissions from Trunk Line's share buying spree.

Ward Pitfield's action in the Husky affair has never been adequately explained. It has been suggested that he was unhappy with the reorganization of the company that Glenn Nielson had been planning, and that he was thus acting in what he saw as the other shareholders' best interests. However, in going behind the backs of the other Husky directors he was considered to have "let the side down" in an unforgiveable way. In some quarters it was seen as a typical example of the East's lack of financial morals when it came to dealing with the West.

But Ward Pitfield had also received his come-uppance. Circumstances had seen that the justice of the Old West had been inflicted on the perfidious Bay Streeter.

Blair's brilliant victory did leave a number of significant loose ends. The principal of these was cleared up when AGTL agreed, in mid 1979, to buy out the Nielsons' stake in Husky for U.S.$48 a share, leaving them, after all their maneouvering, with the tax bill on more than C$100 million to worry about. At the same time, Blair announced that he would be making a similar bid for the remainder of Husky shares. However, as this book went to press, the market price of Husky shares on the American Stock Exchange was above U.S.$48, indicating that if Blair wanted the remainder of Husky, its big American shareholders, many of whom had been burned in the events of June, 1978, were going to make him pay for it.

Nevertheless, with OPEC prices rocketing and even greater insistence by the federal government on energy self-sufficiency, Blair, in controlling Husky, holds one of the keys to Canada's longer term domestic energy supplies.

10 | PetroCan

*Whatever PetroCan was, is, or whether a future
tense applies to it at all, dull is one word that certainly does not apply.*

The fall from grace of the major oil companies after the OPEC
crisis was caused by the new nationalist atmosphere in the energy
industry. Bob Blair proved brilliantly adaptable to such an environment, but the purest creature of the new era was the national oil
company, PetroCanada.

For its opponents, PetroCan was always a hybrid political monster, conceived by the strange bedfellows who formed the federal
government from the latter part of 1972 until mid 1974. For its supporters, it was the only answer to the twin problems of national energy self-reliance and domination of Canadian oil by foreign companies.

Whatever the political viewpoint, however, PetroCanada undoubtedly experienced corporate growth-by-acquisition unprecedented in Canadian history. Within three years of its starting
operations on January 1, 1976, it had grown from two men, a type-
writer and a taxicab account to the largest Canadian-owned oil
company. In balance-sheet terms, its size at the end of 1978, assets
of $3.3 billion, was second only to that of Imperial Oil, assets $3.9
billion.

To say that PetroCan's first three years of operation were spectacular is to underestimate the case somewhat. Its corporate headquarters in Calgary's red-brick Canada Place, soon dubbed "Red
Square" by the hostile local community, were a hotbed of corporate machination and political intrigue. The normal conflicts of
corporate power within companies, which are hardly ever exposed
to the public view, were enormously complicated by the demands
of maintaining an interface with Ottawa.

And yet PetroCan's corporate management made massive steps
in key areas of their mandate, in reviving flagging frontier exploration, experimenting in tar sand and heavy oil technology. Meanwhile, they absorbed two very large oil companies, one of which
represented the largest takeover in Canadian history. Significantly,
they had also been comprehensively outsmarted in attempting to

take over Husky Oil. Whatever PetroCan was, is, or whether a future tense applies to it at all, dull is one word that certainly does not apply.

Perhaps most bizarre of all, however, was PetroCan's relationship to certain other elements of the Canadian oil business. One of the perennial complaints about nationalization or government ownership to any significant degree within an industry is that it kills drive, competition and economic efficiency. Once the heavy hand, and slow-witted brain, of bureaucracy arrive on the scene, or so says conventional wisdom, a kind of molasses of corporate inertia oozes through the sector. The nationalized company just sits there, confident in its political backing and proceeds to live off the fat of the land. PetroCanada, however, has found itself in a most untypical position. National companies can usually claim the excuse of higher, non-commercial objectives for poor economic performance. They rarely find anyone attempting to compete with them in these exalted aims. But PetroCan had not one, but two unofficial rival national oil companies, each combining not only a dazzling ability to think of "national" schemes before the government postulated them itself, but also to produce excellent "bottom line" performances. The companies are the quite extraordinary Dome Petroleum and Alberta Gas Trunk Line, whose managements have displayed a remarkable skill in producing a whole armory of projects, many of which display almost uncanny political appeal.

Indeed, PetroCanada found itself soon engaged in a gigantic game of corporate-political chess, stretching the length and breadth of Canada and incorporating bold new pipeline schemes, heavy oil development plans and projects for tanker transportation out of the high Arctic — all areas of acute political sensitivity. Almost everywhere it found itself engaged in a corporate minuet with either "Smiling" Jack Gallagher or "dour" Bob Blair.

The men who in three short years moulded PetroCan into its present, possibly short-lived, but undeniably imposing, shape were also far from typical in the Calgary oil community. The man originally chosen to breathe corporate life into PetroCanada was Maurice Strong, the closest thing to Renaissance man in the Canadian business community. An unprepossessing personality with a mind of surpassing brilliance, Strong possesses a curriculum vitae like a telephone directory and a social conscience that would put Saint Augustine to shame. The other key individual was Wilbert "Bill" Hopper, a man with a "backroom" background as a geologist, consultant and top bureaucrat, but with an upfront personality and an uncanny ability to make "bottom line" noises.

Strong is a consummate businessman capable of making the most banal political statements, long-winded speeches of almost perfect vacuity. Hopper is a consummate analytical and political brain with the ability of making it sound that his crusade in life is to

teach those damned bureaucrats back in Ottawa what entrepre-
neurialism is all about.

They too, proved to be strange and, at times, somewhat uncomfortable bedfellows.

Like virtually all the events in the Canadian petroleum industry during the 1970's, PetroCanada had at least some of its roots in the OPEC crisis, although it was being considered for some time before the Arab oil-producing nations imposed their unilateral quadrupling of the world oil price combined with an embargo in the fall of 1973.

Its earlier political roots lay in the growing Canadian economic nationalism of the late 1960's and early 1970's. With more than 90% of the Canadian oil industry under foreign, predominantly American, control, it inevitably became a focus for attention. However, the events of 1973-1974 were to provide a much more compelling reason to exercise greater control over Canadian petroleum.

Economic Nationalism

For the Liberal government of Pierre Trudeau energy did not really achieve high priority until the distant rumblings of international oil upheaval were heard at the beginning of 1973.

With exports to the United States at record levels and a very significant firming in prices, the pressure was on the Liberal government to be seen to be doing something. Exports were therefore brought under control, as the NDP demanded. In mid 1973, the Department of Energy produced *An Energy Policy for Canada — Phase 1*. In it, a national oil company was considered. However, from the sequence of for and against points made by Donald Macdonald's energy advisors, it was far from clear just which way the Liberals would jump. Within months, the OPEC crisis, and the need for domestic political survival, were to decide the Liberal government's policy.

On Thursday, December 6, 1973 Prime Minister Trudeau rose in the House of Commons to deliver a truly revolutionary new energy policy. The NDP subsequently claimed most of the credit for the provisions within it, including subsidies of a single Canadian oil price for the whole country, and extension of the pipeline that carried Albertan crude eastward beyond Toronto to Montreal, intensification of research into oil sands, and the creation of a national oil company.

Due to the enormous wrangle over other aspects of energy policy, to the Liberals' defeat in Parliament early in 1974, and to the subsequent election in which the Liberals gained a clear majority, the full debate on a national oil company did not begin until 1975.

Introducing the Act, on March 12, 1975, Macdonald gave a relatively low key speech reiterating the points outlined in Trudeau's keynote energy speech 16 months before. The Energy Minister bent over backwards to play down any great expectations for "early breakthroughs" or great financial success from PetroCan, and noted that private industry had done a "good job". He stressed that "the concerns which have led the government to propose the establishment of a national petroleum company have much more to do with the future than with the past."

He pointed out that development of the industry would require huge amounts of capital which might not be forthcoming from private industry, who might easily choose to invest elsewhere in the world. He also stressed the increased importance of a national concern to help secure critical oil imports.

The most important functions of the new Crown Corporation, he said, would be oil and gas exploration and development in the frontiers. Then came a possible key role in the development of oil sands; the import function; the bringing together of small Canadian companies to compete with larger companies; and finally, a possible entry into the downstream end of the business, into refining and marketing.

These activities, he said, would be based on an initial capitalization of $500 million, plus borrowing powers for another $1 billion.

The clear ideological response to this from the Conservative side of the house was that another Crown Corporation was simply not necessary. All desired policy results could be brought about by general rulings and incentives rather than direct intervention.

The Conservative "party line" was clearly expounded by Toronto M.P. Jim Gillies: "The best way to assure a high standard of living is not for the government to move directly into the production and distribution of goods and services. The evidence is all too clear that in those areas where the government moves in directly, the efficiency of operation is something less than maximum." The horrors of the Canadian Post Office were to be regurgitated again and again during the debate.

The government was vulnerable because of the disastrous impact that the dispute with Alberta had had on exploration activity in western Canada. The implication from the Conservative benches was that the Liberals may have deliberately created the situation so that they could then implant PetroCanada with the claim that it was necessary to boost exploration. If they wanted to boost exploration, and that included the frontiers, said the Conservatives, all the government had to do was create more attractive fiscal rules.

PetroCan was attacked by the Conservatives for being the thin end of the wedge that could lead to nationalization of the whole industry, but the NDP assailed it for being too small and powerless against the might of companies like Imperial Oil.

Tommy Douglas, perhaps predictably, suggested that PetroCan might not go far enough. He reiterated the NDP's desire for Petro-Can to take over one of the major oil companies and to become the sole importer of oil.

With what was to prove an incisive observation, he noted: "My fear is that PetroCanada will be nothing more than a sophisticated method of subsidizing the oil industry by joint ventures, by taking over projects the private sector does not want to take over, and by drilling in areas the private sector thinks are too risky, or too difficult."

For the first two years of its operation, PetroCan perhaps looked as if it was proving Tommy Douglas right.

One of the key issues for the federal government, as it tentatively attempted to put the new Crown Corporation in place, was just who would run it. It was decided early on that to have any credibility, the company would have to operate out of a headquarters in Calgary — where the necks might be red but the politics were pure blue. The environment would be totally hostile, so the man chosen to head the company would have to command respect as a businessman while also reflecting PetroCan's essentially political objectives. The list was obviously a short one. Jack Austin, the Vancouver businessman drafted into the Liberal government as Deputy Energy Minister coveted the job, but there was opposition from within the industry because Austin was not an "oil man". Donald Macdonald had for a while put Arne Nielsen, head of Mobil Canada, at the top of his list. Nielsen held enormous respect in Calgary, was one of the very few Canadians who held a top position in a major oil company, and had insight into government policy through his membership of the select National Advisory Committee on Petroleum. But Nielsen was not considered "political" enough.

In the end, it seems, it was the preference of Pierre Trudeau that led to the choosing of a man who held the somewhat unlikely post at the time of Executive Director of the United Nations Environment Programme, based in Nairobi, Kenya. The man was Maurice Strong.

11 | Maurice Strong— The Reluctant Millionaire

Strong is a man who has always seemed ahead of his time. Indeed, for those who believe in the ultimate imperfection of man, there may be genuine doubts over whether the time will ever come for people like Maurice Strong. Perhaps he really is a mutant.

When God made Maurice Strong, he undoubtedly threw away the mould. Strong is unique in a way that almost demands ungrammatical qualification of the word. He makes you feel that you should really be saying "totally", or "absolutely", or "bizzarely" unique. Indeed, more than throwing away the mould, God has probably grown a little uneasy over the years about the security of his own position, because Strong's progress through life seems to be equipping him for nothing less than the takeover of the Top Job itself. Strong's ultimate ambition is often cited as that of becoming Canadian Prime Minister, but such a post could only be considered as yet another brief stepping stone on Strong's restless path to apotheosis.

What seemed to equip Strong so well for the chairmanship and presidency of PetroCanada was that, in the frenetic pursuit of his multiple careers in public and private life, he had spent, for him, an almost inordinate number of years in the Albertan oil industry. After a stint as an oil analyst with Richardson Securities in Winnipeg, he had joined the fledgling Dome Petroleum as Jack Gallagher's assistant. He had then gone on to found an oil and gas consultancy, taken over an Edmonton-based utility, been instrumental in putting together Canadian Industrial Gas and Oil, Cigol, with Ed Galvin, and then, after moving on to the presidency of Power Corp., had engineered the somewhat reluctant melding of Toronto-based utility Northern & Central Gas with Cigol to form the basis of a "Great Canadian Energy Company."

To say that Strong was respected in the Calgary oil community is perhaps to use the wrong word. He was rather regarded there, as almost everywhere else, as an object of amazement. For a community that tends, because more or less everyone is involved in the same business, to be oil/self obsessed, any individual who leaped in and out of the good, honest pursuit of making money to engage in activities like heading Canada's foreign aid programme and working for the United Nations is regarded less as an oddball than a mutant.

And yet, if Strong did seem to have an overdeveloped social conscience, he was also able to speak to businessmen in the language they knew best, that of pure profit. The ultimate paradox about Strong was that he combined his altruistic pursuits with an equal sensitivity to business opportunity.

Sitting in his small Toronto office early in 1979, the man himself seems the ultimate anti-climax. As a journalist once said of him: "You would not pick him out of a crowd of two." With his greased hair, his slightly pudgy face and his well-clipped moustache, he looks like an escapee from the wrong side of a bank cashier's desk. An asthmatic, his hurried speech — not surprising for a man who obviously has so much to do — is punctuated with short gasps. He is a man who feels that he has to spend a good deal of time justifying his unusual career path. In the spring of 1979, having finally left PetroCanada, backed away from an entry into federal politics, and while in the middle of myriad business deals involving at once ranching and ski-resorts in the United States and nothing less than a potential reorganization of the entire Canadian paper industry, he told the author, rather sadly: "In the world of business, I am treated as a do-gooder, but among the do-gooders I have always found myself an object of suspicion because of my business connections."

But it was not only his dual life that caused suspicion and lack of understanding. His lifestyle, too, bears an almost bizarre stamp of asceticism. He is renowned for wearing "$20 shoes" and travelling economy class on the most gruelling of flights (often spending the whole time dictating letters). Yet he is also a trustee of the Rockefeller Foundation and when in New York, often stays with head of the World Bank, Robert MacNamara.

Strong is a man who has always seemed ahead of his time. Indeed, for those who believe in the ultimate imperfection of man, there may be genuine doubts over whether the time will ever come for people like Maurice Strong. Perhaps he really is a mutant.

Nevertheless, in his championship of the creation of Cigol and Northern & Central into a fully-integrated, Canadian gas company, he had foreshadowed the issues of Canadian energy ownership and the building of a strong nationalist presence in the petroleum industry. Strong was also a champion of causes like ecology before obsession with "Spaceship Earth" had become a cult.

Born in the prairie town of Oak Lake, Manitoba, Maurice Strong was the eldest of four children. His childhood, according to his "official" biography, sounds like an application for cannonization. In a passage that would make any cynical political promoter cringe, it says:

In childhood he often went off into the hills around Oak Lake for solitary communion with nature. "I could never get over the wonder of a hare's turning white in the winter and brown in the summer", he has recalled. "I developed a profound respect for nature, which is at the root of my religious feelings, because the exciting things that were happening in the natural world owed nothing to man."

His mother is reported to have "stimulated her children intellectually with regular readings from literary classics." But the hard truth beneath this somewhat idyllic picture was that Strong's upbringing was both poor and hard. His father had worked on the Canadian Pacific Railway as an assistant station agent, but eventually lost his job in the depths of the Depression. Then his mother had a nervous breakdown from which she never recovered. When Strong was 13, he ran away from home and signed up as a messboy on a merchant ship that was transporting American troops to Alaska.

By the time he was 16, he had returned to Oak Lake to finish high school and had then taken off for a year as an apprentice fur trader with the Hudson's Bay Company in Chesterfield Inlet. Again, the official biography paints a picture of a northern business Leonardo da Vinci in the making: ". . . during his sojourn of more than a year in the Canadian Arctic he learned to speak Eskimo, studied geology in the field, and read books on economics that he had taken with him." He also dabbled in prospecting while in the North and developed an interest in stock promotion.

Flunking out of a pilot's course for the RCAF because of poor eyesight, Strong headed for Winnipeg to join James Richardson & Sons and made a timely entry into oil stock analysis while the post-Leduc petroleum market was still booming. It was while gathering material for Richardson's statistical "Blue Book" that he came across Jack Gallagher, then a young ex-Exxon and ex-Imperial whizz kid who had just started Dome Petroleum. Strong, then in his early 20's, asked Gallagher, then in his early 30's, if he could come and work for Dome. Whether the young Strong could, at that stage, have functioned as "financial advisor" to a man not only 10 years his senior but with oil experience all over the world and powerful connections with the New York investment community seems in some doubt. But that, according to the "official" biography, is what he did.

After a couple of years with Gallagher, Strong took off on a two-year world tour, during which, according to the Strong annals, he, "mastered Swahili, developed a graphite mine in Tanzania, set up petrol stations in Kenya and Zanzibar, and trained natives to run the stations."

When Strong returned, he wanted to become a full-time "do-

gooder". He approached the churches, the YMCA and the External
Aid office but none of them would have him.

"I was very dismayed that nobody wanted a young man with no more than enthusiasm," he told the author.

So Strong then made a fundamental decision. He would not give up his social conscience, but he would transform his position as a "young man with no more than enthusiasm". He would become rich.

Strong returned to Calgary to rejoin Dome, which by now had established itself as an aggressive, although still small, company. There he continued his jack-of-all-trades role. He managed American investment money and he handled the company's land department and administration. A former colleague of Strong at Dome remembers him as a good wheeler-dealer, "but you always had to clear up the mess after him."

Strong had already clearly established the trait that was to mark his business and public life. He had an ability to spin-off brilliant schemes at an astonishing rate, but he did not want to follow them through. He had always to be moving on to the next challenge. Another trait he demonstrated was an obsession with size and empire building. In the early 1950's, after the Bronfmans had established Royalite by buying out Imperial in the Turner Valley, Sam Bronfman Senior approached Gallagher with the offer of a merger. Although Royalite was much bigger, Bronfman realized Gallagher's talents and offered him the majority share of the new company and the position of chief executive. Strong pressed Gallagher hard to take the offer and couldn't understand why Gallagher didn't want to. But Smiling Jack too was marching to his own, ultimately highly successful, drum.

Strong found the opportunity for his next business leap when the management of a small oil company, Ajax Petroleums, was offered to Dome. Gallagher was not interested in taking it over, so Strong formed M. F. Strong Management, moved into Ajax, and within three years had organized it into Canadian Industrial Gas Ltd. He was eventually to be instrumental in the merger of a large group of companies, many of which had themselves been put together by Ed Galvin, into Canadian Industrial Gas & Oil, but by this time he had moved on to the Power Corp. to become president, although he maintained the chairmanship of Canadian Industrial Gas.

Among Power Corp.'s diverse holdings was that of Greater Winnipeg Gas, the Manitoba gas utility. One day, Strong was approached by Spence Clark, head of Ontario utility Northern & Central Gas, about a merger. At the same time, Cigol was being eyed as a potential takeover candidate by Frank McMahon, so Strong came up with the idea of merging Greater Winnipeg and Cigol into Northern & Central, thus forming a gas, as opposed to the more usual oil, integrated company that took its product from the wellhead to the burner tip.

As a result, the entity was formed that was eventually to become Norcen Energy Resources. Strong's concept, however, did not sit all that easy with those who had to organize it. The idea of balancing the ups and down of the exploration and production end of the business with the stability of the regulated utility business looked like a good idea. However, far from everyone agreed with it, and, what is more, things didn't really turn out that way. Indeed, Norcen turned out to be a kind of allegory of the West's perception of their relationship with the East. The oil and gas production arm of the new business, based in Calgary under the brilliant Galvin, ended up producing most of the excitement and the profits, while control resided in the well-decorated walls of Northern & Central's downtown Toronto office. It was seen as another example of the eastern tail wagging the western dog and left a legacy of friction between the Toronto and Calgary offices until Ed Battle, a protegé of Galvin, was eventually installed as president in Toronto under Ed Bovey, the man who, as chairman, had had to try and make Strong's brainchild work.

Strong himself, typically, had moved on before the fruits of his handiwork could ripen. Still obsessed with public service, and now, as head of one of Canada's largest companies, in a position to be taken a little more seriously than when he had returned from his world tour years before, "a young man with nothing more than enthusiasm," Strong was summoned by Lester Pearson in 1966 to become Director General of the Canadian government's external aid programme. Under Strong, the agency was renamed the Canadian International Development Agency.

After four years at CIDA, during which Strong pursued his genuine concern for the underdeveloped nations, he was asked by then secretary of the United Nations, U Thant, to come to the United Nations as undersecretary general with responsibility for environmental affairs. He served at the United Nations until the end of 1975, master-minding the first United Nations Conference on the Human Environment in Stockholm.

Strong demonstrated his remarkable, indeed paradoxical, intellectual diversity during his stay with the United Nations. In a world of increasing specialization he had shown the almost singular ability to make the leap from the corporate machinations of the executive suite to the consideration of such unrelated topics as soil-erosion and man-made diseases.

Strong presents the most fascinating of enigmas. Perhaps the most astonishing thing about Strong is his pervasive sense of insecurity. Despite a list of achievements that would look impressive spread among five men, more than 20 honorary degrees, membership on the advisory boards of an enormous number of charitable

institutions, Strong still seems to feel the need to impress people.
Amazingly, he is inclined to exaggerate the importance of things he did earlier in life. But it was to this man that the Liberal government finally turned in 1975 to head its most controversial creation, PetroCanada.

Wilbert Hopper

The man chosen to go with Strong to Calgary to set up the Crown Corporation was Wilbert Hopper, who, as Assistant Deputy Minister in the Department of Energy, had been behind much of the policy formulated during the critical pre and post-OPEC period. Hopper had been in the running for the Deputy Ministership of the Department of Energy, but was offered the executive vice-presidency of PetroCan as an alternative. Hopper wanted to be president, but was not known in the industry, while a key group within the Cabinet wanted someone from the private sector to handle the top executive position. Strong, it seems, held the same view. However, in the ensuing struggle it was the ebullient figure of Hopper that was to win out in an, at times, bitter political fight.

Hopper, the son of an Ottawa civil servant, grew up in Washington, where his father was a trade attaché. He graduated in geology from American University, Washington, and went to work as a petroleum geologist for Imperial before moving on to a series of backroom consultancy jobs. He worked for consultants, Foster Associates, as a petroleum economist before becoming senior energy economist for the National Energy Board between 1961 and 1965. Then he moved to Cambridge, Mass. as senior petroleum consultant with another leading consultancy firm, Arthur D. Little Inc.

He moved back to Ottawa in 1972 as senior adviser on energy policy and became Assistant Deputy Minister in 1974. Ironically, one of Hopper's original assignments was to make a study of Canadian oil companies and assess the prospects for a national oil company. His report, reflected in the neutral set of pros and antis that appeared in mid 1973 in the *Energy Policy-Phase 1*, was far from enthusiastic. However, the eruption of the OPEC crisis just a few months later was to increase both the pressure for, and the apparent need of, a strong national presence in the oil industry.

On January 1, 1976, or so goes the legend, Strong and Hopper sat down in their temporary office in the International Hotel on Calgary's Fourth Avenue, sharpened their wits, and began to hammer out policy. But what marked the first six months of the Crown Corporation's existence was not only the evolution of a strategy, and a full-tilt plunge into the energy business, but also a power struggle about just who was going to run the show.

There were also a few problems with the PetroCan-government "interface". Theoretically, PetroCanada was responsible directly to the Minister of Energy, but Alastair Gillespie, who had now taken over that role, did not get on with Strong. It was said he resented Strong's access to Trudeau, but whatever the reason, the relationship was not an easy one.

Not surprisingly, reaction from the industry to the setting up of PetroCanada was also a violent one. The walls of the Petroleum Club resounded with indignation at the thought that a "window" should be needed on their activities. The oil community's more general regurgitation of its favourite philosophy: free enterprise good, government bad — intoned with about as much critical analysis as the "four legs good two legs bad" of the animals on George Orwell's farm — was now given a particular, and all-too-close, example against which to rail.

But the fact was that once PetroCan had started business, companies were only too willing to give the Crown Corporation a piece of their action — particularly when it wasn't too attractive! Petro-Can might represent the government, but it also represented money. When companies had acreage for which they held no great hopes, as Shell and Mobil held off the east coast, they were only too willing to let the Crown Corporation come in and drill on it. Within a relatively short time, PetroCanada was wheeling and dealing with the best of them, although it was certainly receiving no favours from its business "partners."

But then, in a speech on April 18, 1977, Maurice Strong dropped a bombshell. Speaking to the Canadian Club in Toronto, he said that while the private industry had, after a year of its operation, accepted PetroCan as a way of life, "some elements in the industry, principally a few large foreign-controlled companies" were waging an "unrelenting underground campaign against PetroCanada, seizing every opportunity to restrict its role and undermine its credibility both with the public and with government."

These were strong words, and Strong might have gotten away with his vaguely alarmist statement, designed perhaps to appeal to nationalistic sensitivities about the oil industry. However, as chance would have it, both Strong and Hopper had to appear the following day before the National Resources and Public Works Committee in Ottawa. Strong was called upon to substantiate his charge with facts, but either could not or would not, and had to resort to waffling. His statement certainly did nothing to improve relations with the industry.

The third "character" to appear in the founding stages of Petro-Canada was Joel Bell — another backroom whizz-kid from the Prime Minister's office. Bell was 35 years old in PetroCan's first year, but had already played a key role in drafting much government policy, including the Act setting up the Foreign Investment Review Agency and the PetroCan Act itself.

Montreal-born Bell, a lean and affable figure with acute political instincts, had studied economics and law at McGill before moving to Harvard where he also started working for the Prime Minister's office. When he left the university, he went straight to work full-time for the government. For a while after PetroCan's formation, he attempted to commute between Ottawa and Calgary, but the strain was too much, so he was eventually taken onto the full-time staff as vice president of corporate planning. Bell was considered to be "Hopper's man," and his appointment reportedly caused some friction in the Cabinet.

Among the fledgling organization's top priorities were getting an exploration programme going and looking around for a sizable company to take over. Exploration needed an exploration man and Strong approached Donald Axford, head of Mobil Canada's oil-finding team. Axford was obviously suffering under the same conditions that had made Arne Nielsen think about leaving Mobil. The New York-based parent had developed a "down" on Canada as a result of the Federal-Provincial dispute, and Axford had seen his exploration budget chopped back from $60 million to just $8 million in the space of a couple of years.

Described by a former colleague as a "wild-eyed explorationist" Axford had known Strong since Strong's early days with Dome Petroleum. PetroCan's chairman knew that Axford had great faith in the east coast offshore, one of the priority areas for PetroCanada's mandate to explore in the frontiers. Axford had enormous belief in the potential for oil and gas finds off Sable Island, and his enthusiasm had been so infectious that Mobil Oil Corp. had even put a picture of the exploration activities there on the cover of their annual report. However, exploration had not produced results and New York had become disillusioned. Axford's faith lived on, however, and the first thing he did after being hired by PetroCan was to go back to Mobil and the other chief landholder off the east coast, Shell, and take farm-outs.

However, Sable Island exploration was initially a flop and Axford also failed to hit it off with Hopper. Hopper decided that Axford had been responsible for a strategic error and wanted to get rid of him. As yet, however, he didn't have enough power. The immediate goal for Hopper was the presidency of the Crown Corporation. Strong had told him that if he could prove himself in the first six months of operations, then he would recommend him, but it seems that Strong had doubts about Hopper's standing with the Calgary community, and he was inclined, along with a number of Cabinet members, to go for an "industry man" for the presidency. Once again, the spotlight fell on Arne Nielsen. Strong called him over to PetroCan and asked him if he was still interested in the job of chief executive and president of the Crown Corporation. If he was, Strong told him that he would do everything in his power to get him the post.

Nielsen, increasingly discontented with the New York stranglehold on Mobil Canada, was interested but told Strong that he wouldn't consider moving for less than his present salary, which, with bonus, totalled about $120,000. Donald Macdonald had told him when he had approached him the previous year that a salary of that level might cause problems for the Crown Corporation. However, in May of 1977, Strong called Nielsen again and told him that the salary had been approved and that he was going to try to clear Nielsen's appointment with the Prime Minister. Hopper even visited Nielsen and declared that he would be "very pleased" to work for him.

However, there was growing concern in Ottawa that PetroCan might be perceived as a private company being funded by the public purse, so the "political" decision was that Hopper would have to be president. The morning that the PetroCanada board was due to meet to go through the motion of deciding on a president, a newspaper story appeared announcing that Hopper would be the new president. There had obviously been a "leak" from the government, and a number of board members, who reportedly included Strong, were deeply incensed. However, at the end of an acrimonious meeting, Hopper was appointed president.

Hopper, keen to assert himself, seemed to have one immediate objective: to get rid of Axford, which he was to do in very short order. The instrument of Axford's downfall was to be PetroCan's first acquisition.

Shortly after setting up operations, Hopper and Strong had started looking for likely takeover opportunities. Strong had decided upon Atlantic Richfield's Canadian subsidiary, Arcan, as a prime candidate. The company was a fairly sizable oil and gas producer that was very obviously up for sale. Its parent, strained by cash shortages as a result of the mounting costs of development of Prudhoe Bay and building the TransAlaska pipeline, had already had to pull out of the Syncrude project. The federal government and the provincial governments of Alberta and Ontario had been forced to step in and bail out Syncrude, and the federal government's 15% stake had already been deposited in PetroCan's care. Now Atlantic Richfield was keen to sell out its entire Canadian operation. Hopper was nowhere near as keen on the acquisition as Strong. Nevertheless, he went down to the United States and negotiated the deal and his basically negative attitude led him to drive an excellent bargain. As Don Getty and Peter Lougheed had demonstrated during the Syncrude negotiations, the best people to make deals are those who are quite prepared to see them fall through. The original price tag placed on Arcan was $400 million. By the time Hopper had finished negotiating, the figure was $342 million.

Arcan, in the words of an industry observer, had been "sitting on its hands", with its 300 or so staff underutilized. It offered PetroCan cash flow of about $50 million a year, derived from production of about 30,000 barrels a day of oil and liquids and 90 million cubic feet of gas. Its total net interest in undeveloped oil and gas acreage was about 11 million acres, while Arcan also had 1.2 million acres of tar sand leases that required in-situ development.

However, for many of Arcan's management and employees, PetroCan's takeover amounted to rape, and three-quarters of the company's top executives left within a relatively short time.

Arcan was also to be the scene of Axford's humiliation. Shortly before Hopper was appointed PetroCan president, Strong appointed Axford to take over Arcan's operations. Within days of Hopper's new appointment, he shoved Axford to one side and appointed Sam Stewart, who had been responsible for tar sands within Arcan, above him. It was then only a matter of time before Axford was forced to leave, albeit with a reportedly attractive financial settlement.

Axford's departure was followed by an uneasy period for personnel all round, during which a great many of Atlantic Richfield Canada's senior employees departed.

However, Hopper and Strong continued aggressively to pursue their mandate. Major moves were made into the frontiers, off the east coast, in the Arctic Islands and in the McKenzie Delta region, and the government's 45% holding in PanArctic Oils Ltd., the multi-company joint venture set up to examine the potential of the Arctic Islands, was also placed under PetroCan's aegis.

Jack and Bob Come Calling

PetroCan was forceful in moving into the frontiers, but its exploration efforts were something less than successful. The major, and expensive, farm-outs taken by PetroCan on land held by Shell and Mobil off the east coast produced little but dry holes. Activity in the Arctic Islands also proved tantalizingly short of commercial prospects, although the promise of finds there was sufficient to cause PetroCan, in 1977, to step into one of the most technologically advanced schemes for moving energy ever considered in Canada, the Arctic LNG (liquefied natural gas) Project.

Under the Arctic LNG scheme, the Crown Corporation, in concert with partners Alberta Gas Trunk Line and a shipping group,

Melville Shipping, developed plans, which were filed with the National Energy Board early in 1979, to liquefy gas produced out of the Arctic Islands at a sophisticated, barge-mounted unit. The gas was then to be shipped aboard special ice-strengthened LNG tankers to a southern facility where it would be once more vaporized before being delivered to markets.

The other highly politicized project in which Petrocan allowed itself to become involved was Alberta Gas Trunk Line's scheme for a Quebec and Maritimes (Q & M) Pipeline. As an ardent nationalist, it was certain that Bob Blair would provide a warmer welcome to PetroCan than many of his United States-controlled colleagues in Calgary. However, Blair also undoubtedly saw PetroCan as an invaluable ally in some of his own schemes. Jack Gallagher, Calgary's other great nationalist, also welcomed PetroCan, although it seems he may have primarily looked at it as so much more potential funding for his grandiose schemes in the Beaufort Sea.

PetroCan was not keen to be used by Gallagher as the financial cat's paw for the Beaufort Sea, but could see a clear rationale for becoming involved with Blair. Not long after the Crown Corporation moved into its second year of operation, it joined with AGTL in two schemes, the Q & M, dreamed up by Blair's management, and the Arctic LNG scheme, which sprang from the head of Petro-Can's Don Walcott. Walcott had been the brains behind Dome Petroleum's early entry into the area of natural gas liquids, which were to provide the bulk of Dome's earnings throughout the 1970's. However, he had become disgruntled at Dome because he felt he had not received the recognition he deserved for his achievements. In 1976 he had joined PetroCan as vice-president of transportation and operations. In 1977, he became senior vice-president in the all-important area for PetroCanada of project development. Walcott got on well with Blair, which also helped the liaison between the two companies.

However, PetroCan was soon to realize that it had perhaps become involved in more than it had bargained for in the Q & M scheme, which involved a good deal of corporate as well as energy politics. And there was also to be a major falling out with Alberta Gas Trunk over the Husky takeover battle, a struggle that was to leave the Crown Corporation with a lot of egg on its face.

As with great chess moves, great corporate schemes tend to do several things at once. The hatching of the Q & M scheme by AGTL seemed to fulfill a whole host of goals. The basic plan was to build a pipeline to carry Albertan gas beyond its existing terminal in Montreal to Quebec City, and then on to the Maritimes. This scheme not only promised a domestic outlet for the excess gas production that had built up in Alberta, but it also promised to displace some of the increasingly expensive imported oil that provided most of the energy in eastern Canada. At the same time, it offered a commercial link to bolster the seemingly increasingly tenuous bonds of confederation with Quebec. As with Blair's Alaskan Highway scheme, it was a pipeline built on the basis of political appeal.

However, corporate politics were also involved, because the line would in fact amount to an extension of the present west-to-east transmission system operated by giant TransCanada Pipelines. For corporate strategists, the key question was: if this line was such a good idea, why hadn't TransCanada thought of it? TransCanada's original answer was that they had never considered such an extension economic. However, for western producers and the Albertan government, which had long considered TransCanada basically as an instrument of the eastern customers it served, the answer was that it was typical of TransCanada's sluggish management style.

There was also an underlying corporate vendetta between Alberta Gas Trunk Line and TransCanada dating back to the struggle over the northern gas pipeline. TransCanada had been a particularly vociferous supporter of the Arctic Gas Group, for which Blair had never really forgiven the company. In the wake of the victory of Blair's Foothills Group, the National Energy Board had recommended that TransCanada, as the largest gas transmission system in the country, should join the Foothills Group, but after some desultory meetings, TransCanada had announced that it would not be going into the consortium. It seemed that the rupture had taken place basically because Blair just did not want TransCanada in his group. However, the reasons were reported to be that TransCanada was not prepared to pay the "entry fee" demanded by AGTL, and that the Toronto-based company was also keen on additional gas exports through its own system that might prejudice the prebuilding of the southern sections of the Alaskan Highway line — which depended on shipping all available additional exports. When TransCanada finally announced, in April, 1978 that it would not be joining the group, Blair was obviously shedding no tears.

When Blair subsequently came up with his scheme to ship gas beyond Montreal, he was quite obviously, and literally, outflanking the eastern transmission giant. PetroCan, meanwhile, by joining the scheme, seemed to have thrown its weight behind AGTL.

The Arctic LNG scheme could also be considered as another outflanking of TransCanada, since it was once again the giant transmission company that was the principal behind the Polar gas pipeline, to which the Arctic LNG scheme was clearly a rival. Blair had other reasons for not being too keen on Polar gas, since that scheme could be considered a competitor to the Alaskan Highway scheme to provide huge new volumes of gas to United States markets.

Blair appeared like a magician, supporting a dazzling array of new projects while TransCanada seemed like a mole, which, having spent too long with its subterranean pipe, could only raise its head and blink. Not only that, Blair had also enlisted the support of the potentially most powerful entity in Canadian oil, PetroCan.

From PetroCan's point of view, it seemed to have become a little too closely involved in what was turning out to be a battle between two giant corporate rivals.

As its second year drew to a close, however, PetroCan had somewhat bigger strategic problems to worry about. Its extensive expenditures in the frontiers had produced virtually nothing; it had ever-increasing amounts of cash tied up in its Syncrude and Panarctic investments, while its other technological research ventures into areas such as heavy oil recovery were a further drain on its resources. As Tommy Douglas had foreshadowed, PetroCan seemed to be doing the industry's dirty work. It soon became obvious that the funds provided from Arcan would be insufficient if PetroCan was to achieve a major impact on the industry. Unless the Crown Corporation had a bigger source of funds under its own control, it would have to keep returning to Ottawa with an outstretched hand, something that would both increase its political profile and its vulnerability to attack. PetroCan needed to buy another company, and it had to be a big one.

Between 1973 and 1975, the backrooms of Ottawa had witnessed many conversations that would have caused yet further shivers of indignation to run through the Petroleum Club. Those conversations were about nationalizing oil companies. One of the first things that Strong and Hopper had done when they sat down together in the International Hotel in Calgary in January, 1976, was to draw up a short list of prospective takeover candidates. They had looked at companies like Mobil and Amoco, two 100%-owned subsidiaries of United States oil giants, as well as majority American-owned companies like Hudson's Bay Oil & Gas, controlled by Continental Oil Co. In the end they had decided on the somewhat smaller Arcan because it was undoubtedly up for sale. Strong and Hopper were perhaps reluctant to become involved in a takeover battle so soon after setting up shop. Now, as 1977 drew to a close, the hunt was on again. At the senior executives' Christmas lunch at the end of 1977, Maurice Strong said that the highlights of the year to come would be the filings with the National Energy Board of the Arctic LNG and Q & M projects, and another takeover.

The Husky Fiasco

A key area of PetroCan's mandate had been in the development of tar sands and heavy oils. In connection with such development, PetroCan, along with Gulf Canada, had been negotiating since June of 1976 with Husky.

It was sometime in the second quarter of 1978, that PetroCan started to plan a takeover of Husky. The affair turned out to be a fiasco for PetroCanada and a victory for the man who had joined them in two proposed major joint ventures, Bob Blair. However, to be fair to Blair, it seemed that his ultimate gaining of control of Husky had more to do with PetroCan's apparent ineptitude in handling the takeover assault than with any desire on his part to embarrass the Crown Corporation.*

For Hopper, keen to establish himself in the shoes of his more-than-dynamic predecessor, Maurice Strong, the debacle meant a significant personal defeat. It left everybody at PetroCan with a bitter taste in his mouth, and it led to a major deterioration in Hopper's personal relations with Blair. The fight led to an inevitable cooling of the desire between the two companies to do business together, as Hopper was determined not to be caught out again.

It was this feeling that PetroCan might turn out to be the fall guy in its partnership with AGTL to build the Q & M pipeline that led to PetroCan's withdrawal from the scheme three months later. Of course, since both sides had more than a little political *savoir faire*, the withdrawal was never called anything so crude. Instead, Petro-Can very quietly announced one day that it was stepping back from full partnership to take "an option" on a 20% participation in the line. In plain language, they were getting the hell out.

It was generally agreed that the line would be feasible only if subsidized in some way. But who was going to come up with the subsidy? The producers did not want to, Premier Lougheed didn't seem prepared to give anything up on the province's part, while consumers in Ontario were none too keen on sharing the financial burden of sending gas to their brothers next door. PetroCan could hear Blair making lots of typically political noises but was finding it hard to pin him down. Hopper felt himself about to become the fall guy once more, so he decided, apparently with Blair's agreement to pull out.

---

* PetroCan was rushed by the apparent stock market leak on June 8, 1978, into revealing its intention to make an offer for Husky stock. The Crown Corporation also had to launch into the bid without the assistance of its top legal brain, David O'Brien, who had become seriously ill a few weeks before the takeover attempt. Most of all, it sprang its takeover offer on the Nielsons under the quite incorrect assumption that the family would go along with it.

American observers were aghast at the Crown Corporation's handling of the takeover attempt. The word that recurred most often was "amateurish". First, PetroCan had been naive enough to think it could approach Husky with a "friendly" offer. Then it had underestimated Husky's ability to mount a counter-offer, which it had elicited from Armand Hammer. Then, finally, when it seemed that the scales were tipping in PetroCan's favour as a result of what many claimed was the "unfair" edge given to it by the Foreign Investment Review Agency's likely blocking of Occidental's bid, Blair had stepped in and blasted his "partner" out of the water with the astonishingly simple but devastatingly effective tactic of buying Husky stock in New York.

For PetroCan in the wake of Husky, it was a matter of bouncing back and bouncing back quickly to re-establish a shattered credibility. Within five months they had done just that, and, in the process, grabbed themselves a prize twice as large as Husky.

Shortly after control of Husky had fallen into the hands of Alberta Gas Trunk Line, Bill Dickie, former Albertan Energy Minister and Husky board member, met Merrill Rasmussen, president and chief executive of Pacific Petroleums Ltd., at the Calgary Golf and Country Club. "We escaped PetroCan," joked Dickie, "but watch out, you might be next."

Rasmussen may have smiled, but inside his feelings were far from happy, for he had reason to believe that Pacific might indeed be next for the unwelcome attentions of PetroCan. In the fall of 1977, when PetroCan, having absorbed Arcan, was gearing itself up to go on the acquisition trail once more, Kelly Gibson, a director and former head of Pacific, had met Wilbert Hopper at an informal gathering. The question arose of whether Phillips Petroleum Co., the American oil giant that held 48% of Pacific's equity, might be interested in selling out. Gibson said he would find out if Phillips would consider selling. Then, in November, Hopper had approached Rasmussen to discuss Pacific's possible acquisition by PetroCan. Shortly afterwards, Joel Bell had gone over Pacific's figures with the company's finance director, Bill Tye. Then, however, Gibson had come back to Hopper and told him that Phillips had not expressed any great interest in selling their block, although they would be prepared "to meet and discuss the matter with PetroCanada further."

For the moment, Hopper allowed the matter to slide, and, within six months, Husky had been singled out as the preferred takeover target. But when the Husky acquisition fell through, PetroCan immediately went on the lookout for another takeover victim. Even as Dickie was jokingly saying "you might be next" to Rasmussen, the analytical tentacles of PetroCan were once more taking a grip on Pacific.

By this time, another rationale for a large company takeover was also becoming apparent. A federal election was approaching and PetroCan was keenly aware of the belligerent noises being made by the Conservative Party about the Crown Corporation's dismemberment. Thus a large takeover was perceived as one means to corporate survival. The larger PetroCan was, the more difficult it would be to disband. Unlike the major oil companies, whose size had landed them in so much trouble in the much more political post-OPEC environment, PetroCan believed that size might be its only chance for survival in the business jungle. For a Crown Corporation, longevity was perceived as being synonymous with

PetroCan's senior executives also adopted a much tighter battle plan than they had for the Husky takeover. The start of the Husky problems had been the "leak" that had sent the market surging and forced the national oil company's hand. The Pacific takeover plans would be kept to as small a group as possible. Although an Ontario Securities Commission inquiry into the Husky leak had drawn a blank, as most such inquiries seem to do, there was a suspicion that the rumour may have emerged in some way from PetroCan's two investment houses, Wood Gundy and Pitfield MacKay Ross.

Thus Hopper and Bell decided this time to do the deal themselves, not bringing in Gundy and Pitfield until the takeover looked like a *fait accompli*. Internal security in Red Square was tightened considerably. A paper shredder became a key piece of office equipment during the takeover and the working out of the strategy was confined to three people, Hopper, Bell, and general counsel O'Brien. Two months after the unhappy conclusion of the Husky affair, the Crown Corporation once again approached the Bartlesville, Oklahoma, head office of Phillips Petroleum.

Phillips had been the most successful of the large American oil companies in recent years. Although its size did not rank with that of the Seven Sisters, its find of the huge Ekofisk field in the North Sea had made it enormously profitable. In 1977, it had earnings of $517 million on sales of $6.3 billion. Its 48% holding in Pacific had dated back to earlier joint ventures with the legendary Frank McMahon, Pacific's founder. Unlike other American holders of large stakes in Canadian oil companies, Phillips had not played the "heavy" with Pacific. It had appointed only two directors to the company's board and had allowed the company to plot its own strategy. Phillips had two wholly-owned subsidiaries, Phillips Canada and Phillips International, through which it was directing the bulk of its Canadian operations.

Phillips also undoubtedly recognized the less hospitable climate for United States oil that had sprung up in Canada in the 1970's. As Atlantic Richfield and Ashland had also decided within the previous three years, Phillips concluded that, if the price was right, now was the time to sell.

For two and a half months, PetroCan and Phillips hammered away at what was a "fair" price for Phillips' 10.3 million Pacific shares. Despite the cloak of secrecy, rumours still trickled onto the stock market. Indeed, on September 26, 1978, PetroCan must have thought that it was facing the same situation that it had with Husky early in June. That Tuesday, Pacific's shares leaped $7, from $41 to $48, as a renewed surge of takeover rumours swept through the Toronto and New York markets. However, PetroCan had no intention of being hustled into the open too soon this time. Phillips admitted to the press that it had from time to time considered selling its stake in Pacific, but Hopper flatly denied that it was Petro-Can that was doing any buying. Eventually, a price was agreed between PetroCan and Phillips of US $55.50 a share, equivalent to Cdn. $65.02. That put a price tag on Pacific of $1.46 billion, making it far the biggest takeover in Canadian history, indeed, one of the biggest takeovers in the world. It also raised another key question: where would the money come from?

The answer was remarkably simple. One day Joel Bell telephoned the Royal Bank's main Calgary branch and delivered that familiar phrase: "I'd like to borrow some money."

"Certainly, Mr. Bell," came the reply. "How much?"

"One and a quarter," said Bell.

"One and a quarter, er," said the hesitant voice at the end of the line, not wishing to be so gauche as to ask "One and a quarter *what*?"

"One and a quarter billion dollars in U.S. funds," said Bell. There was a barely perceptible gulp at the bank-end of the line. "I suppose you'll have to check that out with Montreal," said Bell, tongue in cheek. And indeed, the following day, the PetroCan team was heading east to negotiate the single biggest borrowing in Canadian history.

At the beginning of November, the final touches were being put to the deal, but it was still being kept the most closely guarded of secrets within PetroCan. On November 8, Bob Foulkes, PetroCan's head of public relations, was due to go on holiday, but when he told Andy Janisch, the Crown Corporation's head of operations, Janish told him he thought he ought to go and see Hopper. Hopper told Foulkes to "stick around", although he wouldn't tell him why. He would let him know the following Friday at noon.

That Friday, November 10, members of the media were summoned to a room in the Hotel Toronto where, they were told, Energy Minister Alastair Gillespie would be making an announcement. There, Gillespie blinked into the portable television lights and told them that PetroCan had just bought Phillips' share of Pacific for $671 million. PetroCan would also be making a similar offer for the remainder of Pacific's shares. Pacific's unhappy management was caught in a vise. They were more than unhappy at the thought of government control, but since Phillips had accepted PetroCan's offer, it seemed that they were hardly in a position to recommend that other shareholders not accept it. Nevertheless, they announced that there would have to be an independent evaluation before they could recommend the offer.

Mindful of the Husky fiasco, the stock market did not display overwhelming confidence in PetroCan's offer. When the shares of Pacific started trading after the weekend of the announcement, they rose only to $55 ½, almost $10 short of the offer price. They were discounting, it seemed, that PetroCan might still bungle this takeover as it had bungled Husky. However, the Crown Corporation was taking no chances this time. It moved rapidly to take its holdings above 50% by private purchases from investment institutions. This time it had Pacific in the bag. On January 15, 1979, PetroCan announced its tender offer for all the remaining shares of Pacific. Two days later, Pacific's board recommended acceptance of the offer and on March 12, PetroCan, now with 98% of Pacific's shares, announced that its offer was closed.

Needless to say, the takeover once again attracted cries of indignation from the industry, although Phillips' willing sell-out made it somewhat more difficult to cry "rape". Casting around for heavy objects to heave in PetroCan's direction, critics attacked both the rationale of the bid and its financing. Pacific was recognised as an efficient, well-managed company that, despite its dominant United States shareholder, was clearly autonomous in its management decisions. How could a government takeover improve its performance? The answer, it seemed, was that it couldn't.

The rationale behind the bid was that PetroCan was growing tired of doing the industry's frontier and high technology dirty work. Now it wanted some of the gravy. Pacific was both the "gravy", in terms of its attractive western land position, and a way of financing PetroCan's expensive activities without returning constantly to Ottawa. It was also a way of attempting to preserve the national oil company's corporate survival in the face of a hostile new government.

But the move was also attacked on financial grounds, since, in the long term, it meant that the vast bulk of the $1.46 billion purchase price would find its way into the United States, representing a significant drain on the balance of payments. Also the means of financing, term-preferred shares, was attacked on the basis of PetroCan using "inside information". Term-preferreds had proved a very popular means of financing. They were an "after tax" instrument, which meant that banks were not charged income tax on their interest receipts. This in turn meant that they could reflect their non-taxable income in a much lower rate of interest to the borrower. However, the federal government had grown concerned about the volume of business being done this way, which was rapidly assuming the appearance of a massive "loophole".

Before the November, 1978 federal budget, it was widely rumoured that Ottawa would be removing these facilities, which they in fact did. Since PetroCan obtained the biggest term-preferred financing just days before the provision was removed, the Crown Corporation's many critics quickly turned on it and accused it of having inside information. They pointed out that PetroCan even had the Deputy Minister of Finance, Tommy Shoyama, on its board. Nevertheless, PetroCan staunchly denied the use of any "inside information", and it seems fair to comment that any corporation in its position, knowing that the upcoming federal budget might remove the term-preferred provisions, would have done the financing quickly.

The grudging consensus, however, when the smoke and accusations surrounding the Pacific takeover had settled, was that Petro-Can had done a pretty smart deal, and expunged the memory of the Husky fiasco.

Pacific also appeared a much more attractive all-round package than Husky. The company had a great deal of attractive western acreage, including the central position in the West Pembina oil field of which it had farmed out a portion to Chevron. It was the leader of a consortium that planned to build a heavy oil upgrading plant and had committed to take 9% of the Alsands tar sand project. Combined production of Pacific and PetroCan would make the Crown Corporation the seventh largest oil and natural gas liquids producer in Canada, and second only to Shell Canada as a gas producer, while Pacific also offered PetroCan a position in refining and marketing through its 426 retail and wholesale marketing outlets. Pacific also brought in its 10% stake in the Cochin natural gas liquids pipeline from Edmonton to Sarnia. Perhaps ironically, the man who took most of the credit for thinking up the Cochin line was Don Walcott, so PetroCan would obviously have no trouble coping with that part of the acquisition.

Perhaps most intriguing, Pacific also brought to PetroCan 32% of the equity of Westcoast Transmission, the company that was Bob Blair's Canadian partner in the Foothills consortium to build the Alaska Highway Pipeline.

As with Arcan's executives, some of Pacific's senior management were more than unhappy at the prospect of becoming "civil servants", and the immediate departures included both Rasmussen and Al McIntosh, Pacific's tough and outspoken executive vice-president, who had never made any secret about what he thought of PetroCan. McIntosh went to take the presidency of Home Oil, while Rasmussen moved over to manage the American operations of Husky Oil, by then in the process of becoming 100%-controlled by Alberta Gas Trunk Line.

However, for both Rasmussen and McIntosh, the blow of Petro-Can's assault was somewhat cushioned by the cancellation of their stock options. Some of these options, acquired over the years, had been set at prices as low as $13.25 a share. This meant that, on their cancellation, the holder of a $13.25 option would receive the difference between that price and the PetroCan offer price of $65. The result was that Rasmussen collected about $1.2 million for his cancelled options, while McIntosh collected almost $550,000. It was a case, for once, of "to the vanquished, the spoils".

During the Parliamentary debate on PetroCan, it had been suggested that it might take 10 to 15 years for the Crown Corporation to establish itself as a force in the Canadian oil industry. In fact, aided by a growing sense of power and a government-backed ability to borrow huge amounts of money, it had taken just three years.

The extent of what could be considered real "achievements" by the Crown Corporation was not great. A couple of relatively significant strikes had been made off the coast of Labrador and in the Arctic Islands, the Arctic LNG scheme had been filed, and a number of key contacts had been made with foreign governments on the possibility of future oil supplies. But the most significant events for the company had been the two major acquisitions that it had undertaken.

Nevertheless, it would also perhaps be unrealistic to expect too much in such a relatively short time. For PetroCan's supporters, the main thing was that a significant "presence" in Canadian oil had now been established.

On May 22, however, that presence looked in severe danger of proving an ephemeral one. The lesson of OPEC had been that energy politics can bring sweeping changes with almost the bat of an eyelid. That day in May there was a massive political blink. The following morning, May 23, 1979, the offices of Red Square looked the same as they had the previous day. The grotesque array of Indian masks still glowered threateningly along the hallway leading to the executive suites on the 15th floor; the mini-totem pole still sat behind the receptionist, as if part of an elaborate mystical plan to ward off evil spirits. But the fact was that on May 23 the array of native artifacts had obviously failed to do their job. There were evil spirits stalking the antiseptic, apple green-furnished headquarters of Canada's national oil company.

These spirits had been released the previous day by a ceremony of much more powerful "medicine" and more recent origin that Indian rites. However, in somewhat similar fashion, it had been preceded by several weeks of war-dancing and the repeated incantation of round-sounding but largely hollow phrases. The ceremony, known as a Federal Election, in tossing out the old, tired forces of the Liberal Party, had installed a new group of spirits espousing a quite different ideology. These new spirits threatened to evaporate the political mortar that held PetroCan's now huge edifice together and send its constituent parts tumbling back into the private sector.

There came the cold realization that the cement that bound this huge organization was made of ephemeral, political stuff. As the Progressive Conservatives achieved a clear mandate to take over the government, although their position was somewhat shaky in pure numerical terms, the spirit of potential change blew through the national oil company. The Conservatives had declared themselves staunchly opposed to an organization that they considered an ideological anathema, and had frequently, during their compaign, declared that they would lovingly dismantle the monster once they had gained power.

As the Tories came, if hardly swept, to power, the question was whether this by now Gordian knot of a national oil company would be unravelled, potentially a long and complex job, or whether Joe Clark would attempt a more Alexandrian approach and simply chop the whole thing apart. The latter hardly seemed to be Joe Clark's style, while a more gradual dismemberment also had to take into account practical consideratins, not least of which was the prevailing belief among Canadians that a national oil company might, after all, be necessary. Moreover, perhaps the most unlikely source of support for PetroCan was the very oil community that had four years previously heaped vituperation upon the whole concept of a government presence in oil. Bob Blair continued to speak up for it and even Peter Lougheed seemed to be admitting that it had its uses.

One thing that was in severe doubt, however, was the future of PetroCan's political appointees. Maurice Strong, true to form, had retired from the chairmanship in 1978 to become chairman of the International Development Research Centre, as ever darting from job to job towards that vague ultimate goal.* However, Bill Hopper and Joel Bell, both closely linked to the formulation of Liberal energy policy and to the Liberal party itself throughout the 1970's, remained, for the moment at least. As this book goes to press, their future, and the future of the Crown Corporation they played a major part in building, hangs in a tenuous balance.

---

* By mid 1979, he had left that job too, and was concentrating, once more, on making money. In the meantime, for good measure, he had picked up a membership in Lloyd's of London.

12 | A "Riverboat Man in a Gambler's Industry"

Gallagher has perhaps the most influential teeth in Canadian business. A sighting of his smile on Bay or Wall Streets is enough to send a frisson through stock markets. A flash of his dental work in Ottawa has been known to cause whole Federal budgets to be reworked.

In the hothouse of Albertan corporate growth, there is only one man, and one company whose performance can compare with, and possibly even outrank, that of Blair and AGTL. That man is John Patrick Edward "Smiling Jack" Gallagher, and the company, of which he is chairman, is Dome Petroleum. Gallagher, a slim, elegant and deceptively youthful man in his early sixties, is quite different in corporate style from Blair. He is essentially an old-style promoter, but he has proved remarkably adept at playing the promotion game in a politicized environment. Bob Blair reads the minds of governments. Jack Gallagher plays them like a violin.

In the post-OPEC period, Gallagher and Dome have emerged as the third mighty force in the triumvirate that has seized the Canadian energy initiative from big, foreign-controlled oil. Nevertheless, the main difference between Gallagher and the men at AGTL and PetroCanada is that Gallagher remains at heart an old-style oilman.

In the case of both PetroCanada and Alberta Gas Trunk Line, one might claim that politics is at times the prime determinant of their actions. For Gallagher, however, the wellspring of ambition has always been to pursue the purist goal of the true oilman: to find big oil.

Conventional oil is running out in Canada, but it remains the most fondly sought substance. The West Pembina find in early 1977 represented the biggest conventional oil find in Canada for ten years, but the field's ultimate reserves are unlikely to add even 10% to Canada's dwindling conventional oil reserves of about 7 billion barrels.

But in the summer of 1979, the greatest excitement ever seen in the Canadian stock market surrounded the activities of three drill-ships in the Beaufort Sea, north of the Mackenzie Delta in Canada's Western Arctic. They belonged to Dome Petroleum, the company that had in just three years become the *wunderkind* of North American stock markets. Its shares had risen from $37 in the first quarter of 1977 to the equivalent of $200 by the summer of 1979. The company itself had put up a scintillating growth performance in the 1970's, but the real excitement was about the possibility of finding an elephant, a huge deposit of oil in the murky depths of the Beaufort.

The driving force behind both the exploration and the stock market was the uniquely charming Jack Gallagher.

Gallagher has perhaps the most influential teeth in Canadian business. A sighting of his smile on Bay or Wall Streets is enough to send a frisson through stock markets. A flash of his dental work in Ottawa has been known to cause whole federal budgets to be reworked. Jack Gallagher rates as a "riverboat man" in a gamblers' industry, a visionary among geologists, a wizard among financiers, and, above all, a unique silver-tongue among political lobbyists. In an industry where rapid corporate growth and frenetic stock market activity have become almost commonplace, Dome Petroleum stands in a class by itself.

Unlike Blair, Gallagher has not specialized in winning great corporate battles. The reason is perhaps that Jack Gallagher seldom finds himself with any opposition. Gallagher is a rich man — his stock in Dome alone has been worth as much as $50 million — but his power is not money power either. It is lobby power, the ability of a uniquely charming lone wolf to get what he wants from governments.

His persuasive style is totally different from that of Blair. While Blair is adept at doing what governments want, Gallagher is adept at getting governments to do what he wants. At the intercorporate level, while Blair thrives on confrontation, Gallagher thrives on compromise.

While Blair is a difficult man to reach, Gallagher seems to be always available. If he only had the time, it sometimes seems, Jack Gallagher would like nothing better than to lead the whole world, one by one, to Calgary's Petroleum Club, guide them gently by the elbow to a table and tell them all about his latest venture.

This enthusiasm is behind one of the greatest corporate success stories in Canadian history.

Perhaps the greatest paradox about Dome Petroleum itself is that despite its status as a glamour oil stock, the company has developed into by far the largest public Canadian-owned oil company without ever making a major find! Indeed, in the exploration end of the business, where it is generally acknowledged that it is better

to be lucky than smart, Dome has experienced a dearth of good fortune.

However, if oil is indeed found in the minds of men, then Gallagher's distinguished, perfectly coiffed, silver-haired cranium
may be counted among Canada's potentially more abundant
sources of hydrocarbons.

Jack Gallagher believes there are elephants beneath the murky,
Arctic depths of the Beaufort Sea, an area of about 150,000 square
miles lying due north of the Mackenzie Delta. For any federal government such a find, should it materialize, would be doubly attractive. On the one hand, it would contribute considerably towards
the key target of self-reliance in a politically uncertain world. On
the other, it would tip the balance away from what Ottawa sees as
Alberta's excessive dominance in providing domestic oil and gas.

Gallagher has brilliantly exploited the attractions of the Beaufort
to obtain significant concessions from the federal government. The
principal of these concessions was the introduction in the 1977
budget of "super-depletion" allowances for all wells costing more
than $5 million. Since, at the time it was introduced, this only ap-
plied to wells in the Beaufort Sea, the provision became known as
the "Gallagher amendment" in the "Dome budget". When this
provision was added to the subsequent allowance to individuals to
write off oil and gas exploration expenditures against all personal
income, the result was uniquely generous. It meant that those paying a sufficiently high rate of income tax could actually make
money out of drilling dry holes in the Beaufort!

Stock market interest in the Beaufort Sea has been truly astound-
ing. On September 1, 1978, the Toronto Stock Exchange's oil and
gas share-price index leaped 91 points, its largest ever one day rise,
as a result of rumours surrounding the Beaufort. But the rise was
also, significantly, an act of faith in Jack Gallagher as prophet and
high priest of Arctic exploration.

Almost exactly one year later, on September 7, 1979, the same
index showed an even greater record leap, of 186 points, as the
word swept down Bay and Wall Streets that Dome had at last
struck big oil in the north.

The Fist in the Velvet Glove

In observing an industry prone to throwing up outstanding personalities, it is all too easy to emphasise the individual at the ex-
pense of the corporate team. Jack Gallagher would be the first to
acknowledge this, and with good reason. Dome's management,
under its president, Bill Richards, is perhaps the most talented,

and unconventional, in the industry.*

Richards provides almost total contrast to Gallagher, and could perhaps be described as the iron fist within Gallagher's velvet glove. The contrast even stretches to personal appearance. Where Gallagher, tall and slim, is always immaculately dressed, Richards, short and stocky, tends to be almost scruffy. Where Gallagher's tie usually sports a diamond stud, Richards' is more than likely to feature a gravy stain! At one time, it was a belief in the industry that Richards deliberately dressed badly for regulatory hearings, like the man who goes to court in rags in the hope of having his fine reduced. Another apocryphal story said that Gallagher introduced the clothing vouchers that employees receive as part of their Christmas bonus as a subtle way of getting Richards into a new suit!

However, the contrast in both appearance and style is indicative of the creative diversity that makes Dome what it is. Everybody's ideas are listened to. Lawyers with Afro haircuts who manage pop groups in their spare time can be found coming up with key suggestions. Everybody in the company, to the lowliest junior geologist, feels that he has a chance to make some positive input.

Gallagher is now the symbolic head and financial front man for a brilliant corporate team, but when he started Dome Petroleum in 1950 it was very much a one man show. In 1950, Gallagher had to make the critical decision that separates the entrepreneurs from the "company men", whether to take the risk and go it alone. Then 34, he had been a "company man" for 13 years, a period after which few escape the gravitational pull of corporate security.

Gallagher was born the son of an Irish immigrant railroad worker in 1916 in Winnipeg. He graduated in geology from the University of Manitoba in 1937, in the same class as Jack Armstrong, who was to go on to become head of Imperial Oil. Part of the Gallagher mythology is that his commitment to Arctic exploration was born in 1936 when, during the summer vacation, he trekked the northern wilds as a student worker with the Geological Survey of Canada for a princely $2.50 a day. During that period, so the story goes, a seed was planted that was to take root 25 years later, when Dome first drilled in the Arctic Islands, and would hopefully blossom with a major find in the Beaufort Sea. The vision of the young Gallagher staring up at the Aurora Borealis and declaring: "I'll be back", may have a certain attraction. But if he ever did, then that seed was certainly to lay dormant for a long time.

For a brief period in 1937, after graduation, he did return to work the area from the Great Bear to the Great Slave Lakes, but for

---

* It is also one of the richest. Under Dome's share purchase plan, Dome employees own over 11% of the company's equity. In mid 1979, that was worth a staggering $270 million.

aspiring Canadian oilmen in the late 1930's there was just one place to learn the business: in the United States, where it all started. Gallagher joined the Shell Oil Co. in California as a field geologist. After only a year, he moved back east to Standard Oil Co. of New Jersey, kernel of John D. Rockefeller's trust-busted but still mighty empire, and for the next ten years worked for Standard throughout the world.

Gallagher became a tiny cog in the system, dominated by the Seven Sisters, whose purpose was to find oil wherever it lay. He probed the deserts of Egypt, roamed the forests of Central America and Ecuador and trekked over the mountains of Peru.

Three stories about Gallagher's travels perhaps serve to illuminate key aspects of his personality.

Working for Standard in Guatemala, he was having some trouble coping with local red tape. Somehow, he managed to arrange an interview with no less a person than the country's president. After a "little chat", the president gave him letters of introduction to each regional political supremo, indicating that they should provide "Senor Gallagher" with mules and canoes. When Gallagher wants something, he goes to the top to get it.

While in Egypt, he taught classes in geology at the American University of Cairo, taking his students into the desert for field work at weekends. At that time, he hatched a scheme to fertilize and irrigate parts of the Sahara to form a "Green Belt". During one of the recent Middle East crises, he sent open letters both to Pierre Trudeau and the Secretary General of the United Nations suggesting the scheme as a means of achieving peace in the area. Gallagher is a visionary with a global perspective.

Working for Standard in Peru, he once had to lead a native party 250 miles on foot across the Andes. Gallagher noticed that the native bearers — whom he says he found "easy to motivate" — tended to get rid of their wages, somehow, as soon as they earned them. So he "persuaded" them to let him hold part back so they could have something left at the end of the trip.

Gallagher is a natural leader with strong paternalistic tendencies. He still espouses the philosophy highlighted by these stories. If he wants something, he is not afraid to gently take the Prime Minister by the elbow. Over the years, Gallagher has made a point of acquainting himself with Ottawa's corridors of power. He has perhaps had less luck at the provincial level because his main hydrocarbon ambitions lie outside the province, in the far north. Moreover, Gallagher does not hide his disagreement with Premier Lougheed's struggle for a more powerful provincial representation in Ottawa. Gallagher is profoundly nationalist and federalist.

But this stance is not without its advantages, for it means that Gallagher does not have the "Lougheed stigma" as perhaps Bob Blair has in Ottawa. He has indeed won so many concessions from

Ottawa that it is sometimes said tongue-in-cheek in Calgary that there are two national oil companies — PetroCanada and Dome! This remark tends to cause distinct irritation among PetroCan executives, perhaps because Gallagher seemed to be doing such an effortlessly smooth job in arousing enthusiasm for the Beaufort Sea, while they have struggled off the east coast and in the Arctic Islands.

His corporate style is one of mutual back-scratching, of quiet, behind-the-scenes persuasion and low-key public presentation. But it is a style that has proved devastatingly effective.

Although well-liked and respected, indeed idolized by many of the younger oilmen, Gallagher is not a gregarious man. His corporate style is similar, quite simply because he has enormous faith in his singular ability to "get things done". Part of his strategy is to have good relations with Ottawa. He is a member of the Science Council and the Canada Development Corp., but, tellingly, he turned down an invitation to join the National Advisory Committee on Petroleum, the informal group of top Canadian oil industry executives set up by Liberal Energy Minister Joe Greene in the early 1970's to give some corporate input into government decision making. The reason is that if Gallagher wants anything, he believes that the best person to obtain it is nobody else than himself. In this he has proved perhaps uniquely successful.

In 1948, when Gallagher was manager for exploration in the headwaters of the Amazon in Peru, he was called upon to make a big decision. Standard pulled him out of South America and sent him to Harvard for the Advanced Management course, but then they wanted him to go to the Dutch East Indies as chief geologist for the Far East, including Australia and New Zealand. He was also asked by Standard's Canadian subsidiary, Imperial Oil, to return to Canada. Imperial's discovery of Leduc in 1947 had sparked the modern era of Canadian oil, and the company was attempting to pull in Canadian geologists from wherever it could. Before Leduc, Imperial had been predominantly a refining and marketing company. Indeed, its renowned string of 133 dry holes before it struck Leduc had led the company, almost in desperation, to consider an expensive process for making gasoline out of natural gas. Now, however, the whole complexion of the company changed and it had to build up both its exploration and production departments rapidly.

Gallagher didn't want to head for the Far East so he accepted the job of assistant production manager for Imperial. Gallagher came as a rising young star to Calgary, as a colleague remembers, "the personality boy" of the company. But somehow, he rubbed V. J. "Tip" Moroney, his boss, the wrong way, and says Gallagher, "I soon realized that I didn't fit into a large company." (Whatever the friction between Gallagher and Moroney, it obviously did not

prove to be permanent. Tip Moroney, in 1979, was carrying out
consulting work for Dome.)

Gallagher's statement might sound somewhat paradoxical, since he had just finished a 10-year stretch with the world's largest oil company. But the fact was that Standard was a far flung empire and its head office was more like a central bank. Gallagher had been spoiled by being more or less his own master during his globe-trotting.

In 1950, a discontented Gallagher was approached by a group of Americans representing endowment money from Harvard, Princeton and the Massachusetts Institute of Technology. The United States offered generous tax treatment for investment in exploration, even overseas, and the Americans wanted to get in on the new Canadian oil boom. The leader of the group was Clifford Michel, then managing partner of New York investment house Loeb, Rhoades & Co., and also head of Canadian gold producer Dome Mines Ltd.*

Gallagher agreed to manage their money on a part-time basis and, in 1950, Dome Exploration (Western) Ltd. was born as a private company with a capitalization of $7.5 million in debt and $250,000 in equity. When Dome went public in 1951 (the 1951 share offering and another in 1955 raised a total of $10 million), Gallagher switched to the company full time. Among Dome's earliest employees was Charles Dunkley, who retired from Dome in 1979 as senior vice president. Dunkley, another tribute to the diversity within Dome, is a delightfully cynical man. His definition of a pessimist is someone who has worked for an optimist for five years, "and," he points out, tongue-in-cheek, "I've been working for Jack Gallagher for twenty-five years!"

Looking back at the early days with a modesty reserved only for the enormously successful, Gallagher says: "The oil business is 95% luck. You can be correct as hell and not win. There were some very good people, much better geologically than I was, who came out here and it just didn't fly. But another big thing with building my company is the timing, and it wasn't so much my timing as the fact that then was just a good time to start. There wasn't the competition for land; there wasn't the big money. It's just been a fortunate thing."

Such disarming modesty is a key element of Gallagher's style. Face to face, he wants to know about the other person rather than pressing his own views. When giving one of his slide-accompanied discourses on the potential for oil and gas discoveries in the Beau-

---

* Dome Mines still holds just over 25% of Dome Petroleum, but Dome Petroleum owns 41% of Dome Mines (Dome Petroleum paid $78 million early in 1979 to raise its holdings in Dome Mines from 31% to 41%). This convoluted relationship means Dome Petroleum owns 10% of itself!

fort Sea that have become almost a ritual before financial and political groups in recent years, his voice is soft, his delivery almost self-deprecatory.

When he glides softly through the Petroleum Club — where he has been immortalized by having a lunch (turkey salad sandwich, tinned fruit and cottage cheese) named after him — he positively radiates bonhomie and produces a mirror-image beam in everyone he meets.

In personal life, Gallagher is a man of moderation. Married, with three grown-up sons ("My sons are much better organized than I ever was," he says, deferring even to his own progeny), he has a modest home in Calgary's fashionable Britannia and a ranch in Southern California. Trim and fit, Gallagher is a fine skier and ardent golfer and jogger. Towards the end of 1978, he had an operation to remove a calcium spur on his heel that was bothering him, but he was returning calls that had been put through to Dome until ten minutes before the operation.

Early on at Dome, Gallagher developed the strategy that was to serve the company so well, to spread investment between relatively certain, even dull-looking cash flow building ventures and the occasional "drilling for the moon" rank wildcat project. Dome bought production lands at Crown sales and farmed into lands near production, hovering around the activity of the "big boys". Its earliest bread and butter activities were concentrated in the Redwater and Drumheller fields. Its earliest rank wildcat was one of the earliest and deepest tests in British Columbia, the 11,000 foot Buckinghorse well. It was dry.

Buckinghorse was in fact to set the pattern for Dome's wildcats. The company had very poor luck. However, it was the "dull" projects that were to prove the winners. Indeed, what was subsequently to provide the bulk of Dome's profits during its major growth period came from a section of the oil and gas business a long way from the excitement of plumbing the depths of the earth for its hidden treasures. It came from natural gas liquids. The initial brains behind the system was yet another of Dome's divers geniuses, Don Walcott, a great, sandy-haired bear of a man with an appearance like a farmer but a mind like a tungsten trap.

Walcott was hired from Gulf in 1957 to bring the Provost gas field, in which Dome was a major partner, into production. During the following 20 years, he was to play a seminal role in putting Dome into the leading position in the natural gas liquids business in western Canada, and also into making it a key player in the development of the petrochemical industry in the province. These natural gas liquids which include liquid petroleum gas or LPG's such as propane and butane, are essentially "stripped" from the main flows of gas within the province through "straddle" plants that, as their name implies, sit across its main gas arteries. Dome

built its first such plant outside Edmonton in 1958, but the business
only really started to boom in the early 1970's. In 1970 a further
plant was built at Cochrane, across the transmission line of Alberta
& Southern Gas (negotiations had been carried out while Bob Blair
was still president of A & S) as part of a major new scheme to collect liquids on a large scale. These liquids were then "batched" so
that they could be transmitted through the Interprovincial oil pipeline, with a dramatic saving in transport costs. A further straddle
plant was built across the main TransCanada line at Empress in
conjunction with PanCanadian Petroleum. This plant was also
equipped to strip ethane, a petrochemical feedstock, despite the
fact that there was no immediate market for it. Then Dome came
up with a bold plan to ship LPG's and ethane through a new 1,900
mile pipeline to Green Springs, Ohio, for use by United States distribution giant, Columbia Gas Systems. After a number of years
delay, the go-ahead was finally given as part of a $1 billion scheme
to build a petrochemical complex in the province in which the
major player emerged as the fast-rising Alberta Gas Trunk Line,
with its increasingly high-profile head, Robert Blair.

Throughout this whole period, Walcott played a leading concep-
tual role. Colleagues remember him always turning up at regulatory hearings (in distinct contrast to Bill Richards) looking like a
beefy farm-hand squeezed into a new suit for a country wedding,
his rosy face scrubbed and shining, and his hair slicked down. At
first, opposition lawyers would rub their hands secretly in glee
when they saw him. But somehow, he would always outsmart
them. In this he was in fact more than helped by Richards.

Richards was a young lawyer from Manitoba who joined Dome's
legal department in 1956. Over the following years, he turned out
to be so good at the regulatory hearings covering gas conservation
and liquid plants that he was made Walcott's assistant. Richards
became more and more involved in operations until he was eventually made executive vice-president, and then president of the
company.

Richards bears a distinct physical resemblance to movie gangster
James Cagney, and some who have dealt on the opposite side of
the negotiating table from him would say that his business tactics
are similar. Colleagues admit that he is "not good at compromise,"
and will squeeze the last drop out of a deal. Opponents call him
ruthless. But he has earned enormous respect, including that of the
formidable Blair, who describes him as "one of the strongest oil executives in Canada." Richards has also learned one key lesson
from his chairman, with whom he does not always see eye to eye,
and that is his ability to charm the financial community.*

---

* Richards has made a number of forays to Japan, where there is enormous interest
  in the Beaufort, and is perhaps the only Calgary oilman to have a double sided
  business card with English on one side and Japanese on the other.

"The whole world could be tumbling around their ears," says one ex-Dome employee, "but if a key analyst turned up from Wall Street or Bay Street, either Gallagher or Richards would take two hours off to give him the Dome story." While Gallagher guides his potential converts to the Petroleum Club, Richards chauffeurs his in his oversize Lincoln to the Ranchman's Club, where, in one of the Club's private dining rooms, he puts the Dome case in a perhaps more uncompromising fashion.

But the fact is that both Gallagher and Richards have an impressive story to tell. The growth of Dome Petroleum in the 1980's has been truly phenomenal, as has the performance of its share price. Between 1971 and 1978, virtually all Dome's financial statistics rose by a factor of at least ten. Revenues increased from $41.5 million to $639.5 million, cash flow from $15.9 million to $194.2 million, and net earnings from $6.5 million to $125.1 million. And yet this phenomenal growth had come from those dull old "cash-flow building projects", from the bread and butter business that was just keeping the company going until that "big wildcat" came in.

The Biggest Wildcat

As Dome's size has grown, so has the size of that big wildcat that it is seeking. It started with the Buckinghorse well in British Columbia, then it moved to the Arctic Islands, where Dome was one of the original explorers and operated the first well, at Winter Harbour, in 1961. Again, it was dry. Since 1976, however, Dome has been the leader in one of the biggest and most expensive exploration plays in the world, in the Beaufort Sea, where a single exploratory well can cost up to $50 million.

It is in maintaining an exploration play of this size that Gallagher has shown his chief talent. In a situation where the stakes are obviously too large for any one player, Gallagher has shown himself more than adept at finding partners to help him pursue his lifelong search for the really big discovery. The original "angel", to borrow a theatrical term, for Gallagher's great Arctic exploration show is the federal government, through the budget amendments already mentioned, but Gallagher has persuaded both large companies, like Gulf Canada, and individuals, through popular drilling funds, to pour huge amounts of money into Beaufort exploration.

Gallagher has few enemies. "He could fire you and make you like it," says one of his fellow directors. However, his ability to raise money does arouse a combination of admiration and envy. "He does it all with mirrors," says a rival sourly. "He moves a ton of canaries in a half ton truck by keeping them all flying," says another. One executive, when he heard that Gallagher was due to

visit China in the summer of 1979 said, with a blend of hero wor-
ship and the green eye, and only half jokingly, "He'll be the first
man to sell a drilling fund in Peking!"

That Gallagher has been able to arouse such interest in the Beaufort is a true tribute to his salesmanship, particularly since the
major oil companies that were, in the early 1970's, drilling with
enormous enthusiasm further south on the Mackenzie Delta had
virtually all abandoned their activities by early 1978. They had
found relatively large volumes of gas, but the finds had not been as
large as they had hoped for and the death of the Arctic Gas pipeline in the latter half of 1977 had posed the seemingly insurmount-
able problem of how they could possibly ship the stuff out.

Gallagher, undeterred, drilled on and despite the fact that he
was drilling further north in much more difficult conditions, continued to enthuse a growing band of investors. That growing band
believed that Jack Gallagher, even though he was searching under
an inhospitable sea cloaked half the year in icy darkness, allowing
only brief summer navigation that even then was threatened by
roving icebergs, would lead them to the promised hydrocarbon
pachyderm.

Indeed, from a geological point of view, the Beaufort Sea does
look attractive. The great delta areas of the world, the Mississippi,
the Niger, the Persian Gulf and a number of others, have been discovered to hold major reservoirs of oil and gas. Also, a clear trend
has emerged that shows that the likelihood of larger discoveries increases as one moves out to sea from the Delta area. There, the
sediments in which oil and gas are trapped tend to be thicker. Also
the chance of finding oil as opposed to gas is greater.

However, one piece of evidence that Gallagher leans heavily on
to indicate that there could be something big up there is the find in
1968 at Prudhoe Bay, west of the Beaufort Sea in north Alaska.
There, Atlantic Richfield struck the largest hydrocarbon deposit
ever found in North America, containing 14 billion barrels of oil
and oil equivalent of gas. For reference, that one field contains the
equivalent of exactly twice Canada's total proven oil reserves.

By early 1979, $15 million of seismic work, bouncing sound
waves off the rock formations far below the Beaufort's seabed, had
identified about 40 structures, or potential hydrocarbon traps.

Gallagher has never been shy of pointing out that some of these
structures are potentially as large as Prudhoe Bay, "one, maybe
two or more Middle Easts", he is fond of saying. But these seismic
shadows remain just that, ghosts, until they are drilled. For there is
no way of knowing what they contain without actually drilling
down to them, and that is a very expensive business.

Going into the 1979 season, three years of summer drilling by
Dome's drilling subsidiary, Canmar (Canadian Marine Drilling
Ltd.) had produced tantalizing indications of oil and gas. The com-

pany had hoped to produce the first conclusive test results at the end of the 1978 season, but storms and pack ice had driven the drill-ships off their positions before the tests could be carried out. Rumours of multi-million barrel structures at the two key holes, Kopanoar and Ukalerk, led to the unprecedented share price surges of September 1, 1978, but concrete evidence was missing. Oil was once again being found in the minds of men, but in this case it was the minds of the Bay Street analysts. Using sophisticated numerical techniques, they were publishing precise reserve figures, estimating likely production rates and providing present discounted cash flows. The figures looked impressive, but they had effectively been plucked out of the air!

The fact remains that even if the 1979 drilling season has produced indications of a major oil or gas field, it will still be a number of years before the size of the field can be determined and it can be brought into production. This is the essential problem of the Beaufort, of which Gallagher and his team are only too well aware — that it is a long-term exploration venture but that it needs continued short-term promotion in order to keep up the interest of participants.

To achieve this tricky objective, Dome has therefore to perform what amounts to an exploratory dance of the seven veils. Each season produces a more and more tantalizing spectacle; first a flash of exploratory ankle, then a glimpse of hydrocarbon thigh. However, like the dance of the seven veils, the audience can only be titillated for so long. In the end — and they may not be prepared to wait too much longer — what they want to see standing before them stark naked in all its glory, is an elephant!

Dome's huge drilling subsidiary, Canmar, might also be seen as another huge act of faith in the Beaufort. But it is actually a way of further hedging Dome's bets. Canmar, with its $250 million worth of equipment based in the tiny port of Tuktoyaktuk, acts on a contract basis and drills all Beaufort Sea wells, making a healthy profit in the process. However, the three drill-ships, seven ice-breaking supply boats, three ocean going barges and large supply vessel that made up the sophisticated Canmar fleet as it entered the 1979 season also provided another reason for keeping that alluring dance going. Among the new pieces of sophisticated equipment planned by Canmar in 1979 was a $70 million Ice Drilling Barge, a huge, enclosed drill-ship with a super reinforced hull, capable of swivelling on its moorings into oncoming ice. Canmar also ordered a new ice-breaker at the end of 1978, although plans for a giant "Arctic Marine Locomotive", an ice-breaker of unprecedented power, capable of keeping the Beaufort open all year round, foundered over government concessions sought by Gallagher.

Looking to the longer term future, the critical questions, if the elephant is uncovered, are just how oil and gas can be recovered under perhaps the most demanding conditions in the world, and then how can they be brought to southern markets. Gallagher believes that oil and gas could initially be brought out by enormous ice-reinforced super-tankers, but, for the longer term, he remains a staunch believer in the Mackenzie Valley pipeline, despite the severe blow Justice Berger delivered to its prospects.

TransCanada

It was certainly with an eye to the possibility that the line might be built that Dome, in the later half of 1978, pulled off not only one of the tactically smartest, but also symbolically telling moves among that year's enormous shifts of corporate power in the oil industry: it gained control of TransCanada PipeLines.

Toronto-based TransCanada had, since its stormy birth in 1956, been seen as a conspicuous symbol of the rape of the West by eastern Canada. It took the bulk of Albert's gas to its main markets in Ontario and Quebec, but it was always viewed as the tool of the consumer, keeping down producers' prices, and, as such, had particularly aroused the ire of Peter Lougheed. When, in response to the OPEC crisis, the federal government took over the responsibility for setting both oil and gas prices, its contentious bargaining role ended. But the ill feeling lived on.

TransCanada had, over the years, developed into one of the world's largest gas transmission systems, shifting up to 3 billion cubic feet a day of gas, in highly compressed form, through its 5,800 miles of underground pipe. (For reference, a container with a volume of 3 billion cubic feet would have a base covering 15 football fields and be one and a half times the height of Toronto's CN Tower).

No one had ever claimed that TransCanada was not technically excellent at carrying out that massive job. However, the company's steel arteries had also been a prime carrier of that other west-to-east product, resentment.

The Canadian Pacific Railway had perhaps always been the principal target for western feeling against eastern-dominated transportation systems and, by extension, against the East in general. The feeling is graphically embodied in the story of the Prairie farmer standing drenched beneath a monumental thunderstorm that is destroying his crops. Shaking his fist at the sky, he shouts: "Goddamn the CPR."

TransCanada was not only a major part of the "Goddamn the CPR" syndrome, it had for many years been controlled by the CPR through its investment subsidiary, CP Investments, which held a 13% equity interest in the company. TransCanada had three CPR

representatives on its board, Ian Sinclair, CP's enormously powerful Winnipeg-born lawyer chief executive, and Robert Campbell
and John Taylor, respectively chairman and president of CP's giant
oil subsidiary, PanCanadian Petroleum Ltd.

For years, according to TransCanada's critics, Sinclair had
tended to squash any attempt by TransCanada at diversification
into areas where CP was represented, that is, just about everywhere TransCanada might be expected to look. TransCanada's
management team, under diminutive chairman James Kerr, had in
any case grown staid and unadventurous.

In 1978, the stream of invective hurled at TransCanada seemed
to reach a crescendo. Moreover, the sluggish management team
was also comprehensively outmaneouvered by Bob Blair.

In the wake of OPEC, the federal government's decision to move
towards world prices for oil and equivalent prices for gas had
caused the wellhead price of gas to surge. The result was a burst of
exploration activity and an ensuing greater availability of gas. At
the same time, however, the growth of gas markets in the East declined sharply, a situation aggravated by competition from cheaper
fuel oil and coal.

The combination of these factors meant that TransCanada was
left with the thankless task of telling producers that it could not
take 200 billion cubic feet of the gas for which it had contracted
during the 1978-1979 season. What is more, the TransCanada management told them so none too politely, indicating that they could
cut them back by rigidly enforcing contracts if they did not agree to
a "voluntary" plan. In the end agreement was reached to honour
take-or-pay contracts, under which TransCanada pays producers
for contracted gas not taken, but relations had not improved.

What annoyed the producers most of all was TransCanada's
seemingly adversary attitude. Why, asked the producers, wasn't
TransCanada trying to find markets for the excess gas? It was here
that Blair seemed to be running rings around the giant eastern utility. First he had come up with his Q & M scheme to provide new, if
small, domestic markets. Then, he had proposed major additional
exports to be carried through the "pre-building" of the southern
portions of the Alaska Highway pipeline.

Blair's pre-building scheme was ultimately aimed at easing the
problematic financing of the Alaskan Highway pipeline. His plan
was to split construction into two parts, building the southern sections first and filling them with additional Canadian exports until
the northern section was finished and Alaskan gas became available.

TransCanada had indeed come up with a rival scheme to Blair's
Q & M line — a modified eastward expansion beyond Montreal in
two stages to Quebec City. But the plan appeared like me-tooism,
while its smaller scale lacked the political appeal of Blair's line. The

Q & M line seemed to proclaim proudly: "Never mind the economics, feel the nationalism." TransCanada's scheme just appeared to be saying: "Look, we can do something uneconomic too."

As for exports, TransCanada eventually noticed the significant change in the political-corporate winds, that it was now in vogue for companies to actually come up with new ideas. So it also proposed a plan to shift 235 billion cubic feet to the U.S. market over two years.

However, although this scheme might have found some favour with producers, it certainly found no favour with Blair, who regarded any rival scheme to his own export plan as a threat to the Alaska Highway plan as a whole. It was ostensibly the disagreement over exports that led to TransCanada's failure to join Blair's Foothills consortium. When the National Energy Board had given the nod to Blair's scheme for transporting Alaskan gas in 1977, it had suggested that TransCanada, the Canadian company with most experience in large scale transmission and whose size might add some financial clout, become part of the group. However, there was little enthusiasm from Blair for the new partner. The two companies held desultory discussions after the N. E. B's recommendation, but in April, 1978, after only four meetings in nine months, TransCanada announced that it would not be joining the group after all.

Given the storm clouds, financial and otherwise, that seemed to be gathering around the Alaska Highway project, perhaps TransCanada breathed a secret sigh of relief. But the company was not to be left in peace, for towards the end of the summer of 1978, Canadian Pacific Investments announced that its critical 5.1 million shares of TransCanada were up for sale.

Intense speculation surrounded the block of shares, the move of which to an Albertan company would obviously provide a major symbolic shift of power to the West. However, the federal government, in the shape of Alastair Gillespie, openly declared that he would not like to see that block fall directly into Alberta government hands. It was then that being Calgary-based but truly nationally-oriented, not having the "Lougheed stigma", was to prove to be a great asset. A sparkle, no bigger than a set of teeth, appeared on the horizon.

In mid August, Dome Petroleum unleashed a burst of activity that seemed spectacular even by 1978's unprecedented standards. It not only purchased CPI's stake in TransCanada for $97 million; it launched a $360 million bid for Siebens Oil & Gas Ltd. in concert with a subsidiary of the government-owned CN pension fund; and it announced its membership in a new consortium, the ProGas group, that planned to find new markets for additional volumes of Alberta Gas.

The TransCanada purchase was seen as a tactical masterstroke.

If the problem with TransCanada was its bad relations with the Alberta producers and its lack of dynamism, who better to move into the driving seat than Gallagher — not only an Albertan producer and model of diplomacy but also one of the most dynamic businessmen in Canada? At the October 4, 1978 board meeting of TransCanada, the hulking Sinclair, along with the PanCanadian representatives Campbell and Taylor, resigned their directorships to be replaced by Gallagher, Richards, and Dome senior vice-president John Beddome. The shift represented a good deal more than musical chairs among the minority shareholders; it marked the dawn of a new era for Canada's principal gas transmission company. It also marked a significant symbolic shift of power from that bastion of eastern dominance in Canadian corporate affairs, the CPR, to the bustling phenomenon of western corporate expansion, Dome Petroleum.

With typical financial finesse, Dome paid for the purchase, and that of most of further open-market purchases of TransCanada, with the issue of term-preferred shares. The cost of dividends Dome paid was more than covered by the dividend from TransCanada. In other words, the three seats of power that it now held on the TransCanada board effectively cost nothing!

The Siebens deal — which in any other year would have stood the chance of being the largest takeover in Canada — was another financial masterpiece. It also ranked as one of the most complex takeovers Canada had seen.

Siebens, built up by the legendary Harold Siebens and his son Bill, had long been known to be on the takeover block. It was a land-rich company with earnings in 1977 of over $20 million, but the question, as ever, was one of price. With the Siebens family holding 46% of the equity and Hudson's Bay Co. holding 35%, it was obvious that a takeover would be quick and clean — unlike the Husky affair. More than four-fifths of the company's shares could be picked up by approaching just two groups.

But in the end it was not so much the sale itself as the method of the purchase that drew admiring oohs and ahs from the financial community. Canpar, a subsidiary of the Canadian National Railways pension fund, announced that it was offering $38.50 a share for Siebiens, thus valuing it at $360 million. However, it also announced that it would be selling 76% of the *assets* of Siebens to Dome. Canpar, as a pension fund subsidiary, could sell the assets without paying any tax. Meanwhile, since Dome was buying assets rather than shares, it qualified for tax write-offs associated with asset purchases. Dome also undertook to manage Canpar's remaining share of Siebens. Everybody, it seemed, wound up happy.

But perhaps the most intriguing speculation surrounded Dome's move into TransCanada's scheme for new gas exports, and what

these would mean to relations with the pugnacious Mr. Blair. Blair
had already made clear that he regarded any rival schemes to export gas as "self-interest impediments" to the great scheme to build a pipeline from Alaska — since they would muddy the waters for the "pre-building" of the southern portion of the line — and he had taken unconcealed delight in humiliating TransCanada. However, a TransCanada with Jack Gallagher at the helm was quite a different proposition.

Was this to be the buildup to the corporate fight of the century? But fighting was not Gallagher's style, at least publicly. Where Blair seemed to take delight in standing victorious over the bodies of corporate opponents, Gallagher realized that it was better to beat them almost without them knowing it. Towards the end of 1978, there began intense behind-the-scenes diplomacy between Dome and AGTL over a whole range of major new transmission systems. These included the possiblity that TransCanada might find itself, after all, involved in some part of the Alaskan Highway system, and also the revival of the concept of the Mackenzie Valley pipeline. In the east, Dome hatched a new scheme for serving the Maritimes with Domestic LPG's rather than attempting to build an "uneconomic" pipeline system in one go to the east coast — which seemed to be in direct rivalry to AGTL.

Would there be a corporate showdown? After a period of intense behind-the-scenes diplomacy, the answer appeared in a press release jointly issued by Dome, AGTL and TransCanada on April 25, 1979. It was to be peace.

The statement said that Dome and its effective subsidiary TransCanada PipeLines had reached an agreement "as to major natural gas transmission planning" with AGTL. The three companies would, in future, work together to find new markets for the Alberta gas surplus. TransCanada would, after all, have a part to play in the Alcan pipeline, while Dome and TransCanada would be "joining the maximum effort to ensure early construction" of the pre-built southern sections of the Alcan pipeline, followed by the entire Alaska Highway Pipeline Project. There was even mention of incorporating PetroCanada's scheme to bring liquefied natural gas out of the Arctic Islands.

However, although it appeared as if the hatchet had been buried, a couple of major questions remained unanswered. The first was the rivalry of the schemes to take Albertan gas into eastern Canada. The second was that Dome was still largely in favour of a Mackenzie Valley pipeline to bring out western Arctic Canadian reserves rather than using the Dempster spur. The joint statement declared that TransCanada would have a right of participation in the Dempster Line," but it also stated "Dome and TransCanada may also sponsor studies of other systems for moving Northern Canadian gas."

In the recent, highly politicized energy environment, where new schemes spring fully-formed from the corporate teams of men like Gallagher and Blair only to disappear like phantasmagoria and be replaced by new schemes a short time later, prognosis is very difficult.

The uncertainties in the Middle East in early 1979 — the accession of the Ayatollah Khomeini in Iran, the violent reaction of some Arab States to the signing of a peace treaty between Israel and Egypt, and continuing concerns over the safety of Saudi Arabia — have provided further attractions for Blair and Gallagher's underlying theme: increased national security.

However, the theme has found itself wrapped around massive corporate egos, which, like similar magnetic poles, may have a natural tendency to reject each other.

Whether the tentative dance that Jack Gallagher and Bob Blair are now performing is one of courtship or war, only time will tell.

PART THREE

Making Money in Petroleum: They Never Had It So Good.

"We didn't find any oil, but we sure found a lot of money."
ANONYMOUS INVESTMENT DEALER

"Get off your ass and sell that gas."
JIM GRAY, EXECUTIVE VICE-PRESIDENT,
CANADIAN HUNTER

13 | McMahon & Brown: The Old Timers Had It Tough

Once again, it was as if Sheik Yamani had waved his magic wand over the oil and gas fields of Alberta and turned these economic pumpkins into golden vehicles for taking Alberta's previously Cinderella producers to the ball.

For entrepreneurs throughout oil history, the main attraction of petroleum has been that there is no way of becoming richer quicker. You didn't have to manufacture it, or grow it, or mine it. Once you had discovered it, it came to you. You only had to collect it. The trouble always has been to find it.

Even the most skilled searchers for petroleum spend most of their time being wrong. When it comes to wildcat exploration drilling in western Canada, there has traditionally been a less than one in ten chance of hitting commercial oil or gas. Indeed, in terms of precision, geology, the science of oil finding, seems to rank behind meteorology, the science with the unfortunate task of having to forecast the weather!

However, whereas the failures of meteorology, particularly on holiday weekends, is both legendary and obvious, geologists are more fortunate in having their frequent failures occur many miles beneath the earth's surface, unnoticed by the natives above.

With such a failure rate facing them, it is perhaps not surprising that the psychological predisposition of an oil finder has to be somewhere between that of an inveterate gambler and an eternal optimist. Oil finders thus tend to be supremely self-confident individuals. Indeed, sometimes the problem is prying them loose from an idea.

Luck, and hunches, are of overwhelming importance. There is the story of the exploration team looking at one of the squiggly seismographic maps that provide the clues to what lies beneath the earth's surface. Suddenly, one of them, for no apparent reason, drew in a curved line, like that of an underground oil trap. "What the hell is that?'' asked one of his colleagues. "It's what separates the men from the boys," he replied.

Being a "finder" is as much a matter of psychological predisposition as technical ability. Above all it is an ability to bounce back time and again from failure with a plausible explanation as to why the earth didn't live up to one's expectations!

Wallace Pratt, perhaps the world's greatest oil finder of all time, who worked for many years as chief exploration man for Standard of New Jersey's operating subsidiary, Humble Oil, summed it up perfectly when he said: "Oil is found in the minds of men."

In scientific terms, the key minds belong to geologists — literally "students of the earth". They spend their time mentally roaming the prehistoric globe, recreating seas, beaches, lagoons and rivers that existed when the dinosaurs ruled the planet. It is the geologist's ability to recreate geological history in his mind, to work out where hydrocarbon deposits may have been formed and trapped, that is a key part of his role in finding petroleum.

But merely to have a geology degree is not to become automatically part of that much more elite group of people upon whom the industry depends. It is reckoned that only one in twenty of Calgary's geologists rank as "finders".

To be a "finder" requires something extra, not the smallest part of which is sheer luck, for geology is a far from exact science.

But even more important than having ideas is the ability to promote them. You can't have any luck if you don't drill wells, and drilling is an enormously expensive business. In western Canada, exploration wells can cost well over $1 million. In the Beaufort Sea, they can cost $50 million. At least half the battle for oilmen is to persuade others to part with their money.

When funding wildcat drilling, an investor is essentially supporting a sales pitch. That is why the oil industry has always proved so amenable to financial chicanery. However, as in all other areas of business, the very best sales pitches are delivered by those who believe them themselves. As American oil historian Ruth Sheldon Knowles once wrote: "When a man is exploring for oil, the only reality is the next wildcat, the one that will come in. He lives so completely in his undiscovered wealth that the struggle to pay his bills is what seems like a dream."

This romantic myth persists among Calgary's present day oilmen. But the fact is that things have changed dramatically in the past decade for Canadian finders. Before OPEC came along, the Canadian producers were a corporately frail, boom-and-bust breed, waging a constant struggle against uncertain markets, fluctuating prices and the elusive nature of their hydrocarbon prey. For every success, there were a hundred oil seekers who fell by the wayside. Moreover, if any Canadian company did achieve success, it was almost inevitably swallowed by the great financial maw of the international oil companies. The men who succeeded in such circumstances were exceptional indeed. The two outstanding examples of the great Canadian gamblers of the pre-OPEC era were, fittingly, two of the most flamboyant men in Canadian business history, Bobby Brown and Frank McMahon. These two men were outstanding not only in their relentless search for oil, but also for their desire to play a leading part on the great Canadian energy stage at a time when things were firmly controlled by big, United States-controlled oil. They are the natural predecessors in that respect of Bob Blair and Jack Gallagher, although Blair and Gallagher are playing the pipeline game at a time when the cards are firmly stacked in the favour of Canadian companies.

Frank McMahon

Characters of previous ages sometimes tend to grow in stature as they recede into history, but there is little doubt that Frank McMahon was a giant among oilmen. He founded one of Canada's largest independent oil companies, Pacific Petroleums Ltd., and he built Westcoast Transmission, the first major gas pipeline in the country. Handsome and profane, this hard-drinking, two-fisted entrepreneur went on to become a champion racehorse owner, "angel" of smash-hit Broadway plays and fully fledged member of the Canadian corporate establishment.

In his relentless search for big oil, he showed an ability to bounce back that would have done credit to Robert the Bruce's tenacious spider; in his struggle to gain regulatory approval, he showed an ability to shift with political winds from which his latter day counterpart, Bob Blair, may well have learned something.

McMahon was born in 1902 in the small town of Moyie, British Columbia, the first of three sons of a local hotel owner. He attended Gonzaga College, Spokane, where he ostensibly studied business administration, actually majored in baseball and was a classmate of Bing Crosby. However, he left in his third year to make his fortune. Heading south, he laboured on building the Golden Gate Bridge; he then worked briefly for Standard Oil of California, before, in 1927, setting up his own diamond-drilling business. Two years later, when Wall Street crashed, McMahon crashed too. In 1930, McMahon and a colleague, pipeline builder C. S. Shippy, decided to go into the gas exploration business in British Columbia. They spent $1 million in order to bring gas seeps to a number of local farm houses!

Undeterred, he formed Columbia Oils Ltd., which drilled dry holes in southern British Columbia and Montana, then moved to Peace River, Alberta where the flare from an abandoned gas well provided the symbolic rekindling of his spirit. By 1936, he had spent six years promoting wildcat wells with a lack of success exceptional even for an industry with a low success rate. However, in that year, R. A. "Streetcar" Brown, father of Bobby Brown, and his associates brought in Turner Valley Royalties No. 1, by far the biggest oil find to date in Canada. Poring over maps of local land ownership, McMahon found a lease less than a mile from Brown's well, owned by an employee of the CPR who lived near Vancouver. McMahon sought out the leaseholder and paid him $100 for the option to purchase the lease for $20,000. He then raised the money, bought the lease and incorporated West Turner Petroleums. Despite the success of the Brown well, it took McMahon another eight months to raise the money to start drilling. Then, not untypically, he found that he didn't have enough money to finish the well. However, Imperial subsidiary, Royalite, put up the necessary funds and finally, on April 1, 1938, McMahon brought in the proverbial gusher, flowing at 3,500 barrells a day. Two more successful wells were drilled on the 80-acre lease and the following year, West Turner was merged with another leaseholder, British Pacific Oils, to form Pacific Petroleum. For the next eight years, things were slow. McMahon formed other companies but strikes once more eluded him. However, he never lost his gambler's instinct. In 1948, it was to bring him a wild-well bonanza of unprecedented proportions.

When Imperial brought in Leduc in 1947, McMahon pursued the same strategy as he had in the Turner Valley ten years before. He set about finding where he might pick up some land close to the discovery. He found 160 acres in the area owned by a Scottish farmer. Title to the land was unclear, but he managed to buy off the possible disputant, Imperial, with the promise of 100,000 barrels from future production — if there was any — while the fortunate farmer received $200,000 plus the usual 12.5% royalty. The first two wells were producers, but the third, Atlantic No. 3, proved to be a hydrocarbon genie of incredible power. In March, 1948, the well roared out of control and was untamed for six months, spewing out 10,000 barrels of oil and up to 100 million cubic feet of gas daily. Within two months the gushing well was surrounded by a forty acre lake of oil. Moreover, far from being a disaster, the blow-out proved to be a financial blessing, for the vast majority of the oil was recovered and shipped to market, giving McMahon a million dollar profit. Aided by this bonanza, McMahon bought his way back into Pacific, which he had left because of the conservative nature of the management. Now most of Pacific's conservative management, in their turn, departed and McMahon went on a wildcat gas hunting spree in northeast British Columbia and northeast Alberta. Gas was found in abundance in the Peace River area but now McMahon had to find a way of selling it. That meant he needed a pipeline. On April 30, 1949, Westcoast Transmission was incorporated to build a pipeline out of the area.

McMahon realized that to find sufficient markets to justify a big-inch pipeline, exports would be needed. In a typically profane assessment of Vancouver's gas market potential, he said: "There's no market for gas there except for suicides." Needless to say, he didn't express these sentiments to the regulatory authorities.

However, in the battle to supply the United States northwest, there were two American rivals, the principal of which was Ray C. Fish's Pacific Northwest Pipeline Corp., whose plan was to build a 1,500 mile pipeline to Seattle from Texas. (The name of Fish's second-in-command was Herring.) Over the following couple of years, McMahon put up a virtuoso performance in shifting with the political and business winds. Ironically, in the light of current federal-provincial relations, the federal government, in the shape of C. D. Howe, was pressing Alberta to hurry up and authorize exports. Alberta meanwhile was expressing concern about depletion of supplies and the possible impact on domestic prices. However, after a heated seven-hour debate in the Alberta legislature, Westcoast was finally given permission in March 1952 to export one trillion cubic feet of gas from the Alberta side of the Peace River area. The Board of Transport Commissioners in Ottawa, predecessors of the N.E.B., quickly gave its approval and McMahon seemed to have the issue in the bag. His reserves were more established than those of Fish and he was 500 miles closer to the potential market. It looked like a shoo-in. But then, as was to prove the pattern of pipeline debate for the following 25 years, politics reared its ugly head. The Federal Power Commission in Washington, reluctant to leave the northeast totally dependent on imported gas, turned down Westcoast and approved Fish's line. McMahon, hearing the news in New York, disappeared for a week, presumably to get drunk.

When he returned to his business associates, he summed up the decision thus: "There's one thing strong going for us in Washington, and that's our breath."

Nevertheless, in line with his eternally optimistic nature, McMahon bounced right back, announcing that he would now be exporting the gas to California. A skeptical stock market slashed the value of all the companies with which McMahon was associated by a half, but McMahon knew that the situation was not lost. He realized that Fish needed Canadian gas to supply the northwest market. Also, he was holding Fish up with a potentially damaging lawsuit.

The meeting at which a compromise was reached was presided over by "Boots" Adams, president of Phillips Petroleum of Bartlesville, Oklahoma. Phillips was Pacific's partner in the Peace River area and was destined eventually to gain control of Pacific (and, in 1978, sell that control to PetroCanada).

The meeting was held in the offices of Sunray, another exploration partner, in Tulsa in room 1313, on December 13. There were 13 people present. The numbers turned out to be lucky, but just in case they didn't, "Boots" Adams decided on a little tongue-in-cheek pressure. Those around the bargaining table noticed when he walked in that he had a couple of bulges under his suit jacket. When he sat down he pulled out two Colt 45's and declared: "Right, this is going to be a shotgun wedding."

A compromise was reached and the building of Westcoast Transmission went ahead has planned.

McMahon was always a great showman, and always made a point of looking affluent, even when he was not. Shortly after the FPC decision that seemed to put paid to Westcoast, he gave his daughter — almost certainly on borrowed money — one of the biggest weddings that the West had ever seen.

He also appreciated the importance of appearances in business affairs. While the debate over the pipeline was still in progress, McMahon was coming under pressure from W. A. C. Bennett, British Columbia's premier, to start building. He had three main problems: no export approval, no money, and no pipe. Despite the lack of approval, he went to the Royal Bank and persuaded them to lend him $19 million to buy pipe and then dispatched his genial and brilliant chief engineer, Charles Hetherington, to England to make the purchase. Hetherington returned with about fifty miles of pipe and McMahon told him that to keep Bennett happy they had better start "burying it." "Right," said Hetherington, "I'll get up to Fort St. John (the northern end of the line) and start at once." "Hell, no," replied McMahon, "put it down in the Fraser Valley where they can see you digging up the earth!"

McMahon gave up control of Pacific when Phillips moved into the driving seat. However, by the late 1960's his holdings in the Pacific group were worth well over $20 million and his interests had expanded all over North America, where he had become an internationally recognized member of the jet set.

In Canada, he received almost the ultimate business accolade of being invited to sit on the board of the Royal Bank. He also belonged to Montreal's Mount Royal Club, described as the "most snobbish club" in Canada.

He was a member of the most exclusive hunting club in the country, situated on the island of Ruaux in Quebec. Membership was limited to seven and his co-sportsmen included Edgar Bronfman, Paul Desmarais, head of mighty Power Corp., and Fred Mannix, another Calgarian who mixed in the highest establishment circles.

McMahon's homes included a French colonial mansion in Vancouver, a Spanish "cottage" in Palm Beach capable of seating over 100 for dinner, and an apartment in New York. He spent a great deal of time in New York on financing matters, and while sharing an office with brokerage house Eastman, Dillon, his attention was drawn to the possibilities of financing plays.

One of their financiers explained to him that in return for putting up money, sponsors were given a number of seats for each performance, either to sell or give away. That looked like a pretty good deal, so he and his brother George took a share of a show called The Pyjama Game. At the last moment, another backer pulled out and McMahon took his share, finishing up with half the musical, which turned out to be a smash hit. He followed it up with Damn Yankees, another box office success. He subsequently put money into some flops, but pretty soon was able to expound a comprehensive philosophy for business investment in Broadway: "You put lots of money into the good ones and not much into the bad ones."

He also became deeply involved with horse racing. Along with Max Bell and Bing Crosby he owned Meadow Court, a winner of the Irish Derby, the Epsom Derby and the King George VI and Queen Elizabeth Stakes. Bought for $9,000, the horse was eventually put out to stud for total fees of $1.26 million. McMahon also owned a horse that won the Kentucky Derby and the Preakness.

McMahon is still alive, but has taken no direct interest in the Albertan oil business for many years. As with Brown, his style belongs to another era. In many ways, his skill before regulatory agencies and his ability at bobbing and weaving made him a forerunner of Bob Blair. However, McMahon's personal flamboyance sets him far apart from the very serious men who play today's multi-billion dollar gas transmission game.

Bobby Brown

The memory of Bobby Brown — whose business life tended to be built on hunches, on acting first and working out where the money would come from later — still causes a slight shudder to run through the balance sheet brains of the men who succeeded him at Home Oil.

They are very different men from Brown, but they are the men for the times. Ultimately controlled from the discreetly opulent Toronto headquarters of Consumers' Gas, where financiers and lawyers move carefully in a maze-like world of regulations and interest rates, Home's management is only now emerging from the rule of accountants and legal brains that followed Brown's death.

Brown's story is filled with pathos and his memory still arouses strong feelings, both pro and anti, in Calgary's tight-knit oil community. Some dwell on his alcoholism, claiming that for many years he was not fit to run an oil company; others stress that whatever his failings, he always gave shareholders a run for their money and was prepared to put his own money up too.

Bobby Brown had left the University of Alberta to help his father and Max Bell drill Turner Valley Royalties, which uncovered the biggest field in the British Empire in 1936. It had been financed by selling royalty interests. The method was so successful that the Browns founded a string of similarly financed one-well companies. During the Second World War, Brown Jr. went off to become a naval oil procurement officer. He moved to Ottawa, where he took a suite in the Chateau Laurier and entertained lavishly. At the end of the war he decided to go into business importing appliances from the United States, but the business turned sour when the federal government, concerned about the balance of payments, placed an embargo on such imports.

In those postwar years, and particularly after the discovery of Leduc, Brown and his two colleagues, John Scrymgeour and W. H. Atkinson, presided over an enormously rapid corporate expansion in Brown's main company, Federated Petroleums Ltd. Neil McKinnon, brilliant head of Canadian Imperial Bank of Commerce, took a financial and personal liking to Brown and helped finance his companies' growth both through exploration and acquisition. In 1950, helped by McKinnon, he managed to merge with Home, and then, through some financial legerdemain, finished up with effective control through an intricate corporate pyramid of holding companies. Under Brown's leadership, Home made one of Canada's most important oil discoveries, at Swan Hills. Brown's modus operandi was simply summed up. He once said: "I have an effective arrangement with the senior employees who manage the operations of Home Oil. I find the money, and they find the oil."

But Brown's tendency to walk the financial tightrope in pursuit of bigger and bigger things was to prove his ultimate undoing. One of his major tactical errors was to pursue control of giant utility TransCanada PipeLines, on the purchase of whose shares he spent $30 million in the late 1950's. By the end of the decade, both Home and Brown were deeply in debt. He managed to extricate himself, however, and kept Home moving along until, in the wake of the huge Prudhoe Bay discovery in 1968, he embarked on his biggest gamble. In Alaska, he both committed huge sums to earn interests in acreage held by Atlantic Richfield, discoverer of the field, and spent more than $50 million of his own and Home's money on purchases of Arco shares. But the Prudhoe bubble burst, Home's exploration efforts were fruitless and the stock market slump of 1970 sent Home shares plummeting from a high of $81 to less than $10.

Finally, the man who got Home was Oakah Jones, the "rock-ribbed Boston Yankee" who headed Consumers Gas. Brown was

saved financially and remained on as president and chief executive. However, his position was made more clear when, about to
seat himself at the head of the table in his plush executive suite in
Home's Calgary office at the first meeting after the takeover, he
was quietly but firmly guided from the seat by the towering Jones,
who then took it himself. Brown lived only eight months after the
takeover.

The death of Bobby Brown was the death of an era. The alcoholism that wrecked his body towards the end of his life prevented
many from feeling any sorrow for him.

There were certainly men at least as dynamic and clever as
Brown left in the industry after he departed, but his passing was as
much one of personal style as business substance. Even when he
was in deep trouble in the late 1960's he still flew everywhere in his
$3 million Grumman Gulfstream II. The most luxurious executive
aircraft available, Brown's sported gold-plated dolphins on the
bathtaps. He had three lavish homes, in Calgary, in Qualicum
Beach on Vancouver Island, and in the millionaires' retreat at Palm
Desert. He entertained regally on both sides of the Atlantic. At the
opening of Home's gas plant in Yorkshire, he regaled the local
gentry with champagne in a marquee that boasted crystal chande-
liers.

The climate in which both McMahon and Brown operated was
very different from that of the modern Canadian oilmen. They
lived in an industry dominated by big foreign, predominantly
American, oil — although to them that seemed like the natural
state of affairs. They constantly had to fight against the financial
odds, trekking to the East to find the money to pursue their ambitions (Bobby Brown is reputed to have spent more time in the
Royal York in Toronto than in Calgary).

Brown and McMahon would have loved to operate in Alberta in
the wake of the OPEC crisis. In a nationalistic energy environment,
the pendulum of control was firmly swinging back towards domestic companies. Symbolically, Pacific had fallen back into Canadian
hands (even if they were those of the national oil company) while
Ashland, the company that would have merged with Home, had
sold out its Canadian interests. Eastern bankers now made pil-
grimages to the West, bearing, it seemed, almost limitless funds to
Alberta's oilmen. Albertan companies had clearly taken the initiative on new pipeline projects, with powerful provincial and federal
support. But, perhaps most of all, it had never been so easy to
make money out of finding oil and gas.

Once again, it was as if Sheik Yamani had waved his magic
wand over the oil and gas fields of Alberta and turned these economic pumpkins into golden vehicles for taking Alberta's previously Cinderella producers to the ball.

14 | Canadian Hunter: Making a Myth as Natural Gas Fuels the Canadian Initiative

Anecdotes about significant stages in Canadian Hunter's development — about Masters' and Gray's departure from Kerr McGee; about what Alf Powis, chief executive of Toronto-based Noranda Mines, said before committing funds to support Canadian Hunter; about the discovery of just how big the Elmworth field was — are recounted almost like secular Stations of the Cross, stories to be told to the faithful.

Only hermits or those with mediaphobia could be unaware that the great world economic crisis of the 1970's has been about oil. But the fact is that Alberta's biggest and fastest growing empires, and its largest and most recent personal fortunes have been built on natural gas. Similarly, most of the new multi-billion dollar energy transportation schemes on which Calgary's finest corporate brains spend the majority of their waking hours are related not to oil, but to natural gas.

Gas provides about 20% of Canada's energy needs and, in 1979, brought in a massive $3 billion from export sales of about one trillion cubic feet to the United States. In the fall of 1979, the National Energy Board was considering a number of new export applications that could boost Canada's sagging balance of payments by a further $1 billion or more.

And yet gas has reached this precious status almost as an afterthought, a sideshow to the great circus of the OPEC crisis. Natural gas and oil are frequently produced in tandem, and the OPEC nations produce vast volumes of gas with their oil, yet gas played little or no direct part in the OPEC struggle because there is only a very small world market for it. This limited market, in turn, arises from the essential nature of gas. Oil is easily collected, easily stored and easily transported, but gas is bulky and thus correspondingly much more expensive both to store and ship. Its "thermal density"

relative to oil, that is, the volume of gas required to produce the 197
heat equivalent of a given volume of oil, is about 900 times greater
than oil. In other words, to produce the equivalent heat as a barrel
of oil requires a container full of gas in uncompressed form about
the size of an average apartment!

In the early years of the petroleum industry, gas was considered
an undesirable substance unless local uses could be found for it.
Geologists seldom, if ever, looked for gas in Canada until the start
of the 1950's. However, since the western Canadian basin is "gas-
prone", they often found it. Before the turn of the century, engineers for the Canadian Pacific Railway would curse when they
struck gas while drilling for water. As larger deposits were found,
they were linked up with local communities to provide a cheap
source of fuel. Gas found by the CPR in 1890 was used to provide
the towns of Medicine Hat and Redcliff with an abundance of
cheap fuel. The sight of those flaming gas lights led Rudyard
Kipling to describe it as "the city with all hell for a basement."

Gas was thus always a "second class" resource, and had only a
very small place in the mythology of the oil industry. The great
search was always for the dark, slippery genie, oil. If gas emerged
from a wildcat well, it often seemed like a raspberry from below, a
rude exhalation of insubstantial matter indicating failure. Young
Imperial geologists who found gas were told by the company's oil
hands: "We're an *oil* company sonny". The gas produced in association with early oil discoveries in Alberta's Turner Valley was simply flared. For many years in the 1920's and 30's a Satanic glow lit
up the sky west of Calgary as gas roared day and night into the Albertan sky. The present market value of that gas is around $5 bil-
lion.

However, after the Second World War, the energy industry in
the United States began to look at the attractions of gas. It was domestically abundant, clean burning, and, once it was connected up
by pipelines, convenient and dependable. The post-war period in
the United States was marked by a boom in the gas transmission
and utility business as a huge spider's web of pipelines was built
across the continent to link up a seemingly endless supply of this
"wonder fuel" to grateful customers. Canada lagged behind, and
in 1950 only 2% of the nation's energy came from gas, mostly
consumed locally in Alberta. However, during the 1950's, Canada leaped into the gas age. A concentrated effort was made to
find markets for the fuel and pipelines were built to the East (the
TransCanada PipeLine) and the West (Westcoast Transmission) in
the mid-50's. These systems also carried increasing supplies to the
United States.

The leap, however, was a controversial one, and the controversy
arose, once more, from the nature of gas itself. With oil, the chief
value lies in the product. The cost of piping oil from the wellhead
to the refinery is small relative to the value of the oil. With gas, by

contrast, most of the capital, and the risk, is tied up in the transmission system. The oil industry has always been about finding, producing, refining and selling. The gas industry has always been about running transmission systems and utilities, that is, about building and running pipelines.

Running gas pipelines and utilities in North America has inevitably been a growth business. Once the system is in place, income is regulated by federal and provincial authorities, but as long as demand and supply both keep growing, then the expansion of the system and the growth of the company are assured.

However, it is the building of gas pipelines that has always been a highly politicized and risky business. Since transmission systems cost so much, it is critical to have supplies and markets both lined up and linked up quickly. It is also critical to know that both the supply and demand are going to enable the pipelines to run close to capacity over a long period. The risks inherent in pipeline transmission have meant that governments have often had to step in to assist in their construction. The classic example was the TransCanada PipeLine, the giant system that links Albertan supplies to their major markets in Ontario, Quebec and also in the United States. In order to get the pipeline built, the federal government had to construct the section of the line through northern Ontario itself, and then lease it to the company. (It was eventually sold to the company).

The ramming through of legislation by the Liberal government in 1956 to provide federal financial assistance to build the Trans-Canada PipeLine led to the government's fall. The colourful Frank McMahon's fight to build Westcoast Transmission, the line that moved Albertan gas to Vancouver and into the United States, was also marked by years of regulatory delay and a great deal of political infighting. However, following this burst of controversy, the Canadian gas industry seemed to settle down to a steady growth pattern, both domestically and in terms of exports to the United States. In the 1960's, Canadian gas use almost trebled, from 321 billion cubic feet a year in 1960 to 917 billion cubic in 1970. Exports, meanwhile, soared, increasing more than sevenfold between 1960 and 1970, when Canada shipped 780 billion cubic feet over the American border. Almost all of this gas was produced in Alberta.

As the 1970's opened, gas consumers in Canada were paying an average of 63¢ a thousand cubic feet (mcf) for their gas supplies, but the vast bulk of that cost was in transportation charges. Producers were, in most cases, getting below 15¢ an mcf.

It was to be these high fixed transportation charges, combined with the impact of OPEC, that was to be one part of the secret of success for Alberta's "gas men."

Even with the world price for oil at little more that $3 a barrel in the early 1970's, gas still seemed relatively cheap.

Although gas, once again because of its bulky nature, could not substitute for oil in its crucial functions of fueling road, rail and air transport, it did provide a viable alternative in "static" situations, such as industrial and home heating. Indeed, since it was clean burning and piped all the way to the "burner tip", it was considered preferable. Western producers, however, felt that eastern consumer interests were artificially keeping the price of gas down. The finger was pointed at TransCanada, which not only transported the gas, but also was the middle-man in setting price between producers and consumers.

Once Lougheed had swept to office in 1971, he had soon picked energy as the means of asserting the province's status. One of his key objectives was to haul up the price of gas to eastern consumers to a more "reasonable" level. This brought him into a head-on confrontation with TransCanada PipeLines. A report commissioned by Lougheed from the Energy Resources Conservation Board estimated that gas was underpriced by between 10¢ and 20¢. Lougheed called in TransCanada to negotiate new contracts but the giant transmission company persisted in squeezing the lowest price possible out of the province. One incident during the negotiations summed up both Alberta's perceptions of the commercial arrogance of the East and Lougheed's mounting hatred for "Traps". At a meeting in Edmonton, James Kerr, TransCanada's diminutive and aloof chairman, (there are only a couple of select individuals in the whole company who dare to address him as anything but "Mr. Kerr"), presented what Lougheed considered a derisive offer and flatly refused to go any higher. Lougheed was so enraged that he simply closed the brief in front of him, got up and stormed out of the room, leaving the somewhat embarrassed negotiating parties to draw the abortive meeting to a close.

Indeed, TransCanada always was associated with the eastern consumers rather than the western producers, but it also had a corporate reason for keeping prices down. Since TransCanada's income was regulated, and based on the size of its transportation facilities, the route to corporate growth lay in increasing throughput and the size of its operation. Increasing throughput could best be achieved by stimulating eastern demand. This, in turn, seemed best achieved by holding down the price of gas. TransCanada's attitude to western producers thus perfectly paralleled that of the Seven Sisters to OPEC before 1973. TransCanada's income was calculated as a fixed amount deducted from the price at which it sold each unit of gas to the eastern utilities, who in turn, took the gas on the last leg of its journey into the homes and factories of Ontario and Quebec. Once TCPL had taken its cut of this unit price, then another regulated slice was taken by Alberta Gas Trunk Line, the transmission system that collected gas within the province and delivered it to TransCanada at the Alberta border. Once TransCanada and Trunk Line had taken their cuts, then what was left went to the producer.

It was this system, which left the producer as the last man in line for a share of the gas dollar, that was to prove the route to riches for the gas producers once the OPEC crisis struck.

Following the decision to move domestic oil prices to world levels, the federal government made another crucial decision, under pressure from Alberta, to link the price of gas to that of domestic oil. The key formula was that gas was to be priced at 85% of the equivalent value of domestic oil at the "Toronto City gate", that is, the point at which TransCanada sold it to the eastern utilities.

The system whereby a large fixed chunk of the wholesale gas price was taken as a fixed charge by the transportation companies had meant that when prices were low, only a trickle of money reached the producer. When wholesale prices began to move upward rapidly, however, the fixed charges remained relatively stable. The previous trickle to the producer turned into a financial gusher.

Through the 85% formula, the consumer price of gas was inextricably linked to domestic oil, which in turn was firmly declared to be heading towards the OPEC world price. But the fixed charge element of transportation meant that the amount the producer received increased much more rapidly than the overall price. In 1970, domestic consumers paid $581 million for 917 billion cubic feet of gas. In 1977, they paid a whopping $2.3 billion for 1.43 trillion cubic feet. Thus, between 1970 and 1977, the average consumer price for gas in Canada increased more than two and a half times. However, the price received by the producer before royalty payments leaped by a factor of ten, to over $1 per cubic foot. The OPEC increases looked almost modest by comparison.

But if the increase in domestic prices produced a bonanza for the gas producer, then the flowback of cash from gas exports caused something of an even higher magnitude. The great federal-provincial dispute after OPEC had started with Ottawa's desire to grab the fruits of higher oil export prices. This they did through an export surcharge that effectively creamed off the difference between Canadian domestic prices and the world price charged to the United States.

There was a clear economic rationale for this move, in that once the government had decided to hold domestic oil prices below world levels, they had to subsidize the imports that came into eastern Canada. An export surcharge was not only an obvious but also a directly related source of revenue.

Once again, a decision was made to charge world oil-related prices for gas exports. However, since no gas was imported, the economic rationale for taking the increased revenue did not exist. Moreover, after the tremendous battle over oil, Ottawa in any case probably lacked the financial will to do battle over the extra gas revenue. The provincial government decided to hand out the additional export revenue to Albertan producers based, pro rata, on their total gas sales, whether they were exported or not. Two other factors virtually gilded the lily for the Albertan gas producers. Not only was the export price higher than the domestic price, but transportation charges to the American border were much smaller than for domestically destined gas. Finally, the export price was set in United States dollars, providing a further boost when the Canadian dollar declined in value. By late August 1979, the United States was paying around $3.25 an mcf for Canadian gas, with the prospect of higher prices to come in the new decade. Of this price, more than $3 was going to be divided among producers, about *twenty times* before royalties what they were receiving at the beginning of the decade. Even some of the OPEC nations might have looked on with envy.

Masters and Gray: The Tigers

It is the morning of January 18, 1979. John Masters, president of Canadian Hunter, has just been told that his company, in consortium with others, has picked up two thirds of the acreage in the biggest individual land sale in Alberta's history.

"We're still the Tigers," says Masters, smiling out of his ruddy, weather-beaten face.

The moment, and the words, are significant.

Hunter, only formed in 1973, has spent $18 million in the sale, an amount that even Imperial Oil would consider twice. However, it is a typically bold move for an entity that has become in six years not only one of the most spectacular growth stories in a spectacular growth environment, but also one of the most controversial companies in Calgary.

The words are significant because they were said to be recorded, to be written down in the history books. John Masters is a man who very clearly perceives himself as being at the centre of the making of a myth.

Masters and Jim Gray, Hunter's executive vice-president and co-founder of the company, could easily be brothers. Squat and muscular, both with short-cropped sandy hair, they look like the sort of men it would be wiser not to get involved with in a barroom brawl. But their rise to prominence has been as a result of the intellectual rather than the physical impact they have had on the oil industry.

Their theories are under constant attack, and they have provided the hottest geological debate in Calgary for years. Yet they are responsible for one of Canada's largest gas finds, at Elmworth in west central Alberta. And, despite their controversial views, Canadian Hunter, was, by mid 1979, estimated to be worth more than $500 million. To the end of 1978, backers had come up with $150 million to fund their exploration efforts, and the mighty Imperial Oil had agreed — under the largest farm-in agreement in Canadian history — to spend between $150 million and $179 million to earn an interest of just 15% in their properties.

In an industry renowned for its individualists, Masters and Gray are fascinating case studies. Although so similar in appearance, their characters are totally different. Gray is perhaps the most gregarious man in Calgary. His energy, and enthusiasm, are seemingly boundless. His barrel chest seems to contain some great and unstoppable motive force that demands that he keep constantly in motion.

Masters, however, is more reclusive by nature, an intellectual who avoids, indeed looks with distaste on, the Petroleum Club cocktail party circuit of the Calgary corporate establishment.

One thing they do have in common, however, is their selling ability. Again, their styles are different. Gray sweeps you along with a tidal wave of enthusiasm; Masters bears you along more gently, but just as firmly, with a seemingly impregnable, almost hypnotic logic.

Many people are unaware of Masters' existence, since Gray has served as the "front man" for the company since it started. But Masters is really the intellectual driving force behind Canadian Hunter. Gray may go around spreading the word, but if he is the prophet, Masters is Allah.

Although he was for a number of years the head of Oklahoma-based Kerr McGee Corp.'s Canadian operation, Masters is in many ways outside the mainstream of Calgary corporate life, partly because of the controversy over his geological views but also significantly through choice. He attributes a great deal of the industry's suspicion of him to its unwillingness to adopt new ideas, or move beyond the conventional wisdom.

His approach to both geology and Canadian Hunter is a supremely intellectual one, and his conversation abounds with images and analogies. His corporate style is unusual to say the least. He recommends that his staff read books that he feels may have some bearing on the course of Canadian Hunter's development — for example, a book on the development of the Japanese company Sony, *The Sony Vision*, so impressed Masters that he sent memos to his staff to get hold of it. Some of his memos are almost philosophical in style, containing phrases like "we all see the world through the lenses of our self image." He is one of the very few oilmen likely to bring Samuel Johnson into the conversation.

Self-image is an important thing with John Masters. It goes

beyond mere ego, which is such a powerful force among the real movers in the oil industry. It is an extreme self-awareness. Like Jack Gallagher and his efforts in the Beaufort Sea, Masters wants most of all to be rememberd as a great "oil finder". Even now, he is acutely aware that a myth is being created. Anecdotes about significant stages in Canadian Hunter's development — about Masters' and Gray's departure from Kerr McGee; about what Alf Powis, chief executive of Toronto-based Noranda Mines, said before committing funds to support Canadian Hunter; about the discovery of just how big the Elmworth field was — are recounted almost like secular Stations of the Cross, stories to be told to the faithful.

Wealth is not the driving force behind Masters, it is recognition, a desire that others should see him in the role he perceives himself playing. Above the fireplace of his huge, modern, open-plan home, just outside Calgary on a bend in the Bow River, there is a striking portrait of an Italian monk standing among the bombed-out ruins of his monastery. The man is dressed in a cassock made out of an old army blanket, but his face has a marvellous self-composure. It displays inner calm. Masters almost certainly identifies himself with this man. He too, knows exactly where he is and what he is at, despite the skepticism of others.

But Masters is neither surrounded by ruins nor cloaked in rags. Although he still prefers to pad around the house in an old tennis shirt and sneakers, he can look forward, without any trace of boasting, to being one day among the richest men in Calgary. As yet, the real fruits of success haven't come to Masters or Gray, but under the deal they worked out with their backers, they receive jointly 12.5% of net profits from every venture they undertake. They have shared out about half that amount to attract top employees, but the remainder, once gas from Elmworth starts to flow in large quantities, ensures they will be multi-millionaires.

Masters' story begins in Iowa, where he was born in 1927. He spent most of his formative years in Tulsa, Oklahoma, in an oil town, surrounded by an oil family. His stepfather, John G. Bartram, was a well known scientist and geologist, and the young Masters was hearing about overrides, drill-stem tests and other oil industry terms as soon as he could hear. He studied geology at Yale University, whence he graduated in 1951.

During the Korean war, he practised his geological skills looking for uranium in Arizona, New Mexico, Colorado and Utah. He became district geologist for the U.S. Atomic Energy Commission, and while in that job he was asked to give a presentation to Dean McGee, head of Kerr McGee, which had just bought a uranium mine in his area.

When his talk was over, Masters was approached by McGee, who put an arm around his shoulder and asked him if he had ever thought about working for an oil company. That was to be the beginning of a 20-year association with the company.

The young geologist made one condition. He didn't want to work in uranium, he wanted to work in oil. Oil had much more intellectual appeal for Masters. Uranium was too much of a field operation, where one spent a great deal of effort mending flat tires and digging trucks out of mud holes. Most of the time was spent collecting the data. Not much time was spent interpreting it. Even then, it was "intellectualizing and interpreting" that held all the appeal for Masters. He worked in Oklahoma City for a year, but then moved to another of the great American oil towns, Midland, Texas. Masters enjoyed the intellectual stimulation of the town but was having trouble living on the salary. What is more, the uranium boom hit in the Colorado Plateau when a drifting prospector stumbled across the giant Mivida field. Geiger counter sales suddenly rocketed, penny uranium companies sprang up like dandelions and Masters saw all his old friends from the Atomic Energy Commission being picked off with hefty salary increases. Masters made it known he was "looking around" and was approached by Tidewater Oil, a subsidiary of Getty Oil, to work in uranium. However, when he told Dean McGee, McGee offered him the management of the company's uranium operations. He also said that Masters could run the oil business in the Rockies from his Denver base. Masters was about to receive his first real stroke of luck. One day he received a call from the office where the company ran a free uranium service for prospectors. The superintendent told Masters that they just had a man come in all the way from Grants, New Mexico with a bunch of samples, all of which were black uranium ore. He had taken the samples to every geologist in Grants, but all had said that there couldn't be uranium deposits that far north of town. It was a long and bumpy ride out to the site anyway, so they just couldn't be bothered.

Masters could, and he set out for the prospector's site. What he found when he got there was a series of drill holes 100 feet apart, with neatly piled samples arranged by depth beside each hole. Masters ran his geiger counter over the samples, assayed them, and, by late afternoon, had mapped out on the back of an envelope the biggest uranium find in the United States. It was to make Kerr McGee the largest uranium company in the country.

Masters places great significance in the story of the find, which, not surprisingly, raised his corporate status enormously. Its significance, he believes, is that the find had been dumped in the lap of at least half a dozen other geologists, who were all too intellectually and physically lazy to follow it up.

Action is a key element of Master's philosophy. Despite the fact that he teaches a course in geology at the University of Calgary, he has little time for the academics, the "grey-beards", who rank in his mind with the Calgary oilmen who have become tied to their desks, who have become, in his words "catchers instead of pitch-ers." Another of his seminal mental images is of the scene around "Dad" Joiner's well in east Texas in 1931, the well that opened up the greatest oilfield to date in the United States. There were per-haps 200 people gathered around that well, but only one of them, H. L. Hunt, who earned his living as a card sharp and gambler, set out to control the surrounding leases, and went on to become one of the world's richest men. For Masters, the example is a potently symbolic one.

Masters too has devoted a great deal of thought to the theory of organizations, corporate strategy and managerial interraction. His relationship with Gray is a close one, and he stresses the "mental leapfrogging" that takes place between them as they bounce an idea back and forth and in the process move it farther forward than either of them could do individually.

In terms of corporate strategy, self-image is once again all impor-tant. "I believe we could have been pretty good generals. We are constantly assessing risks, hitting, bluffing. The psychology of at-tack is never far from my mind. How do we gain an advantage over our thirty biggest rivals, some of them 100 times larger than us. How do we attack them, how do we overcome them."

However, in those early days in the mid 1950's, Masters was completely absorbed by becoming a "finder". He was a man whose body and brain were always on the move. In 1957, he was sent up to Kerr McGee's Canadian operation, but the intense activity of the uranium area had taken its toll. Not only had they been two years with a wild west atmosphere — when Masters and his team had been claim-jumped, had their tires slashed and were even shot at — but they were years when Masters became almost obsessed with exploration and geological theory. He found himself con-stantly turning over data in his mind, lost the ability to relax, and eventually had a form of nervous breakdown that debilitated him for several months. But again, Masters sees this now as an essen-tial part of his development, as a critical testing from which he eventually emerged with a great maturity and an ability to be able to switch off.

After nine months in Canada, he returned to Oklahoma City and in 1958 became Kerr McGee's chief geologist for oil. He was just 31 years old. In the following years, Masters worked all over the United States, on the Gulf Coast, in the Rocky Mountains, west Texas, Kansas, Oklahoma, but his success was not outstanding. This lean spell is constantly thought over by Masters, who, in his ongoing critical self-analysis, feels it necessary to explain it to him-self as much as to others. Again, the answer, as he sees it, has played a critical part in his subsequent exploration philosophy.

"The answer," he says, "is that too many people were jiggling my aim, or telling me not to shoot just yet. From that, I became aware that exploration does, and should, go on in the minds of just a few men."

The intricate processes within John Masters' head are very obviously the control centre of the phenomenon of Canadian Hunter.

The years in Oklahoma City, between 1958 and 1966, were fallow ones for Masters, years of frustration because he was not making the big finds he, and McGee, so badly wanted. So in 1966, he was sent back to Canada to head Kerr McGee's Canadian operation. Soon after, he hired Jim Gray, then a geologist with Great Plains, the subsidiary of Burmah Oil that would eventually be taken over by Norcen. The two immediately hit it off as a team, except in one highly significant way — that big strike still eluded them. They found Keg River reefs of the type responsible for the Rainbow and Zama discoveries, but they contained water. They moved into exploration in the Foothills of western Alberta and into shallow gas fields. But everything they did was marginal. They weren't "ringing the bell," says Masters, "people were still jiggling my aim."

On the Street

However, for Masters and Gray, as for the oil world in general, 1973 was to be the critical year. As world supplies tightened and the OPEC nations got ready to flex their new-found political muscle, Dean McGee, down in Oklahoma City, was getting a little nervous about the situation in Canada. He saw that the other major oil companies had pulled out of the West and he wanted to wind down the operation and bring Masters back to head office, leaving Gray in charge in Canada. Masters, for a variety of personal reasons, just didn't want to go. However, his ultra self-confident approach had earned him some enemies at head office and the pressure began to mount: come back to Oklahoma City or leave. Masters made the critical decision. He was going to leave.

Masters headed south to give McGee his decision. McGee said he was sorry to see him go. "By the way," he asked, "what's Jim going to do?"

Masters suddenly thought "By gosh!" and he said: "Why, Jim is going to quit too."

As soon as he left McGee's office, Masters headed for the first telephone he could find. The saga of Canadian Hunter was about to begin. Masters telephoned Gray and said: "Jim, I've got some good news and some bad news."

"What's the good news?" asked Gray.

"I finally quit today," replied Masters.

"That's fantastic," said Gray, "now what's the bad news."

For the first time in their careers, Masters and Gray were outside the corporate womb, out on the street with no money and no plans. Gary Last, who was to go on to buy Sabre Petroleums, and Vic Kloepfer, one of the industry's most respected petroleum engineers, at that time had a consulting practice, and they offered Masters and Gray a spare room in their office. They started with one table, two chairs and a telephone. What they needed more than anything else was financial backing, so while Masters pored over maps and thought about exploration strategy, Gray spent all day long on the telephone, approaching, and being turned down by, various companies.

In the end, what got them their start was not the brilliance of their exploration strategy, but Jim Gray's family connections. Gray had been born in Kirkland Lake, Ontario, and his father had operated a mine for Noranda, the giant Toronto-based mining group. Bill Rowe, executive vice-president of Noranda, had been a great friend of Gray's father. Rowe found out from Gray's mother that Jim and John Masters had gone out on their own, and persuaded Noranda's chief executive, Alf Powis, to stop over in Calgary on a trip to Vancouver in order to hear what the two had to offer.

What Gray and Masters were after was $5 million a year to spend on exploration for a period of five years. The presentation they made to Bill Rowe and Alf Powis was based not so much on the promise of great new finds as on economics and technology. They pointed out that expected higher gas prices and improved drilling and production technology would make many areas previously considered uneconomic worthwhile. The West, they claimed, still had lots of promise, despite the pull-out of the major oil companies.

The four had dinner at the Petroleum Club, then Gray and Masters drove the two Noranda men to the airport, where they had a final drink.

Powis said two things which the financial supplicants, with the eager philosophical deference those who need money always pay to those who have it, heartily accepted.
Thought One:
"When everyone else is leaving somewhere and you can see a reason to stay, then you have a real opportunity."
Thought Two:
"When all the wise men are saying something, then it is very often wrong."

Amen to all that, thought Masters and Gray as they saw Powis and Rowe on their way. And the word was made folding money shortly after, in June, 1973, when Powis' assistant, Ossie Hinds telephoned and said that Noranda would be prepared to put up half the money but would deposit $100,000 in the bank right away.

It wasn't the whole deal, but they both felt that Noranda's commitment aided their own credibility and would make it much easier to raise the remainder.

It was in fact twelve months before the final agreement was signed with Noranda, but the show was on the road. One small problem was what the show should call itself. First, they thought of Everest Oil, with all its overtones of the major geological conquests they planned. But a check with corporate registers established that that name had already been taken. Then they settled on Chimo Oil and Gas, with a cosy native element. But that had gone too. So then Gray talked to Bill Rowe, who suggested that "Canadian" should be in there somewhere. Then someone came up with Hunter as having a certain romance, and Canadian Hunter was born.

But they still had to find the remainder of the money. Top of the list of companies most likely to provide the other half of the $25 million was Steel Company of Canada Ltd., the country's largest steel producer. Jim Gray had knocked on Stelco's door many times, and J. Peter Gordon, the company's chairman and chief executive, and John D. Allan, its president, had expressed great enthusiasm for the scheme.

In December, 1973, Masters and Gray trekked to Toronto to make a presentation to Stelco's board of directors. But the decision had the misfortune to come before the board at the same time as the announcement of a rapid escalation in the cost of Stelco's enormous new plant at Nanticoke, on Lake Erie. Faced with rapid inflation, the board decided it had no money to risk in oil and gas exploration.

Masters and Gray were crushed. They had been spending money as if everything was assured. In the event, however, Stelco's $12.5 million would have been more than well spent. Eventually, since Noranda had such a good financial year in 1974, the Toronto-based mining giant decided to take on the whole deal. Masters and Gray were off and running. Initially, they proved far more expert at spending money than finding petroleum. After proceeding fairly carefully for the first two years, they horrified Noranda by spending their entire exploration budget for 1975, $8 million, in the first three months of the year.

After moving into heavy oil in Lloydminster in a small way, and a couple of other exploration ventures, they eventually decided that the Elmworth area in west central Alberta might be the place to test out their theories. Wells had been drilled in the area and had come up with shows of gas, but possible levels of production had been too low to make the wells economic. They had been declared dry.

However, what Masters and Gray believed was that this whole area, known as the deep basin, extending far to the northwest and the southeast of the Elmworth area and covering almost 26,000 square miles, contained a huge volume of gas in low quality reservoirs. This gas, they believed, had not previously been economic but now much higher prices for gas to the producer — increased by a factor of more than ten since the early 1970's — plus more sophisticated technology, would enable these low quality reservoirs to be exploited, and produce an enormous amount more gas.

According to subsequent claims by Masters and Gray, the whole area might provide an additional 50 trillion cubic feet of gas at the 1978 wellhead price of $1 a thousand cubic feet. Such a volume, for reference, would virtually double Alberta's proven gas reserves.

Their figures were treated with the greatest skepticism by the industry, and indeed still are, so one may well ask, if their theories were considered so shaky, how did they become a half billion dollar company?

The answer lies in the geologist's greatest resource, luck. For, drilling early in 1976, what Canadian Hunter found was not a third class reserve of dubious economic value. They found a first class reserve, and it turned out to be a very big one.

The genie was waiting for them in a sedimentary formation known as the Falher Sands. When drilling the discovery well, they almost missed the critical Falher zone completely. However, they had it recorded in their geological prognosis as a possible gas bearing section. When they tested it, it "came up and hit them in the eye" with a flow of 10 million cubic feet, much greater than anything they had expected. It was not an enormous flow but it was a good one. They drilled on and found a number of other "pay zones", that is, oil or gas-bearing rocks. However, these other finds were lower quality reserves that would require "fracing", a technological tool that Masters and Gray thought could help them tap low quality reserves economically.

Fracing is by no means a new concept. It had been used at the discovery well of the Pembina Field more than 20 years previously. The process essentially breaks into "tight" rock formations, that is, formations that allow the oil and gas contained in them to flow only very sluggishly. The breaking, or fracturing, is carried out by pumping a fluid under enormous pressure into the rock. This causes fissures to open. To keep these cracks open once the fluid is withdrawn, an agent such as sand is also pumped down to prop open the cracks. Once the fluid is withdrawn, then these cracks allow oil or gas to flow more freely to the wellbore.

Fracing can increase the flow rate of a well by as much as a factor of five, but even then, many of the zones being tested remained uneconomic.

However, the discovery in the Falher was a free-flowing gas genie, albeit, it seemed at first, not a very large one. But that was to be Canadian Hunter's second pleasant surprise.

The reason the find in the Falher zone had not caused enormous excitement was that it was in a formation of rock collectively known as conglomerates. These are a sort of consolidated gravel, composed of pebbles of various sizes held together by a cementing material. These formations are usually the result of sands lying at the bottom of an ancient river channel that have gone through the conventional process of being buried beneath other sediments, along with their organic contents, and being turned into rock. They usually do not cause great excitement, because river channels are usually narrow and sinuous, and thus not very promising as large gas or oil traps. When the word got out that this was what Canadian Hunter had found it caused very little interest.

However, Canadian Hunter had a Houston-based geological consultant, Bob Sneider, who, when he looked at the findings from the well turned to Masters and said: "Goddamn it John, that's a beach conglomerate."

A beach conglomerate changed the whole possible complexion of the find, for beaches, unlike river beds, can be of very large areal extent. Thus, depending on its size, a beach conglomerate offered a lot more attractions. Sneider had provided the geological key for the unlocking of what was to be a huge find. Now there were two problems: to find out just how big and then to start snapping up land before the word got out.

As with the tiny company Nairb's activities at West Pembina, the fact that it was Canadian Hunter who was doing the exploring in Elmworth tended to dampen the interest of the larger oil companies. Texaco had access to Canadian Hunter's well information, but they didn't use it. They went along with Canadian Hunter in a number of sales, but in most cases took less than the still-small company, and in some cases did not participate at all.

Initially, however, Canadian Hunter's problem was to gauge the size of the potential discovery. By the summer of 1976 they had mapped out what they thought could be a very large field. One key test would be if the conglomerate "outcropped", that is, had been pushed out of the ground towards the west in British Columbia, where the upsurge of the Rocky Mountains occurred. So, in the autumn of 1976, Dave Smith, one of Canadian Hunter's key exploration men, and Larry Miekle, another Houston-based consultant, hired themselves a helicopter in Fort St. John, British Columbia, and flew westward along the successive outcrops to see if they could find the remains of a prehistoric beach bursting out of the ground. After the fourth outcrop Miekle found his way to a telephone and reached Masters. "Did you find the beach?" asked Masters. "John," replied the consultant, "you could hear the seagulls."

In deference to real geological age, perhaps he should have said, "you could hear the pteradactyls", but his find marked a key piece of support for Hunter's geological theory, and it meant that the field was a big one. It also meant that Hunter had to start picking up as much land as it could on the British Columbia side of the border, where the field extended. Masters phoned Powis at Noranda and told him they had to hit the land sales "like a ton of bricks". It is important to remember that nobody else was as advanced in terms of geological theory as Hunter was; however, a certain amount of interest was aroused because of the prices Hunter was paying. Masters' all-important bidding strategy for the land was that they should place priority on bidding successfully for the land, rather than risking bidding too low as a result of the desire to avoid attention. Attention was eventually aroused. Amoco, which had a lot of land in the southeast of the area, was slow to start but subsequently moved in strongly. A team of PanCanadian Petroleums, Ashland Canada, Canadian Superior and Dome Petroleum outmuscled Hunter financially a few times, although they were not quite so sure what they were bidding on. The French-owned Total Petroleum N.A. and Edmonton-based Chieftain Development also emerged as key players in the area.

A couple of times at the sales, Masters admitted that he "flinched", bidding on the low side, and lost the acreage. "I thought I would see if anyone else was in there bidding against us. They were, and I kicked myself."

As far as Hunter's own backers were concerned, one of the really key early players was Gus Van Wielingen, the dynamic head of Sulpetro, who quickly recognized what Hunter had found. Sulpetro had been buying land in the Elmworth region since shortly after the Canadian Hunter discovery, but later in the year Van Wielingen put up what seemed like a massive $24 million to jointly acquire acreage and do exploration with Hunter. (Sulpetro subsequently farmed out half its interest to CanDel Oil Ltd. for $18 million, thus finishing up with half its original interest for just a quarter of its original cost.)

As far as Hunter's original backer was concerned, Noranda gave away 25% of its interests in the company's properties to Kerr Addison (which is controlled 41% by Noranda) which in turn gave up 10% of the total to Petromark, a highly successful exploration company based on West German money funnelled into the country by young financier Klaus Hebbern.

In 1978, Canadian Hunter received what some consider perhaps the ultimate accolade for a Canadian-owned company. Throughout the history of Canadian oil, it had usually been the majors who had initiated the big exploration plays, with a number of key exceptions. The big boys, Imperial, Gulf, Shell, Texaco, Amoco, Mobil and Chevron, had done the majority of the work and the Canadian independents had gathered around them, trying to get just a peripheral piece of the action.

However, in the late 1960's and early 1970's, the majors had headed for the frontiers, abandoning, to a greater or lesser degree, hopes of further major finds in the conventional exploration areas of the West. Perhaps the company which abandoned the West most comprehensively was Imperial Oil. In 1978, Canada's largest oil company found itself badly, and embarrassingly, left out of both the West Pembina and Elmworth plays. It paid big money both in West Pembina and Elmworth land sales, but in early 1978, a symbolic change occurred. The mighty Imperial came cap in hand to little Canadian Hunter, almost desperate to get a sizable presence in one of the two major exploration plays in Alberta, and asked if it could farm into their acreage. After a good deal of haggling, Masters and Gray typically squeezed more money out of Imperial than they originally intended to spend. But on August 1, 1978 an agreement, the biggest of its kind in Canada, was signed whereby Canada's largest oil company agreed to spend $150 million over 30 months on drilling and well completions in return for 12.5% of Hunter's acreage in Elmworth and 17.5% of its other western Canadian acreage. Imperial also committed to spend a further $29 million conditionally on Hunter acquiring certain new acreage.

John Masters was Allah, Jim Gray was his Prophet, and the Mountain — in the shape of Imperial Oil — had come to Mohammed.

Imperial had come up with a huge financial commitment, but even that was not enough for Masters and Gray. Indeed, for "finders" with geological bees in their bonnet, there is *never* enough money.

If Masters can be considered the prime mover in finding the petroleum, Gray is undoubtedly the genius at finding money and promoting Canadian Hunter's activities. He has also been in the forefront of promoting the whole domestic gas industry. Aware that, with a gas oversupply situation in the West, the enthusiasm for Elmworth depends significantly on finding new markets, Gray has been a vociferous proponent of exports. In 1978, he was distributing lapel badges declaring "Get off your ass and sell that gas." (With an eye to additional domestic markets in Quebec, he even had a slightly tamer French version produced, saying "Bouge et fait marchez ce gaz la.")

As with all great salesman, the words "no" and "can't" fail to register in Gray's mind. Early in 1979, paper giant Domtar Inc. agreed to put up $10 million towards a new $50 million land-buying programme. The way in which Gray got the money is a tribute to his relentless salesmanship. Gray had been introduced through *eminence grise* Bob Wisener of Walwyn, Stodgell to Alex Barron, chairman of Domtar. Barron had told Gray to go and see Alex Hamilton, Domtar's president. Visiting Hamilton, Gray's argument was that since Domtar spent more than $40 million annually on energy, the company should have a deeper direct involvement in oil and gas.

Gray said to Hamilton: "When you hear about energy, you tend to forget it. When you read about it you may remember it. But

Hamilton, nevertheless, was still wavering, so Gray decided on one final blitzkrieg. He telephone Hamilton's secretary for an appointment, but she said that Hamilton had a heavy schedule for the following few days and that there was no way in which Gray could be fitted in. That in itself presented the sort of challenge in which Gray revels. "Well," he asked "where is he going to be tomorrow?" She replied that he was flying to Toronto for a board meeting of the Canadian Imperial Bank of Commerce, but that he had a very busy schedule.

"Well," said Gray "perhaps I could take him down to the board meeting." The secretary couldn't think of any response to that, so, the following day, as Alex Hamilton descended the escalator at Toronto's Terminal Two, there, waiting at the bottom, stood Jim Gray's smiling bulk. Gray shepherded Hamilton into an awaiting limousine. As they travelled down route 427, Gray found out what was bothering Domtar's president. Travelling east along the Gardiner Expressway he allayed Hamilton's worries and reiterated the wisdom of Domtar's involvement. By the time they drew up at Commerce Court, Gray had his $10 million.

Despite this almost unparalleled ability to find financial backers, skepticism still surrounds Masters and Gray because of their controversial claims that the deep basin is capable of yielding more than 50 trillion cubic feet at current prices. Judging from Imperial's rather modest estimate of western gas reserves delivered to the National Energy Board during hearings in late 1978 and early 1979, it seemed that they didn't believe them either. Indeed, when the NEB delivered its findings in mid 1979 — focusing on the ability of Canada to approve major new exports of gas to the United States — it included what amounted to a rebuff to Masters and Gray for the sort of reserve figures they had been throwing about.

In the report, the NEB said: "The Board has devoted considerable attention to the prospects of the Deep Basin of Alberta and British Columbia. The established reserves of the Elmworth/Wapiti area, an area under active development within the Deep Basin, are estimated to be in the order of 1 Tcf (trillion cubic feet), all in conventional reservoirs. No gas in the low permeability (tight) sands of the Deep Basin has been placed in the established category at this time. Further advances in technology which might lead to economic recovery of a portion of this resource would permit its inclusion in the future."

One trillion against 50 trillion! Further advances in technology! The report would have put the cap on the well of lesser men's enthusiasm.

But of course in the case of Master and Gray it didn't. Again, as with all finders, their belief in the Elmworth discovery goes beyond support of a theory. It amounts to a psychological commitment.

15 | The Newest and Largest Fortunes: Gas and Land

"$100 Million Speaks Much Louder Than Words"

The achievements of John Masters and Jim Gray, in finding western Canada's possibly greatest gas pool, had not been significantly turned into vast wealth by the end of 1979, although they could take some comfort in the fact that vast wealth was coming! But there was a select group of men who had already cleaned up on gas by the end of the decade. The foremost of these were J. C. Anderson, the beefy Nebraskan with a salty turn of phrase; Gus Van Wielingen, the urbane Dutchman who appears more like a banker than an oilman; Verne Lyons, the reclusive geologist from Saskatchewan who has built a huge diversified corporate empire in just a few short years; and Syd Kahanoff, another compulsively hard worker from Saskatchewan who was the only one of the quartet to turn his company into cash — personally emerging with $55 million from the sale of Voyager Petroleums.

Van Wielingen, Anderson, Lyons and Kahanoff were by no means the only ones to achieve millionaire status as a result of their gas finding ability, but they were the most spectacularly successful.

Gus Van Wielingen — A Different Category

Gus André Van Wielingen is not by nature inclined toward self-doubt. He is neither embarrassed by his wealth nor shy about his achievements. If the West is going to make its way into the boardrooms of the eastern Establishment over the next ten years, it will be men like Van Wielingen who will lead the charge. Charge is perhaps the wrong word, for the process will be a subtle one; there will be few visible signs of change, no open conflict. It will simply be a gradual assumption of corporate influence in line with personal wealth.

Van Wielingen already possesses considerable personal clout. A long-time friend of Peter Lougheed, his personal $20 million holding in Sulpetro Ltd., the company he controls, is just the visible tip of a financial iceberg involving finance and real estate as well as oil and gas.

A stocky, handsome man with penetrating brown eyes, Van Wielingen has the air and the self-confidence of a European merchant banker. Where it is sometimes impossible to differentiate between oil millionaires and their staffs, Van Wielingen's impeccably cut suits and velvet waistcoats tell you straight away that this man is the boss.

Van Wielingen obviously revels in the trappings of wealth; in his Mercedes, the Learjet that Sulpetro leases, and his homes in Calgary, Los Angeles and Dallas, where another of his companies, Sulpetro International has its headquarters. He even has two lavishly appointed offices within a couple of blocks of each other in downtown Calgary, the one where he wears the hat of Supeltro chairman, chief executive and main shareholder, and the other where he dons the headgear of Vangus Resources, his personal holding company.

Outside of Sulpetro, one of Van Wielingen's main business partners is Dick Bonnycastle, multi-millionaire financier and founder of the Harlequin empire. Van Wielingen is also involved in joint ventures both in Canada and the United States with the ubiquitous Maurice Strong and Toronto financier George Gardiner, head of Gardiner, Watson — one of the outstanding successes among Toronto institutional brokerage houses in recent years. His holdings include a share in the exclusive Arizona Biltmore hotel, and, along with Bonnycastle, he has an interest in about 20 thoroughbred racehorses.

Van Wielingen revels in being an entrepreneur, a risk-taker at the multi-million dollar level.

He likes to draw a clear distinction between the "company men" and the entrepreneurs in Calgary. "I'm one of the relatively few people in town who actually owns something. I don't know many other people in town who have personal control of a $200 million company," he says. "It puts you in a different category."

Van Wielingen emphasizes that he has not achieved his position without effort. He puts in 15 hour days and probably clocks a quarter of a million miles a year flying between Toronto, Calgary, New York, Dallas and Los Angeles. But that degree of effort, he believes, plus his business acumen, has put him in a "different category".

Jack Gallagher and Bob Blair may perceive themselves as corporate empire builders in the national interest, but Gus Van

Wielingen perceives himself rising swiftly and surely in a purer corporate hierarchy, in a group of people where words are covered by personal cheque books, in a world where not only personal reputation but personal wealth are being put on the line. He admires both Blair and Gallagher as corporate risk-takers, although he points out that Blair is taking risks with other people's money. But he has open disdain for much of the remainder of Calgary's professional corporate management. "They are not owners," he stresses, implying that proprietorship is really the only way to corporate grace.

Van Wielingen has built Sulpetro not once but twice since 1966, when he started the company. In 1975 he sold out to Hudson's Bay Oil and Gas for $102 million, paid back bank loans, bought out a majority of his partners and started again. Aided by rocketing gas prices and the experience of having done it once already, it only took him three years to build up assets of $100 million plus the second time around. Early in 1979 the company made its first public offering, raising $18 million from the sale of 1.65 million shares, but Van Wielingen still sits firmly in control with more than 50% of the company's voting stock.

Van Wielingen's route to riches has not been an easy one. He has worked long and hard for his success. Born and raised in Holland, he joined the United States Navy at the end of the Second World War as a pilot in the Pacific and Australia. He returned to Holland to study mechanical engineering, and then joined Standard Vacuum, a company jointly owned by Standard of New Jersey (subsequently Exxon) and Standard of New York (Mobil), for whom he returned to work in Indonesia. He went back as a fighter pilot in the United States Navy during the Korean War and had the distinction of having survived being shot down in the Sea of Japan before he eventually came to Canada in the early 1950's to work for Gulf.

Van Wielingen became fascinated by gas processing, that is, extracting liquids from the flows of gas, and he left Gulf and borrowed $1 million to build two extraction plants, one near Edmonton and the other near Stettler, Alta. The plants extracted the liquids and provided "scrubbed" gas to local authorities. The idea was similar to the one on which Dome Petroleum was later to build the majority of its earnings, but the market in the mid 1950's was not good. Van Wielingen had borrowed the money for the plants from the Chase Manhattan Bank in New York, who, unknown to him, had written off the loan as a bad debt. However, Van Wielingen managed to sell the plants and, to the Chase's surprise and delight, paid them off. His reputation might have risen among the banking community, but his first full-scale attempt at entrepreneurial success had been abortive.

He then joined consultants J. C. Sproule and Associates as chief gas engineer, and was almost immediately assigned to the Borden Commission, set up by the Diefenbaker Tory government to look at the whole issue of Canadian oil and gas policy. Van Wielingen became an expert on liquefaction of natural gas and on the pipelining of liquid petroleum gas (LPG). He hatched the idea of building an LPG pipeline to the west coast as a step towards serving Pacific markets with Albertan LPGs. He got Peter Bawden, the millionaire drilling contractor who later became a federal Conservative MP, to finance the research, and was joined by a young lawyer named Peter Lougheed as the third director of Mountain Pacific Pipelines, the corporate entity set up to carry out the scheme. Lougheed had for some time been Van Wielingen's personal lawyer, and a director of his personal holding company.

However, entrepreneurial flare was to be doused once again, this time not by markets but by Gulf Oil, who contracted to sell LPGs to Japan in refrigerated tankers and thus squashed Van Wielingen's scheme.

It was then, still undaunted after entrepreneurial strike two, that Van Wielingen decided that he didn't want to be the middle man in the oil and gas business any more. He decided he would go and see if he could find the stuff himself. He incorporated Sulpetro in 1967 with $50,000 of his own money and $350,000 from West German investors that he had been introduced to in New York, the vanguard of the West German money that was to provide an enormous boost to the industry in the mid 1970's.

Through his experience with Sproule, Van Wielingen knew where there were large undeveloped reserves of gas. He spent a year researching the likely target areas and then went to the CPR and made a deal on a huge block of land in east-central Alberta. Van Wielingen agreed to drill one well in each nine sections of a 225 section parcel (a section equals 640 acres) in return for a 100% working interest on the lands. The CPR would get a 20% royalty of anything discovered. Van Wielingen did most of the geological work himself, hiring some land men and geologists on a contract basis.

By 1975, after this and a number of other highly successful joint-venture deals, Van Wielingen had built the company into a very significant entity. However, some of the American shareholders were getting nervous about the size of the appreciation of their investment. They wanted to take their profits, so the company was sold for $102 million. Bank loans were paid off, as were many of the shareholders, and Van Wielingen was able to start again and this time keep control of the company.

Van Wielingen set about building the company up once more with an aggressive programme of buying undeveloped acreage. In 1976 he spent $15 million acquiring 766,000 acres from Mesa Petroleum (N.A.) and later in the year entered into a $24 million joint venture with Canadian Hunter in order to gain major acreage in the Elmworth region. Between December 1975 and October 1978, Sulpetro drilled or participated in 396 wells, of which 236 brought in commercial oil or gas. As a result of the finds, proven gas reserves jumped from 6 billion cubic feet to 171 billion cubic feet, while proven reserves of oil and natural gas liquids increased from 164,000 barrels to 2.3 million barrels. Land inventories increased from 500,000 net acres to 1.7 million net acres.

Van Wielingen remains very close to Premier Lougheed, acts as a chairman for a number of political functions and in 1978 organized the Premier's Dinner. He often breakfasts with Lougheed and has accompanied him on a number of trade missions. Van Wielingen, like Bob Blair and Jack Gallagher, is more than aware of the importance of political connections and influence in the present day oil industry. The fact that he could "in no way" be considered a supporter of the Liberal party has not stopped him from making contributions to it. Moreover, before a corporate fund raising trip to Europe a few years ago he prevailed on Don Getty, the provincial energy minister to give him a letter confirming that he was a "friend" of the provincial government. That is the sort of mutual back-scratching that Van Wielingen believes those who support the provincial government deserve.

And he certainly does support Lougheed and his attack on Ottawa. "I think that central power should be challenged," he says. "I think its unrealistic to think that because someone has something in Vancouver they should have it in Halifax too.

"I think Alberta is discharging its responsibility. I often think, if all this oil and gas was in Ontario, how *they* would discharge their responsibility."

The views are conventional Alberta-corporate-conservative, and despite his cosmopolitan air, Van Wielingen has obviously fully absorbed his dose of Western resentment. "Why," he declares indignantly, "they still think we are a colony out here."

Van Wielingen's self-confidence and unbashed admission of his own success does not sit well with all his Calgary counterparts. Says the head of another fast growing gas company: "Van Wielingen has a pilot with two jobs. His second job is to fly Van Wielingen's plane, the first to kiss Van Wielingen's shoes."

Humility may admittedly not be part of Van Wielingen's make-up, but then he has little cause to be humble. Moreover, he feels that his achievements are only just beginning. "All my ventures are still in their formative stages", he says. Asked if he expects to get a bank directorship — the equivalent of knighthood for the business community — within the immediate future, he says: "I don't want bank boards just yet. I'm too busy."

But for Van Wielingen there is no trace of doubt that "bank boards" will come.

If you met Verne Lyons, you would certainly not suspect that he was one of Calgary's greatest corporate empire builders and richest men. But then, the chances of bumping into Verne Lyons are not that great. He likes to keep himself to himself.

A big bear of a man, Lyons is responsible for finding, along with colleague Bob McCullough, the third largest gas field in North America. He has built the private company he started in 1972 and took public in 1973, Ocelot Industries Ltd., into a diversified energy concern with a market value of over $300 million; and he owns stock in Ocelot worth, in mid 1979, over $100 million.

Lyons went to the University of Saskatchewan and the London School of Economics before going to the University of Alberta in the late 1940's to earn a degree in geology. After graduating in 1951, he worked for Shell Oil Co. and Charter Oil Co. before forming his own consulting firm in 1958.

His partner, Bob McCullough, had graduated from the University of Alberta with a Commerce degree in 1938 to spend thirty years in the oil industry, finally as general manager and secretary treasurer of Charter Oil from 1964-1967 before he teamed up with Lyons.

The success of the two men was a classic example of the dramatic impact of economics on the gas finding business. The story starts, perhaps somewhat improbably, in 1883, when one of the CPR's drilling rigs, searching for fresh water in southeastern Alberta, hit a flow of gas in the Milk River formation at about 1000 feet. This was the first gas discovery well drilled and completed in western Canada. The old well was used for a year or two by the CPR camp nearby and then abandoned. The field, apart from some scattered drilling, was to lay dormant for the following 80 years.

In 1968, Lyons and McCullough, funded by a group led by Max Bell, set about examining the extent and the commercial possibilities of the Milk River field. The reason that nobody had showed much interest in the field was simply because its economics were too marginal. However, by innovative techniques that cut the cost of drilling a well from $20,000 to $8,000, and by increasing the number of wells in a given area, they believed that they could make the field pay. The other rather interesting feature they discovered about the field, once they had worked out its geology, was its areal extent; it covered about 10,000 square miles!

However, enormous skepticism surrounded the two oilmen. "We were the joke of the town," says McCullough. However, they were convinced that the price of gas would escalate, and with it the commercial viability of the field. In June, 1968, a company, Alberta Eastern Gas, was formed, and by November, 1969, when a first public offering of $3 million was raised, the company had acquired interests and options to 664,000 acres of gas rights in Alberta and Saskatchewan. The company's cost-cutting techniques proved effective and, as the gas price escalated in the early 1970's, so their operation became more commercial. But when gas prices began to surge after the settlement of the federal-provincial dispute on energy pricing, things really took off. By mid 1976, AEG had proven and probable gas reserves, discounted at 12%, totalling $177 million.

However, in the meantime, Lyons had left the management of AEG to concentrate on Ocelot, the private company he set up in 1972. In April, 1973, Ocelot raised $4 million via a public offering of shares and, by June, 1976, the estimated value of its oil and gas reserves had grown, again discounted at 12%, to $205 million. In the event, this estimate proved to be over-optimistic, but it was an important basis for Ocelot's next move.

One morning in late September, 1976, Lyons telephoned his old colleague, McCullough, who was still working at AEG, and said: "Bob, your shares have just been delisted."

"Oh," said McCullough, "why is that?"

"It's because," said Lyons, "I'm taking you over."

So, on the basis of one Ocelot share and $9 cash for each AEG share, Lyons moved back as the undisputed master, owning 39.1% of the new company (he now directly owns 43.6%). Before the takeover, Lyons had been moving aggressively in acquiring drilling, pipeline and oilfield equipment supply, so, by 1978, he could look back on a truly astonishing growth performance. Between 1975 and 1978, Ocelot's earnings had grown by a factor of 50, from 2¢ to $1.04.

Lyons is essentially a very private man, and reportedly an uncommunicative one, prone to grunting more often that he speaks. McCullough says that they used to work by a "kind of telepathy." Still, $100 million speaks much louder than words.

J. C. Anderson "The Thrill of the Chase"

Of all the shapes and sizes in which Calgary's gas finders come, J. C. Anderson perhaps most looks the part. Tall and beefy, he appears like the model of the rough and tough drilling man. However, what has made Anderson one of the select band of finders — and one of the richest men in Calgary — is a brilliant technical brain and an outstanding ability to make deals. 1979 was the tenth year since Anderson made the big break from the executive offices of Amoco. During that ten years, he has built the companies under his control to an asset value of more than $300 million and his personal worth to something in excess of $50 million.

J. C. Anderson likes nothing better than to get out his "singing pen" or his "old spinning map" for visitors. With his pen, he likes to draw the elaborate corporate pyramid at the top of which he sits. On the map, he likes to explain how he came to discover one of the largest gas fields in Alberta. All this with a pride that manages to steer clear of self-importance.

J.C., as he is universally known (even his wife calls him J.C.) is a man with a smart mind and a novel turn of phrase. He has not featured greatly in the public eye because most of his interests are still private. However, in mid 1979 he was considering reorganizing that complex corporate pyramid and saving his "singing pen" a little work.

The company that stands at the top of the pyramid is Anderson Exploration Ltd. Through it, Anderson runs the business interests of four groups: Alamo Petroleum Ltd.; Fairweather Gas Ltd.; the oil and gas investments of his brother Bob; and finally his own two companies, Anderson Oil & Gas and J. C. Anderson. Alamo Petroleum is the wholly-owned subsidiary of New York-based Rosario Resources Corp., a very large producer of gold and other precious metals in the United States and Central America. Fairweather, in which he and his brother each have a 20% stake, is the oil and gas exploration arm of Vancouver-based B.C. Sugar. These four groups generally participate equally in new deals while Rosario and B.C. Sugar pitch in a major chunk of Anderson's overheads.

Anderson is proud of what he has achieved but avoids the pomposity of some of his entrepreneurial counterparts. He lives with his wife and four teenage children on a 680 acre farm just 16 miles from downtown Calgary. His huge, rambling house has an unobstructed view both of downtown Calgary and the mountains. Anderson is not the sort of man who would go out of his way to seek a place in the "Establishment", which perhaps explains why he has had so little trouble in becoming part of it. His wife and children are all very keen riders and six of Anderson's horses are stabled at Ron Southern's enormous riding centre at Spruce Meadows.

Anderson's origins were relatively humble. He was born in Oakland, Nebraska, where his father worked for a local bank. (He only retired in 1978, at the age of 83!). After leaving high school J.C. went to Midland College, Texas on a basketball scholarship. His original intention was to study physical education and eventually become a coach. However, along the way he became interested in geology and eventually transferred to the University of Texas to study petroleum engineering. He started work for a subsidiary of Standard of Indiana (Amoco) as a roustabout in west Texas, but after only five weeks found himself summoned into the army, where he spent two years and finished up working for counter-intelligence. Eventually, he returned to the Amoco subsidiary to work as a junior engineer. He worked the Gulf coast and was then transferred to Tulsa, then Denver and eventually, in 1966, to Calgary.

Within a short time, Anderson became Amoco's chief engineer in Canada. However, he was so impressed with the potential of Alberta that in August, 1968, he decided to go it alone. Anderson remains a great fan of Amoco where, he says "I never spent a bad day during twelve working years."

However, the decision to go it alone was not an easy one. He was 38 years old, had a wife and child to think about and had a bright future at Amoco. "If I hadn't come to Canada I would still be with Standard of Indiana. But having worked most areas of the United States, I thought I could see tremendous potential for going it alone here. Alberta hadn't really been scratched, and still hasn't. But when I was thinking about it, I certainly didn't get much sleep for two or three months."

Anderson's initial strategy was the classic one of finding attractive looking deals and then getting someone else to put up the cash for them. In return, Anderson would get a "free ride" in the shape of a piece of the action. Anderson Exploration was formed with his brother Bob and a lawyer from San Antonio who introduced them to a group of investors willing to put up $400,000 as seed money. At the end of 1975, Anderson Explorations bought the original group's stake for $12 million, an appreciation of thirty-six fold in just six years.

Anderson's first significant success came within a year of "hitting the streets". He came upon some old gas wells that had been drilled by Imperial Oil and capped in the early 1950's at a place called Belloy. Anderson decided that he could make the property commercial so he turned up at the offices of the mighty Imperial and asked if they would sell to him. Since they were at this time shifting their exploration emphasis toward the frontiers they said they would sell the wells and the leases for $422,000. Basically, Imperial thought Anderson was crazy. "They thought to themselves," says Anderson, "here's a guy with a size two hat and 48 inch belt." But Anderson soon went to work to prove them wrong. Today, the value of the Belloy gas field, using a discount factor of 15%, is a staggering $137 million.

To get the money to buy the Belloy field, J.C. headed south in the summer of 1969. At first he knocked on doors unsuccessfully, but eventually was introduced to David Fagin, now president of Rosario, who came up with the cash and started the long relationship between Rosario and Anderson.

Imperial was suitably impressed and has done a number of deals with Anderson since. The symbolic irony, of course, is that in some cases Imperial Oil has to come to Anderson to get a piece of *his* action. In 1978 for example, Imperial put up $7 million for the drilling of 52 wells on Fairweather's properties in order to earn a one-third interest in the lands.

However, there was a much bigger success to come. Anderson became intrigued by the Peace River Arch area of northwest Alberta, north of the presently-booming Elmworth exploration play. Four wells had penetrated the Dunvegan Arch, in the middle of the region, but had found nothing commercial. However, Anderson went over the old well data and massaged it in every way, including the use of computers. In the end, the prospects did not look outstanding, but at this point the classic "hunch" came into effect and Anderson decided to drill. The result was the discovery of one of the ten largest gas fields in Canada, seventeen miles long and four miles wide, with present reserves totalling 1 trillion cubic feet. A very significant factor in financing the deal was Alberta and Southern Gas. Anderson sold them on the deal and they agreed to lend him 1¢, interest free, for every thousand cubic feet of oil he discovered in the field. In the end, that modest agreement led them to lend him $11 million.

In 1976, the deal was done with B.C. Sugar that led to the creation of Fairweather. B.C. Sugar put up $7.5 million to buy a 20% interest in the lands of Anderson Exploration and another $7.5 million for exploration. In return, they got 60% of the equity of Fairweather.

Anderson may now be on the point of moving into the really big time. Early in 1978 he led Fairweather in an unsuccessful takeover attempt on Bridger Petroleum Ltd., which eventually went to Home Oil for almost $60 million. Then, far more ambitiously, the bulky figure of J.C. appeared in the background of the spectacular battle for Husky Oil in the summer of 1978. Anderson had extensive heavy oil interests himself and realized the value of Husky, so as the principal players fought their battle in an arena that stretched from Los Angeles to Calgary to Ottawa to New York, Anderson attempted to sell his own deal to both the Nielsons, who controlled Husky, and to Bob Blair. "I'd done studies on a whole number of companies, and of those of medium size the one where you could really make something happen was Husky," says Anderson. However, in the end the prize went to Bob Blair.

J. C. Anderson has far more money than he will ever need, so why does he carry on working? The answer quite simply, is that for Anderson, as for so many of his counterparts, business is also a pleasure.

"I'm not in this game for the money any more. The money is now only there as a way that other people can keep score on how well you are doing. It's the thrill of the chase, matching your wits against big guys and little guys and always making new deals," he says.

Most oilmen find themselves taking work home, but for Anderson this has taken a new twist. There was once a small gas producing gas well on his farm. He looked at the well data and decided that there just might be something more there. However, the min eral rights to his land are held by the previous owner. "So make sure you don't write anything about this until I've done the deal", he says with a twinkle in his eye.

Not even J. C. Anderson's own backyard is safe from his compelling urge to find petroleum, and do "deals".

Kahanoff: Small is Beautiful

In a town thoroughly imbued with the work ethic, Syd Kahanoff still rates as something extraordinary. It was only the knowledge that he had cancer that forced him to turn his paper worth into hard cash, collecting $55 million personally when the company he started in 1969, Voyager Petroleums, was sold to Calgary real estate dynamo Ralph Scurfield at the end of 1978 for $197 million.

However, Kahanoff set about dealing with cancer the way he set about dealing with his business, and by mid 1979 it seemed that this remarkable man might have actually beaten the most feared of diseases. Three months after the doctor told him he should be dead, he was thinking about re-entering the business.

Kahanoff admits, however, that he had not enjoyed the business so much in recent years. What he didn't like was the administration. It is worth pointing out that administration for Kahanoff meant a staff of less than 40. An eastern manufacturing company with earnings the size of Voyager's ($12.3 million in 1978) might easily employ 5,000 people. But for Kahanoff and so many of his confreres in the oil business, small is beautiful.

Voyager employees know a good deal more about hard work than their counterparts in the East, but they also know more about rewards. All the executives may have been at work by 7.00 am (Kahanoff used to like to hold breakfast meetings at 6.30) but then one-fifth of Voyager's staff are millionaires as a result of the company's generous stock option scheme. "There would have been more if they maintained their stock position," says Kahanoff.

For Kahanoff, money for what it could buy ceased to be the object of the exercise a long time ago. "I wanted to be successful, and success is measured in profits." Even then, however, Kahanoff firmly believes that the only really enjoyable profits are those that are earned. Shortly after he started out so successfully on his own he bought 40 acres of land on what was then the edge of Calgary. The growth of the town ensured him a seven figure profit on the land. "But," he says, "I got no charge out of that, because I didn't deserve it."

Kahanoff was born in Winnipeg, the son of immigrants from Kiev in the Ukraine. Then his father took a job as a fur trader in north Saskatchewan at the tiny town of Mildred, close to Shell

Lake, the scene of some particularly unpleasant axe murders. Kahanoff, the only non-Indian child around, went to the classic one-
room schoolhouse, left when he was 14, and just "kicked around"
until he went to the University of Saskatchewan after the war to
study engineering physics. Kahanoff wanted to do research, but
lacked the money, so he went and got a job building the Interprovincial Pipeline, which remains today, although much expanded,
the main artery for Alberta's oil to the East. He started as a welder's
helper, but then somebody discovered that he was an engineer.
"So they gave me a little red truck and a cut in pay and they made
me an inspector." Kahanoff early on learned the anomalies of
being employed by other people.

After working for a while as a geophysicist in Regina — for no
better reason, he points out, than because his girlfriend was
there — he joined Union Oil. He went with Union to Australia,
and was instrumental in discovering Australia's first significant oil
field. In the mid 1960's, he returned to Calgary just after the major
oil finds at Rainbow Lake in the northwest of the province. Together with a colleague from Amoco, George Longphee, Kahanoff
made the decision to go it alone. Many of Alberta's oilmen started
out in the service end of the business, but few have been so spectacularly successful so quickly as Kahanoff and Longphee. They set
up a geophysical service, Geocan, on the basis of a loan of $50,000
(half of which they immediately lent to another colleague). Introducing revolutionary new techniques that greatly increased the
productivity of their seismic crews, they soon had so much business that their monthly payroll was $375,000! At the end of their
first full year of operation, they showed a net profit of $800,000!
(An observer on a normal crew earned perhaps $600 a month. An
observer on a Geocan crew could pull in $2,500 a month. The crews
were aware that they were the best in the industry and, like most
oilfield workers, were not slow in pointing that out to rival crews.
Once two Geocan crews happened to meet in a local tavern in a
small town. The ensuing fight nearly wrecked the place!)

Kahanoff and Longphee then put their profits into producing
properties and also began looking for oil and gas on their own account. They knew that a gas transmission line was being built
towards the TransCanada system in east central Alberta, so they
set out to find gas within striking distance of the line. They were
enormously successful. Equally important, they made a contract
with TransCanada to sell the giant company all the gas they found
in a huge 4.4 million acre area. Some producers thought that the
contract was not wise because it meant that the gas could not be
sold in possibly more remunerative markets. At that time, with gas
prices below 15¢ an mcf, there were more markets than gas. Kahanoff thought he could foresee a time when the reverse would be
true. He was right. As the price of gas soared, so major new pro-

duction emerged and a shortage of markets followed. However, TransCanada had to pay Kahanoff for everything he produced, whether they could take it immediately or not.

By 1969, Kahanoff had found lots of gas but had effectively run out of money, so he took Voyager public. Many new companies had been floated during the stock market boom that followed the Prudhoe Bay discovery in 1968, but the market had taken a dive by the time that Kahanoff brought Voyager Petroleums public. The boom had broken. Nevertheless, the company raised $4.5 million from its public offering. That money soon ran out and Kahanoff went East to raise some more. His trips to Toronto and Montreal produced, for the time, typical results. He spoke to 32 eastern companies and all turned him down. In the end, and again typically, it was New York who came up with the money in the shape of financial and shipping conglomerate W. R. Grace. Grace invested a total of $6 million and, when Voyager was sold at the end of 1978, pulled out with $45 million.

For the moment, Kahanoff is helping his old friend Scurfield, and Voyager's new president, Earl Joudrie, who headed Ashland Canada before it was taken over by Kaiser Resources in mid 1978, to take over the reins at Voyager.

"I have this dream," he says. "It is to go back and start again with a two-man outfit."

The Siebens — If You Have Land You Don't Have to Be Lucky

In terms of the truly outstanding accumulation of wealth experienced in the past decade, another family name should be added to the gas millionaires. It is that of the Siebens. Along with Kahanoff and the Nielson family at Husky Oil, the Siebens are one of the few groups of individuals that have "realized" the vast amount of wealth they had created through the sale of their company.

In Calgary's obsessively hard-working, wheeler-dealer environment, both Kahanoff and Siebens are outstanding. Kahanoff is recognized as perhaps the hardest-working oilman while Bill Siebens and his father Harold rate as the greatest of land dealers. Their stories are testimonies to the fruits of application in Alberta within the past ten years. But they are also testimonies to the fact that, after the first six noughts, personal wealth ceases to mean very much. Except, perhaps, to create unwanted pressures.

Indeed, Bill Siebens sleeps with a loaded shotgun under his bed. His father Harold is reported to have an atomic fallout shelter in his basement. The Siebens family is obviously a little worried about security. With a very conspicuous joint realization of $160 million from the sale of their company, that isn't surprising.

That huge sum of money represents the achievement of being Canada's outstanding exponents of the art of dealing in oil and gas land.

If the phrase "It's better to be lucky than smart" might appear under any geologist's coat of arms, then the motto: "If you have land you don't have to be lucky" might easily serve for the many dealers in the industry who either accumulate blocks of land for themselves or work out land positions for companies.

A number of companies have been built merely by knowing where the action is, or where it is likely to be next, and then accumulating a land position and waiting for the explorationists to beat a path to their door. Land dealers concentrate on having an excellent nose for exploration trends. They just make sure they know where the action is. It doesn't matter why.

If explorers are the industry's great gamblers, the land dealers are its bookmakers, concentrating on hedging their bets by having a large spread of land and winning, whichever exploration "horse" comes in.

The conventional wisdom around Calgary is that neither Harold nor Bill Siebens ever found a barrel of oil or a whiff of gas. The statement is not true, but it is meant as a compliment. It serves to emphasise that what the Siebens family was good at was not finding petroleum, but at spotting the places where the industry was going to look for it next. They dealt in that ultimately most precious and fixed of commodities, land. What is more, when they sold Siebens Oil & Gas to Jack Gallagher's Dome, it was not the Siebens family selling out, it was just the most recent time they had sold out.

Their attitude to business has always been typically "oil", at once more basic and purer than the machinations of businessmen in eastern boardrooms. Whereas wheeling and dealing in Montreal or Toronto is directed, at the highest levels, toward empire building, toward achieving the pinnacle of power, being the centre of the Establishment, old Harold Siebens never looked at it that way. His wheeling and dealing was always directed to the pursuit of the purest of capitalist aims — turning the Big Profit. Empire building was never his way. Money making most certainly was.

The Siebens family wasn't exactly poor before it entered the oil business. Harold had built up a giant sporting goods store in St. Louis, Missouri in the 1930's and 1940's. He had an extensive catalogue business and supplied equipment to the United States armed forces, a customer that helped him to achieve the position of being the third largest sports supplier in the whole country. But in 1948, Harold decided to sell out and enjoy a little recreation. He bought two trucks and two trailers and announced to the family that it was heading north. Bill Siebens' elder sister was a photographer and part of the scheme was to produce a travelogue about a "family on the move".

The convoy moved off in the spring of 1948 and motored into Alberta as the Leduc and Redwater oil booms were reaching their peak. In Edmonton, they camped out on the grounds of the Legislative Building where, somehow, Premier Ernest Manning got to hear about their adventure. Manning was very keen to get the tourist business going in Alberta, so he was particularly interested when he heard that the Siebens family was involved in making a film. He also wanted to publicize the now-booming oil business.

In the spring of 1948, Frank McMahon's Atlantic Number Three well had blown out of control. Over a six month period it was to disgorge 1.25 million barrels of oil and 10 billion cubic feet of gas. Manning saw a way of killing two promotional birds with one stone, and he arranged for the Siebens family to be taken to view the spectacularly angry gusher — Bill remembers having his boots checked for any nails that might make a spark and ignite the well. Pictures of the phenomenon duly taken, Manning in return helped the family obtain permits to become the first group of civilians to travel up the Alaska Highway after the war. Harold and his clan fished all the way up the highway and hunted on the way down, although Bill and his younger sister had to miss the return journey to go back to school.

The remainder of the family drove all the way down to California before concluding their odyssey, but Harold had been so impressed by the potential of what he had seen in Alberta, that soon afterwards he returned to Calgary and set up an office in the Palliser opposite the Sun Room, where imported U.S. oilmen did a lot of entertaining and were eventually to form the basis of the Petroleum Club. Harold was not completely ignorant of the oil business. While still in St. Louis he had formed a syndicate of businessmen to drill on some acreage held by his father and himself. The hole had been dry but Harold had made a critical observation. The key to financial success lay not in drilling the hole, but in owning the land. That was to be the basis of his business philosophy in Canada, and it was to prove spectacularly successful.

Early in 1950, Harold set up Alberta Leaseholds Ltd. and began to pick up petroleum and natural gas leases, primarily in Alberta. The cost of these acquisitions was a relatively modest $50,000. However, toward the end of the following year, when Harold had built up some 400,000 acres, he sold out for a cool $1 million to Bailey Selburn Oil & Gas Ltd., which was ultimately to be taken over by Pacific Petroleums.

Harold decided to do it again. Another company, Alberta Minerals Ltd., was formed, and within a year Harold had picked up a further 1 million acres at nominal cost. In April, 1952, he sold out to Pathfinder Petroleums, ultimately to become part of Canadian Industrial Gas & Oil Ltd. which in turn formed most of Norcen Energy Resources, for $1.15 million.

Not wishing to change a winning formula, Harold then did it once more. In March, 1954, he set up two companies, Siebens Minerals Ltd. and Siebens Oil Producers Ltd. This time the process of the accumulation of low cost acreage took a little longer, but late in 1957, Fargo Oils Ltd. paid a weightier $3.4 million for the land spread, with Siebens retaining a gross overriding royalty. (Fargo went on to be absorbed by Canadian Reserve Oil and Gas Ltd.)

Earlier in 1957, as his next "vehicle", Siebens had formed Siebens Leaseholds Ltd. The following eight years were to be slow ones for the industry, coming between the original Pembina field in 1954 and the discovery of Rainbow in 1964. The sell-out of Siebens Leaseholds can perhaps be considered the only "bad" deal Harold ever did, for two weeks after the company had been sold to Canadian Export Gas and Oil Ltd. in 1965 for $1.1 million, Banff Oil made the discovery of the Rainbow field on lands just a spitting distance away from 1.5 million acres of the land Siebens had given up. Siebens had not actually signed the agreement when the discovery was made, but hands had been shaken, and that was what counted in the oil industry.

While Harold had been very quickly getting his feet wet in the land-dealing business in the early 1950's, Bill had been picking up a degree in petroleum engineering from the University of Oklahoma. He had then joined the United States Air Force. While flying, Bill had achieved a certain heroic status by being the first pilot to ever land a fighter with a jammed undercarriage at night. He could have baled out but claims that he was too "frightened."

When, in 1959, having made far more money than anybody could hope to do justice to in one lifetime, Harold decided to retire to E. P. Taylor's millionaires' subdivision at Lyford Cay, Bill flew into Canada to take over.

The company that was sold at the end of 1978, Siebens Oil & Gas Ltd., was formed in 1965, by which time Bill had firmly taken over the reins. Bill proved to be every bit as adept as his father at spotting key acreage before it became "hot", but the company also started moving into the exploration business for the first time. Landholding, however, remained the focus of corporate attention. At the end of the 1960's, there was a massive shift of emphasis in the industry towards the frontier areas. The huge find at Prudhoe Bay in Alaska led to a rush for land in the Arctic Islands, the Mackenzie Delta and the Beaufort Sea. And who did the majors find when they got there? Why, of course it was Siebens Oil & Gas.

In January, 1970, Siebens decided to go public and sold just 18% of its equity for $10 million. The company's frontier land holdings were huge. Panarctic Oils Ltd. had made finds in the Arctic Islands, Imperial Oil had struck significant amounts of gas in the Mackenzie Delta and Mobil had had some success off the east coast, so it seemed that the frontiers were the shape of things to come. In the event, it did not turn out that way, at least immediately, but that created little problem for Siebens, who had merely been sitting on cheaply acquired acreage, waiting for larger companies to come to him.

Bill Siebens also moved enthusiastically with the international trend in the industry during the early 1970's, picking up interests from Sicily to South Vietnam, Ethiopia to the North Sea. However, in 1973 he acquired possibly his biggest break, and it came literally to his doorstep with a visit from executives of the Hudson's Bay Company, who were looking for a small exploration company into which they could inject their very sizeable land holdings.

Hudson's Bay had 4.5 million acres of mineral rights in the three western provinces left over from the lands granted to them under their original charter. The lands were held by Hudson's Bay Co. Resources, which operated with a skeleton staff. Under changes in the tax rules, Hudson's Bay was forced either to build up its staff and become an active explorer to retain its royalty income, or else find someone else to do it. They looked at a number of companies but eventually decided on Siebens, who received mineral ownership of the 4.5 million acres in return for 2.8 million shares. Thus Siebens acquired one of the most powerful land positions in western Canada, and the Hudson's Bay Company one of its most valuable shareholdings.

Meanwhile, in the spring of 1974, Siebens was a partner in drilling three wells in the North Sea, and became involved in Abu Dhabi. The North Sea was providing some disappointments, but in 1975, with a typically Siebens-like move, Bill managed an end run around no less an entity than the British Government. Britain had welcomed foreign capital into the North Sea, but Siebens managed to raise the money for his drilling activities in England! Also, in 1976 it sold half its interests in the North Sea Brae Block to Marathon in return for the recovery of *all* its expenditures.

Bill Siebens' sense of international adventure seemed far out of proportion to the still relatively modest size of the company. He even dared to move into the preserve of "big oil" in the Middle East, where the company drilled offshore at the island of Socotra, a still-medieval place south of the Saudi Arabian peninsula. There the inhabitants, many of them the descendants of shipwrecked travellers, still live in the most primitive conditions. Siebens had spotted a giant anomaly south of the island that looked as if it might echo the huge pools that lay beneath the Saudi desert. Drilling proved disappointing, but failed to dent Bill's drive.

It seemed at one time as if Bill Siebens, a tough-looking, stocky, bald-headed man, might have ambitions to break the circle of constant purchase and re-sale in another attempt to build the "Great Canadian Oil Company". But in the end, it seems, the pressure to sell came both from old Harold and from the Hudson's Bay Company, each of which held 34.8% of the company to Bill's 10.9%. With land prices surging, the potential market value of the company was obviously something that the larger shareholders just couldn't resist.

In 1978, Siebens was at last bought out by a wheeler-dealer of a class to whom perhaps even Bill and Harold Siebens would bow, Jack Gallagher, head of Dome Petroleum.

The takeover was far from simple, and involved an intricate mesh of tax considerations and the use of an intermediary, Canpar, a subsidiary of the CN Pension Fund, to pull it off. Effectively, Canpar bought the shares of Siebens while Dome purchased the assets of Siebens from Canpar. But the simple end of the deal for Bill and Harold Siebens was that they got the money. Almost $40 million went to Bill and $120 million to old Harold.

Publicizing, even enjoying, their wealth seems to be quite another thing for the Siebens. Harold takes comfort in his bomb shelter and one of his major preoccupations early in 1979 was reported to be supervision of the compost heap at the local Bahamian golf club! Modest pleasures indeed. Bill and his wife have developed a great concern about kidnap and extortion, hence the shotgun and other security precautions, and they are reported to indulge in little conspicuous consumption.

Indeed, Mrs. Siebens still heads for "Bay Days" bargains, as she always has. That isn't meanness, it's just a philosophy of life.

Meanwhile, in early 1979, Bill Siebens, facing an enormous tax bill, was gearing up to put that money the only place he can keep it — and also where he is indisputably best at keeping it — back in the ground. Bill Siebens, inevitably, was getting ready to start all over again.

Rostoker and Gillespie: A Little Wistful

As a sidelight to Siebens' spectacular success, it is perhaps worth mentioning a couple of men who looked on rather wistfully when Siebens Oil & Gas was sold. The men were George Rostoker and Roy Gillespie, whose company, Transalta, had been a 50-50 partner in many of the Siebens deals. Because a third partner, Sioma Schiff had not wanted to go public, they finished up selling out their company for a "mere" $6 million to Dome Petroleum in the early 1970's. They had subsequently all moved out of the business. However, the sight of what was happening to the oil industry in 1978 was just too much for them and they formed a new company, Cherokee, and took it public in early 1979.

Rostoker, a tiny, white-haired man with penetrating blue eyes, looking like a younger Dr. Armand Hammer, explains, with a twinkle in his eyes, how he got into the oil business. He left the family textile business in France in 1951 and headed for Canada with his "fortune" of $25,000. Reaching Montreal, he contacted a friend who worked for a stockbroker. The "friend" sat him beside a stock exchange tape machine. There, indulging his natural gambling instincts, his fortune fast began to disappear. Then he fell in with another investment advisor who persuaded him to put money into land deals in Calgary. It was to clear up the ensuing mess that he at last found himself in the bustling little town that was still enjoying the benefits of the post-Leduc boom.

In Calgary he teamed up with Schiff, an urbane "investor" who was interested in making money out of oil but much preferred to spend his time in London or New York in more cultural pursuits. They invited Gillespie to join them because, although he didn't have any money, they liked his approach to dealing.

Rostoker says that he soon learned that the thing to do was to take options on as much prospective acreage as possible rather than tying up money in buying it. But he waxes almost lyrical about the joys of parlaying a quarter section of land (160 acres) into 50,000 acres by an astute series of deals. For him, that was the real pleasure of the business.

Their company became involved in a great many fifty-fifty deals with Siebens, and Rostoker admits that: "We always let Bill do the dealing." However, at the beginning of the 1970's there was that parting of the ways that eventually left Bill and Harold Siebens with $160 million, while the Transalta trio had to be content with their paltry $6 million. The regret of Rostoker and Gillespie is not so much that they missed out on all that money, but that when they withdrew from the business in the mid 1970's, they missed out on all that *dealing*. Now they are coming back to put that straight.

16 | Ringing Out the Good News: The Financial Boom

*Of course, relatively few investors actually dab-
bled in the stock. However, for every one who did
buy Bonanza, there were a thousand who heard
the tale and looked on in awe, mentally multiplying their modest nesteggs into yachts, furs, diamonds, or just security. Now if only they could
grab a stock like that.*

Money shows a number of similarities to petroleum. It flows
freely from one place to another, it is easily transported, and it has
a pervasive grip on the minds of men. However, under the right
conditions, it is a great deal easier to find. Whereas the actual effort
necessary to release the pressurized genie, petroleum — a pricking
of his rock enclosure — is a relatively simple one, much greater
flows of hard cash can be released by the promise of a single word:
profit.

Oil and gas have always offered the potential of great profit because they can be found in huge amounts with a relatively small
expenditure. That is, if you are lucky. Thus when new fields are
found, such as Elmworth and West Pembina, money rushes
towards them. However the great post-OPEC boom was also
caused significantly because the economic rules of the game were
changed. It now became profitable to search out smaller, less powerful genies than before, genies that in many cases, like undersized
fish, had been "thrown back".

Elmworth and West Pembina did offer outstanding profit potential, as indicated by the share price surge of their participants, the
record prices paid for land and the huge amount of exploration activity surrounding them. But what OPEC did more significantly
was to spread the boom all over the province of Alberta.

Big profits are pursued inevitably by big money, but when the
long term potential of those profits is also large, then money's
human servants dutifully pack and follow in its wake. In the past
few years, Calgary has seen an unprecedented inflow of bankers,
investment dealers, security analysts, underwriters and financial
advisers. The city, and the province as a whole, has undergone a
massive uprating of its status in the financial world.

Before the boom, the heads of western oil companies had to trek east to plead their case within the bastions of the big five banks or before the sharp-eyed, financial brains of Bay Street. Now the bankers and the investment dealers come, accompanied by huge lines of credit, to visit their western customers. In many cases, senior personnel have been moved permanently to Calgary, in recognition that the town is destined to take over, indeed may have already taken over, as the financial capital of the West, second only to Toronto in all of Canada.

Moreover, the West, typically, soon injected its own brand of dynamism, and enthusiasm, into the rather more staid ways of the eastern financiers. The symbol of that different approach was a bell that appeared in downtown Calgary during the hectic days of late 1977.

Like any wealthy group, the financial community tends not to publicize its "killings". Indeed, it often seems to prefer to emphasize its misfortunes. The classic example of the latter is the doleful Lutine Bell, which stands in the giant insurance underwriting syndicate, Lloyds of London, and is rung whenever a major disaster occurs.

However, even for the traditionally low profile Canadian financial community, it was particularly hard not to express joy in the bonanza that came its way as a result of the post-OPEC western oil boom. Indeed, downtown Calgary developed a kind of Lutine Bell-in-reverse, a visible, and audible, symbol that business had never been so profitable.

Rob Peters, head of one of Calgary's fastest growing small investment dealers, Peters & Co., had decided, in typically forthright western fashion, to take a higher profile and ring out the *good* news: literally.

So he, too, went out and bought himself a bell, mounted it outside his small, bustling downtown office on Fourth Avenue and whenever he did a block share trade, he went out and rang it. The whole idea was a little tongue-in-cheek, but Peters decided that a little publicity wasn't bad for business either.

By the end of 1977, when West Pembina oil fever had a firm grip of Canadian investors, the bell was resounding around downtown Calgary as often as 10 times a day.

The bell may no longer be rung (only because it became a little embarrassing) but a more pervasive sound has taken over. It is the din of construction. Towering temples to the genie oil and the greater Mammon, money, began to take shape in downtown Calgary at an accelerating pace. By 1978, building permits in the city of Calgary had reached a staggering $1 billion, as oil companies big and small beefed up their operations, new oil companies were created, and the servants of money sought premises to carry out their business.

Sizable new reserves of both oil and gas have been found in the past few years in Alberta, but the new flow of hydrocarbons out of the ground has been but a trickle compared with the massive gushers of money trying to find their way into the province.

The greatest source of funds for new activity was generated by the swelling coffers of the oil companies themselves. Aided by rocketing prices for their oil and gas, their production income soared. However, for them, the fiscal catch 22 was that, under more "generous" taxation incentives, the only way they could keep most of their money was to reinvest it. It was rather like the monkey who grabbed for the fruit in a jar but then found that the mouth of the jar wasn't big enough for him to withdraw his hand. The only way for him to retain the fruit was to keep his hand in the jar. For the oil companies, the only way to retain most of their profits was to return them to the ground.

Tax Pornography

The reinvestment of profits has provided the largest source of funds for Alberta's petroleum boom, but the industry has found enormous funds from a number of other sources. Indeed, the first significant amount of money for the great oil and gas investment party came from a somewhat unlikely quarter: West Germany.

The Germans have always held a misty vision of the United States' northern neighbour as a country of virtually limitless space, resources and opportunities. For West Germany, a country in which fear of inflation amounts to a national paranoia, investments in land and resources — the ultimate "real" basis of value — have always held particular attractions. However, in the early 1970's investment opportunities became available to the Germans that were indeed unprecedented.

The Germans had a phrase for it. They called it "tax pornography", a financial deal so generous that it had a trace of fiscal obscenity. And yet this loophole enabled perhaps $400 million of German money to be invested in the Canadian oil industry between 1973 and 1979, thus providing one of the earliest impetuses for the boom. When the federal-provincial dispute was at its murkiest, West German investors became "the only bank in town."

Financial brains roam the jungles of international tax law like predatory creatures, looking for slow-footed loopholes to leap upon and devour. Early in the 1970's, a Munich-based investment manager, then only in his late 20's, discovered such a juicy creature. The man's name was Klaus Hebbern, and what he saw was to provide enormous funds for a bevy of small Canadian oil companies, help spawn a great many more companies and, incidentally, make him extremely wealthy. "Hebbern's harem" embraces some of the brightest and best of the small Canadian oil companies. Hebbern has also had a hand in some of the more significant deals of the past few years. He funneled funds into Amalgamated Bonanza when it was carrying out the drilling in Texas and was to cause its share price to rocket, and he took a 10% interest in the fledgling Canadian Hunter before the company became a phenomenon of the post-OPEC oil boom.

What Hebbern discovered was that, under Germany's somewhat loose tax laws, investors could claim anything up to 250% write-offs for investment in drilling for oil and gas, that is, for every $100 they invested, they could write $250 off against taxable income — tax pornography indeed. What it effectively meant was that the West German government was paying for all the drilling and giving the lawyers and doctors who "invested" a premium on top of that.

German investment prospectuses tend to incorporate a good deal more sales pitch than their North American counterparts, in some cases looking more like holiday brochures than a balanced appeal to investors. Once Hebbern had established that such deals could be done, prospectuses promising "the deal of the century" and displaying vistas of "Oil in the West" started proliferating from the group who followed his lead. But with the sort of write-offs they were promising, the glossy sell was hardly necessary.

Hebbern, smooth, sleek and superior, became interested in Canadian oil companies while following their activities in the North Sea. The first Canadian company into which he funnelled German drilling fund money was the highly successful Skye Resources, during the period when youthful whizz-kid Bob Lamond was its chief geologist. When Lamond decided to go out on his own, Hebbern put him in touch with another young Teutonic *eminence grise*, Rudi Siegert, who was also to go on to play a significant role in funding a number of companies. Hebbern had another colleague, Dr. Helmut Roeschinger, who also started chanelling money into the country. Then the German-based DEB group arrived, represented by Don Copeland and Dr. Richard Bowens, and, as a final key player among the principals, Jurgen Hanne, who brought eager and claustrophobic cash out of West Berlin to the wide open spaces of the West.

What some of the Germans sought was not only to provide an investment outlet, but also to take a piece of the equity in each of the companies for which they provided funds. The result was that Hebbern and Siegert finished up not only providing funds for companies but also in owning siginficant equity positions in them.

Some of Calgary's brightest young geologists today sit in brand new offices as the heads of their own companies as a result of the cash ferried in by men like Hebbern. He and Roeschinger put up money for Petromark and Bluesky, run by Doug Hunter, which in turn puts money the way of companies like Focus run by Uldis Upitis, and Conuco, bought out in mid 1979 by Brinco. They have also provided drilling funds for companies like Coseka and Peyto as well as for more spectacular success stories such as Amalgamated Bonanza and Canadian Hunter.

By far their biggest individual investment is in Canadian Hunter. Hebbern first met John Masters, Hunter's president, through contacts at brokerage house Walwyn Stodgell. Hebbern was so impressed by Masters that he tried hard to negotiate a deal. However, Masters and he could not come to terms. In the end, Hebbern went to Hunter's main backer, Alf Powis at Noranda, to get a piece of the action, and eventually came away with 10% for a commitment to spend $28 million. The shrewdness of this investment is clearly demonstrated by the fact that Imperial Oil was willing to commit $179 million late in 1978 to earn 15% of Canadian Hunter's acreage. Hebbern has since then committed to raise another $20 million for Canadian Hunter.

Rudi Siegert was also originally brought into Canada through Hebbern to invest in Czar, one of the most spectacular success stories in recent years. Siegert went on to form a very lucrative relationship with Bob Lamond, setting up new companies with personnel found by Lamond and money found by himself. As a result, Siegert not only provided funds for Czar, and the companies he subsequently formed with Lamond, Focus, Tristar and Orbit, but he also gained significant chunks of their equity.

Hanne provided funds for another two small companies that enjoyed enormous success in early 1979, Westfort and Delta, run by colleagues Paul Conroy and Roger Bethel, respectively an Irish ex-architect and a Welsh geologist.

In the end, tax pornography became too much even for the highly liberal West German government, so, deciding it had to step in to guard its fiscal morals (and stop being an involuntary investor in oil drilling in Alberta) it challenged the oil investment deals in the courts.

Following radical financial censorship of the more bizarre examples of exploitation of the West German tax system, perhaps the great days of West German oil investment had ended by 1979. Nevertheless, that money, via "tax pornography" played a significant part in fueling the great Alberta oil boom.

Man on the Move

German funds can take some of the credit for giving a start to some of Calgary's brightest and most technically gifted entrepre neurs. Perhaps the most outstanding success story among his peer group is Bob Lamond, a geologist of outstanding ability who has established an even more impressive talent for high finance and corporate promotion.

Conversation with Bob Lamond tends to take place in 25 second bursts, as he arranges appointments, fixes up trips to Munich or Zurich, consults with business associates, or simply leaps up and runs out of the room, a shining lightbulb just having appeared above his head.

Lamond, just 35 years old in 1979, may not yet have reached the upper echelons of the corporate elite, but his rate of acceleration towards the really big time is almost frightening. Already clearly established as a first-rate geologist — one of the magical 5% whose ideas carry the industry along — he has proved in the past couple of years to be even more successful as a stock promoter.

Totally unselfconscious about his wealth, he admitted, early in 1979, to being worth "somewhere between $12 and $15 million". He didn't know because he hadn't stopped lately to count. What was perhaps more important, the figure wasn't likely to stand still for too long. Lamond, president of Czar Resources Ltd. and major shareholder in a whole flock of companies that he has been instrumental in setting up with German money, is a man on the move.

Lamond's career in the Canadian oil industry started, perhaps surprisingly, one day in 1965 at the University of Edinburgh, when a man named Barnie Clare walked into a laboratory where Lamond was working and offered him a job as a geologist with Imperial Oil. The Rainbow field had just been discovered in northwest Alberta, and Imperial found itself short of geologists, as did most companies every time a major new field was discovered.

Lamond at first was not very interested. He had been planning to move on to do a Ph.D at either Edinburgh or London in Paleontology. However, his parents encouraged him to seize the opportunity, so he took both the airline ticket and the advance offered by Clare, and, after a month's holiday in Berlin, headed for his "new life" in Alberta.

Clare returned from his recruiting drive with a good haul from Britain's post-war baby boom. What was more, most of them, like Lamond, were unusually short in stature. The joke went around that Clare had gone over to Europe and purchased geologists "by the pound".

Within weeks of arriving in Calgary, Lamond found himself, in his own words, "sitting in the weeds with a bunch of Limeys and Welshmen", the rest of Clare's British haul. What Imperial wanted the young geologists for was to "sit" wells, that is, examine rock cuttings as they were brought up by the drilling mud from thousands of feet below ground. It was one of the lowest of technical jobs but was indispensable experience for the aspiring oilman.

Lamond worked for Imperial for three years, but began to feel stifled by the inevitable bureaucratization of such a large organization. Moreover, the carefully planned ascent through the corporate hierarchy to the upper echelons of the company was too slow a route to an objective that Lamond was not sure that he coveted anyway.

Lamond was a case study of how individual brilliance can be stifled in large organizations. Basically an untidy person, it irked him that every night he had to wrap all his maps up and then lock them in a vault, only to have to get them all out again in the morning. The emphasis was on conformity rather than on results. Imperial's committee approach tended to obfuscate who did what. There was no immediate reward for individual sparks of brilliance. Says Lamond: "I found myself a middle of the road lazy person becoming a totally lazy person. I found that I could do everything quickly and I was turning into a drone."

The time had come to move on.

The young Scotsman phoned the Manpower department in Calgary and said he would like to work for a medium-sized American company. He was sent to Mesa Petroleum and hired on the spot. However, he was there only two months when one of Mesa's vice-presidents, Frank Podpechan — who had been an independent oilman in the United States before joining Mesa and being sent up to organize the Canadian operation — suggested that they move out and start their own oil company. Thus was born the subsequently extremely successful Skye Resources. Over the following five years, during which he was Skye's chief geologist, Lamond discovered that he really did have a talent for finding oil and gas. Three quarters of the wells he drilled produced commercial finds — a remarkable success ratio. However, after five years, having established that he could find oil and seeing that financing didn't look that difficult, he decided to go out on his own.

Some of the funding for Skye had come from Klaus Hebbern, so Lamond asked the smooth young German stockbroker if there was any chance of funding a venture with Lamond at its head. Hebbern was enthusiastic, but thought there might be some conflict with Skye, so he introduced Lamond to another German financier who was to spend a great deal of time in subsequent years shuttling between Germany and Calgary, Rudi Siegert.

Czar Resources was incorporated as a private Alberta company on April 11, 1974. It went public on July 5, 1975 and was listed for trading on the Alberta Stock Exchange in April of 1976. On May 1, 1979 it started trading on the Toronto Stock Exchange. Between its first trade on the ASE and the middle of 1979, the shares increased thirty times in value as Lamond continued his exploration success and the Germans kept on coming up with the money, mainly through the Siegert-run Copetrex drilling fund. Copetrex put up the original $1.8 million grubstake for Lamond and by mid 1978 had come up with five more tranches of money. Lamond, always quick to catch on to a good idea, soon organized his own drilling fund, Aurora Energy Fund, which in late 1978 was organizing the sale of its third set of investment units.

He was showing the trait that separates the truly great oilmen from the rest. He was not only good at finding oil, he was even better at finding money.

A United States subsidiary was set up as another recipient for German drilling money.

Lamond's corporate strategy was typical of the small oil company. The top priority is to find oil or gas for production in order to gain cash flow, a record of success, and, above all, credibility. So he has concentrated his efforts in two main established exploration areas: Alberta south of Edmonton to the United States border, and northeast British Columbia. So far he has been very successful.

Lamond is deeply interested in business per se. When he saw Klaus Hebbern running around Calgary, founding oil companies and funding them, he began to wonder why he couldn't do the same. Soon, he discovered an activity even more lucrative, and much more certain, than finding oil. Getting together skilled teams of young geologists, he put them in touch with German drilling money, then just sat back and took a piece of the equity action.

Typically, Lamond makes no claims for the efforts involved in setting up these companies. There is very little. However, when he has introduced the Canadian geologists to German investors, he has emerged in most cases with 20% of the new company. Once he has picked the geologists and made the introductions, he takes no further part in the running of any of the companies, except perhaps to guarantee loans. He just enjoys his equity position.

The first company he helped to start was Focus Resources Ltd. Then he formed Orbit Oil & Gas Ltd., then Tristar, Tiber and Penn Energy. In all cases, he used the same basic technique. To run Focus, he got an old friend and geologist of Imperial vintage, Uldis Upitis; to head Orbit, he picked a young geologist out of Dome Petroleum, George Ongyerth.

However, the facility with which Lamond has pulled off these deals has created a certain resentment among those now heading the companies, such as Upitis. Meanwhile his former partner at Czar, Verne Lindberg, also departed the company under strained circumstances. Lamond seems to have trodden on a few toes in the process of being in a great corporate hurry.

But Lamond's pugnacity is somehow very likeable. Short and stocky, with snub features, broken teeth and reddish crinkly hair, he looks like the prototype of the fighting Scotsman. Nevertheless, he is perhaps one of the most intellectual members of the oil community. His hobbies include collecting antiquarian books and archeology; one of his heroes is Heinrich Schliemann, discoverer of the City of Troy.

Lamond comes from farming stock near Angus in Scotland,

where his father was the chief horticultural officer for the Civil Service. He went to one of Scotland's best private schools, Heriots, before going on to study geology at the University of Edinburgh.

Lamond might easily have finished up putting dinosaur bones together as a paleontologist. Instead he seems to have found his true vocation first in piecing together geological exploration plays and now in assembling larger and larger financial deals. There is a certain symmetry in all these activities, erecting something large from small pieces, and Lamond has demonstrated not only skill, but enormous enthusiasm for all of them. Now it's just a matter of waiting to see how large Lamond's ultimate creation will be.

Lamond has no illusions about his relative clout in the oil industry as a whole. He knows that he is still too small to become involved in a major exploration activity. "When one of those plays like West Pembina come along we have to head for the hills. We know that we'll be million-dollared to death".

However, Lamond obviously has the talent to make the big time. His self-confidence is enormous, but somehow it has avoided shading into self-importance. Nevertheless, he has been known to mouth what is perhaps the greatest geological heresy, denying a tenet incanted by most geologists with a roll of the eyes towards the heavens. "Luck," he says, "is a big myth."

Such sentiments might be considered an invitation to the wrath of the gods, but the prospect doesn't worry the smiling Lamond too much. Moreover, it seems uncertain whether even the mighty oil industry will be able to hold him for too long. Early in 1979, he spread his wings by offering a new tax-sheltered fund for investment in gold through his Aurora Energy Fund.

Although he has rubbed many associates the wrong way, Lamond also has a remarkable way with all types of people. He seems just as at home in the meticulously furnished financial offices of Munich and Zurich as he does drinking beer in his shirtsleeves at home with a group of Czar employees.

However, the only thing that might give him away in the latter set of circumstances would be the home itself, an enormous million dollar mansion in Mount Royal built by one of Calgary's earliest and most successful petroleum explorers, Eugene Marius Coste.

Lamond is a man with no paranoia about wealth or how to spend it. He obviously enjoys both what he does and its financial fruits. "Things", he says, "are just beginning to become really fun".

Drilling for Money

For the young Scotsman, the drying up of German drilling money which had given him his start presented no great problem.

It merely meant that he had to seek funds elsewhere. Fortunately, as the German tax door began to close, another door, this time in Canada, began to open. The new source of drilling funds promised an even greater inflow of cash to an already booming industry.

Death may still be certain, but the taxes part of life's supposed twin inevitabilities has been placed in some doubt in recent years. The wealthy have always been prepared to pay large sums of money to specialists for seeking ways to avoid rendering unto Caesar, but it took no predatory tax genius to spot the potential of the legislation relating to personal investment in oil and gas exploration introduced in Canada in the 1976 budget. For many years, American investors had had the advantage over their Canadian counterparts of being able to write off 100% of the cost of oil and gas exploration. Of course, with the cost of a single conventional well in some cases running beyond $1 million, very few individuals could, or wanted to, go out and drill a single "glory hole". However, a much more attractive proposition was to become part of an exploration syndicate, known as a "drilling fund". Drilling funds had for many years been big business in the United States, providing about 6% of annual exploration expenditures, but until 100% write-offs were available for Canadians in 1976, because of the government's desire to put as much money as possible into making Canada energy self-sufficient, there had been little market for drilling funds in Canada.

Once the legislation was introduced, however, the Canadian investment community took after drilling funds like dogs after a car. At first, however, their problem was rather similar to that of the ambitious canine if he caught his prey; just what would he do with it! The tax provisions might be superficially generous, but they were far from simple, so considerable fiscal wrestling with the authorities was necessary before funds really started to take off.

The investment dealers could see a whole army of doctors, dentists and lawyers with more disposable income than they knew what to do with, a petroleum industry begging for funds, and highly desirable write-offs (and commissions for themselves) in the middle; it was only a matter of time before the link was made. The legislation relating to the generous write-offs was due to end in June 1979; however, it was extended to 1981 by the outgoing Liberal government, and by mid 1979 the funds were really beginning to take off.

All sorts of permutations and combinations of features were being incorporated to make the funds as attractive as possible, but the main thing was that investor suspicion had been overcome. Investors were quickly won over and industry sources estimate that as much as $300 million might be raised in 1979 and perhaps as much as $500 million in 1980. What is more, due to another piece of legislation in 1977 giving accelerated allowances for drilling in the

Beaufort Sea of well over 100%, Canada even had its own somewhat milder form of "tax pornography". If an investor was in a
sufficiently high tax bracket, and invested in one of the growing
Beaufort Sea funds, sponsored by the ever-innovative Dome Petroleum, then he could actually make a net return on his investment even if Dome drilled dry holes!

The Beaufort Sea drilling provisions made Dome the prime recipient for drilling funds in Canada, with more than $200 million
committed to Beaufort Sea drilling by early 1979. What was offered
to investors in terms of acreage in return for their massive investments was more than modest. However, investors didn't care because in many cases they stood to gain *whatever* Dome either found
or didn't find in the murky depths north of the Mackenzie Delta.
Their satisfaction was to come with their next tax return. The possibility of Dome making a big find, and producing it, represented
merely some distant icing on the cake. For Dome it represented additional costless funds to test their geological theories. For the government, it spurred the programme of finding out Canada's frontier geological potential.

Drilling funds certainly fitted into the means of doing business
favoured by all oilmen and practiced most successfully by Jack Gallagher: the method has the initials OPM, "other peoples' money".

But the greatest volume of money changing hands around the
growing oil boom of the mid 1970's was in the stock markets. Starting in 1977, building through 1978 and moving into 1979, almost
everybody who knew anything about the stock market decided
that the place to be was in oil shares.

The Biggest Boom

In the first half of 1979, Canadian stock markets outperformed
those of every other major country. While the Dow Jones Industrial
Index in New York jerked sideways in an agony of indecision, London markets faltered and the Tokyo Exchange wondered whether
to go up or down, the Toronto Stock Exchange soared. In June the
TSE 300 reached an all-time record of 1,619.76. The group of shares
that stood in the vanguard of this unprecedented rise were the
Canadian oil stocks.

Petroleum shares provided the momentum for the greatest sus-
tained stock market boom in Canadian history. In the first half of
1979, share prices rose to all time highs on Canada's stock markets
as an unprecedented number of shares changed hands. In that six
month period, almost $500 worth of shares were traded for each
man, woman and child in Canada, a total of more than $10 bil-
lion.

In less than five years there had been a magical transformation. At the end of 1974, Canadian oil shares emerged from a financial bloodbath. The federal-provincial dispute over the spoils of OPEC had created a bleak investment environment. However, by Christmas, 1974, both parties had pulled back. Not only were major exploration incentives introduced, but the federal government decided that Canadian domestic oil prices would have to move to world levels. Then they decided that gas, too, should move toward the equivalent of international oil prices (although there was no significant international market in gas). The main motive force behind previous stock market booms had always been primarily speculation. News had, in particular, always been a poor substitute for rumour in the market for petroleum shares. But the situation after 1974 was quite different. The underpinning for the boom was that the oil and gas reserves that all petroleum companies held in the ground suddenly had their value multiplied. It was as if all the depositors in a certain bank had suddenly been told, "for every dollar you have invested here, we will give you another five dollars." For gas, whose value showed an even more spectacular increase, it was as if the fairy godmother had said, "I will turn every one dollar into 10." The fairy godmother, once again, was OPEC. That is not to say that the market was without its speculative element.

At the beginning of 1975, the oil and gas producers' share index stood just above 600, having dived a disastrous 200 points in the closing weeks of 1974. However, it recovered all this lost ground and more during 1975, finishing the year at around 1,000. It moved ahead once more in 1976, standing close to 1,300 by Christmas. By mid 1977, it had risen again to 1,500 and stock market analysts began to get nervous about a downward "correction".

But they hadn't seen anything yet. It all really started with a company called, appropriately, Amalgamated Bonanza.

A Star Is Born

Bonanza proved to be the precursor of a mammoth firework display that delighted oil and gas investors for well over two years. Like all good pyrotechnics, the show revealed not only a dazzling array of glittering objects, in this case shares, shooting skywards. It also provided lots of noise, in fact booms; the West Pembina boom, the Elmworth boom, the Beaufort Sea boom, and a set piece — taking the form of a bomb-burst — that went under the name of "takeover fever".

But Amalgamated Bonanza was the first stock to ignite the interests of the general investing public. In 1977 it became the darling of the Canadian stock market. The trading in its shares, for a company of its size, was phenomenal. During 1977, more than $140

million worth of its stock was bought and sold, making it the third
most heavily traded oil company on the Toronto Stock Exchange. It traded 40% more volume than the mighty Imperial Oil, which ploughed along like an ugly dinosaur. Bonanza, by contrast, soared and its shares rose from $7 at the beginning of the year to almost $50 by the end.

Of course, relatively few investors actually dabbled in the stock. However, for every one who did buy Bonanza, there were a thousand who heard the tale and looked on in awe, mentally multiplying their modest nesteggs into yachts, furs, diamonds, or just security. Now if only they could grab a stock like that. The urge for the quick killing in oil was being stirred in the brains of investors, both large and small. The story was all in the name.

Paradoxically, however, Amalgamated Bonanza's success had very little to do with Canada. It was indeed a Canadian-based company, but it ultimately struck its motherload midway between Houston and Dallas, Texas, in the historic heartland of North America's first really gigantic oilfinds.

Like the Elmworth gas play in Alberta, the significance of the find that was to cause Bonanza to soar was not acknowledged at first. The company discovered a reasonable flow of oil in a formation known as the Woodbine Sands in Brazos County, Texas. However, step-out drilling revealed that the field was a large one. The more they stepped out from the original discovery, the more oil they found. It seemed to be everywhere. So they followed the typical route of snapping up as much land as they could, and pretty soon found themselves worth a lot of money. The gusher may still be the symbolic orgasm of oil discovery, but long lasting satisfaction comes with the realization that the source is a big one. Amalgamated Bonanza had found the big one.

By the end of 1977, Bonanza, a company that had three years before been worth $3 million, had a market value of $180 million. Its shares had risen seven-fold in twelve months to $50, and all shareholders were looking back on tremendous gains.

The man looking back on the biggest gain of all was the individual who organized the original investment in Bonanza, Dr. Frank Natoros. Natoros had been a wealthy optometrist operating in British Columbia who held property in downtown Calgary. It was through these interests that he was introduced to oil investment. By the end of 1977, Natoros' stake in Bonanza was worth a mind-boggling $34 million.

Natoros had by this time become far too rich to afford to live in Canada. A small, bald man in his late 40's, Natoros now spends his time between a ranch in upstate New York, a house in Phoenix, and another home in La Paz, Mexico, where he has taken on the responsibility of educating his children himself. His recreations include an 85 foot yacht and a passion for hunting and fishing.

A lot of Natoros's friends also became rich as a result of Bonanza.

There were so many doctors who were major shareholders originally that annual meetings were held on Saturday mornings because that was the only time they were free to attend.

A lot of Alberta's oilmen object strongly to being called "blue-eyed Arabs", but some of Bonanza's medical shareholders took a more light-hearted view of the name. One Vancouver doctor turned up at an annual meeting in the Calgary Inn in complete Arab regalia and, tongue-in-cheek, was led by one of the hotel's beefeater-clad doormen to a seat that had been roped off from other shareholders.

At the time of writing, the final chapter of the Amalgamated Bonanza story had yet to be written. In January of 1979, Bonanza Oil & Gas Ltd., formed to hold the company's Canadian properties, was split out from the main company and its shares were distributed pro rata to Amalgamated Bonanza shareholders. The intention was to sell off the main company and start, once again, from scratch. By mid 1979, Amalgamated Bonanza had not been sold. Moreover, the combined price of the two groups of shares was just half what it had been at the height of enthusiasm for the company, mainly because of technical problems with the Brazos field.

Now John Fleming found himself disturbed in the middle of dinner and called to the telephone while on the golf course in order to explain just why Amalgamated Bonanza's shares were dropping.

John Fleming, the brilliant young accountant brought in by Natoros to manage Bonanza, found himself suffering more brickbats than bouquets in early 1979, while there were also reported to be personality conflicts within the company that led to the departure of its mercurial head of exploration, Bill Bell.

It seems almost certain that a buyer will be found for Amalgamated Bonanza, but a pall of disillusionment now hangs over the company's new downtown Calgary office. The lesson from Amalgamated Bonanza is perhaps that although the company found abundant oil, it could not hope to live up to the expectations of the stock market.

Amalgamated Bonanza's shareholders were an outstanding example of the enormous success that the oil boom has brought to amateurs. But, not surprisingly, the success brought to professionals by oil fever was even greater.

The Professional

The scene is a small Hudson's Bay store in a little town in the northern wilds of Alberta. A select party of oil investors, visiting a drilling site, stops off to buy odds and ends. Somewhat strangely, it seems, one of their number, a big, heavyset man with a youthful, aristocratic face behind silver-framed spectacles, moves towards

one of those circular wire-framed book displays. The store manager notes, to his amazement, that the man seems to be rearrang-
ing the books. Later, he discovers that all the Harlequin Romances
have been placed in a more prominent position!

The action is not quite as bizarre as it seems, for the slightly
portly man is Dick Bonnycastle, and his minor readjustments represent just a little attention to detail in one facet of his many-sided
business interests. Bonnycastle, the scion of Canadian family
money that is about as old as Canadian family money can get, has
an empire that spreads from publishing through real estate and
department stores to manufacturing. Most of all, he has emerged
in the 1970's as one of the most spectacularly successful backers of
small oil companies, multiplying his already multi-million dollar
oil investments many times over.

Where the Siebens family saw their route to riches in land and
the Seaman family saw theirs in servicing the petroleum business,
Bonnycastle has clearly seen the potential of the oil industry in
finding talented entrepreneurs and backing them with cash.

His first oil venture was in the late 1960's, when he moved into a
little company called Ulster Petroleums, whose main asset was a
lot of what seemed like "whale-pasture" in the Beaufort Sea. Two
weeks after his investment, at 10¢ a share, the Prudhoe Bay discovery was made and Arctic acreage suddenly became the hottest
game in town. The value of Ulster soon increased more than tenfold (in mid 1979, Ulster was trading at almost $5). Bonnycastle,
not surprisingly, was bitten by the oil bug. His other major moves
have included backing the rangy Joe Mercier, joint founder of Universal Gas, by purchasing a large chunk of shares for 60¢ a share
(Universal was sold to Aquitaine in 1978 for $12 a share) and sup-
porting Gus Van Wielingen, urbane head of Sulpetro. Bonnycastle
was also instrumental in forming other companies like Canadian
Obas, Tiger Resources and Rupertsland.

Calgary is not a town given to much regard for social pedigree.
Nevertheless, Bonnycastle's background gave rise to a little suspicion among some of his early partners — "he was so damned
rich", emphasizes one, who now counts his own net worth in
seven figures. A descendant of one Sir Richard Bonnycastle, Bonnycastle's great-great-great grandfather sat for a time under sen-
tence of death during the Riel rebellion.

Born in Manitoba, Bonnycastle came to Calgary in the early
1940's as a boy to work on an uncle's farm during the summers.
After a couple of years, he decided that his efforts were due some
reward, a proposition that he put to the surprised uncle. As a result, he received "one of the scruffiest little heifers" he had ever
seen. The heifer was however to teach him a lesson in genetics.
The scrawny animal produced six very hefty calves. He was also to
be taught something about timing when his uncle sold out his little
"herd" just two weeks before a bout of disease ravaged local cattle.

Bonnycastle's father — Oxford educated like most of the family — had been a chief trader with the Hudson's Bay Company before he got into the publishing business and in 1949 formed the seed of the company that was to become the world's leading romantic fiction company — Harlequin Enterprises. Bonnycastle sold out Harlequin to Torstar, the Toronto-based publishing conglomerate, in 1975 for $30.5 million, but continues to hold a management interest since he sits on the Torstar board.

The formula romances published by Harlequin are snapped up today in their millions. They almost uniformly feature a winsome heroine and a superficially ruthless, but deep-down vulnerable hero who pursue an emotionally torrid but physically antiseptic love affair through to its illogical conclusion of their living happily ever after. In 1978, Harlequin afficianados around the world paid around $80 million for more than 100 million books.

The enormous diversity between Harlequin and oil investments is no paradox; it merely exemplifies that Bonnycastle is an entrepreneur with financial accumulation in his blood, and is prepared to look literally anywhere for his opportunities. Such *Nth* generation inbred belief in free enterprise, particularly in such a fertile environment as Alberta, finds it very hard to understand why everyone could not at least aspire to such a state of laissez-faire grace. Sitting, feet up, in the plushly furnished 23rd floor corner office of his Calgary-based holding company, Cavendish Investing, Bonnycastle expounds political views in a tone that does not brook argument. His ideal system is one in which everybody holds equities and supports an elite managerial class which singlemindedly goes about increasing share values.

Indeed, one of his complaints about the East is that not enough individuals hold shares in the companies they work for. "They finish up as wage slaves," he says. The terminology is Marxist but the solution is not. Bonnycastle believes that the West is far more "democratic" in that share ownership is more broadly spread. He has taken measures to increase this tendency, and it was partly his suggestion that led application forms for the publicly offered shares of Alberta Energy Company to become available through banks as well as investment dealers so they would be more available to the general populace.

Bonnycastle's emotional attachments to the West are clearly based on ranching rather than oil, and his support for Alberta is more ideological than geographical. He likes Calgary because it is a bastion of free-enterprise, but he has some harsh words to say about Peter Lougheed's government, which, for Bonnycastle's mind, is far too interventionist. He saves his strongest words for the Heritage Fund. For him, the crime is not that the fund exists, but that it is not bigger, which he believes it would be if under the control of "real" money managers rather than bureaucrats.

Bonnycastle shies away from the idea of direct political involve-

ment in order to push his views, although he was national conven-
tion leader for Jack Horner, the Albertan Conservative MP who fell
from grace with his constituents when he crossed the floor of the
House to become a Liberal cabinet minister. Perhaps it was this experience that finally disenchanted Bonnycastle with national politics. "I'm not impressed with the political system, and I couldn't
possibly live in Ottawa," he says.

Between expounding his strong, if for Alberta somewhat conventional political views, and getting on with the serious business
of making money, Bonnycastle finds time for more pleasurable
pursuits, principally the "Sport of Kings".

Bonnycastle is in the forefront of reviving the province's position
in thoroughbred horse racing, a position lost after the departure of
Frank McMahon and the death of men like Max Bell and Wilder
Ripley. A steward of the Jockey Club of Canada, his immaculately
clad figure is recognized both at North American and other international race tracks. In 1978 one of his fillies, Enstone Spark, won
the British 1000 Guineas classic, and another horse in which he
held a share was nosed out of the winner's enclosure at the Epsom
Derby.

As well as being a close business associate of Gus Van Wielingen, the opulent looking head of Sulpetro — their joint interests
include part ownership of the luxurious Arizona Biltmore and partnership with the ubiquitous Maurice Strong in Rostland Corp. —
their two well-padded and immaculately dressed figures can often
be seen heading for Van Wielingen's private Lear jet enroute to the
races. Van Wielingen has part ownership in a number of Bonnycastle's horses.

Bonnycastle is also firmly plugged into one of the most successful racing syndicates in the world through his relationship with
Robert Sangster, the British head of the Vernons family empire
based on the English Football Pools. Sangster, who controls worldwide operations that bring in more than $600 million annually, has
revolutionized horse racing in recent years, transforming it from an
aristocratic sport to an international business. Bonnycastle is one of
a select group of international multi-millionaires that have been assembled by him to bid at key sales against the likes of Nelson
Bunker Hunt and the Firestone family.

Bonnycastle is the model of self-confidence in everything he
does, but if his style is that of the eastern Establishment, his instincts are firmly those of the dynamic West. The idea of revolving
among a series of large Establishment boardrooms doesn't appeal
to him, because he basically doesn't like to be involved in too many
things over which he doesn't exercise a considerable degree of control.

"I could be on a bank board if I wanted," he says with no trace of
immodesty, "but frankly that would be a bit of a pain in the neck at
the moment."

PART FOUR

Petroleum and the New Alberta

"One hundred million dollars are more dollars than the mind can comfortably conceive. Laid end to end, they would stretch from here to — well, a hell of a long way. Piled up they would surely topple over."

MAX GUNTHER

The Very, Very Rich And How They Got That Way

17 | Peter Lougheed: The Bucks Stop Here

Examining the power structure in Alberta is like peeling back the layers of an onion. Each layer fits, but comes away easily. There are no great conspiratorial connections. The seeker for the centre of power is left with a single man, Peter Lougheed, who very clearly believes that his political position sets him apart. Other segments either fit themselves around Lougheed's central concept, or else have no part in the great shape of things.

For Mao Tse Tung, power may have grown out of the barrel of a gun, but for Peter Lougheed it has undoubtedly grown out of a barrel of oil. The roots of his strength clearly lie in Alberta's petroleum wealth and the enormous price increases that the OPEC nations forced on world oil throughout the 1970's. Southam Press's Ottawa bureau chief, Charles Lynch, summed it all up in a little recitation he delivered before Lougheed early in 1974:

> I'm the Sheik of Cal-gary
> These sands belong to me
> Trudeau says they're for all
> Into my tent he'll crawl
> Like Algeria did it to DeGaulle.
> The gas we've got today
> We just don't fart away
> Gas pains don't worry me
> Cuz I'm the Sheik of Cal-gary . . .

The assessment may have seemed a little crude, both in words and rhyme, and would almost certainly not have appealed to a man who, it was once written, has "deep convictions about his own sanctity". However, the verse provided a neat summary both of the source of Lougheed's power and the western attitudes he embodied. Petroleum provided both the battleground and the weapon for the assertion of Albertan rights. It was Alberta's successful fight to maintain a large share of the "spoils" of higher oil prices that gave it both a new identity and the funds to become the wealthiest province in Confederation.

Envisaging wealth is as difficult as trying to grasp any large number. As Max Gunther said in *The Very, Very Rich And How They Got That Way,*: "One hundred million dollars are more dollars than the mind can comfortably conceive. Laid end to end they would stretch from here to — well, a hell of a long way. Piled up they would surely topple over."

In terms of Alberta's wealth, even a hundred million dollars seems like nothing. Alberta's oil revenues are accumulating at the rate of more than $3 billion a year. That works out at around $8.64 million a day, or $6,000 a minute, or $100 a second. To attempt to give these numbers some perspective, they mean that the Albertans would theoretically be able to buy:

- One ton of gold (based on a price of U.S. $300 an ounce) every 31 hours, 22 minutes.
- Assets of General Motors of Canada (Canada's largest company by sales) in 188 days.
- All the shares of Imperial Oil (Canada's largest oil company) in one year, 156 days.
- La Communiante, by James Morrice (The most expensive Canadian painting every sold at auction) in 16 minutes, 20 seconds.
- The Bank of Nova Scotia in 116 days, 23 hours.
- All the teams in the Canadian Football League in three days, three hours.
- Rembrandt's portrait of his son Titus in five hours, 54 minutes.
- Affirmed, the horse that in 1978 won the Triple Crown, in 40 hours.
- Toronto's Eaton Centre (the largest shopping complex in the world) in 29 days.
- The Montreal Canadiennes in two days, 16 hours.
- The 35 largest publically-owned oil companies in Canada (based on December 31, 1978 share prices) in five years, 211 days.

Having laid out these impressive possible purchases, the next key feature of the province's wealth is that it probably couldn't, in reality, buy any of these things without arousing a cry of protest from some group or other. For these resources are flowing not to the feckless princes of the desert who have to answer to nobody but Allah for their actions. They are flowing into the hands of democratically elected provincial politicians, subject to enormous pressures and constraints in their actions. Nevertheless, what this huge transfer of wealth has provided is the means by which old scores could be settled.

As Larry Pratt pointed out in his book *The Tar Sands*: "What Peter Lougheed articulates so well are the politics of resentment, the frustrated aspirations of a second tier elite for so long dismissed as boorish cowboys, as yahoos with dung on their boots, by the smug, ruling Anglo-French establishment of Ontario and Quebec." If oil was the means, the end was the elevation of Alberta to its long-denied rightful place within Confederation.

Having been tempered in the fires of Canada's greatest federal-provincial battle, presiding over an unprecedented period of Albertan growth, and having been carried to power in the past two provincial elections with overwhelming landslide victories, it is perhaps not surprising that Lougheed has grown in stature to something more than a mere politician. As during the long years of Social Credit domination of the province under Aberhart and Manning, the mantle of premiership has become almost inextricably welded to the man. Peter Lougheed has an unmistakable aura of the Divine Right.

A Tin Ear

Yet the flesh and blood vulnerability of Lougheed contrasts sharply with the magnitude of the political persona. Beneath the armour of the knight who came out of the West in the early 1970's like an avenging whirlwind to settle old scores, sits a quiet, shy and intensely compassionate man who can be turned to tears at the misfortune of a friend; a little man with a tin ear who has mimed the national anthem since unwittingly delivering an off-key rendition in front of a live microphone before a tittering audience.

It has been said of Lougheed that he is uniquely able to "compartmentalize" his public and private lives, a perhaps essential psychological adjustment given the pressures of his uncompromising political image. However, it seems he is not always aware of the "compartments" in other peoples lives. Don Getty recalls with a wry smile that Lougheed is quite capable of calling a meeting for Superbowl Sunday. Once, Getty was just sitting down to watch the Stanley Cup final when he received a call from Lougheed. When he told the Premier what was happening on the television, Lougheed said, "Really. Who's playing?" Coming from a one-time fully fledged superjock, the question was mildly shocking.

But Lougheed's single-minded hard work has a powerful motivating force on those around him. Getty, who emerged as Lougheed's champion during the federal-provincial dispute, is a good case in point. Tall, rangy and good looking, Getty was an outstanding quarterback with the Eskimos. Soft spoken and personable, everybody liked him. In the words of a colleague: "Getty had no great driving ambition. He was just an easy going kind of guy, until Lougheed got hold of him."

Under Lougheed, however, Getty emerged not only as an intractable proponent of Albertan control of natural resources, but also the most capable provincial energy minister ever seen. Lougheed and Getty formed a kind of two-man hit team, working out their strategy for dealing with the federal government and the oil companies as if it was a glorified football match. Quite often they would pre-arrange to storm out of meetings, or Getty would go in and play the "heavy" to soften up the opposition before Lougheed came in to clinch the deal with a more "reasoned" approach. (A top provincial aide remembers one federal-provincial energy meeting where both men had pre-arranged to "stomp off." However, as the meeting unfolded everything seemed to be going Alberta's way, so they decided that they had to stay!)

Getty and Lougheed were doing more than just being tough and applying games theory to their political approach, they were asserting the whole case for western equality (and then some). Getty told the author: "Our premier met with their (that is, Ottawa's) ministers. Our ministers met with their deputies. We were determined to change that." And, in the process, lay the West's chip on the shoulder to one side forever.

Getty, like so many of his colleagues, left the provincial government just before the 1979 election, obviously having had enough of the killing pace set by Lougheed. The good news as far as Getty was concerned was that he had become perhaps the hottest piece of property on the corporate job market.

By May of 1979 he was sitting, symbolically, in a naked office in an executive suite on the outskirts of Edmonton, ready to start a new, less strenuous, and more remunerative, life. His gigantic hands, which had once thrown touchdown bombs and more recently been formed into an intimidating fist shaken in the direction of Ottawa, now held a copy of a slim booklet — "Duties and Responsibilities of Directors in Canada". And the directorships were just pouring in. He had already accepted positions on the boards of Brinco, Interprovincial Steel and Pipe Corp. (Ipsco), Celanese, Placer Development, and, perhaps most significantly, on the board of Alberta Gas Trunk Line, spearhead and symbol of Albertan corporate power.

It is in Lougheed's clear support for Alberta Gas Trunk Line that political opponents who are to Lougheed's left see indications of some dark government-corporate conspiracy. Yet business in general feels nervous with Lougheed, whom it thinks has "socialist" tendencies. Many people accuse Lougheed of "croneyism", and yet his close friends and associates say that he works them as hard as he works himself. Peter Lougheed is a much misunderstood politician.

Examining the power structure in Alberta is like peeling back the layers of an onion. Each layer fits, but comes away easily. There are no great conspiratorial connections. The seeker for the centre of power is left with a single man, Peter Lougheed, who very clearly believes that his political position sets him apart. Other segments either fit themselves around Lougheed's central concept, or else have no part in the great shape of things.

Lougheed may be a Conservative, but his conservatism is not of the classical school of non-intervention. He had learned not to trust big business before he came to power. He believes in creating a free enterprise climate, but the ultimate goal is not free enterprise itself, but free enterprise for the good of Alberta. If Lougheed thinks Alberta can be better served by government ownership, then he has no compunction about moving in that direction.

It is perhaps the fact that Lougheed runs the Albertan Cabinet like a corporate boardroom that is sometimes mistaken for a big business bias. In fact, the attitude inherent in such political style — that Alberta needs to be "managed" — is completely anathema to big business, which, in Alberta in particular, is of the "clear the decks and let free enterprise get on with it" school.

Lougheed has no real friends among the executives of the major oil companies in Calgary (his brother Don is a senior vice-president of Imperial Oil, but is renowned as a hard-line anti-interventionist, who, when called upon to testify at any sort of regulatory hearings, usually gives it to governments straight between the eyes. The brothers seldom mention oil in each others' presence because it leads to massive arguments.)

Says an executive of one of Calgary's largest foreign-controlled oil companies: "I could get to see Gerald Reagan tomorrow. Blakeney is accessible, but Lougheed is really difficult."

In Calgary's corporate towers, the Premier is sometimes referred to as "Litmus" Lougheed, because he "went in blue and came out pink." His grab for the spoils of the OPEC increase by raising provincial oil royalties, his takeover of Pacific Western Airlines, and the creation of the Alberta Energy Company were all seen as dangerously "leftist" tendencies.

Alberta Energy: The People Get a Share

What particularly roused the ire of the oil industry was the creation of the Alberta Energy Company. The basic idea behind Alberta Energy was to give the people of Alberta a chance to participate in the equity side of the oil business as well as reaping the indirect benefits of lower taxes due to the province's swelling natural resource coffers. The concept was originally thought up by Don Getty but soon received the premier's whole-hearted support. Lougheed announced the creation of AEC in September, 1973 in connection with the building of the Syncrude tar sands plant. The company would, among other things, operate the plant's power supply and pipeline facilities, and would also have an option to take an equity interest of between 5% and 20% in the whole project. When 50% of the company's equity was offered to the Albertan public in 1975, more than 50,000 of them subscribed for part of the issue. Early in 1979, 95% of the company's public shareholders remained in the province. About 85% of them owned less than 100 shares while just over half held less than 30 shares.

This whole posse of relatively unsophisticated shareholders, combined with the political nature of the beast, means that the company places very great emphasis on its public relations, which is handled with a kind of charming superficiality above which it never attempts to rise. Proud possessors of five AEC shares, down from Peace River for the day, will drop into the company's Calgary head office to ask "what interest am I getting on my money?" A mention of "Her Majesty" in the company's prospectus provoked a lady to write in and indignantly ask what the Queen of England was doing involved in this company that was meant for Albertans. The summer crop of letters in 1979 produced a request for "20-30 lbs of Syncrude tar sands for me and my friends." A $3 cheque for postage was included.

From a political point of view, AEC seemed a laudable venture, but the reverse side of this exercise in wilder public ownership was that the provincial government could hardly allow the shares to go *down* in price. The result was that AEC was spoon fed some of the juiciest projects and pieces of land in the province. It was given the rights to the giant Suffield and Primrose military blocks; it was granted the contract to build the utilities plant and pipeline for the Syncrude project; and it also became half-owner, with the redoubtable Alberta Gas Trunk Line, in Steel Alberta and Pan Alberta Gas.

Whereas 50% government ownership might in most cases be a cause for concern among public shareholders, in AEC's case the potential bureaucratic burden was turned into a silver spoon. "My kid sister could run the Alberta Energy Company," one disgruntled, but not atypical, oilman told the author.

The Mannixes: Far from Cosy with Peter

Among those who claim that Alberta is run as some great conspiracy, the supposed close relation between Fred Mannix Senior and Lougheed is often cited as a key axis. Yet Lougheed's obsessive desire not to show any personal favours has in fact led to a souring of his relationship with the patriarch of the Mannix clan.

No examination of the Albertan establishment would be complete without mention of the Mannixes, whose tightly held corporate empire makes them perhaps western Canada's richest family. Although coal and construction form the basis of their $500 million-plus business conglomerate, they have considerable oil and gas interests through Western Decalta and Pembina Pipe Line — the only one of their subsidiaries that is not 100% controlled.

Former Mannix employees are dotted throughout Alberta in key positions. They include Peter Lougheed himself; Chip Collins, deputy provincial treasurer and the man charged with the thorny task of controlling the province's massive and mounting Heritage Fund; Harold Millican, former key provincial advisor and now administrator of the Northern Pipeline Agency, the federal entity installed to oversee construction of the $14 billion Alaska Highway Pipeline; Harold Milavsky, head of property empire Trizec; and David Wood, a close friend of Lougheed's who handles the Premier's publicity.*

Patriarch of the clan, Fred Mannix, Sr., is a staunch conservative and has been described as a "rabid Albertan". Although he has left the day-to-day running of the business to his two sons, Fred Junior and Ronnie, his is still the dominant voice within the company. Whether grouse shooting in Spain, playing golf in Palm Desert or hunting in Alberta, Fred Sr.'s finger is never far from the pulse of the giant empire he built on the foundations laid by his own father.

As befits such a powerful family, it sports not one but two bank directors. Fred Sr. sits on the board of the Royal while Ronnie, the younger and more outgoing of the two sons, who now effectively manages the running of the huge business, is on the board of the Bank of Montreal.

The family is compulsively secretive and shies from publicity. Not without reason. In the early 1970's the original meeting of the Canada West Foundation, an organization set up to promote the interests of the West and behind which Fred Mannix was one of the founding forces, was cancelled when the RCMP discovered a plot by members of the Quebec separatist movement, the FLQ, to kidnap Mannix and other wealthy Calgary businessmen. It took the Canada West Foundation another three years to get off the ground. It is not generally known that during the period of the War Measures Act, it was the RCMP in Calgary who took the greatest number of extraordinary measures of any city force in Canada in order to protect the city's wealthy. The extended Mannix clan, of which there are reported to be 64 in Calgary, is acutely aware of its vulnerability and Fred Sr. makes strenuous efforts to keep pictures of his children and grandchildren out of the newspapers.

---

* David Wood spent 13 years as head of Mannix's "public relations," during which time he reportedly was not called upon to issue a single press release.

This secrecy has tended to enhance the reputation of Mannix Senior as a "heavy". Up close, however, acquaintances claim that he is in fact "about as frightening as the Wizard of Oz."

Lougheed spent six years with the Mannix organization, leaving in 1962 as a vice-president and director. It has even been suggested that Mannix provided an ersatz father for the serious young man destined one day to make a massive mark on provincial politics. It is doubtful if this ever was the case, but if it was, the enchantment of the relationship has certainly worn off in recent years. The very suggestion of some kind of cosy corporate-cabinet relationship betrays a basic misunderstanding of Peter Lougheed's style. Very much his own man, Lougheed is in fact acutely sensitive to any suggestion of undue influence from "non-elected" advisors. Also, Lougheed has almost bent over backwards to avoid any accusation of political favor. In some cases, Lougheed's desire to be seen to be fair seems to have worked against the interests of friends or colleagues.

Indeed, there is speculation that the Mannixes are far from happy with Lougheed's approach. The company's plans to develop its Gregg River metallurgical coal property were delayed, and greatly escalated in cost, by the Lougheed government's determination not to be hurried on its provincial coal policy. What may really have blighted relations between Mannix and Lougheed was the compulsory purchase by the province of a large part of one of Mannix's farms, at Fish Creek, south of Calgary, for a provincial park. The government decision, made in 1973, was undoubtedly an embarrassing one for Lougheed due to his previous close relationship with Mannix. Mannix was upset because the province for which he had done so much seemed to be depriving him of his home. Nevertheless, in order to avoid any haggle over a "fair price" for the property, valuation was at once put in the hands of the courts. It took the courts six years, during which the value of the land had increased tenfold, to come to a decision. The province thus had to pay Mannix $41 million for what amounted to less than one-half of his property. Such an amount might seem to be no cause for disappointment, but the fact was that Mannix was deeply hurt by the dispossession. He in fact offered to bequeath the land to the province provided he could keep it until his death, but the offer had been turned down. The eventual court settlement also brought great, and extremely unwelcome, publicity about Mannix's personal wealth.

The Mannix success story started at the turn of the century when Mannix's father, Fred S. Mannix, moved out of Manitoba into Alberta to pursue his interest in construction. Fred S. started the family's tradition of quite literally "shaping the land". He dug irrigation ditches, became involved in highway construction, earth moving and coal stripping. By the start of the Second World War, he had expanded the business into building harbour facilities and

dredging. A two-fisted entrepreneur, Fred S. was reported to have
lost two fortunes before ill health decided him, in the early 1940's,
to sell out majority control of the business. He sold to the giant
United States construction company, Morrison-Knudsen, on the
condition that his son Fred Charles who, at the age of 21 was already superintendent on a dam project, stay with the company.
Fred C. pursued his job with such single-mindedness that in 1950,
under a highly complex financial arrangement, he was able to buy
back the company. The relationship with Morrison-Knudsen
proved to be a valuable one, for it enabled Mannix to move into the
big league of construction projects. These included involvement in
the Toronto subway system, the St. Lawrence Seaway, the Trans-
Mountain oil pipeline, the Interprovincial pipeline, the Quebec
North Shore and Labrador Railway, and major railway construction projects in Australia.

Although nowhere near as tough a personality as he is sometimes painted, Fred C. is obviously no slouch when it comes to corporate arm wrestling. Peter Lougheed is quoted as saying of Fred
C.: "He wasn't afraid to take on large corporations, large organizations . . . I saw him many times eyeball to eyeball against the big
eastern corporations — and they blinked."*

When, in 1954, he wanted to build the pipeline from the giant
Pembina field, it took him just 20 minutes with James Muir, then
head of the Royal Bank, at the bank's Montreal office to secure a
$14 million loan for the construction.

In line with its low profile, the Loram Group (for Long Range
Mannix) to which the empire's name was changed in 1975,
operates out of one of the most unassuming of Calgary offices, a
building on Seventh Avenue that does not even bear the company
name. But there is nothing unassuming about the scale of the business operations. Loram International, the construction subsidiary,
is reported to have annual sales of more than $100 million; Manalta
is the biggest coal producer in the country, mining more than 8
million tons a year; Loram Maintenance of Way Inc., based in Min-
neapolis, is one of the six leading specialists in the U.S. in tracklay-
ing and repair; Manalta Holdings runs the 1,400 acre Bar X ranch
and provides management services, while 52%-owned Pembina
Pipe and Western Decalta make up the oil and gas presence. Loram
also has distribution and consulting subsidiairies.

The main concern with any dynasty is obviously continuity and
it seems that the reins of the empire have now slipped into the
hands of the younger rather than the older Mannix son.

Ronnie, known as "Redfat" while at Ridely College because he
was so rosy and round, is reported to have been wild in his youth,
but has developed the leadership qualities and the personality to
run the business. His elder brother Freddie is reportedly much

---

* Allan Hustak, *Peter Lougheed* (Toronto, McClelland and Stewart, 1979).

quieter and, according to associates, a "little stuffy." Ronnie took over the presidency and chief executive position from Freddie when Freddie departed in mid 1978 for the one-year leadership course at Queen's University. The course, run for a select group of about 50, involves extensive travel and meeting with world leaders and is a kind of advanced finishing school for the super-influential. Freddie's passion is reported to be espionage and military affairs and his current hero, William Stephenson, alias "Intrepid".

All the Premier's Men

Lougheed's relationship with Fred Mannix Sr. probably never took the hand-in-glove form that some outsiders imagine. If it ever did, it certainly does no longer. Nevertheless, Lougheed retains a close relationship with a number of men he has known since his school days, when his tenacious running as a football player earned him the title of the "swivel-hipped" half. These include Harold Millican, also a member of the ex-Mannix mafia, who now runs the Northern Pipeline Agency; Harold Hobbs, who moved from the Calgary parking authority to the Legislative building in Edmonton as deputy minister of the executive council; Jim Seymour, who runs the Premier's Calgary office, and Fred Wilmott. Harry Irving is a friend from football days who recently moved off the AGTL board to make way for Don Getty. Joe Healy is another friend who serves on the AGTL board.

Among the key civil servants upon whom Lougheed has leaned heavily during his rise to power, the foremost are Chip Collins, the personable former army captain who spent 22 years with Mannix before moving to the post of deputy provincial treasurer, Dr. George Govier, the brilliant engineer and former University professor who headed the Alberta Energy Resources Conservation Board and is now a consultant (he also rates as one of the snappiest dressers and best dancers in the West), Wayne Minnion, at the Alberta Petroleum Marketing Commission, and Barry Mellon, deputy energy minister during the dark days of federal-provincial confrontation.

Chip Collins is a member of the so-called "Patio Group", that derived its name from a meeting one day on the patio of the Legislative Assembly to discuss the takeover of Pacific Western Airlines (they met there for no more sinister reason than that Lougheed was eating his lunch outside because it happened to be a nice day). The other members of this group were Cabinet members Merv Leitch, Lou Hyndman, and Don Getty, along with Peter Macdonnell, the Edmonton lawyer who is perhaps Lougheed's most constant friend and adviser outside the government.

Macdonnell, a partner of leading Alberta law firm Milner &

Steer, is firmly plugged into the national Establishment through his family (his father, J. M. Macdonnell, was a Conservative Cabinet Minister and his uncle, Vincent Massey, former Governor General) and his board membership of the Royal Bank. His position in the oil industry at large is affirmed by his directorship of Home Oil, while he holds unparalleled status in Alberta's political-corporate interface by his membership on the boards of both Alberta Gas Trunk Line and the Alberta Energy Company. (He also sits on the board of Century Sales & Service Ltd., the Edmonton company run by Hugh Pearson, chairman of AGTL.)

From within the oil industry, Lougheed's associates are all noted for their prominent stance as Albertans. The foremost of these are Bob Blair and Dave Mitchell, who head the twin "spears" of Albertan diversification, AGTL and AEC. Mitchell used to be a next door neighbour of Lougheed before he was appointed and knew the Premier well. Lougheed's colleagues, however, stress that Blair is not among Lougheed's close friends.

Among petroleum consultants, Lougheed's two closest advisers are Rod McDaniel and Hoadley Mitchell. McDaniel is perhaps the most prestigious consultant in Calgary. His reserve estimates, says oilmen, "are a little on the conservative side," although given his political affiliations, that is perhaps appropriate.

McDaniel is a very prominent citizen as well as being a very prominent consultant. He sits on the Stampede Board and is a past president of the Calgary Chamber of Commerce, and is chairman of PWA. Hoadley Mitchell sits on the boards of PWA, Ipsco, the West's biggest steel producer, in which Steel Alberta (half-owned by AGTL and AEC) has a 20% stake, and the Bank of British Columbia, as well as a number of smaller companies (including, once again, Century Sales & Service).

Among the Calgarian oilmen, or oil service industry men, off whom Lougheed "bounces" ideas are Bud McCaig, chief executive of Trimac, Doc Seaman, head of Bow Valley Industries and Bob Brawn, president of Turbo Resources.

The affiliations of McCaig and Seaman are clearly evident in the identical Karsh portraits of Lougheed that they keep in their headquarters — mementoes that Lougheed presented to all the original select members of the "Lougheed Club" which helped finance his early political efforts. Both serve on the board of AGTL, both head large and growing family companies, and both are models of Albertan entrepreneurial talent. Both also chuckle a little at the thought that they have any "special relationship" with Lougheed.

"People sometimes come up to me," McCaig told the author, "and say, 'as one of the advisors to the Premier . . .' They obviously don't understand the Premier."

"Peter Lougheed is the best long-range planner I've ever known. He thinks everything through very carefully, but he is totally and completely his own man," says McCaig.

McCaig is typical of the sort of businessman to whom Lougheed looks for the growth of the province's corporate strength. His father, J.W., started the business as a haulage firm with a small fleet of trucks, hardy vehicles with grills like fencers' masks, smooth, curvaceous fenders and headlights like eyes mounted on stalks. J.W. was a model of the work ethic and the entrepreneurial spirit, driving along roads so horrendously dusty that you had to stop every hour and sleep in the coffin-like tool boxes by the side of the rig. Bud seems a long way from that hard past. Immaculately smart in velvet waistcoats and with hair so tonsorially perfect that it appears that he must keep a barber permanently somewhere in the wings, he could easily be mistaken for a smooth denizen of Bay Street. But underneath is that western toughness and drive that sets Albertan businessmen apart. McCaig now runs one of the ten largest trucking companies in North America and Trimac has considerable interests in drilling and servicing as well as in waste recycling. But the fact that he is "second generation" business almost ensures him a place in the local establishment, a position sanctified by a position on the board of the Calgary Golf and Country Club.

For Lougheed, all these man are useful. He invites small select groups of such men to occasional dinners at Government House where the "bouncing" of ideas takes place. The dinners are not a regular affair but are held when a particular issue arises. For example, the issue of Alberta within Confederation has been one on which Lougheed has been particularly keen to have the views of Albertan businessmen. The election of the Parti Quebecois was the occasion for another dinner. But that, essentially, is all they are. Lougheed makes a very deliberate, and strenuous, effort to distance himself from business. Says Getty: "The Premier is very sensitive to the feeling that it is elected people who put their names on the line, not their advisers. Thus he makes it very clear that he is the one who makes the final decisions. The men down in Calgary are powerful individuals either because of their brains or their wealth. But they don't make any decisions in Alberta."

The man who makes the decisions is Peter Lougheed.

18 | The Empire Builders

Their chief executives are not always as polished as their eastern counterparts, but they are men with vise-like handshakes who have usually known what it is to work long and hard in the field.

Borne on a tide of petroleum wealth, Albertan business empires have sprung up at an astonishing rate in the past ten years. By far the most prominent have been those of Bob Blair at Alberta Gas Trunk Line and Jack Gallagher at Dome Petroleum. These two men have, however, been both models and the psychological inspiration for an upsurge in provincial self-confidence and corporate aggression.

Writing in *The Canadian Establishment*, Peter Newman said of Albertan businessmen: "They feel alienated from the political process, suspicious of the eastern Establishment, certain that the Toronto and Montreal crowd's proximity, contacts, and affiliations allow them to play a better game of Ottawa poker, to be constantly receiving more favourable consideration."

This assessment may have been true 10 years ago, but it is certainly not true now. Bob Blair and Jack Gallagher have established that their skill at "Ottawa Poker", far from being inferior to that of the East, is unparalleled anywhere in the boardrooms of Toronto or Montreal.

Peter Lougheed is obviously keen to see the growth of powerful Alberta-based companies, but again, the relationship is not quite as hand-in-glove as many outsiders imagine.

A widespread misconception is that Lougheed in some way controls Alberta Gas Trunk Line, regarded by most people as the spearhead of provincial corporate growth. In fact, however, the province seems to have considerably less direct control over the actions of Trunk Line than it did when Blair came along. What Blair has done, however, is to anticipate the desires of Lougheed.

When Blair joined Trunk Line, none of the company's executives was represented on the board. Now, the board not only contains Blair but also his second-in-command, executive vice-president

Bob Pierce, and senior vice-president Robin Abercrombie. Trunk Line has also diversified considerably outside the province. It is true that Lougheed still officially appoints four of AGTL's 15 directors, and has considerable influence over the appointment of others, but the AGTL board should be looked at as a list of the top tier of Alberta's corporate elite rather than an instrument for provincial control of the company.

The AGTL board is not only packed with outstandingly successful businessmen, it is packed with men profoundly committed to the growth of the province. It represents the single largest grouping of Albertan corporate clout.

In 1979, apart from Blair, Pierce and Abercrombie, the board members were: Arthur "Art" Child, president of Alberta's largest non-oil related company, Burns Foods; Joseph "Joe" Healy, a close friend of Lougheed's who runs an Edmonton-based motor distributorship; Ron Southern, president of pre-fabricated construction and oil service company, Atco Industries; Don Getty, the former provincial energy minister; Ernie Pallister, a leading Calgary oil consultant; Fred McKinnon, an ex-senior executive of British Petroleum Canada from one of Alberta's oldest ranching families; Hugh Sanders Pearson, AGTL's chairman and head of Edmonton-based Century Sales & Service; Harley Hotchkiss, one of Calgary's most successful and individualistic entrepreneurs, who built Sabre Petroleums from scratch and sold out in 1976 for $24 million; and two of the province's leading lawyers, Bill Howard, Q.C., and Peter Macdonnell, Q.C.

Art Child, who owns 25% of Burns Foods, a company with annual sales of more than $1 billion, ranks with Fred Mannix Senior as a "rabid" Albertan. He is one of the founder members of the Canada West Foundation, of which he was chairman in 1979. Child has an autocratic and almost militaristic style. He has no time for consensus-style management. For corporate inspiration, he looks instead to figures such as Julius Caesar, "who," he was once quoted as saying, "was an exceptionally brilliant leader whose qualities of leadership apply equally well to business as military matters."*

Southern is another leading light of the Albertan corporate establishment. Atco, with revenues in the year to March, 1979 of $368 million, is best known for its pre-fabricated buildings, which not only dot the construction sites of Alberta but are found as far away as Saudi Arabia. However, last year, Southern acquired Thomson Industries (the company started in Alberta by John Thomson but

---

* Mannix Senior is another admirer of military style in business. The current president of Loram is Stanley Waters, a former lieutenant general, while J. M. Rockingham, the general who led the Canadian contingent in the Korean war was also a Loram senior executive for a time.

with its headquarters now in Texas), which now provides the bulk of revenue and earnings. Southern is perhaps represented on more boards than any other western businessman.* He also stands firmly at the centre of the province's obsession with horses through Spruce Meadows, the giant riding complex he built just outside Calgary which is now the scene of a number of international events.

Blair and Gallagher would rate as exceptional entrepreneurs at any time or place in Canadian history, although the present climate is uniquely suited to their talents. However, for many of the other Albertan companies the growth they have experienced in the past decade has come as a great surprise to them. It would be easy to get carried away with the idea that Alberta has risen because of the corporate talents of its businessmen. Nobody could deny that they do have talent, but it should not be forgotten that the single most important element of their success has been the huge rise in domestic Canadian oil prices as a result of OPEC, and the unprecedented boom climate that resulted. Because of the OPEC boom, a whole group of Albertan companies have been expanding like nothing so much as nuclear-irradiated insects from some 1950's "B" movie.

Nevertheless, this exceptional rate of growth does mean that they have been able to achieve the unusual corporate combination of size and flexibility. The corporate arteriosclorisis of bureaucracy has not had time to set in. Where businesses of a similar size in the East may have seen ten or twenty generations of professional management come and go, many of the West's burgeoning business giants still have their founder, or his son, in the top spot. Huge family businesses are still identified with the men who started them from scratch: the Mannixes and Loram, the Seamans and Bow Valley Industries, the McCaigs and Trimac, the Siebens and Siebens Oil & Gas, the Neilsons and Husky Oil. All have built huge corporate empires or achieved great financial worth within a relatively short time.

The important thing about having a "founder" in control is not only that he inevitably knows the business well, but he is also usually the major shareholder. His is not the bureaucratic concern of the professional manager, attempting to achieve a merely satisfactory rate of return without wielding the corporate axe too much. These individuals have no trouble in making multi-million dollar

---

* Apart from AGTL, he has served on the board of, or is currently a director of: Canadian Pacific Investment Ltd.; Canadian Utilities Ltd.; Rothman's of Pall Mall Canada Ltd.; Royal Insurance Co. of Canada; Mercantile Bank of Canada; Scott & Easton United Securities Ltd.; Crown Zellerbach Canada Ltd.; Pacific Western Airlines Ltd.; Canada Cement Lafarge Ltd.; Northern Telecom Ltd.; Westburne International Industries Ltd.; and Trimac Ltd.

corporate decisions overnight that a whole bevy of committees in an eastern corporation would take many weeks to pore over. "Founder" management is a management with a deep pride in proprietorship and an almost religious belief in hard work and achieving the maximum possible returns — an entrepreneurial purity that usually disappears long before any company reaches the size of the Albertan giants. Their chief executives are not always as polished as their eastern counterparts, but they are men with vise-like handshakes who have usually known what it is to work long and hard in the field. Few of them have to thank anyone in Ontario and Quebec for their success.

Inevitably, however, the family businesses are passing into new hands. The Siebens and the Nielsons have now sold out (although they are now controlled, respectively, by the ubiquitous Dome and Alberta Gas Trunk Line). The second generation runs Trimac and Loram, and the Seaman brothers are looking to retire in the early 1980's.

Since the modern age of Canadian oil only started a little over thirty years ago, with the Leduc find in 1947, there is obviously no really "old" oil money in Canada. But of the "older" oil money — that is, any that was well in place before the OPEC crisis of the early 1970's — much of it was based not in finding and producing petroleum but in servicing the industry. Just as much of the fabulous fortune of Howard Hughes was based on the seemingly mundane base of drilling bits, so many of the Albertan fortunes were made out of building roads and pipelines, out of running rigs that were contracted to the industry, and out of a hundred other activities that served the great god petroleum. The service industry was both a good deal more stable than the exploration industry and tended to avoid the acquisitive depredations of the majors.

It was largely through service activities that the family fortunes of the Mannixes, the McCaigs, the Seamans, the Bowlens (Regent Drilling) either were started or boosted and that the great individual wealth of men like John Thomson (Thomson Industries) Peter Bawden (Peter Bawden Drilling Services) and Bill McGregor (Numac) took off.

Sometimes, it seems, the "company men" who work for American-controlled big oil find it a little hard to come to terms with the phenomenal success of some of the entrepreneurs who started out doing small contracting jobs in the long shadows of the giant oil companies.

This feeling comes out in the occasional throw-away line by one of big oil's old timers. "Why," declares some crusty old executive with unconcealed irritation, "Ron Banister (founder of bustling pipeline company Banister Continental) started out just laying small inch pipe around Leduc for Imperial. Bill McGregor (founder of Numac) was once the *milkman* in the Turner Valley."

Bill McGregor was never a full-time milkman, although when he was young he did cart milk around the Turner Valley from his father's farm. Now, he certainly is rich. His holdings in the company he started in 1963, Numac Oil and Gas Ltd., were worth about $30 million in mid 1979.

McGregor fits perfectly into the mould of self-made men in Alberta who revel in hard work. Indeed, it goes beyond work. It is a way of life. McGregor talks enthusiastically about the structuring of deals as other men might wax lyrical about the form of sculpture or the tonal effects in a great painting. He admits to playing the occasional game of golf, but for him, as for so many others in Alberta, work is not only the greatest good, it is also the greatest source of pleasure.

Sitting in his Edmonton office before the unlikely decorative combination of an 8½-foot Narwhal tusk and a limited edition replica of the sword (made by Wilkinsons of England) that the Queen presented to the RCMP on their 100th anniversary, McGregor is the very model of the solid Albertan citizen. A past president of the Edmonton Petroleum Club, his place in the national business establishment is attested to by his board membership of the Bank of Nova Scotia.

Numac is not a huge company. In 1978, it had cash flows of $12.8 million, but it has grown spectacularly, and has even more spectacular things to come.

The company's share of a giant uranium find in Saskatchewan, in which its partners are Imperial Oil and Bow Valley Industries, could multiply its cash flow many times over by the mid 1980's, while another deal, with Gulf Canada — under which the major is paying Numac $25 million over five years for a farm-in to some of its heavy oil acreage at Surmont, Alberta — offers the company a major position in heavy oil development.

"I could just sit here now and watch the company grow by itself," McGregor says, "but we'd have to pay some pretty hefty tax bills." And if there's one thing that Albertans hate with a passion unseen even in the East, it is taxes.

McGregor was born in Saskatoon, but came to the Turner Valley when he was still a young boy. When he left school, he went to work for Anglo-Canadian Oils and stayed there ten years until he decided to go into the construction business. After Imperial's Leduc find, he and a bunch of friends got together to drill a well and discovered the MicMac pool, run by Mic Mac Oils Ltd., of which McGregor was president and managing director. In 1953, Consolidated Mic Mac was formed as Mic Mac was merged with Skyline and Banner Petroleums. Over the following ten years, McGregor steadily built up the company until, in 1963, it was sold to Hudson's Bay Oil & Gas for $15 million. Then McGregor formed Numac. By mid 1979, McGregor had built Numac to a company with a market capitalization of over $350 million. Speculation that McGregor might be forced into spending some of his money, by Numac being taken over, made Numac one of the most hotly traded oil shares in a sizzling market in 1978 and 1979. But McGregor shows little interest in moving off into gentle retirement. He leans forward and says, with an infectious enthusiasm, "Let me tell you about the deal with Gulf . . ."

Doc Seaman: Growing like Topsy

As with Numac, the prospects of many Albertan companies are as, or even more, outstanding than the growth they have witnessed in the latter half of the 1970's.

The best example of this is Bow Valley Industries, started 30 years ago by the man who still heads it, Daryl K. "Doc" Seaman. Seaman would slip easily into any establishment. The 15th floor offices of Bow Valley seem to have a touch more "class" than the other rather stereotyped oil company headquarters of Calgary. The carpets are a little deeper, the wood panelling of higher quality, the wall prints, 19th century winter scenes, a little more imaginative. Seaman, easy-going and self-assured, has the very best corporate connections both nationally and provincially. He serves on the board of Crown Trust, an important force within the mighty Argus Corporation (although not actually part of it); Bronfman money is represented by Cemp Investment's 15% holding of Bow Valley and the presence of Cemp's president, Leo Kolber, on the board; while Seaman's seat on the board of Alberta Gas Trunk Line is perhaps the symbol of his standing within the province of Alberta.

Doc Seaman's spot in the Albertan Establishment, or at least the power establishment, is also signified by the presence in the Bow Valley headquarters of the Karsh portrait of Peter Lougheed. However, the presence alongside it early in 1979 of another photograph, that of Pierre Trudeau, indicated a deviancy from "Alberta First" that in fact means that Seaman is not one of Lougheed's closest sounding boards.*

Only the crushing handshake — which has obviously rearranged quite a few metacarpals in its time — indicates that this is a man who has served his stint in the field. Doc and his two brothers, B.J. and Donald, are, along with the Nielsons, the Siebens and the McCaigs, among Calgary's outstanding family

---

* Two months after the election, Trudeau's picture had disappeared but had not, as yet, been replaced by a picture of Joe Clark!

success stories. Their shareholdings in Bow Valley were, in mid   271
1979, worth $22.5 million, $22.3 million and $13.9 million, respectively. However, the really phenomenal statistics relating to Bow Valley are not the wealth of its managers (president Dick Harris has $3 million worth of Bow Valley shares too) or even its spectacular growth in the past five years (53% per annum!) but its prospective growth. Bow Valley's involvement in uranium in North Saskatchewan, with Numac and Imperial, and its interests in oil and gas fields in the North Sea and in Abu Dhabi, mean that the company is forecasting a sixfold increase in its 1978 cash flow, to $175 million, by 1983.

That projection is more than just a very large number, it means that Bow Valley is moving into a whole different corporate league within Canada.

Significantly, what it also meant early in 1979 was that the giant Argus Corporation, bastion of eastern corporate power, had to back out of a plan to buy into the company, because it simply could not afford it! Early in 1979, Argus, through its subsidiaries Hollinger Mines and Labrador Mining and Exploration, had proposed to buy $40 million of Bow Valley treasury shares immediately and commit to buy out the Seaman brothers' holding in 1983 on a formula based on asset value. However, the Ontario Securities Commission ruled that Hollinger might have to make a similar offer to all shareholders, involving a total takeover that could have involved them spending over $1 billion.

Bow Valley is still not a name that is particularly well known in the East, and yet, like so many other Albertan companies, it is growing at a phenomenal pace. The prospect of attempting to swallow such a creature when it had grown to even more horrendous proportions five years down the road caused even the giant Argus to gulp and step back.

"I must admit that it does take me back when I consider that we are bigger than someone like Labatts or Molsons," says Seaman. However, Bow Valley has been thinking in world-scale terms for some time. The $130 million it borrowed from the Royal Bank early in 1978 to buy a Denver-based U.S. oil company, Flying Diamond, was at that time the biggest single bank loan in Canadian history. In mid 1978 it was in the running right down to the wire to buy out Ashland Canada in one of Canada's biggest takeovers. During the crucial stage of the negotiations for the company, the Ashland negotiators, Orin Atkins, the man whom Bobby Brown had so badly wanted to merge with Home Oil, and Earl Joudrie, head of Ashland Canada, were shuttling up and down University Avenue in Toronto between Edgar Kaiser and the team from Kaiser Resources, who were staying at the Harbour Castle Hotel, and the Seaman brothers in the Four Seasons. Seaman's final offer of $32 a share was the same as Kaiser's but Kaiser's was all cash, as opposed to the cash and share package of Bow Valley, so the Vancouver-based resource company won.

The Ashland takeover was one of the few situations where Doc Seaman misread the business signs. The night before it was announced that Kaiser would be taking Ashland, it had seemed that Bow Valley was 90% certain to make the acquisitions. More typical of Seaman's shrewdness was the takeover of Flying Diamond. Bow Valley had, in 1977, realized that overseas ventures in the Middle East and the North Sea would provide enormous cash flow down the road, so they started looking for an acquisition to provide some boost in earnings during the interim. One of Seaman's New York contacts told him that American corporate giant, Gulf & Western, was interested in selling its 40% stake in Flying Diamond, so contact was made and, just before Christmas of 1977, Gulf & Western sent engineering reports on Flying Diamond's position up to Calgary. After mulling these over, Bow Valley's management decided the company was worth $30 a share. G. & W. thought this was a bargaining stance and attempted to coax Bow Valley higher. However, the company would not budge. Finally, one day Charles Bludhorn, Gulf & Western's redoubtable head, phoned Doc Seaman and proceeded to launch into a tirade about how his company couldn't possibly let their stake in Flying Diamond go for less than $40 a share. Such was the decibel level of the onslaught that Seaman had to hold the receiver away from his ear. When Bludhorn had finished his attempt to bludgeon Seaman into submission, Doc quietly told him they had done their homework and that was the price they were prepared to pay. Bludhorn hung up.

A little while later, the American executive called back, somewhat more reasonably in tone, and suggested that Gulf & Western might be prepared to take some Bow Valley shares as part of the deal. Doc told him that Bow Valley shares were under-valued and that they didn't want to issue any more without really good reason. Bludhorn once more began to rant and rave, but at the end of half an hour, when it was clear that Seaman wasn't going to budge, he said, "Alright, you can have them for $30 a share. You're the toughest goddam Canadian I've ever met."

The three Seaman brothers were born within a couple of years of each other in the early 1920's in Rouleau, Saskatchewan, where their father was in the construction business. Doc, the eldest, had gone straight from high school into the air force at the beginning of World War II, which meant that when he returned to the University of Saskatchewan in 1945 to study engineering, his two younger brothers were already there. When Doc got out of university in 1948, most of his fellow graduates were heading "down East" to the golden triangle of industry in southern Ontario. However, Doc and his father and brother B.J. decided to go and have a look at the oil boom they had heard about in Calgary. Doc was so excited by what he saw that he signed up almost immediately to work as a field engineer for a seismic contractor. After a year, he and a partner, Bill Warnke, scraped together the money, $20,000, to buy a shot-hole drilling rig. Doc had to travel down to Texas and pick up the rig, which was truck mounted, and then drove it back. Originally, the two young men had no contracts and spent a couple of weeks just knocking on doors. Finally, one Friday night, Doc Seaman found the right door. Upon being hired, he announced that they would be ready to go first thing Monday morning. "The hell you will," came the reply, "You'll start tonight." That directive was to set the cracking work pace that was to be at the root of the company's growth.

Soon, Warnke sold out and Doc was joined within two years by both brothers. In May, 1951, the name of the company was changed to Seaman Engineering and Drilling Co. (Sedco). The company expanded rapidly in providing services for oil companies and within five years had four complete seismic crews that it rented out, and a dozen rigs. The brothers followed each other Indian-style through the various parts of the business as Doc moved on to pioneer new areas of development. By the mid 1950's, Doc had decided to get into long-term contract drilling. He was keen to get into exploration, but by this time he had seen lots of promotional companies go under when their first large lump of exploration money had disappeared down a dry hole.

Again typically, Doc had enormous trouble interesting the East in the company's operations and, in the end, he had to turn to Charterhouse Canada, the Canadian subsidiary of the British finance group, for seed money. In 1956, Charterhouse obtained 25% of Sedco for a payment of $35,000 for common and $150,000 for preferred shares. This act of faith was well rewarded, although Charterhouse's policy of selling off equity worth more than $1 million in any one company meant that they missed out on the chance for really massive capital accumulation. Nevertheless, an ex-Charterhouse man, D'Alton Sinclair, now a Toronto-based consultant, still sits on Bow Valley's board.

The brothers rode the cycles of the business throughout the 1950's — the boom after Pembina in 1953-54, the surge following the Suez crisis in 1956, and the subsequent slumps — but at the very end of the decade they made their biggest move, buying control of Hi-Tower Drilling for $1.2 million and then merging it with Sedco. On June 1, 1962, Bow Valley Industries was born. The company grew both organically and by acquisition throughout the 1960's, moving into metal fabrication, a business where earnings could be set against exploration expenditures. But the main thrust was to move into exploration. By the end of the 1960's, the company had enough oil and gas production to create a small oil and gas department run by Harley Hotchkiss, who had just left the

Bank of Commerce, where he had been the expert in oil and gas. Harry Van Rensaeller, the company's finance director, had powerful New York connections and was able to raise drilling fund money from the eastern United States. Then, in April, 1971, the company took the really big plunge into exploration and production with the takeover of Syracuse Oils, a company built up by Angus McKenzie, an elusive figure whose main vehicle is now the highly successful Sceptre Resources.

The Syracuse merger not only brought them into exploration, it brought them into exploration in exotic places, such as Abu Dhabi and the North Sea. McKenzie was one of the first Canadian oilmen with a truly international perspective, and he is responsible for putting many Canadian companies into foreign areas. The Syracuse merger also brought in talented explorers like Dick Harris, now Bow Valley's president, and Fred Wellhauser, senior vice president.

In some ways, Bow Valley was like the majors when OPEC struck in that it had underestimated the future potential of the western basin and reasoned that the only likely area of economic potential in Canada was the frontiers. Nevertheless, the service side of the industry has been just booming since 1975.

Doc Seaman is one of the few Calgary oilmen who will admit that it has been easy to make money in the past few years. "The first twenty years were the toughest," he says. However, those twenty years of concentrated effort laid the basis for one of the most powerful Canadian presences in the oil industry. However, Doc is like so many of the other Calgary oilmen. Having worked so long, and so hard, he would find it hard to stop. Even the abortive agreement with Hollinger meant that the Seamans would have continued to manage Bow Valley for another five years. "I don't want to retire now," he told the author, "we're all too young. I've tried to play golf for two weeks solid. It's not much fun. I couldn't go and spend a winter in Hawaii. I've seen too many people slip out of the business and be frustrated."

The View from the East: Bank Boards

This growth of western business power is obviously a source of fascination to those who wield the boardroom clout in the East. It is also a source of concern for those intent on the position as king of the Canadian corporate castle.

"Conrad Black does ask me quite a lot about Bob Blair and Jack Gallagher, particularly Bob Blair," says Seaman. Black, the youthful driving force behind the reorganization of the Argus empire, is

obviously concerned that Blair might just be an example of a more
powerful corporate being than himself.

However, as long as they do not dare to enter the energy field, most eastern boardrooms have little to fear from the West. The corporate machinations of the East's slow growing business empires — whose main excitements come with reshuffling the old rather than venturing into the new — hold little interest for most Albertan businessmen. When he looks to expand, the western businessman looks south, not east. Access to eastern money is still highly desirable, so a board membership on a bank or other financial institution is considered useful.

The presence of Albertan corporate power has become more prominent on bank boards in recent years. The Bank of Montreal has not only Bob Blair, but also Donald Harvie, influential son of Eric Harvie, Ronnie Mannix, scion of the Mannix dynasty that now runs the biggest family empire in the West, and H. J. S. Pearson, an Edmonton businessman with very strong provincial political ties who is also chairman of Alberta Gas Trunk Line.

The Albertan presence on the board of Scotiabank is represented by Bob Pierce, Bob Blair's tough second-in-command; Dave Mitchell, head of the provincially-blessed Alberta Energy Company, and Bill McGregor.

The western oil presence in the Toronto Dominion boardroom comes from Arne Neilson, widely respected head of Canadian Superior, and Edgar Kaiser of Kaiser Resources. The Bank of Commerce seems to be lagging behind its confreres somewhat since it has Mack Jones, influential senior partner of law firm Jones, Black as its only Calgary representative.

The Royal, however, largest of the "big five", has the most impressive array of both Albertan and oil talent on its board, fittingly perhaps for a bank that has placed its vice-chairman, Hal Wyatt, permanently in Alberta. It boasts not only Fred C. Mannix, patriarch of the Mannix dynasty, but also Kelly Gibson, chairman of the board of the Foothills pipeline consortium, Merrill Rasmussen, ex-head of Pacific Petroleums and now in charge of Husky Oil's United States operations following its takover by AGTL, and lawyer Peter Macdonnell, one of Peter Lougheed's closest advisers. Oil muscle is rounded out with the presence of Jack Armstrong, head of Imperial, and Pierre Nadeau, chief executive of Belgian-controlled Petrofina. Bill Twaites, outspoken former boss of Imperial, is now one of the bank's two vice-presidents, along with the powerful head of Canadian Pacific, Ian Sinclair, whose oil interests include PanCanadian Petroleum.

The western businessman wants far more than to be merely absorbed into the East's power structure. Nevertheless, the ease with which they are slipping into such circles is a measure of their new self confidence.

Although he hasn't made it into any eastern bank boards yet, another outstanding example of the self-confidence of western businessmen is Bob Brawn, president of Turbo Resources. Like so many of his colleagues, going through the exercise of toting up just how many millions of dollars he is worth seems pointless to him. What does mean something to him is that Turbo, a company started in 1970, is now one of the 300 companies that make up the Toronto Stock Exchange index — the barometer of the equity market.

Brawn is yet another of the young lions to whom Peter Lougheed is looking to build the corporate power of Alberta. Brawn is home-grown — his father, Gerry, now retired, as a well-respected figure in local Calgary journalism — and self-made, the essential twin credentials for membership of Calgary's natural corporate elite.

When Brawn states that he is looking forward to annual sales by the mid 1980's of $1 billion from Turbo, a company less than 10 years old, there is no suggestion of doubt about the matter. His implicit faith in the "Anglo-Saxon" work ethic and in his own abilities have been tempered by Alberta's unprecedented economic boom into the type of corporate self-confidence that is found these days only in Alberta.

In a town where phenomenal corporate growth is almost commonplace, where sales and earnings graphs in annual reports surge upwards at 45 degree angles in awe-inspiring financial flights, Turbo has a place of its own. It is not simply the hundred-fold increase in earnings per share that the company has achieved during the 1970's; it is that Turbo, alone among Calgary's home-grown oil companies, is integrated. Its operations stretch from producing oil to selling it through its 220 gas stations. Although the scale of its business is dwarfed by the major, foreign-controlled integrateds, the fact that it has dared to enter what was considered their preserve and not only survive, but blossom, is seen as a great symbolic achievement for a domestic oil company.

Its push into refining and manufacturing were also sure to endear it to Peter Lougheed, whose concern with upgrading Alberta's petroleum resources within the province and with diversifying away from them altogether has become a critical industrial strategy.

Apart from its incredible success record, the other peculiarly western trait about Brawn and Turbo is the sheer enthusiasm shown by both the man and the company. Emblazoned on the wall on the rather cluttered way to the washroom in the Turbo head office is a large sign: "Turbo shares closed at . . ." followed by a daily record of the company's escalating share price. It hardly amounts to any deliberately sinister attempt at conditioning, but it must have appeared to Turbo employees that the rise in price of their company's shares in 1977, 1978 and 1979 was almost as inevitable as the need to go to the bathroom! (The share price is also prominently displayed in Turbo service stations). Trading as low as $2.10 in the first quarter of 1977, Turbo shares by mid 1979 were flying at over $14, making Bob Brawn's paper worth close to $10 million and that of Ken Travis, chairman and co-founder of Turbo, well over $20 million.

The thought that this makes Brawn, at the ripe old age of 42, theoretically able to retire to a life of luxury is one that never crosses his mind, as it seems to be absent from the whirring crania of most of Calgary's bustling entrepreneurs. Brawn sees any suggestion that people should be enjoying their millions as ignorance about the ethos of the West. Spending money in large quantities he sees as part of the "English inherited wealth" syndrome, something only done by effete generations in which the entrepreneurial genes have been weakened by the soft life, groups operating in a country where personal drive has been slowly but surely bred out of the system by punishing taxation and a cloying social stratification.

"People in this part of the world use wealth to create more wealth," says Brawn.

As with his "English inherited wealth," many of Brawn's observations about the good and bad environments for business life relate to a national or racial background. "I think the Anglo-Saxon spirit and work ethic is that you can do *anything* provided it isn't against the law. By contrast, the Napoleonic code or French civil law tells you what you *can* do and thus dampens initiative. Everybody just wants a little piece for themselves."

19 | Calgary

*"If you don't play golf, are not in the horse and
cattle set, don't drink or ski, what the hell could
you do here? But the main thing is that nobody
gives a damn what your pedigree is."*

There are two social establishments in Calgary with the name
"Ranchman's". The one is a wood-panelled private club, home of
old Calgary money and many of today's actual and aspiring corporate elite. The other is a giant barn-like dance hall where Dolly
Parton look-alikes sing doleful country and western music to a
stetsoned clientele. The two places represent the extremes of Calgary's social life, but it is still possible to graduate from one to the
other within a relatively short time.

Inevitably, there are elites within the province, but they tend to
be "natural" elites of talented people thrown together by their
business interests and common goals. They are not secretive
groupings of inherited wealth attempting to shore up a crumbling
world of privilege.

That is not to say that they have been without privilege. But their
privilege has been to operate in an industry where the profit potential has been spectacular.

Due to this spectacular business environment a great deal of Albertan money is so new it is still wet; so recently acquired and so
enormous in amount that it has to keep pinching itself to see that it
is still there. At no time or place in Canadian history has such a
proliferation of personal wealth occurred.

Gigantic fortunes, beyond the dreams of avarice, have been
built. However, they have been built so quickly that they have
achieved little real significance to their owners.

Although many Calgarians owe the sheer, enormous extent of
their fortunes, if not their relative personal success, to their dusky
brethren within OPEC, their attitude to wealth is very different.
Perhaps what is most disappointing about modern-day Alberta is
the intense seriousness of it all. Very few people seem to be enjoying their wealth. Indeed, there is a considerable body of opinion

that holds it as bordering upon the immoral to enjoy wealth at all. Wealth is there to create more wealth. Far from bestowing freedom, it seems to impart only the weight of great social responsibility.*

For some of the new rich, the mantel of affluence seems to fit like a glove; the sense of pride in financial achievement comes through loud and clear.

But for others, great personal wealth has obviously created problems. Many of Alberta's super-rich are not high rollers. Their fortunes have come about as a result of playing the business game in an exceptionally amenable environment. At another time in Canadian history, they might have earned enough to live in comfortable obscurity. However, in recent years, with enormously escalating oil and gas prices, and huge amounts of money trying to find a home in Calgary's hothouse financial environment, the rewards have been unprecedented, the publicity great.

Indeed, personal wealth should create fewer personal problems in Calgary than in any other still relatively small Canadian city, because there are so many other wealthy people. Moreover, the number realistically aspiring to that status, and thus seeing it as a "good thing", must be higher than in any other place in Canada.

In part, the reason why wealth has not always brought proportionate happiness in its wake has nothing peculiarly Calgarian about it. Financial paranoia often accompanies first generation riches. A common fear, and one that is quite justified, is that of kidnapping, the ultimate horror for all those with young families. It is an obvious reason to play down personal wealth.

There are other general pressures on the wealthy. The accumulation and conspicuous enjoyment of large amounts of money have always attracted envy, but now they also attract the more tangible attentions of the taxation authorities to a degree never known in the old days.

But sometimes it seems that for both Calgarians and their city, it is a matter of having been swamped by their own wealth. Calgary is at once the least typical and most typical of Albertan cities. Least typical because much of its tenuous culture and social structure has been swept away by the influx of new wealth, because it is filled

---

* Perhaps part of the difference between Albertans and Arabians is that the sheiks of the desert are in no doubt that their wealth is a gift of god, for which they have had to make no effort. Arabs abroad delight in spending their money in the most bizarre ways. In Paris, a young Kuwaiti playboy purchased an imitation James Bond car and drove it down the Champs Elysees, spewing clouds of pink and green smoke from special smokescreen attachments. The son of the ruler of Abu Dhabi, Sheik Khalifa bin Zayyid, caused some consternation in the V.I.P. lounge at Orly airport when he was discovered to be travelling home in the company of 75,000 French bees, which he was carrying in garbage bags. Sheik Sabah Salim Al Sabah, the Emir of Kuwait, ran up a hotel bill in France for $150,000 before spending a similar amount for the purchase of two million flower pots.

with outsiders come to make their fortunes. Most typical because that brand of unstructured dynamism is what modern-day Alberta is all about.

Calgary is a city of potentials, living in the aspirations of its new inhabitants. Dick Whittington viewed medieval London as a place where the streets were paved with gold. Those who move to Calgary look upon it as a city where the sidewalks ride on petroleum. Calgary is a bastion of free enterprise and personal initiative. Its inhabitants tend somewhat conveniently to ignore the fact that the basis for their profitable "free enterprise" activities lies in an enormous cartel which has its origins half the world away in the deserts of Saudi Arabia. Nevertheless, despite that minor detail, the Albertan oilmen, most of whom operate out of Calgary, represent the flower of Canadian entrepreneurial spirit. This spirit is abundantly reflected in the town itself.

When Are You Going to Finish It?

You can almost see it grow before your eyes. If someone had installed a time-lapse camera over the city, the hothouse expansion of Calgary would, in a matter of cinematic minutes, produce a marvel to behold. In recent years, anybody absent from Calgary for more than a month or two has been forced into a double-take on his return. The "golden crescent" of the city's core, bounded on the south by the railway tracks below Ninth Avenue and on the north by the slow curve of the Bow River, has sprouted a proliferation of giant new office blocks at a rate little short of bizarre. Seeded by petroleum fever, fertilized by a huge influx of money and cultivated with consummate care by its business inhabitants, the city has grown at a rate unprecedented in Canadian history.

Ten years ago, the Calgary Tower stood as an architectural wonder of the West. The old Palliser Hotel still lorded it over a sprawling but still relatively small urban area. In 1979, four years into the great post-OPEC oil boom, the Calgary Tower now appears like an oddity from another era, gawking in long-necked awe at the massive office blocks rising to the west of it in the city's booming downtown core; the Palliser, like some dowager duchess caught in the middle of a hockey crowd, has been jostled on all sides by the breakneck pace of new construction.

Approached on a crisp January day, the city rises like a glittering man-made commercial mountain out of the rolling Alberta Foothills. The misty-white plumes of vapour that rise from the office blocks make it look as if the buildings themselves are panting with exertion.

Calgary is by no means a town without a past, but in the 1970's it has been like an urban 90-pound weakling turned into a metropoli- tan Mr. Universe, an entity so different as to be almost unrecognizable.

Booms are not new to Calgary, a town built, after all, on the perpetual uncertainities of oil. But the latest surge is not only the greatest, it is also different. It has been founded not on the inevitably ephemeral surge of activity following a major new oil strike, but on the more secure and financially rewarding effect of a truly dramatic change in oil economics.

Sheik Yamani is the city's patron saint. There has been a clear and logical sequence of events leading from the fateful night of October 11, 1973 in Vienna, when negotiations between oil company representatives and Yamani had broken down, to Calgary's becoming one of North America's great boom towns. More than that, it now ranks as one of the greatest oil towns in the world.

In the United States the oil industry has a large number of centres of activity, of which the principal are Denver, Tulsa, Houston and Dallas. Calgary, however, stands pre-eminent as *the* oil city in Canada. Even the majors, whose operations were previously tightly controlled out of Toronto, have now shifted a great deal of corporate decision making to Calgary. Because of the enormous expertise built up around the Albertan industry, Calgary has also become a world-recognized centre of oil technology.

The boom is most dramatically indicated in the building permits issued by the city covering every form of construction from apartments to churches. Between 1973 and 1978, the value of these permits quadrupled, from $242 million to the magic $1 billion mark in 1978. The most spectacular component of the increase was permits for offices. In 1973, they were worth $16 million. By 1978, the figure had risen to $338 million, a 21-fold increase.

At the beginning of 1979, downtown Calgary faced a $1 billion office building boom. That was the value of offices either under construction or proposed for the burgeoning downtown core. The joke going the rounds was that of the visiting Easterner who declared: "Calgary's a fine city, but when are you going to finish it?"

The answer, it seems, is that Calgary still needs a great deal of "finishing". Any urban community is a great deal more than a population statistic and a vacancy rate for office space. The danger, perhaps is that the blanket of giant, antiseptic new office blocks will smother the city's somewhat tenuous cultural past.

Calgary is above all a business city, dominated by office blocks and lacking geographical focus. Many of those who wheel and deal in the rising canyons of the golden crescent know the city as little more than a series of numerical coordinates; one gigantic urban office block with 40 floors stretching between Fourth and Ninth Avenues and Centre and Tenth Street southwest. Limousines speed them the 15 minute drive along smooth new highways from the glistening new airport to downtown, and then out again. The whole experience can be as personal as a conference call.

Calgary is, however, an attractive city. The Bow and Elbow rivers that meander around the downtown core, and its gently rolling, and fast expanding, suburbs, give it a topographical interest lacking in a city like Toronto. And then, of course, there are the mountains, appearing to Calgarians like a Siren-call out of the West. Indeed, the attractions of Calgary's surroundings are the key gravitational pull against which the city has to assert itself. Calgary is a city without city dwellers; Calgarians are still overwhelmingly an outdoor breed. At weekends the downtown core becomes a deserted place, populated only by visitors to the Bay and Eatons, and by the occasional stranded oil company representative from out of town.

It is still essentially a town from which most of its inhabitants seek to escape. Those on their way to making their pile head for the mountains at weekends; those well on their way head south or to Hawaii as often as possible; and those who have made it most often depart permanently for sunnier climes.

Old Harold Siebens officially retired in 1958 to E. P. Taylor's millionaires subdivision at Lyford Cay in the Bahamas, leaving the management of Siebens Oil and Gas to his son Bill.

John Scrymgeour, chairman of giant Westburne International Industries, a conglomerate with interests from oil drilling to plumbing supplies, moved his permanent residence several years ago to the opulent surroundings of Tuckers Town, Bermuda. Scrymgeour, one of the more urbane of the oilmen, was the brains behind many of Bobby Brown's initiatives at Home Oil. Although Scrymgeour spends much time on the financial tour between New York, Calgary and Toronto, he now administers a personal fortune from Tucker's Town that includes more than $30 million worth of Westburne shares.

Frank McMahon retired to Palm Beach long before Calgary's present hectic boom and is now seeing out his final days aboard his huge yacht.

Fred Mannix Senior, patriarch of the Mannix clan, the richest family in the West, retired some time ago from full-time management of the tightly controlled half-billion dollar family empire, although he still keeps a watchful eye from his luxurious villa in Palm Desert, and returns to Calgary often.

Among those whose empire building keeps them in Calgary full time, the Palm Springs residence, or the house in Vancouver are almost *de rigeuer*. However, the ranching instinct of westerners remains close to the surface among oilmen, and a great many have "spreads" within commuting distance of town. Among the most deeply involved — a man whose energies seen superhuman even by Calgary standards — is Joe Mercier, the brains behind Universal Gas, sold out for $23 million in 1978 after a start from scratch in 1970. During the whole two months of calving at his ranch south of town, the tall, rangy figure of Mercier, who looks just right for a starring role in a Western, can be seen riding through the herds after dinner in the evening, then at 11 pm, again at 2:30 am and once more when he gets up at 5:45 am. All this before driving the 25 miles into town for a full day's oilpatch wheeling and dealing. Mercier's other sidelines include raising eight children and playing basketball at the "Y" at least three times a week!

Among the city's other major ranchers are Jack Pierce, head of Ranger oil and an aviation fanatic, whose ranch, 40 miles from Calgary, boasts not only an airstrip and a $1.5 million house but also the only six-car garage in Alberta with its own fully automated car wash; the Seaman brothers, Doc and B.J., who jointly run a spread near town; Dick Bonnycastle, leading oil financier and businessman-about-the-world, who owns two ranches, one a short distance from town, where the famous Bonnycastle Stampede breakfast is held — one of the highlights of Calgary's social calendar — and another about 200 miles from his opulent downtown office; Gus Van Wielingen, Bonnycastle's business associate and founder of the enormously successful Sulpetro, has houses in Dallas and Los Angeles as well as a residence in Calgary, and also has a ranch outside it.

Among the most beautiful of the ranches of Calgary's oil commuters is that of J. C. Anderson, the colourful Nebraskan who came to Calgary with Amoco and took the plunge, more than successfully, 10 years ago. On a clear day, the view from Anderson's rambling cedarwood house embraces both downtown Calgary and the mountains. Showing visitors around his rolling, full-section spread, "J.C." takes a justifiable pride in the trappings that taking the plunge have brought him: the thoroughbred horses, the cattle, the new machine shed that looks as if it could house 20 combine harvesters — "I think I may have overdone it a bit," drawls J.C. — the garage full of cars and four-wheel drive vehicles, including two Mercedes.

But Anderson also typifies how easy it is for a newcomer to rise into the social elite in a city where achievement counts for significantly more than "family" or inherited wealth. Through his wife and children's interest in riding, J.C. has found himself suddenly to be a fully fledged member of the "horsey" set. In 1978, the Andersons held a bloodless "hunt" stamped with the full seal of establishment approval by the presence of Fred Mannix Senior. After one of the big international events at Ron Southern's massive riding establishment, Spruce Meadows, it seemed in no way unusual for Mark Phillips, husband of Princess Anne, to turn up for a party at the Andersons. In Britain, the presence of such a figure — epit-

ome of the "upper classes" — would lead to much social flutter-
ing. At the Anderson Ranch, he was just a British guest, who by all
accounts, played shuffle-board and drank a little too much. "He
wasn't half a bad guy", notes J.C.

The qualities that make Calgary at once the narrow, but open,
place that it is are aptly summed up by "Diamond Jim" Brady, a
relative newcomer to Calgary who had tasted financial disaster in
the East before turning his massive energies to the oil business
where the company he now runs, Seagull Resources, has made
him a multi-millionaire in short order.

"If you don't play golf, are not in the horse and cattle set, don't
drink or ski, what the hell could you do here? But the main thing is
that nobody gives a damn what your pedigree is."

Philanthropy and Eric Harvie

Part of the problem of enormous personal wealth is that it devel-
ops no meaning until it is given a life of its own. There is obviously
just so much that one person can consume and in many cases, for
Alberta's oil rich, that still leaves a lot of spare cash in the bank. In
the end, it seems, the very rich are almost *driven* to philanthropy.

In many cases the wealth is "paper wealth", that is, tied up in
the equity of a company. In some cases, the individuals involved
have been working so hard they do not realize that they have it. In
other cases, they realize that they have it but they have no idea
what to do with it. But in almost no cases have the problems of
new wealth created any overwhelming desire to give it away.

The financial conservatism of a number of Alberta's new rich
also has an historical origin. Many of the relatively older people
who have found their fortunes in the past five or ten years have
known real financial hardship. A whole group emerged from the
Saskatchewan dust bowl. For them, frugality is a lesson deeply ingrained.

However, some of yesterday's oil millionaires had humble origins too. The differences with today's oil-rich are partly ones of
personality, but also due to the anti-wealth political environment
of modern Canada.

One frequently voiced criticism against Calgary's new super-rich
is that their philanthropic tendencies are underdeveloped. Despite
being perhaps the richest city in per capita wealth terms in all of
Canada, Calgary's contributions to the United Fund leave it well
down the list of large Canadian urban areas. Nevertheless, there
are notable personal and corporate exceptions to this. Moreover,
what is not generally known is that one of Canada's greatest individual philanthropists was a Calgarian oil entrepreneur. His name
was Eric Lafferty Harvie, Q.C.

Harvie was the greatest philanthropist of his generation. Although stories about his personal frugality abound, he, and his estate, distributed well over $100 million to support art and historical collections, preserve Canadiana, and finance parks, gardens and scientific research.

In 1979, the rump of Harvie's fortune, administered through the Devonian Group of Charitable Foundations, was finally being distributed, but Harvie's memory will live on not only in Alberta but throughout Canada as a result of his gifts.

Harvie's career as a full-time oilman lasted only eight years, from the discovery of Leduc until 1955, when he decided to devote himself to charitable work. In that eight years, it is estimated that he laid the groundwork for a fortune of more than $100 million.

Like John Paul Getty, the U.S. oil billionaire who once installed a payphone in his London house because guests were making too many long-distance calls, the stories most often told about Harvie are related to his meanness.

He once closely questioned an accountant when a $3 charge for a car wash appeared among the minutiae of corporate expenses. Harvie was used to only paying $2.50. However, the accountant explained that the extra 50¢ was for cleaning the whitewall tires.

An elderly couple, who had served for years as caretakers on Harvie's ranch west of Calgary, took $5 of groceries with them when they left Harvie's employment. He deducted that amount from their final pay.

Harvie never moved from the small bungalow in Mount Royal that he had inhabited since a young lawyer and he always drove the most dilapidated of cars. Shortly before he died, in January, 1975, he is reported to have gasped one of the more prosaic secrets of his success to Peter Newman, author of *The Canadian Establishment*: "Never throw away old socks, old underwear or old cars".

But just how did Eric Harvie become so rich? The answer lay not in finding oil, but in having land, acreage right in the middle of the Leduc and Redwater fields that were discovered by Imperial Oil in 1947.

Harvie was certainly not young when he struck it rich. He had started working in Calgary in 1915, at the age of 23, when he joined his uncle, Dr. J. D. Lafferty, in his law firm. During the 1920's and 1930's, like almost every other professional man in the West, he had dabbled in the Turner Valley, where successively large finds had been made between 1914 and 1936, when Turner Valley Royalties blew in. But in 1944, he decided to take the big plunge, purchasing half a million acres of freehold rights from Anglo-Western Oils, a company that had been in receivership for three years. The land had originally been purchased in 1906 by a British-backed land colonization venture that sold lands to settlers. However, the company had maintained the underlying mineral rights. Starting out as the Western Canada Land Co., it then became the British

Dominions Land Settlement Corp. By 1931, all the land had been sold, so Anglo-Western was formed to look for oil. The search was an unsuccessful one and by 1941, Anglo Western was in receivership.

In 1942, the provincial government put a mineral taxation act in force that placed a levy of 5¢ an acre on freehold mineral rights. The amount seemed modest, but proved to be excessively burdensome when it meant paying $25,000 a year for what were considered worthless subsurface rights. So, in 1944, Anglo-Western was only too glad to sell out to Harvie in return for his paying the back taxes of $50,000 plus an undisclosed sum. Harvie formed Western Minerals to hold the mineral rights, and Western Leaseholds as the operating end of the business. Western Leaseholds was meant to be the company that raised finances, gave farm-ins and did exploration and development work. Western Minerals was there to sit back and enjoy the royalty and fee income — if there was any!

Initially, development was far from easy. There was no income from the land and that $25,000 tax bill had to be paid every year. Shell gave Harvie $30,000 for an option on 300,000 acres, but never exercised it. Then, in November, 1946, he leased 480 acres to Imperial in the area of a little town known as Leduc. This was to be Imperial's final exploration play in western Canada after drilling 133 consecutive dry holes. Harvie leased Imperial another 193,000 acres in February, 1947, and then, just nine days later, the modern era of Canadian oil blew in with Leduc Number One. Shortly afterwards, the Redwater field was struck, northeast of Edmonton, where Harvie also had land, and the seeds of Harvie's huge fortune were planted. In the three years following Leduc, Harvie's companies received $4.3 million in cash royalties and rentals, as well as large amounts of production. By 1951, he had interests in 84 producing wells and Western Leaseholds was generating net earnings of $1.5 million a year. The same year, he went public, but business declined over the following four years and in 1955 he sold out Western Leaseholds to Canadian Petrofina for $50 million, of which he netted $20 million. Western Minerals however carried on collecting royalties from up to 200 wells until 1973 when it too was sold out, for $30 million, to Brascan.

By that time, however, Harvie had long devoted himself to his first love, collecting almost anything and everything relating not only to Canadian but world history. Many of the more than 14,000 items he accumulated had a good deal more novelty value than historical significance — for example, a set of Queen Victoria's bloomers — but the range of the collection was, and is, enormous. It includes: a cannon ball from the Prussian siege of Paris in 1871; a sled from the British Antarctic expedition of 1910; a pair of pistols once owned by the Archduke Nicholas of Russia; the drum that announced the start of the Battle of Little Big Horn and Custer's last stand; Sir Robert Peel's penny farthing bicycle; and the complete panelling from a French chateau.

Some of Harvie's benefactions also appeared a little whimsical, such as the identical four-ton bronze statues of Robert the Bruce that appeared simultaneously in 1955 in front of the South Alberta Jubilee Auditorium and 30 miles northwest of Edinburgh at the site of the Battle of Bannockburn.*

The Glenbow Foundation, preserving the heritage of the Old West, probably still stands as his crowning achievement, but he was also the driving force behind the Calgary Zoo and the Banff School of Fine Arts. In more recent years, the Devonian Foundation has become involved in conservation, research and museum projects in the Maritimes as well as parks in Ontario and British Columbia.

The now dwindling funds in the Devonian group are overseen by Harvie's son Donald, a low profile figure who is however, very powerful within Calgary's oil industry and a key member of the Albertan Establishment. For many years a senior executive with Petrofina after it took over Western Leaseholds, he is a director of the Bank of Montreal and vice-chairman of PetroCanada.†

Donald Harvie rates as possibly the pinnacle of "old" oil money in Calgary, and yet the making of the family fortune goes back less than 30 years. Probably three-quarters of all the significant oil fortunes in Alberta have been made in the 1970's. That even applies to the bulk of the oil wealth of those who were firmly part of Calgary's "establishment" before the OPEC crisis.

Carl O. Nickle: Worthy of Immortalization

If Eric Harvie has a modern day equivalent it is Carl O. Nickle. Nickle was well known before Harvie started making his millions, but the real growth in his personal wealth has all taken place in the past five years, when he has been approaching retirement. Nevertheless, Nickle's philanthropy and his somewhat eccentric trap-

---

* One of the more unusual features of Calgary's huge, bustling new international airport is a proliferation of glass cases containing often unusual foreign artifacts as well as the more traditional bronze embodiments of the rough and tough nature of the Old West. These divers trappings of old civilizations and glorifications of more recent ones are all from Eric Harvie's collection.

† For PetroCanada, one of the side benefits of having Eric Harvie on the board is that Red Square too is bedecked with artifacts from the Devonian Foundation. Some of the native works, however, seemed to take on ominous significance for the Crown Corporation after the federal election. For example, outside senior vice-president Joel Bell's door hung the print of an animal that looked as if it had seen a ghost. Its title was "Avingaluk. The Big Lemming."

pings firmly establish him as a man who has come to terms with wealth.

Nickle's office looks like a store room for a struggling art collection; his home looks as if it is about to open as one of those "Believe it or Not" museums; the man himself is a phenomenon worthy of immortalization somewhere in wax. Carl Nickle is one of the greatest tributes to the diversity of the Calgary oil community.

Nickle is second generation oil, but the family wealth is hardly old. Carl's father, Sam, did not become independently wealthy until the early 1960's, when he was already 70 years old, but the Nickle family has become a pillar, perhaps even the cornerstone, of the Calgary oil establishment. Such an assessment might cause an uneasy shuffling among the rest of the community, because Carl has just that very slight suggestion of kookiness that often accompanies compulsive art collectors. His cluttered office stands in marked contrast to the chromium, smoky-glass and deep-piled extravaganzas of the town's other oil offices. The scattered collection of artwork lacks a certain homogeneity. Indian paintings overlap with scenes of Dutch windmills and copies of the Magna Carta; western bronzes jostle with huge 18th century French vases; a fading photomontage of the "Calgary Chamber of Commerce Orient Tour 1962" is framed by two bizarrely realistic pictures of his parents, old Sam's smile blatantly sporting a monumental set of false teeth, and his mother playing a violin (she was in fact a concert violinist).

Again, there is something a little unusual about the reports put out by Nickle's oil company, Conventures. In an age of slick and glossy financial publications, Conventures' statements not only retain a staunch attention to the most minute detail, but also have obviously been run off in the basement. The front page of the annual report has very clearly been put together by some loving, if slightly amateurish, family hand. "A Canadian-owned, Independent, Energy Company," it proudly states, the misaligned letters going up and down like musical notes on a stave, the tune, perhaps, for the national anthem.

Yet Carl Nickle is not a man to be taken lightly. A brilliant mind, he has for many years been the unofficial "Ambassador" for the western oil industry both in the East and throughout the world. As the chief spokesman for the Independent Petroleum Association of Canada when its representatives travelled to Ottawa in 1969, he told disbelieving Ottawa energy mandarins, and Pierre Trudeau himself, that Alberta oil should be pumped into the East for security reasons. Four years later the OPEC crisis proved him right. The federal government staged an about face in policy that incorporated Nickle's strong recommendation that the Interprovincial oil pipeline should be extended beyond Ontario to Montreal.

Nickle has an encyclopaedic knowledge of the world oil in-

dustry, which he is prepared to display at the drop of a hat. He is
equally quickly prepared to pull out the western oil soapbox that
he keeps in his back pocket. This, well, slightly loquacious tendency means that attempted conversation with Nickle often turns
into a filibuster. His analysis of the Iranian situation, or Mexican
potential, or the growth of Russian naval power throughout the
globe, can be fascinating topics, except when you want him to talk
about something else. An apocryphal story tells how a member of
the National Energy Board emerged from a conversation with
Nickle totally exhausted. "Goodness," he is reported to have said,
"that's the last time I ask Carl Nickle what time it is. He just spent
two hours telling me how to build a watch."

But if a little fun is occasionally poked at Nickle, there is also
genuine respect and affection for him in Calgary. He has done a
great deal for the social and cultural life of the town, and, despite
his father's late-made wealth, he is recognized as an "achiever", a
man who is where he is because of his own efforts. His colourful
career has embraced the newspaper business, broadcasting, being
a member of Parliament, and now, in his mid 60's, running a junior
oil company.

Nickle's family knew hardship in the "dirty thirties". Carl's
grandfather had been a shoemaker, "following the routes of the
early railroads to practice his trade". His father, Sam, had been
born in Philadelphia before the family had moved on to Winnipeg,
Los Angeles and finally settled in Calgary to run the "Nickle Boot
Shops". Carl's father had originally gone into the shoe business,
but his "Slipper Shop" had foundered during the Depression. Sam
then became the western distributor for "Habitant" pea soup —
providing a sound if somewhat uniform basis for the family's nu-
trition — and also for home-study accounting and business
courses. However, old Sam had developed the condition of "oil in
the blood" early on in his career, and whenever he found himself
with any spare cash, it went into buying leases and backing wildcat
ventures.

When Bob Brown Senior's Turner Valley gusher blew in in 1936,
Sam decided to devote himself full-time to oil. He put all his lease
interests into a company called Northend Petroleums and proceeded to do what wildcatters in those days spent most of their
time doing — wearing out their shoes looking for money. In 1941,
Sam drilled the deepest well in the British Empire. It was dry.

By the end of the Second World War, Sam Nickle had established himself as a name in the oil business and in 1944 he founded
Anglo-American Oils. Later he moved into exploration in Nova
Scotia, and acquired mineral rights in Manitoba and Saskatchewan. In 1953 he became fully integrated by buying refining and
marketing operations from the late A. H. Mayland. The tax authorities forced him to sell out these "downstream" activities to British

American (later to become Gulf Canada), but he continued to build his producing properties, folding them into Canadian Gridoil and eventually selling out to Ashland Canada in 1969. Like so many of his dynamic generation, he died in the early 1970's.

Carl, had, in the meantime, been pursuing his own career. When he left high school, he too had worked in a shoestore. His original salary was $15 a week. However, as things got tougher, the manager, announced that the shoeshine boy would have to go and that Carl would have to double-up. His salary would also be reduced to $12 a week. Shortly afterwards, as business deteriorated further, the manager fired the store's repairman and announced to Carl that he would be doing three jobs for his new salary of $10 a week. At this point, Nickle decided to head for the "relief-camps", where government logging or roadbuilding work brought in only 20¢ a day, but you also received your board — and nobody was likely to get fired!

Nickle eventually found his avocation in journalism. At first he worked for radio station CFCN in Calgary, but then, after the 1936 Turner Valley discovery, he decided to start his own paper, "Nickle's Daily Oil Bulletin", destined to become the bible of the industry. Chugging up and down the bumpy road to the Turner Valley in his Model T Ford, the chubby figure of Nickle, and the slim mimeographed sheets of his bulletin, soon became well known around the oil business. After the war, the oil business, and the bulletin, suffered a flat period, but the Leduc boom changed all that.

In 1951, Calgary sent Nickle to spread the good word in Ottawa, where he served as a Tory MP. During his period in Ottawa, he became the Conservatives' energy spokesman, and played a significant part in the acrimonious "pipeline debate", over the financing of the TransCanada PipeLine that was to bring down the Liberal Government. However, disillusioned with politics, Nickle had already returned to pursue his business interests in Calgary before the Tories took power.

The great post-OPEC boom has made little difference to Nickle's outlook on life, except that since he can fairly claim to have seen it coming, he tends perhaps to quote himself a little too often. What it has done, however, is to make him a good deal richer. Conventures was originally just a hotchpotch of family investments (it is still effectively 40% controlled by Nickle). However, shrewd wheeling and dealing on Nickle's part, moving, in the classic fashion, to take a small piece of bigger exploration plays, has greatly increased the size and value of the company. In particular, Nickle moved quickly, and early, to establish a strong position — for a company of Conventures' size — in the West Pembina and Elmworth oil and gas fields. The company's wide-ranging portfolio of oil investments has also escalated enormously in value during the

booming oil markets of 1977-1979. In 1977, shares of Conventures
were trading for just over $1. By mid 1979, they were going for
more than $8, making Conventures' market value over $50 million.

By 1979, the 65 year old Nickle was beginning to become a little
worried about estate duties, so he announced that Conventures
was up for sale. As this book went to press, no buyers had as yet
come forward.

Sale of Conventures is hardly likely to quieten the authoritative
sound of Nickle's voice around Calgary, and he maintains an influential presence in each aspect of the town's cultural life. He is a former chairman of the board of governors of the University of Calgary and of the Alberta Securities Commission; a governor of the
Glenbow-Alberta Institute, the cultural foundation started by Eric
Harvie; he is a past president of the Calgary Philharmonic Society,
which his mother helped start; and associate director of the Calgary Stampede; a director of the Calgary Community Foundation,
and a past president of the Calgary Allied Arts Foundation.

If any one aspect of the Nickle family places them clearly among
the Calgary "Establishment" it is their philanthropy and sense of
civic responsibility. Old Sam set up the Nickle Family Foundation
in 1955 and in 1970 donated $1 million towards the building of an
art gallery at the University of Calgary, the Nickle Arts Museum,
officially opened by Carl in January, 1979. Carl has a long history of
philanthropy dating from the time he gave away his whole salary
when he was an M.P.

If Carl has a model, it is almost certainly Eric Harvie, whose public benefactions, continuing long after his death, have probably totalled well over $100 million. "I tried to follow Eric's example," he
admits, "but on a much smaller scale".

Among Nickle's contributions to the Nickle Arts Museum is part
of the huge coin collection he has built up over the years. His childhood collection started with 25-cent Canadian notes (sometimes
referred to as shinplasters), the first Canadian issue of paper currency dating back to 1870, and over the years has expanded to contain examples of the world's most exotic ancient currencies as well
as complete collections of Canadian coinage. His Canadian collection includes notes issued by the Hudson's Bay Company before
Rupert's Land joined the Dominion and Alberta Social Credit's
"velocity dollars", more popularly known as "funny money." His
foreign treasures include one of the only two known silver coins
minted for King Hormuzd, ruler of the Sassanian Empire in Meso-
potamia between 579 and 590 AD and one of the very few King Edward VII 12-sided, nickle-brass three penny pieces (which cost
$10,000 in 1965).

However, even Nickle's benefactions sometimes seem to have
an element of wheeling and dealing about them, while his man-

agement of Conventures — the major value of which lies in its portfolio of holdings of other oil companies — seems at times to have skated perilously close to conflict of interest with his outside board memberships. In particular, Conventures bought a large block of Ashland Canada, on whose board Nickle served, shortly before the company was taken over by Kaiser Resources in 1978. Conventures made a clear profit of $2.6 million on the acquisition. Nickle never made any secret of the deal, indeed he broadcasted it as a shrewd buy, and there was no complaint from any security commission. However, it is perhaps the sort of deal that only Nickle could have pulled off. It is certainly not any lack of probity on Nickle's part, it is just that perhaps the spirit of his share dealing belongs more to the age of Bobby Brown than the present. There are not many of Nickle's kind left.

Clubs and Elites

Although Calgary is not an elitist city by the standards of Toronto and Montreal, what feeling of stratification there is tends to centre around the city's clubs. The Ranchman's Club peers ever-so-slightly down its nose at the Petroleum Club, which in turn feels itself several cuts above the 400 and the Professional Clubs, where the oil industry's "lower echelons" do their entertaining. The remnants of Calgary's "old" ranching money and the cream of the modern day elite play golf in the opulent surroundings of the Calgary Golf and Country Club, while the best families play a whole variety of sports at the — for Calgary — aging pile of the Glencoe Club.*

The Ranchman's Club perhaps comes closest to exuding establishment. Sunbeams, crossed with strata of cigar smoke, fall on leathery old members in deep, comfortable, leathery old chairs. As you enter the club's front door, you are confronted with a discreetly wood-panelled hall leading to a wide staircase which splits to either side and moves aloft to the club's dining rooms. Down the hallway to the left, which also leads to the billiard tables, sits a sanctum affectionately known as the "Kremlin". There, the very leatheriest of leathery old members sit immersed in newspapers. An excessive rustle from an upstart member, that is, one under 70 years of age, may produce the iciest stare that rheumy eyes can muster.

Women are allowed into the club only at certain times, on certain floors, and may enter only via the back door (this amounts, in fact,

---

* In Edmonton, the Edmonton Petroleum Club and the Mayfair Golf and Country Club are the haunts of the provincial capital's oil "establishment."

to no great abasement, since the car park is behind the club and virtually *everybody* enters by the back door).

The dining room is a more leisurely place than that of the Petroleum Club, where most members sit down at noon and rise at one. Members linger longer over pre-lunch drinks and take their time over consuming the club's good, if miniscule, luncheon portions. Old oil money is represented by men like Donald Harvie, heir to the fabulously wealthy but equally philanthropic Eric Harvie. It is through the membership of men like Harvie that the Ranchman's can afford to look at the Petroleum Club as perhaps a haunt of the *nouveau riche*.

However, the Petroleum Club is not really a haunt of the *riche* at all. It is the almost sanctified lunchtime assembly point for Calgary's corporate, legal and banking elites. Three-quarters of the club's 1,550 memberships are tied in with companies, some of which have 20 or more places reserved for their executives. Many of the personal memberships belong to older members, now long retired, who cling to memories of a wilder group than the dignified men who now meet and shake hands in the downstairs lobby before moving off to one of the club's dining rooms. With only a little jogging of memories, some of these older members will almost gleefully point out that the very same dignified men often had far from dignified origins. Some of the most elevated members of the oil establishment had their "start" in stock promotions that would make the collectively thinning hair of modern day securities commissions curl. One oilman now close to the premier is reported to have made his start by slipping a "micky" into the drink of a rival and then stealing his geological maps.

A lot of the more dynamic activity of the past few years seems to have passed by the Petroleum Club. The club is still indisputably the focus for Calgary's big oil corporate elite, but it is perhaps because the giant companies have in many cases looked flat footed during the past few years that the Petroleum Club is no longer the place where the younger movers and shakers hang out. Many of those who have made it big in the 1970's were either too far down the corporate hierarchy during their "big company" days to have ever been considered for membership, or were not very enthusiastic members before striking out on their own.

Nevertheless, the Petroleum Club — whose unspecacular, low-rise building sat, in mid 1979, typically surrounded on all sides by the swirling dust of hectic construction projects — has always, and will always, enjoy a central position in Calgary life.

Since the modern oil era dates only from Leduc in 1947, the Petroleum Club is, not surprisingly, a relatively new institution. In the early days of the post-Leduc oil boom, the Renfrew Club was the only downtown business and luncheon club. Filled with bankers and lawyers, the Renfrew held one thing more valued than the aura of establishment — a liquor licence. As new companies, and oilmen, spilled into town, they frequently held cocktail parties in the Sun Room of the Palliser Hotel. After a short time, the Sun Room became the recognized spot for oilmen, who decided that they would like to found a petroleum club. The oilmen had lots of money and no liquor licence, the Renfrew Club had a liquor licence but not too much money. So the stage was set for a marriage of convenience that produced the modern Petroleum Club. The early days of the club were characterized by a good deal more whooping and yipping than is now heard around the club's newly renovated interior. There was a big crap game every Saturday night where the money, in the words of the old oilmen, "used to flow like water". The rather mild-sounding game of gin rummy has been inherited from the Renfrew Club and continues every lunchtime in a large cardroom-cum-dining room downstairs. The game may be mild but the stakes are not. Small fourtunes have been won and lost at the tables.

But the "wild times in the card room" seem now to have passed, along with many of the club's characters. Gone is the lone individual who had official permission to sleep at the bar after lunch — while others with somnolent objectives were firmly escorted out. Gone too is Bobby Brown, who had his own personal exit for those occasions when lunchtime left him feeling a little the worse for wear.

The modern day oilmen are a much more sober lot, and their eating habits are regular to say the least. Most materialize from the huge office blocks that surround and dwarf the club a few minutes either side of noon. They depart at one-o'clock on the dot to make sure they catch the final action of the eastern stock exchanges.

Their views tend to be as regimented as their eating habits, and they are capable of whipping each other into a rage against the imputed arguments of never-present ideological foes. A few key words (or phrases) — PetroCan, federal government, energy policy — can stir an irate and almost Pavlovian reaction. Of course, nobody within the club would ever dare to defend any of the above. (Wilbert Hopper, in fact, while president of PetroCan, inherited a Petroleum Club membership when the federal oil company took over Atlantic Richfield Canada, but had to give it up to Andy Janisch, who later became PetroCan's president, when Janisch joined the national oil company from Gulf Canada.)

The Petroleum Club is thus certainly a bastion of free enterprise views, but has undoubtedly lost much of its mystique in recent years. No so long ago, it was the place in Calgary where "deals" were done on napkins over lunch. Eyes darted around the lunchtime crowd to see just who was dining with whom. Now it is filled with company men who have opulent offices in which to do their deals. Many of them have in any case to Telex to Chicago or Tulsa or New York before they can do any significant dealing at all.

Among the truly big noises who can still be seen at the club are Jack Gallagher, who has achieved a kind of immortality in the unlikely form of a lunch that is named after him, the "Gallagher Special", consisting of Turkey sandwich, fruit and cottage cheese. Gallagher, however, is seeking his immortality elsewhere.(Several years ago, Gallagher, who was not happy at the quality of the turkey going into the sandwich that bore his name, came into the club's manager and asked if beef could be substituted. The club's manager, it seems, deserves a place in history because he managed somehow to resist Gallagher's persuasive tongue. He told "Smiling Jack" that the club was prepared to have *two* Gallagher sandwiches, but that the turkey had to stay.)

However, the fact that the Petroleum Club has become an establishment institution is one key reason for the decline of its dynamism. The official three year waiting list (which, in reality, is estimated to be ten years) means that the younger entrepreneurs have in most cases not even bothered to apply for membership. There is in any case a tendency to more or less mock the club's fuddy-duddy image and its introspective nature; to poke gentle fun at some of the members to whom social status has become more important than finding oil and gas. "Some of them," says John Masters, the outspoken head of Canadian Hunter, "think that the oil business consists of belonging to the Petroleum Club, being on a bank board, becoming a member of the CPA (the Canadian Petroleum Association) and going to cocktail parties".

J. C. Anderson, refers, with a twinkle in his eye to "all those old hard legs", who trot down faithfully to the club at noon.

Joe Mercier says: "Belonging to the Petroleum Club used to be a big status symbol, like graduating to a walnut desk. But it really isn't so much any more." Mercier would rather go and play basketball down at the YMCA.

Bob Brawn says: "There used to be a clique that made all the deals. They met every day at the Petroleum Club at noon. They're not nearly as predominant as they used to be."

The renovated club is an attractive place, deep carpeted, covered with wood veneer and liberally dotted with the cowboy and Indian bronzes that are *de rigueur* decoration in any western Canadian office or club. The main upstairs dining room, a great circular, terraced affair — referred to a little tongue-in-cheek as the "Vegas room" by some of the members — is now the club's focus. There, aging Latin American beauties and their "combos" provide entertainment to nightly revellers.

The attitude toward the varied collection of artwork that graces the club's walls is summed up by the ex-club manager. Proudly showing a visitor around, he points to a medium-sized, nondescript work: "This is a $4,500 painting," he confides. Then, moving on, "this is a $6,000 painting", and finally, with a burst of true aesthetic appreciation, "and *this* painting (of a group of flying ducks) cost $12,000".

This is, of course, in no way to pass judgment on the general aesthetic appreciations of the Petroleum Club's membership, although it is perhaps surprising that the Westburne group, headed by the cultivated John Scrymgeour, should have chosen a painting of such surpassing awfulness as "The Hunt", which now hangs halfway up the club's main stairway, to present to the institution. Perhaps fortunately, the painting — featuring a couple of stuffed animal heads, the rear end of a foxskin and a variety of hunting bric-a-brac set against an evening sky — is very difficult to see during the day due to bad lighting.

As is often the case, the Petroleum Club's real snobbery resides in some of those who manage, or have managed, the institution. The mortar of any class system is often as much its servants as it members.

The same former manager bemoaned to the author the decline in the quality of the members' tastes — literally. Although, he pointed out, the club continues to import some of the best wines directly from France — including the best "boozejolay" — newer members "just don't have the pallets any more". In particular, the movement out of Calgary of men like John Scrymgeour, "a real connoisseur", was deeply regretted. Wine experts remain, but this former guardian of the cellars obviously regards them as a dying breed. They include Kelly Gibson, former head of Pacific Petroleums and for a long time one of the main movers and shakers in the oil business; Carl Jones, former head of Hudson's Bay Oil and Gas and another of the industry's powerful personalities; Al Ross, who resigned in mid 1979 as head of Mannix subsidiary Pembina Pipe and was head of the Calgary Chamber of Commerce in 1979; and Rod McDaniel, perhaps Calgary's leading oil consultant and a close personal friend and advisor to Peter Lougheed.

"Its not that the newer members don't drink", the Club's former manager hastens to add. "In fact, they are heavier drinkers than ever before. They just aren't willing to experiment." Indeed, in most dining clubs, liquor represents about half the takings from food. At the Petroleum Club, the proportion is about two-thirds. For 1978, which was, of course, a record year, the Petroleum Club's food sales were $1.4 million and its liquor sales not far short of $900,000.

Women are not allowed into the club until after 3:30 pm, the reason given being the great noon-hour rush, although the problems of the increasing number of women geologists and executives in the industry has yet to be squarely faced.

As for the town's two other "industry" clubs, the Petroleum Club's former manager puts them firmly in their place: "The Professional Club is for the second echelon of engineers and geologists; the 400 Club is for a similar echelon, salesmen, people like that, the second and third echelon."

There is no doubt that the Petroleum Club is considered important by top corporate executives — Andy Janisch wanted to make sure that he kept it when he moved from Gulf to PetroCan; Arne Nielsen made it part of the package he demanded to induce him to move from Mobil to head Canadian Superior. The simple reason is that once your company bestows one of its memberships upon you, it means that you have corporately "arrived". But as a scene of wild revelry or multi-million dollar deals, its days seem numbered. Many of Calgary's new guard of oil entrepreneurs either haven't had time for lunch in the past few years, or if they have, would prefer to spend it elsewhere. When they develop a little more time, and they decide at last to take life a little more easily, then Petroleum Club membership may become a little more desirable. For the moment, however, the club, like many of its corporate members, is perhaps lagging a little behind some of the dynamic activity going on without its hallowed portals.

Postscript

The struggle that took place between Edmonton and Ottawa in 1974 has left a legacy of bitterness that will not easily be forgotten, although by 1979 most of the men who engaged in the shouting, the finger pointing and the name-calling had left political life. The man whose political persona was tempered by the struggle, Peter Lougheed, remains. Bill Dickie, never a heavy puncher politically, returned to the law after the 1975 election. He still speaks like a politician, refusing to admit that any tactical or strategic errors were made in the great grab for the spoils of higher oil prices. His claims that it was the provincial government that was "caught in a squeeze play" between the federal government and the oil companies certainly stretches the imagination.

Don Getty is prepared to take a much more objective view of the events of 1974, admitting that the province probably "over-reached". Getty is the individual who has perhaps grown in stature the most since the days of the crisis. He became Energy Minister when Dickie left in 1975 and was personally responsible for regaining the respect of the oil industry.

During the dispute, the exchanges between "Thumper" Macdonald and Getty were among the most vituperative. After Syncrude was saved by government intervention, Donald Macdonald gave Bill Mooney, the head of Canada Cities Service and a man who fought very hard to keep the project afloat, a desk diary. In it, Macdonald wrote, with an undetermined degree of humour: "To Bill Mooney — the great supporter of national oil policy." Mooney showed the diary to Getty, who, with rather more barbed wit, inscribed: "If you understand national policy, you're a genius."

However, Getty went on to gain a grasp of the industry that he perhaps had not had during the dispute, and negotiated subsequent key agreements on oil and gas pricing. He calmed down considerably, although his occasional frustration with Macdonald's successor, Alastair Gillespie, could not always be restrained.

However, burned out with the heavy and thankless burden of political life under Lougheed, Getty left provincial politics to return to the oil industry after the March 1979 election.

By the end of 1979, John Turner, who, as Finance Minister, introduced the royalty non-deductibility provisions that raised Albertan temperatures most, remained in the political wilderness, although he was still being touted to receive the call to lead the freshly-defeated federal Liberal Party.

Donald Macdonald, the Thumper, had also returned to the law. Although he was perhaps the key target for Albertan abuse, his forthright approach and brilliant mind won over many of his former opponents.

By the spring of 1979, that left only Lougheed and Trudeau of the protagonists. The real relationship between these two very different men had always been an enigma. The contrast between the mercurial brilliance and charisma of Trudeau and the staid, staunchly unilingual and studied image of Lougheed is very great. Perhaps René Lévesque was the only provincial Premier in a position not to be intimidated by Trudeau's intellect, and Lougheed certainly wisely steered clear of open debate with the Prime Minister during the dispute.

However, in terms of political achievement, Lougheed entered 1979 with the strongest support in Confederation, while Trudeau danced on the edge of electoral oblivion. Their fates were of course related, since they were at opposite ends of the seesaw of Confederation, where Lougheed's successes had to be counted as Trudeau's failures.

In May, 1979, Pierre Trudeau danced off the political precipice. Then there was one: Peter Lougheed.

Just how high Lougheed was riding in the spring of 1979 was clearly underlined by the provincial election in March, when the people of Alberta, or at least the 40% of the electorate who could be bothered to turn out for such a foregone conclusion, gave him his second landslide victory.

The election was one of the dullest in Canada for years. On the Canadian television channels in Alberta on the evening of March 14, 1979, political pundits attempted to breathe life into a non-event. The most fitting comment came as the "scoreboard" appeared on the CBC announcing that the Progressive Conservatives had won, or were leading, in 74 seats out of 79. Through a microphone unintentionally left live, one of the talking heads let loose an enormous sigh of boredom!

From a federal point of view, however, this overwhelming popular support for Lougheed could have frightening ramifications. If he regards it as a mandate to continue his hard line on negotiations with Ottawa, the strains on an already struggling Confederation could be considerable. Lougheed stands for provincial wealth and for eyeball-to-eyeball confrontation with the still much resented eastern political and corporate Establishment. The economic boot has now undoubtedly changed feet in Canada. The key question is whether that will be enough for Lougheed, or whether he will want to apply the boot to the sagging flesh of the East's rulers.

On the night of the provincial election, Nick Taylor, leader of a still seatless provincial Liberal party, asked about the result's significance, emphasized that it depended on whether Lougheed used it to "push with his shrill screams against central Canada." Social Credit leader, Bob Clark, said it looked as if "The people of Alberta have endorsed the Premier's fight with Ottawa." Later that evening, Taylor said: "This man wants to pull Canada apart," and then, with perhaps the most chilling words of all: "The milk of human kindness and forgiveness runs thin in Lougheed's veins."

Whether that stands as the embittered personal assessment of an unhappy loser, or as a prophetic warning to Ottawa, only time will tell. The fact remains, however, that after the March election, Lougheed stood as master of all he surveyed. Admittedly, the halo of disinterested public service had slipped slightly at the end of 1978 when it was learned that Lougheed had accepted free airline tickets from Canada's major airlines, but that obviously made little difference to the people of Alberta.

The success of Joe Clark in the 1979 federal election arouses intriguing possibilities about federal-provincial relations in future. Joe Clark is an Albertan but he was never fully accepted into the essentially jockish clique of provincial Conservative politics. However, the fact that Lougheed may regard him as a "known" and above all manageable quantity, may lead to a moderation of the province's hard line towards Ottawa.

The 50% increase in OPEC prices in the first half of 1979 has placed enormous pressure on the federal government to escalate the rise in domestic prices. Canada was importing about 500,000 barrels of oil a day into the eastern part of the country in the latter half of 1979. Following the meteoric escalations in the OPEC price in the first half of the year, this oil was now costing over $24 a barrel. Under the previous Liberal government's "one-price" policy for oil, the federal government has to provide a subsidy to importers to bring the price of oil down to the domestic price. By the third quarter of 1979, this meant the federal government was paying out more than $10 for every barrel of imported oil, or a total of over $5 million a day. These payments amounted to a severe additional burden on an already strained public purse. However, for

the federal government, the obvious way to reduce the subsidy
seemed to be to increase the domestic price of oil at a faster pace
than that of its predecessor government. There was widespread
speculation after the resurgence of open economic militancy in the
first half of 1979 that instead of domestic Canadian prices rising by
$1 every six months, they might rise by $2 or even more.

However, it seems certain that no federal government can permit Alberta to enjoy a further acceleration in the growth of its
wealth when it already has patently more than it knows how to utilize. Depending on how hard a line Lougheed decides to take on
higher oil revenues, another federal-provincial dispute may be in
the making. Alberta's increasing wealth is a foregone conclusion.
The dispute will merely be over the matter of degree.

Once again, it seems, the noise of OPEC's militancy, so frightening to most of the rest of the industrialized world, is sweet music to
the ears of Peter Lougheed and the rest of Alberta's blue-eyed
sheiks.

Appendix

The Petro-Rich.

Some of the Calgarians with multi-million dollar stakes in the companies they built. This table represents only these individuals' shareholdings in their principal company. Their total wealth is in many cases considerably larger.

Name	Company	Value of shareholdings(1)
Harold and Bill Siebens	Siebens Oil & Gas Ltd.	Harold — $123.4 million(2) Bill — $38.6 million(2)
Glenn and James Nielson	Husky Oil Ltd.	$107 million(3)
J. V. "Vern" Lyons	Ocelot Industries	$112.4 million
Jack Gallagher	Dome Petroleum	$52.4 million
Bill Richards	Dome Petroleum	$12.5 million
Seaman family	Bow Valley Industries	D.K. — $23.6 million B.J. — $23.4 million D.R. — $14.6 million
Bill McGregor	Numac Oil & Gas	$33.2 million
Syd Kahanoff	Voyager Petroleums	$55 million(4)
Gus Van Wielingen	Sulpetro	$25 million
John Scrymgeour	Westburne International	$34.2 million
Jack Pierce	Ranger Oil	$22 million
Bob Brawn	Turbo	$11 million
Ken Travis	Turbo	$18.9 million
Stan Milner	Chieftain	$13.6 million
Bud McCaig	Trimac	$19.4 million

(1) Based on 1979 year's high for stock on August 1, unless otherwise stated.
(2) Money received when Siebens was sold in 1978 to Dome via the CN pension fund for $355 million.
(3) Received under an agreement with Alberta Gas Trunk Line under which AGTL has bought the Nielson's 18.4% of Husky for US$48 a share.
(4) Personal proceeds from sale of Voyager to Nu-West Development in 1978.

SOURCE: *Financial Post*, Wood Gundy

Who Owns The Canadian Oil Industry?

This chart, ranking Canada's top conventional oil and gas producers, clearly shows that the U.S. still has a strong hold on ownership of the Canadian industry. The top five oil producers in Canada are all either majority or wholly-owned by U.S. companies. In all, nine of the top 20 producers are U.S.-controlled.

Company	Daily prod. of oil and natural gas liquids (bls)	Daily prod. of natural gas (thousands of cub. ft.)	Major shareholder	Country of origin
Imperial Oil	231,000	345,000	Exxon Corporation — 69.6%	U.S.
Texaco Canada	122,800	71,500	Texaco Inc. — 89.7%	U.S.
Gulf Canada	112,000	373,000	Gulf Oil Corp. — 68.3%	U.S.
Hudson's Bay Oil & Gas	74,874	377,300	Continental Oil — 52.9%	U.S.
			Hudson's Bay Co. — 21.1%	Can.
Chevron Canada	73,000	179,000	Standard Oil of California — 100%	U.S.
Shell Canada	65,800	601,500	Shell Investments — 78.8%	U.K./ Holland
PetroCanada	64,658	394,520	Federal government — 100%	Can.
Mobil Oil Canada	63,000	221,000	Mobil Oil Corp. — 100%	U.S.
Amoco Canada	52,000	261,000	Standard Oil of Indiana — 100%	U.S.
Husky Oil	48,253	80,302	Alberta Gas Truck Line — 67.8%	Can.
Canadian Superior	38,377	241,946	Superior Oil Co. — 49.7%(1)	U.S.
PanCanadian Petroleum	36,482	304,110	Canadian Pac. Investments — 87.1%	Can.
Home Oil	30,685	125,700	Consumers Gas — 49.7%(2)	Can.
Aquitaine	29,700	145,500	Societe Nationale Elf Aquitaine — 74.8%	France
Union Oil of Canada	25,576	64,479	Union Oil of California — 86.5%	U.S.
Ashland Oil Canada (now Kaiser Oil)	25,200	66,300	Kaiser Resources Ltd — 100%	Can.
Norcen Energy Resources	23,187	155,700		Can.
BP Canada	20,465	109,534	BP Canadian Holdings — 65.5%	U.K.
Petrofina Canada	17,900	73,300	Petrofina S.A. — 71.5%	Belg.
Dome Petroleum	13,241(4)	164,300	Dome Mines — 25.75%(3)	Can.
Amerada Hess Corp	12,583	79,426	Amerada Hess — 100%	U.S.
Sun Oil Co.	10,250	15,625	Sun Oil Corp. — 100%	U.S.
Total Petroleum(NA)	9,858	41,931	Campagnie Francaise des Petroles	France
Murphy Oil	9,401	28,275	Murphy Oil Corp. — 77.4%	U.S.
Canadian Reserve	5,764	18,231	Reserve Oil & Gas — 88.3%(5)	U.S.
Asamera	5,645	247		Can.
Bow Valley Industries	3,795	63,200	Seaman Family — 20% Cemp Investments — 13.5%	Can.
Candel Oil	3,437	52,768	St. Joe Mineral Corp. — 92.3%	U.S.
Francana Oil & Gas	3,375	11,000	Hudson Bay Mining — 54.9%	Can.
Amalgamated Bonanza	2,357	6,500	Analind Corp.(Dr. Natoros) — 10.6%	Can.
Westcoast Petroleum	2,278	30,500	Westcoast Transmission — 54.4%	Can.
Canadian Occidental	1,715	39,145	Hooker Chemical Corp. — 82%	U.S.
Numac Oil & Gas	1,542	7,381	The Pitcairn Co. — 10.2%	Can.
Ranger Oil	1,307	15,243		Can.
Canada Northwest Land	594	15,438	Thor Dahls Group — 27.4% Imasco Ltd. — 20.8%	
Ocelot Industries	478	77,890	J. V. Lyons — 43.6%	Can.
Alberta Energy Co.	420	74,000	Alberta Government — 50%	Can.
Coseka Resources	312	23,852	Brinco — 25.4%	Can.
Turbo Resources	298	3,792	Liberty Holdings & Ind. — 19.7% Bob Brawn — 11.5%	Can.

(1) Superior Oil is attempting to buy out the Canadian shareholders and achieve 100% ownership.
(2) Consumers is negotiating for 100% control of Home.
(3) Dome Petroleum in turn owns 41% of Dome Mines.
(4) Does not include Siebens Oil & Gas or Mesa Petroleum.
(5) Denison Mines of Toronto has made a US$525 million bid for Reserve Oil & Gas

SOURCE: Wood Gundy. Annual reports.

The Seven Sisters and Their Canadian Subsidiaries.

The Canadian subsidiaries of the Seven Sisters all rank in the top hundred Canadian industrial companies but their size is dwarfed by that of their parents.

Company	1978 sales (US$ million)	Canadian subsidiary	1978 sales (C$ million)	Rank among all Canadian industrial companies by sales.
Exxon	60,334	Imperial Oil	5,671	4
Royal Dutch/Shell	44,054	Shell Canada	2,715	12
Mobil	34,736	Mobil Canada	649	52
Texaco	28,607	Texaco Canada	1,902	17
British Petroleum	27,390	BP Canada	749	42
Standard Californ.	23,232	Chevron Canada	379	87
Gulf Oil	18,069	Gulf Canada	2,550	11

SOURCE: *Time magazine. The Financial Post 500.*

The Refiners. How International Oil Dominates Canadian Refining.

Refining Capacity, Throughput and Operating Rates

Company	Refining Capacity (bbls./day) 1978	Average Crude Processed (bbls./day) 1978	Operating Rate % 1978
Canada			
Imperial	490,000	435,000	89
Gulf	385,900	301,000	78
Shell	295,000	262,550	89
Texaco	261,500(1)	163,600	63
BP	160,000	112,778	70
Petrofina	95,000	72,400	78
Husky	21,500	15,493	72
Other	804,000(2)	456,379	57
Total	2,512,900	1,819,200	72
United States			
Husky	60,000	44,585	74
Total Pete	89,200	70,866(3)	79

(1) Includes the 48,000 bbl/day Port Credit, Ont. refinery where crude oil refining was suspended in 1978.

(2) Includes Irving Oil, Golden Eagle, Petrosar, Sun Oil, Consumers' Co-op, Chevron, Pacific as well as Newfoundland's Come By Chance 100,000 bbl/day refinery which is currently mothballed.

(3) Includes only 9 months of throughput at Total's Arkansas City refinery purchased on April 1, 1978.

SOURCE: Wood Gundy

The Federal Government's Secret Energy Advisors:
The National Advisory Committee on Petroleum.

Nacop was set up by Liberal Energy Minister Joe Greene in the early 1970s to provide secret consultation with the Federal Government. Membership was by invitation and members were sworn to the same vow of secrecy as taken by the Cabinet. The committee met at irregular intervals to discuss specific policy topics. No minutes of the meetings were ever taken. The committee is still in existence, although the new Federal Conservative government had not, by the fall of 1979, decided how they would "use" it.

Present Members

James Allan—Golden Eagle
Jack Armstrong—Imperial Oil
C.W. Daniel—Shell Canada
K.F. Heddon—GCOS (formerly Sun)
W.H. Hopper—PetroCanada
J.W. Kerr—TransCanada PipeLines
D.F. Mitchell—B.P. Canada
P. Nadeau—Petrofina Canada
C.D. Shepard—Gulf Canada
R.W. Sparks—Texaco Canada
E.C. Phillips—Westcoast Transmission
R.B. Bailey—Canadian Reserve Oil & Gas
R.W. Campbell—PanCanadian Petroleum
A.R. Nielsen—Canadian Superior
R.F. Ruben—North Canadian Oils
D.G. Waldon—Retired, formerly of Interprovincial Pipeline

Past Members

E.C. Bovey—Northern and Central (before Norcen formed)
H. Bridges—Shell Canada
A.F. Campeau—Petrofina Canada
A.G. Farquharson—Texaco Canada (before Tex. Can. Tex. Inc. amalgamation)
K.H. Gibson—Westcoast Transmission and Pacific Pete
A.L. Irving—Irving Oil Ltd.
K.C. Irving—Irving Oil Ltd.
O.L. Jones—Consumers' Gas
Jerry McAfee—Gulf Canada
F.A. McKinnon—B.P. Oil & Gas (before amalgamation with B.P. Canada)
D.E. Mitchell—Great Plains (defunct), later Alberta Energy Company
M. Paulson—Home Oil
L.J. Richards—Hudson's Bay Oil and Gas
G.E. Roark—Husky Oil
A.H. Ross—Western Decalta
W.O. Twaits—Imperial Oil

Oil Men Who Sit On Bank Boards

Bank of Montreal

S. Robert Blair, Calgary
President and CEO, The Alberta Gas Trunk Line Co. Ltd.

C. William Daniel, Toronto
President and CEO, Shell Canada Limited

Louis A. Desrochers, Q.C., Edmonton
Partner, Messrs. McCuaig Desrochers

Donald S. Harvie, Calgary
Chairman and CEO, The Devonian Group of Charitable Foundations

Ronald N. Mannix, Calgary
President, Loram Co. Ltd.

H. J. S. Pearson, Edmonton
Chairman and CEO, Century Sales & Service Ltd.

Canadian Imperial Bank of Commerce

Edmund C. Bovey, C.M., Toronto
Chairman, Norcen Energy Resources Limited

M. E. Jones, Q.C., LL.B., Calgary
Senior Partner, Jones, Black & Company

The Royal Bank of Canada

John A. Armstrong, Toronto
President, Chief Executive and Chairman of the Board,
Imperial Oil Limited

Kelly H. Gibson, Calgary
Chairman of the Board, Foothills Pipe Lines (Yukon) Ltd.

P.L.P. Macdonnell, Q.C., Edmonton
Partner, Milner & Steer

F. C. Mannix, Calgary
Company Director

Pierre A. Nadeau, Montreal
Chairman of the Board and CEO, Petrofina Canada Ltd.

L. Merrill Rasmussen, Calgary,
President and CEO, Pacific Petroleums Ltd.

Bank of Nova Scotia

William S. McGregor, Edmonton
President and Managing Director, Numac Oil & Gas Ltd.

David E. Mitchell, Calgary
President and CEO, Alberta Energy Company Ltd.

Robert L. Pierce, Q.C., Calgary
Executive Vice-President, The Alberta Gas Trunk Line Company Limited

The Toronto-Dominion Bank

Edgar F. Kaiser, Jr., Vancouver
Chairman and CEO, Kaiser Resources Ltd.

Arne R. Nielsen, Calgary
President and CEO, Canadian Superior Oil Ltd.

Clarence D. Shepard, Toronto
Chairman of the Board and CEO, Gulf Canada Limited

SOURCE: Annual Reports 1978.

Company	78 Sales $000,000	Base salary	Variable Compensation(1) $	Total	Common shs. held (last yrs end)
Ashland Oil Canada Ltd. $216					
Vernon Von Sant. Jr., pres. & CEO		104,445	49,400	*153,845	n.a.

*Includes $25,000 credited to deferred compensation account; excludes $225,000 paid as retirement allowance on Oct. 3, 1978.

Company	78 Sales $000,000	Base salary	Variable Compensation(1) $	Total	Common shs. held (last yrs end)
Banister Continental Ltd. $94					
R. K. Banister, Chm. Banister Pipelines Intl. Inc.		50,847	*90,000	140,847	144,034
R. T. Banister, chm. & pres.		77,706	*50,000	127,706	

*Bonus

Company	78 Sales $000,000	Base salary	Variable Compensation(1) $	Total	Common shs. held (last yrs end)
Bow Valley Industries Ltd. $232					
D. K. Seaman, chm. & CEO		65,625		65,625	750,646
B. J. Seaman, vice chm.		55,419		55,419	743,532
D. R. Seaman, sr. v/p		49,588		49,588	462,764
Canadian Occidental Petroleum Ltd. $92					
R. S. MacAlister, pres.		71,207	2,683	73,890	15,453
Canadian Superior Oil Ltd. $228					
A. R. Nielson, pres. & CEO		225,000		225,000	1
Dome Petroleum Ltd. $639					
J. P. Gallagher, chm. & CEO			154,448	154,448	
W. E. Richards, pres.		111,666	121,129	237,795	
Hudson's Bay Oil & Gas Co. $394					
S. G. Olson, pres.		135,331	4,980	140,310	16
Husky Oil Ltd. $703					
J. E. Nielson, pres. & CEO		144,688	196,250	340,938	
Imperial Oil Ltd. $5700					
J. A. Armstrong, chm. & pres.		258,800	195,020	453,820	18,405
J. G. Livingstone, exec. v/p		167,500	130,507	298,007	7,830
J. W. Flanagan, sr. v/p		132,300	95,772	228,072	3,202
J. H. Hamlin, sr. v/p		133,133	85,306	218,439	5,084
D. D. Lougheed, sr. v/p		124,050	89,195	213,245	6,146
Interprovincial Pipe Line Ltd. $286					
D. G. Weldon, chm.		64,500	53,128	117,628	
Norcen Energy Resources Ltd. $n.a.					
E. G. Battle, pres.		131,300	6,500	*137,800	8,134
E. C. Bovey, chm.		166,500	5,700	172,200	15,606

*Excludes benefits received on exercise of options ($1.2 million paid for stock by him vs $1.8 million market value of shares on date taken up).

Company	78 Sales $000,000	Base salary	Variable Compensation(1) $	Total	Common shs. held (last yrs end)
Numac Oil & Gas Ltd. $17					
W. S. McGregor, pres.		70,040		70,040	759,612
Pacific Petroleums Ltd. $471					
L. M. Rasmussen, pres.		*201,813	98,125	299,938	
A. M. McIntosh, exec. v/p		123,100		123,100	

*Includes $13,188 received from Westcoast Transmission Co.

Company	78 Sales $000,000	Base salary	Variable Compensation(1) $	Total	Common shs. held (last yrs end)
Ranger Oil (Canada) Ltd. $10.4					
J. M. Pierce, pres.		101,000	6,413	107,413	705,816
Westburne International Industries Ltd. *$482					
J. A. Scrymgeour, chm.		US240,000		US240,000	680,800

*Yearend Mar. 31/78

Company	78 Sales $000,000	Base salary	Variable Compensation(1) $	Total	Common shs. held (last yrs end)
Westcoast Petroleum Ltd. $26					
R. H. Lawrence, pres. & CEO		90,000		90,000	9,000
Westcoast Transmission Ltd. $844					
E. C. Phillips, pres. & CEO		137,150	10,938	148,088	91,023

(1) Cash equivalents, including directors fees, commissions and bonuses.

SOURCE: *Financial Post*

Bob Blair's Domain

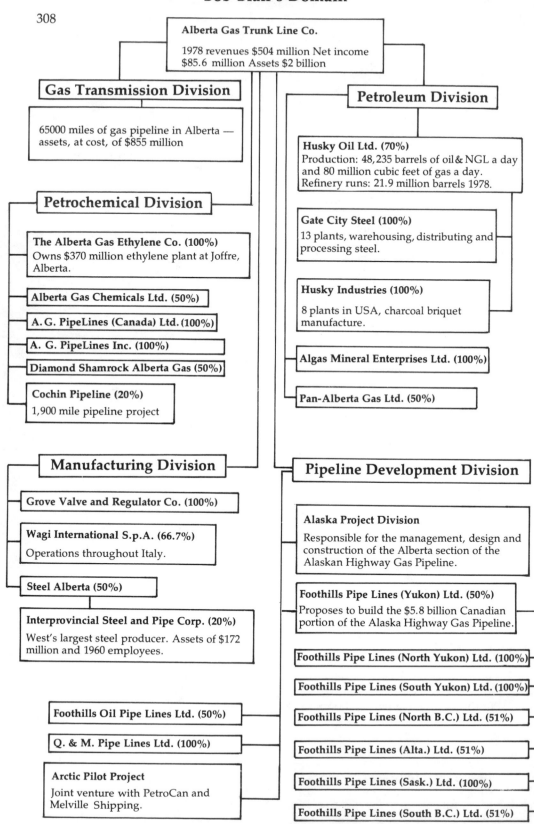

Alberta Gas Trunk Line Co.

1978 revenues $504 million Net income $85.6 million Assets $2 billion

Gas Transmission Division

65000 miles of gas pipeline in Alberta — assets, at cost, of $855 million

Petroleum Division

Husky Oil Ltd. (70%)
Production: 48,235 barrels of oil & NGL a day and 80 million cubic feet of gas a day. Refinery runs: 21.9 million barrels 1978.

Gate City Steel (100%)
13 plants, warehousing, distributing and processing steel.

Husky Industries (100%)
8 plants in USA, charcoal briquet manufacture.

Algas Mineral Enterprises Ltd. (100%)

Pan-Alberta Gas Ltd. (50%)

Petrochemical Division

The Alberta Gas Ethylene Co. (100%)
Owns $370 million ethylene plant at Joffre, Alberta.

Alberta Gas Chemicals Ltd. (50%)

A.G. PipeLines (Canada) Ltd. (100%)

A. G. PipeLines Inc. (100%)

Diamond Shamrock Alberta Gas (50%)

Cochin Pipeline (20%)
1,900 mile pipeline project

Manufacturing Division

Grove Valve and Regulator Co. (100%)

Wagi International S.p.A. (66.7%)
Operations throughout Italy.

Steel Alberta (50%)

Interprovincial Steel and Pipe Corp. (20%)
West's largest steel producer. Assets of $172 million and 1960 employees.

Foothills Oil Pipe Lines Ltd. (50%)

Q. & M. Pipe Lines Ltd. (100%)

Arctic Pilot Project
Joint venture with PetroCan and Melville Shipping.

Pipeline Development Division

Alaska Project Division
Responsible for the management, design and construction of the Alberta section of the Alaskan Highway Gas Pipeline.

Foothills Pipe Lines (Yukon) Ltd. (50%)
Proposes to build the $5.8 billion Canadian portion of the Alaska Highway Gas Pipeline.

Foothills Pipe Lines (North Yukon) Ltd. (100%)

Foothills Pipe Lines (South Yukon) Ltd. (100%)

Foothills Pipe Lines (North B.C.) Ltd. (51%)

Foothills Pipe Lines (Alta.) Ltd. (51%)

Foothills Pipe Lines (Sask.) Ltd. (100%)

Foothills Pipe Lines (South B.C.) Ltd. (51%)

All figures are for 1978 or 1978 year-end unless otherwise stated.

Jack Gallagher's Empire

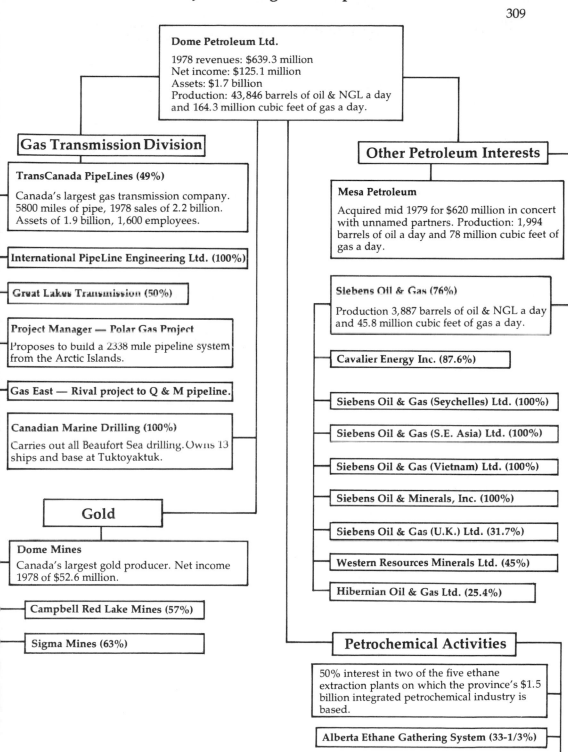

Dome Petroleum Ltd.

1978 revenues: $639.3 million
Net income: $125.1 million
Assets: $1.7 billion
Production: 43,846 barrels of oil & NGL a day
and 164.3 million cubic feet of gas a day.

Gas Transmission Division

TransCanada PipeLines (49%)

Canada's largest gas transmission company.
5800 miles of pipe, 1978 sales of 2.2 billion.
Assets of 1.9 billion, 1,600 employees.

International PipeLine Engineering Ltd. (100%)

Great Lakes Transmission (50%)

Project Manager — Polar Gas Project

Proposes to build a 2338 mile pipeline system
from the Arctic Islands.

Gas East — Rival project to Q & M pipeline.

Canadian Marine Drilling (100%)

Carries out all Beaufort Sea drilling. Owns 13
ships and base at Tuktoyaktuk.

Gold

Dome Mines

Canada's largest gold producer. Net income
1978 of $52.6 million.

Campbell Red Lake Mines (57%)

Sigma Mines (63%)

Other Petroleum Interests

Mesa Petroleum

Acquired mid 1979 for $620 million in concert
with unnamed partners. Production: 1,994
barrels of oil a day and 78 million cubic feet of
gas a day.

Siebens Oil & Gas (76%)

Production 3,887 barrels of oil & NGL a day
and 45.8 million cubic feet of gas a day.

Cavalier Energy Inc. (87.6%)

Siebens Oil & Gas (Seychelles) Ltd. (100%)

Siebens Oil & Gas (S.E. Asia) Ltd. (100%)

Siebens Oil & Gas (Vietnam) Ltd. (100%)

Siebens Oil & Minerals, Inc. (100%)

Siebens Oil & Gas (U.K.) Ltd. (31.7%)

Western Resources Minerals Ltd. (45%)

Hibernian Oil & Gas Ltd. (25.4%)

Petrochemical Activities

50% interest in two of the five ethane
extraction plants on which the province's $1.5
billion integrated petrochemical industry is
based.

Alberta Ethane Gathering System (33-1/3%)

Cochin Pipeline (32-1/2%)

Source.   Annual reports. Company press releases

The $4 Billion Trading Spree
Value of Canadian Oil Shares
Traded During 1978

**How Oils Have Dominated
the Toronto Stock Exchange**

More than half of the top 50 stocks by trading
volume on the TSE in the year to June, 1979 were
oil or oil related.

		Stock Symbol	Trading Value ($000)
1.	Dome	DMP	792,077
2.	Husky	HYO	640,020
3.	Asamera	ASM	291,050
4.	Imperial	IMO	284,884
5.	Bow Valley	BVI	254,628
6.	Numac	NMC	244,440
7.	Norcen	NCN	210,062
8.	Total Pete	TPN	209,568
9.	Amal. Bonanza	ABN	162,718
10.	Home	HGA	153,966
11.	Ranger	RGO	126,208
12.	Chieftain	CID	106,580
13.	Cdn. Superior	CAS	106,227
14.	Gulf	GOC	104,561
15.	BP	BPO	98,810
16.	HBOG	HBO	89,741
17.	Shell	SHC	67,262
18.	Texaco	TXC	51,413
19.	Aquitaine	AQT	48,682
20.	Ocelot	OIL	42,399
21.	Merland	MOC	40,720
22.	North Cdn.	NCO	31,360
23.	Alberta Energy	AEC	30,924
24.	PanCanadian	PCP	27,149
25.	Westcoast	WPL	26,536
26.	Canada NWL	CNW	26,186
27.	Coseka	CKS	21,091
28.	Union	UCN	19,234
29.	Murphy	MO	17,301
30.	Cdn. Occidental	CXY	16,936
31.	Cdn. Reserve	CRG	13,596
32.	Turbo Resources	TBR	11,233
33.	Francana	FOG	8,969
34.	Petrofina	PFC	5,171
35.	Candel	CDY	252

SOURCE: Wood Gundy

	Stock	12 Month Dollar Vol.
1	Dome Pete	$472,026,368
2	Brascan 'A'	299,200,512
3	TR-C Pipeline	298,182,912
4	Bell Canada	295,407,872
5	Inco Ltd.	279,294,208
6	Imp Oil 'A'	253,622,048
7	Cdn Pac Ltd.	252,297,328
8	Alcan Alum	237,377,824
9	Hud Bay Co.	213,522,688
10	Noranda Mns	197,824,016
11	Norcen Enrgy	191,267,440
12	Asamera Oil	178,899,344
13	Bank of Mtl	176,561,280
14	Numac Oil	166,017,904
15	Abitibi Papr	165,794,240
16	Royal Bk Cda	151,691,056
17	Cdn Imp Bank	137,522,864
18	Moore Corp.	132,737,584
19	Amal Bonanza	125,719,824
20	MacMillan Bl	125,309,728
21	Bow Valley I	119,039,248
22	Alta Gas 'A'	117,314,896
23	Home Oil A	115,165,584
24	Total Pete	112,994,544
25	Steel Co. 'A'	111,994,592
26	Seagram Ltd.	111,469,984
27	Gulf Cda Ltd.	111,348,992
28	Husky Oil	106,775,088
29	Dome Mines	104,247,280
30	Hud Bay Oil	103,706,992
31	Cdn Sup Oil	99,229,696
32	Bank Nova Sc	98,307,760
33	Tor-Dom Bank	97,639,408
34	Nrthn Tele	92,806,976
35	Walker-G 'A'	88,928,896
36	Denison Mine	77,133,280
37	Genstar Ltd.	76,250,864
38	Kaiser Resrc	75,852,944
39	Cmrs Gas	69,305,504
40	Cominco Ltd.	67,671,088
41	Calgary P 'A'	66,676,976
42	Domtar Inc.	66,580,032
43	Westburne	65,540,144
44	Falconer N A	64,645,488
45	Westcoast Tr	64,452,928
46	Shell Canada	63,338,032
47	IAC Ltd.	60,629,184
48	Dom Fdr & St A	59,918,880
49	Intprov Pipe	58,402,112
50	Ranger Oil C	58,239,536

SOURCE: *The Graphoscope*

In line with its colleagues in the developed industrialized world, Canada's consumption of oil products has appeared almost insatiable since the second world war. Since 1947, consumption has virtually doubled every ten years. In the 1970s it has become clear, as it should have been clear all along, that that sort of growth could not go on forever.

Year	Refinery Crude Runs(1)	Net Product Imports (exports)	Apparent Consumption of Crude Oil & Products
1947	33,656(2)	6,579	40,235
1948	37,948	8,724	46,672
1949	41,890	7,230	49,120
1950	47,518	8,788	56,306
1951	55,395	11,902	67,297
1952	60,228	9,537	69,765
1953	67,181	9,466	76,647
1954	73,798	8,067	81,865
1955	84,815	16,107	100,922
1956	98,572	14,697	113,269
1957	103,871	13,691	117,562
1958	104,679	12,224	116,903
1959	116,011	15,818	131,829
1960	121,696	14,261	135,957
1961	129,085	12,080	141,165
1962	134,809	11,187	145,996
1963	144,242	11,826	156,068
1964	148,534	15,228	163,762
1965	154,508	24,503	179,011
1966	165,492	24,817	190,309
1967	169,848	28,376	198,224
1968	180,353	30,292	210,645
1969	188,653	30,659	219,312
1970	202,986	28,715	231,701
1971	221,641	18,431	240,072
1972	243,450	7,458	250,908
1973	266,075	1,155	267,230
1974	281,215	(4,031)	277,184
1975	270,681	(7,287)	263,394
1976	271,173	(3,515)	267,658
1977	286,909	(5,054)	281,855
1978	288,666	(12,699)	275,967

(1) Includes condensate and pentanes plus propane/butanes/mixes.
(2) All figures are cubic meters per day.

Note: Export/Import numbers above do not reflect total foreign trade transactions.

SOURCE: Canadian Petroleum Association

OPEC Prices Have Surged in the Seventies Canadian Prices Have Soared . . . But Still Lag Behind.

When OPEC prices took off in the winter of 1973-74, they left Canadian prices a long way behind. Between April, 1974, when Canadian prices took off in pursuit, and the latter half of 1978, Canadian oil prices were making up ground on the world price, even though world oil was priced in $US and the Canadian $ had fallen sharply against the currency of its U.S. neighbour. However, the upsurge in world prices in 1979 has left Canadian domestic oil prices lower relative to the world price than they have ever been. Taking US$20 as the average current world price (= C$23.50 at the end of 1979), the Canadian price was C$10 cheaper.

World price of oil[1]		Price US$/barrel
	1960-1970	1.80
15 February	1971	2.18
1 June	1971	2.29
20 January	1972	2.48
1 January	1973	2.59
1 April	1973	2.74
1 June	1973	2.90
1 July	1973	2.96
1 August	1973	3.07
1 October	1973	3.01
16 October	1973	5.12
1 November	1973	5.18
1 December	1973	5.04
1 January	1974	11.65
1 November	1974	11.25
1 October	1975	12.38
1 October	1976	12.38
1 July	1977	12.70
1 Jan	1979	13.34
1 April	1979	14.54
July	1979	18.00[2]

(1) Saudi Arabian light crude, to which prices of other OPEC countries have usually been linked.

(2) This represents the "floor" price for OPEC oil, the official price of which now ranges between 18.00 and 23.50.

Domestic Crude Oil Price Changes: Alberta Average Wellhead

Date	Cdn. $/BBL.	Reason for Change
1970 January	2.76	
1970 December 15	2.85	Reflect OPEC Price Increase
1972 November 15	2.95	General Increase
1973 January 5	3.15	Reflect OPEC Price Increase
1973 May 1	3.40	U.S. $ Devaluation & OPEC Increase
1973 August 1	3.80	Reflect OPEC Price Increase
1974 April 1	6.50	Federal/Provincial Agreement
1975 July 1	8.00	Federal/Provincial Agreement
1976 July 1	9.05	Federal/Provincial Agreement
1977 January 1	9.75	Federal/Provincial Agreement
1977 July 1	10.75	Federal/Provincial Agreement
1978 January 1	11.75	Federal/Provincial Agreement
1978 July 1	12.75	Federal/Provincial Agreement
1979 July 1	13.75	Federal/Provincial Agreement

SOURCE: Shell Canada, B.P., The Petroleum Economist

How the province dominates the country's reserves of oil and gas, and accounts for more than four-fifths of production.

Remaining Established[1] Canadian Crude Oil & Natural Gas Liquids (NGL) Reserves, Production and Life Indices

Province	Conventional Crude Oil & NGL Reserves at December 31, 1978 (000's bbls)	1978 Crude Oil & NGL Production (000's bbls)	Life Index 1978 (years)
Alberta	7,210,301	427,088	16.9
Saskatchewan	747,384	60,296	12.4
British Columbia	174,824	14,239	12.3
Other	168,616	5,994	28.1
Total Canada	8,300,126	507,616	16.4

(1) Established Reserves equates to the former proven plus probable category

Remaining Established[1] Canadian Natural Gas Reserves, Production and Life Indices

Province	Natural Gas Reserves at Dec. 31, 1978 (Mmcf)	1978 Natural Gas Production* (Mmcf)	Life Index 1978 (years)
Alberta	54,760,283	2,007,434	27.4
Saskatchewan	1,248,516	41,661	30.0
British Columbia	7,716,078	262,615	29.4
Other(2)	18,332,120	27,280	672.0
Total Canada	82,056,997	2,330,000	35.2

(1) Established Reserves equates to the former proven plus probable category.
(2) Includes 18.0 trillion cubic feet of reserves in the Northwest Territories, primarily in the Mackenzie Delta area, and the Arctic Islands.

* Preliminary Estimates

Canadian Daily Production of Conventional Crude & NGL and Natural Gas, 1978

Province	1978 Crude Oil & NGL Production (Bbls./day)	% of Cdn. Production	1978 Natural Gas Production (Mmcf/day)	% of Cdn. Sales
Alberta	1,170,789	84.1	5,500	85.6
Saskatchewan	165,290	11.9	123	1.9
British Columbia	39,033	2.8	723	11.3
Other	16,430	1.2	75	1.2
Total Canada	1,391,542	100.0	6,422	100.0

SOURCE: Canadian Petroleum Association. Wood Gundy

Index

Abercrombie, Robin, 133, 266
Aberhart, William, 37
Abu Dhabi, 230, 271-74
Aquitaine Ltd., 247
Adair, Red, 103-105
Adams, "Boots", 191-92
AEC. See Alberta Energy Company.
AEG. See Alberta Eastern Gas.
Ajax Petroleums, 147
AGTL. See Alberta Gas Trunk Line.
Alamo Petroleums Ltd., 221
Alaska Highway, 110, 118, 178
Alaska Highway pipeline, 106, 108-109,
    119, 121, 132, 155, 162, 179, 181, 259
Alberta
    eastern Canada, uneasy relations
        with, 35, 40, 42, 177
    federal-provincial relations, 14, 29,
        35-36, 41-42, 44-45, 82-83, 91-94,
        106, 142, 298-99, 300-301
    oil exploration, incentives for, 40, 44,
        55, 79, 100
    oil markets (1947-1970), 27
    oil prices 12, 41, 43-44, 54
    oil production, 13, 29
    Syncrude and, 80ff., 152
Alberta & Southern Gas, 107, 113, 173
Alberta Eastern Gas, 219-20
Alberta Energy Company, 63, 84, 248,
    257-58, 263, 275
Alberta Energy Resources Conservation
    Board, 40, 262
Alberta Gas Trunk Line, 16, 63, 106ff.,
    132ff., 153ff., 165, 173, 178, 181, 199,
    200, 256, 258, 262ff., 267n., 274-75
Alberta Heritage Fund. See Heritage
    Fund, Alberta.
Alberta Leaseholds, 228
Alberta Minerals Ltd., 228
Alberta Natural Gas Co., 111n.
Alberta Oil Sands Technology and
    Research Authority, 86
Alberta Petroleum Marketing
    Commission, 262
Alberta Securities Commission, 291
Alcan project, 118, 119, 181
Allan, John D., 208
Alsands project, 73, 79, 81, 85, 162

Amalgamated Bonanza, 95, 236-37,
    244ff.
American Eagle, 102
American Stock Exchange, 132, 136-37
Amoco, 32, 74, 79, 211, 221-22
Amoco Canada, 88, 100, 102-104, 156,
    283
Amouzegar, Jamshid, 25
Anderson Explorations Ltd., 221-22
Anderson, J. C., 220, 283-84, 295
Anglo-American Oils, 289
Anglo-Canadian Oils, 269
Anglo-Western Oils, 285-86
Arab-Israel War of 1967 (Six Day War),
    23
Arab-Israel War of 1973 (Yom Kippur
    War), 25
Arab Oil Embargo (1967), 23
Arctic Gas, 63, 67, 71-72, 110-12, 115,
    118-20, 175
Arctic Islands, 38, 53-54, 93-94, 136,
    153-54, 163, 168, 170, 174, 181
Arctic LNG (liquefied natural gas)
    project, 153, 155-56, 163
Arctic National Wildlife Refuge, 119
Argus Corp., 270-71
Armstrong, Jack, 60-62, 64-65, 80, 168
Ashland Canada, 159, 211, 226, 271-72,
    290, 292
Ashland Oil, 194-95, 272
Atco Industries, 266
Athabasca River, 84
Athabasca Tar Sands, 55, 81
Atkins, Orin, 271
Atlantic Richfield, 114, 152, 159
Atlantic Richfield Canada, 45, 82-83,
    152-53, 156, 158, 162, 175, 294
Aurora Energy Fund, 240-41
Austin, Jack, 143
Axford, Donald, 151-53

Bahamas Exploration, 70n.
Bailey Selburn Oil and Gas, 228
Baird, Joe, 128, 130
Banff Oil, 229
Bank of Montreal, 135, 259, 287
Bank of Nova Scotia, 135, 254, 269, 275
Banister Continental, 268

Banister, Ron, 268
Barron, Alex, 212
Battle, Ed, 148
Bawden, Peter, 217, 268
B.C. Sugar, 223
Beaufort Sea, 38, 53-54, 73, 79, 154,
    166, 167-68, 170-71, 174-76, 188, 203,
    243-44, 247
Beddome, John, 180
Bell, Bill, 246
Bell, Joel, 150, 158-59, 160, 164, 287n.
Bell, Max, 193, 219, 249
Bennett, W. A. C., 112, 192
Berger, Justice Thomas, 63, 111-12, 117,
    119, 177
Berger Report, 111, 117, 119
Bethel, Roger, 62, 237
Black, Conrad, 274
Blair, Bob, 16, 63, 81, 87, 106ff., 131ff.,
    139-40, 154-55, 157, 162, 164-66, 169,
    173, 178-79, 181-82, 189, 193, 215ff.,
    263, 265-67, 274-75
Blakeney, Allan, 133, 257
Blaser, Lorenz, 71
Bluesky Corp., 237
Bonanza Oil & Gas Ltd., 246
Bonnycastle, Richard 215, 247-49, 283
Borden Inquiry, 28
Bovey, Ed, 148
Bowens, Dr. Richard, 236
Bowlen family, 268
Bow Valley Industries, 108, 263, 267,
    269, 270ff.
Brady, "Diamond Jim", 284
Brawn, Bob, 263, 276-77, 295
Bray, Dick, 66, 68-69
Bridger Petroleum, 24, 223
Brinco, 237, 256
British American Oil, 70n., 289
British Dominions Land Settlement
    Corp., 285
British Petroleum, 21, 22, 120
British Petroleum Canada, 266
Bronfman, Edgar, 192, 270
Bronfman, Sam, Sr., 147
Brooks, Ralph, 119
Brown, Bob, Sr., 187, 190, 193ff., 282,
    289, 292, 294
Brown, Bobby, 271, 274
Buckinghorse (B.C.), 172, 174
Bullion, J. Waddy, 129
Burns Foods, 266

Calgary, 14-15, 68, 104, 108, 280ff.
Calgary Allied Arts Foundation, 291
Calgary Chamber of Commerce, 296
Calgary Community Foundation, 291
Calgary Golf and Country Club, 264,
    292
Calgary Philharmonic Society, 291
Calgary Stampede, 263, 291
Campbell, Robert, 178, 180
Canada
    national energy policy
        Joe Clark, 163-64, 300-301
        John G. Diefenbaker, 23, 28-30
        Pierre E. Trudeau, 31-34, 41-44, 91,
            131, 300
    exports — U.S., 52, 141
    imports — 28, 31, 41, 65

industry, foreign control of, 32, 139-41
Canada Cities Service, 298
Canada Development Corp., 170
Canada West Foundation, 259, 266
Canadian Arctic Gas PipeLine, 112,
    116-17
Canadian Establishment, The (Newman),
    265, 285
Canadian Export Gas and Oil Ltd., 229
Canadian Hunter, 55, 69, 74, 94, 134,
    196, 201-203, 206, 209ff., 218, 236-37,
    295
Canadian Imperial Bank of Commerce,
    274-75
Canadian Industrial Gas and Oil Ltd.,
    144-45, 147, 228
Canadian International Development
    Agency, 148
Canadian Marine Drilling Ltd., 175-76
Canadian National Railway, 180
Canadian Occidental Petroleum Ltd.,
    24
Canadian Oil Companies Ltd., 79
Canadian Pacific Investments Ltd., 179,
    267n., 275
Canadian Pacific Railway. See CPR.
Canadian Petrofina, 286
Canadian Petroleum Association, 38,
    91, 295
Canadian Reserve Oil & Gas Ltd., 229
Canadian Superior Oil, 90, 93-94, 275
CanDel Oil Ltd., 211
Canmar. See Canadian Marine Drilling
    Ltd.
Canpar, 180, 231
Carter, Jimmy, 121-22
Cavendish Investing, 248
CDC Oil & Gas, 93
Cemp Investments, 270
Century Sales & Service Ltd., 263, 266
Charterhouse Canada, 273
Chase Manhattan Bank, 216
Cherokee Ltd., 231
Chevron Standard Ltd., 55, 79-80,
    88-90, 95ff., 162, 211
    West Pembina, discovery at, 95-96,
        102
Chieftain Development, 211
Child, Arthur, 266
Chretien, Jean, 110
Christiensen, Jay, 134
Cigol. See Canadian Industrial Gas &
    Oil.
Cities Service Canada, 81-82, 84
Clare, Barnie, 238
Clark, Bob, 300
Clark, Joseph Charles (Joe), 64, 164,
    270n., 300
Clark, Spence, 147
CN Pension Fund, 231
Cody (Wyoming), 123-24, 126, 132
Cold Lake (Alberta), 68, 81, 86-87
    exploration cost at, 68, 81
Collins, Chip, 259, 262
Columbia Gas System, 173
Columbia Gas Transmission Corp.,
    111n.
Columbia Oils Ltd., 189
Conroy, Paul, 237
Conservative Party. See Progressive
    Conservative Party.

Consolidated MicMac, 269
Consumers' Gas Co., 72, 111n., 112, 115
Continental Oil Co., 156
Conuco, 237
Conventures Ltd., 102, 288, 290-92
Copeland, Don, 236
Copetrex drilling fund, 239
Coseka, 237
Coste, Eugene Marius, 241
CPA. See Canadian Petroleum Association.
CP Investments, 179
CPR, 110, 177-80, 197, 217, 219
Creber, Ted, 115
Crowe, Marshall, 132
Crown Trust, 270
Crown Zellerbach Canada, 267n.
Czar Resources Ltd., 237-40

Daniel, Bill, 78, 80
Davis, William (Bill), 40
Deep Basin, 213
Desmarais, Paul, 192
Dempster Highway Line, 110, 118-19, 181
de Souza, Ivan, 130
Devonian Group of Charitable Foundations, 285, 287
Dickie, Bill, 41, 83, 117, 158, 298
Diefenbaker, John G., 23, 28-29
Dome Exploration (Western) Ltd., 171
Dome Mines Ltd., 171
Dome Petroleum, 16, 54, 61, 63, 79, 144, 146-47, 151, 154, 165ff., 211, 227, 231, 240, 243, 265-68
Dominion Securities, 134
Domtar, 212
Dorsey, Bob, 70
Douglas, Tommy, 33, 143, 156
Drury, C. M. "Bud", 110
Dunkley, Charles, 171

Economic Council of Canada, 133
Edmonton Petroleum Club, The, 269, 292n.
Elmworth field, 55, 68-69, 74, 94, 134, 196, 203, 208, 211-13, 233, 244-45, 290
El Paso project, 110, 118
Empress, 173
Energy Policy for Canada, An — Phase 1, 141, 149
Energy Ventures Inc., 132-33
Esso Resources, 66, 68, 82
Evans, Cal, 69
Exxon, 21ff., 32, 57-59, 61, 63ff., 78, 114, 120, 216

Fairweather Gas Ltd., 221, 223
Fargo Oils Ltd., 229
Farrell, Bryce, 130
Federal-provincial energy meeting (1974), 42
Federal Power Commission (U.S.), 118, 191-92
Feldmeyer, Art, 93
Financial Times of Canada, The, 82
FIRA. See Foreign Investment Review Agency.
Fish, Ray C., 191
Fleming, John, 246

FLQ, 259
Flying Diamond Ltd., 271-72
Focus Ltd., 237, 240
Foothills Pipeline Consortium, 110, 119, 133, 155, 162, 179, 275
Foreign Investment Review Agency, 124, 130-31, 137, 151
Fotheringham, Allan, 120
Foulkes, Bob, 160
FPC. See Federal Power Commission
Gallagher, Jack, 16, 61-62, 140, 144, 146-47, 154, 165ff., 189, 215-16, 218, 231, 243, 265, 267, 274, 295
Galvin, Ed, 144, 148
Gardiner, George, 215
Gardiner, Watson Co., 215
Garvin, Jim, 59
Gas Arctic Systems Study Group, 112
General Motors of Canada, 254
Getty, Don, 44, 83, 101, 133, 153, 218, 255-57, 262, 264, 266, 298-99
Getty, John Paul, 285
Getty Oil Corp., 204
Gibson, Kelly, 117-18, 122, 158, 275, 296
Gillespie, Alastair, 64-65, 131, 133, 150, 160, 179, 299
Gillespie, Roy, 231-32
Glenbow-Alberta Institute, 291
Glenbow Foundation, 287
Gordon, Peter J., 208
Gordon, Walter, 115
Govier, Dr. George, 262
Grace, W. R., 226
Gray, Jim, 55, 69, 185, 201ff.
Great Canadian Oil Sands, 80-81, 85-86
Greater Winnipeg Gas, 147
Greene, Joe, 51, 91, 170
Gulf & Western Corp., 272
Gulf Oil Corp., 21-22, 32, 49, 55, 70-72, 75, 211, 217
Gulf Oil Canada Ltd., 43, 52, 70-73, 79, 81-82, 84, 111n., 112, 124, 157, 172, 269-70, 290

Haider, Mike, 66
Haight, Gordon, 68
Hamilton, Alex, 212
Hammer, Dr. Armand, 23, 127, 130, 231
Hanne, Jurgen, 236
Harlequin Enterprises, 247-48
Harradance, Milton, 37
Harris, Dick, 271, 274
Harvie, Donald, 275, 287, 293
Harvie, Eric Lafferty, Q.C., 275, 284ff., 291, 293
Hawkins, Dallas, III, 102
Haynes, Arden, 68
Healy, Joe, 262, 266
Hebbern, Klaus, 211, 235-37, 240
Henderson, Gerry, 96
Heritage Fund, Alberta, 12, 14, 109, 248, 259
Hetherington, Charles, 192
Hobbs, Harold, 262-63
Hodgson, Stuart, 116
Hollinger Mines, 271, 274
Home Oil Co., 72, 102, 162, 193, 195, 263, 271, 282

Hopper, Wilbert "Bill", 125, 127, 130, 140, 149ff., 156ff., 164, 294
Horte, Verne, 115, 119
Hotchkiss, Harley, 266, 273
Howard, Bill, Q.C., 266
Howe, C.D., 191
Hudson Institute, 82
Hudson's Bay Company, 180, 230, 248
Hudson's Bay Oil and Gas Co., 79, 156, 216, 269, 296
Hunt, H. L., 205
Hunt, Nelson Bunker, 249
Hunter, Doug, 237
Husky Oil, 24, 73, 86-87, 106, 108, 113, 123ff., 140, 154, 157ff., 180, 223, 267, 275

Imperial/Esso. See Imperial Oil.
Imperial Oil, 28, 38, 41, 49, 52, 54-55, 57, 59ff., 65, 67-69, 72, 78-79, 81-83, 85, 87, 90, 95-96, 111n., 112, 134, 168, 170, 211-13, 222, 229, 238-40, 245, 254, 257, 269, 271, 275, 285-86
Independent Petroleum Association of Canada, 30, 288
Interprovincial PipeLine, 29-30, 41, 261, 288
Interprovincial Steel & Pipe Corp., 256, 263
IPAC. See Independent Petroleum Association of Canada.
Ipsco. See Interprovincial Steel & Pipe Corp.
Iran, 13, 22, 64, 66, 80, 182
Irving, Harry, 262
Israel. See Arab-Israel War of 1967; Arab-Israel War of 1973.

Jamieson, Ken, 24, 66
Janisch, Andy, 160, 294, 297
Jennings, Rob, 129 30
Johns, Joe, 97
Jones, Carl, 296
Jones, Mack, 275
Joudrie, Earl, 226, 271

Kahanoff, Syd, 224
Kahn, Herman, 82
Kaiser, Edgar, 271, 275
Kaiser Resources, 226, 271, 292
Kennedy, Senator Edward M., 122
Kerr Addison, 211
Kerr, James, 178
Kerr McGee Corp., 202-203, 205-206
Khomeini, Ayatollah, 80, 182
Kloepfer, Vic, 207
Kolber, Leo, 270
Kopanoar, 176
Kuwait, 22

Labatts, 271
Labrador, 163
Labrador Mining and Exploration, 271
Lamond, Bob, 62, 236ff.
Last, Gary, 207
Leduc field, 15, 27-28, 61, 79, 90, 96, 170, 190, 268, 285-86, 293
Leitch, Merv, 262
Lévesque, René, 299
Liberal Party, 33, 43, 83, 141, 163, 299
  gas pricing policy 42, 45, 141

oil policy (1973), 41-42, 141
  oil pricing policy 41, 42-43, 45, 141
Liberal Party (Alberta), 300
Libya, 23-24, 67, 87
Lindberg, Verne, 240
Litt, Justice Nahum, 118
Lloydminster field, 86-87, 127
Loeb, Rhoades & Co., 132-34, 171
Long, Gus, 75
Longphee, George, 225
Loram Group, 261, 266n., 267
Loram International, 261
Loram Maintenance of Way Inc., 261
Lougheed Club, 37
Lougheed, Don, 38, 257
Lougheed, Peter, 39, 45, 68, 84, 133, 152, 169, 248, 253ff., 275-76
  Alberta Petroleum Exploration Plan and, 44-45
  background, 36ff.
  Liberal Party, clash with, 36, 40, 42, 44, 91, 142, 298
  TransCanada PipeLines and, 177, 199, 218
Lynch, Charles, 253
Lyons, Verne, 219-20

Macdonald, Donald, 33, 41-42, 44-45, 114, 141-43, 152, 298-99
Macdonnell, J. M., 263
Macdonnell, Peter, Q.C., 262, 266, 275
MacEachen, Allen, 133
MacKenzie, Alexander, 84
Mackenzie Delta, 38, 42, 53-54, 67, 110, 112, 117-19, 153, 166-67, 175, 229, 243
Mackenzie Valley Pipeline, 42, 110, 117-19, 177, 181
Mackenzie Valley Pipeline Inquiry. See Berger Report.
Maclean's, 120
Manalta Holdings, 261
Manning, Ernest, 36-38, 228
Mannix Corporation, 37, 296
Mannix, Fred, Jr., 192, 259ff., 274
Mannix, Fred, Sr., 258-59, 262, 266-68, 282 83
Mannix, Ronny, 259ff., 267-68, 274
Maple Leaf Line, 118-19
Marathon Corp., 230
Maritimes, 22, 154, 181
Massad, Alex, 92-93
Masters, John, 55, 69, 134, 196, 202ff., 237, 295
Matthews, Dick, 125, 129
Mayfair Golf and Country Club, 292n.
McAfee, Jerry, 70-72, 78
McCaig, Bud, 263-64, 267-68, 270
McCaig, J. W., 264, 267-68, 270
McColl-Frontenac Co., 77
McCullough, Bob, 219-20
McDaniel, Rod, 263, 296
McDougall, Hartland, 135
McGee, Dean, 204, 206
McGregor, Bill, 268-70, 275
McIntosh, Al, 162
McIvor, Don, 66
McKenzie, Angus, 274
McKinnon, Fred, 266
McLeod Young Weir, 129
McMahon, Frank, 147, 159, 187, 190-92, 198, 228, 249, 282

318   McMillian, John, 118-19, 122, 132
Medland, Ted, 123-24
Mellon, Barry, 262
Melville Shipping, 154
Mercantile Bank of Canada, 267n.
Mercier, Joe, 247, 283, 295
Mesa Petroleum (N.A.), 217, 239
Michel, Clifford, 171
Michigan Wisconsin Pipe Line Co.,
    111n.
Mic Mac Oils Ltd., 269
Miekle, Larry, 210
Middle East, 22, 67, 175, 182, 272
Millard, Mark, 133-34
Millican, Harold, 259, 262
Minnion, Wayne, 262
Mississippi River Delta, 175
Mitchell, Dave, 266, 275
Mitchell, Hoadley, 263
Mobil Canada, 88ff., 95, 143, 151, 153,
    156
  Mobil Oil Corp. and, 89, 91-93, 152
Mobil Oil, 21-22, 32, 38, 88-89, 91-92,
    94, 151, 211, 216, 229
Mooney, Bill, 298
Morgan Stanley, 121, 131
Moroney, V. J. "Tip", 170-71
Morrison-Knudsen, 261
Mountain Pacific Pipelines, 217
Mount Royal Club, The, 192
Muir, James, 216

Nadeau, Pierre, 275
Nairb Petroleums Ltd., 97ff.
Nanticoke refinery, 53, 78
Narvik, Dianne, 133, 135
National Advisory Committee on
    Petroleum, 91, 143, 170
National Energy Board, 33, 40, 118-19,
    132, 149, 154-55, 179, 191, 196, 213,
    289
Natoros, Dr. Frank, 245
Natural Gas Pipeline Co. of America,
    111n.
NDP. See New Democratic Party.
NEB. See National Energy Board.
New Democratic Party, 33, 111, 119,
    141
Newsweek, 110
New York Stock Exchange, 135
Nickle Arts Museum, 291
Nickle, Carl O., 30, 287n.
Nickle Family Foundation, 291
Nickle, Sam, 288
Nickle's Daily Oil Bulletin, 30, 290
Nielsen, Arne, 38, 89ff., 143, 151,
    267-68, 270, 275, 297
Nielson, Glenn, 124ff., 135-37
Nielson, Jim, 123-24, 132, 135-36
Nixon, Richard M., 31, 71n., 110
Noranda Mines, 134, 207-208, 211
Norcen Energy Resources Ltd., 97-98,
    102, 148, 228
Northern and Central Gas Corp.,
    111n., 112, 144-45, 147-48
Northern Natural Gas Co., 111n.
Northern Pipeline Agency, 259, 262
Northern Telecom Ltd., 267n.
North Sea, 91, 104, 159, 230, 236,
    271-72, 274
Northwest Energy Corp., 118, 132-33

NorthWest Project Study Group, 112,
    114
Nova Scotia, 89
Numac Oil & Gas Ltd., 268ff.

Oakwood Petroleums Ltd., 102
OAPEC, 25
Occidental Petroleum Corp., 23, 106,
    127ff.
Ocelot Industries Ltd., 219-20
Ongyerth, George, 240
Ontario, 14, 21, 82, 152
Ontario Securities Commission, 136-37,
    159, 271
OPEC, 11, 12, 44, 199-201, 257, 267
  effect on Canadian producers, 188,
    196-98, 200, 233-34
  formation of, 22-23
  1973-74 oil crisis, 13, 19, 22ff., 66, 80,
    106, 110, 124, 139, 149, 206, 244,
    268, 274, 281
  oil embargo — U.S. (1973), 51
  price increases, 11, 24, 25-26, 51, 74,
    81, 87, 96, 300
Orbit Oil & Gas Ltd., 237, 240
Organization of Arab Petroleum
    Exporting Countries. See OAPEC.
Organization of Petroleum Exporting
    Countries. See OPEC.
Ottawa Valley Line, 29, 42

Pacific Lighting Gas Development Co.,
    111n.
Pacific Northwest Pipeline Corp., 191
Pacific Petroleums Ltd., 74, 79, 97ff.,
    118, 158-59, 189-91, 228, 275, 296
Pacific Western Airlines, 262-63, 267n.
Pallister, Ernie, 266
Pan Alberta Gas, 258
PanArctic Oils Ltd., 93, 153, 229
PanCanadian Petroleum, 81, 88, 173,
    178, 180, 211
Panhandle Eastern PipeLine Co., 111n.
Pearson, H. J. S., 263, 266, 275
Pearson, Lester, 148
Pearson, Stan, 72
Pembina field, 96, 102, 229, 261
Pembina PipeLine, 259, 261, 296
Pembina, West, field. See West
    Pembina field.
People, Peregrines and Arctic Pipelines
    (Peacock), 115n.
Pepin, Jean-Luc, 40
Persian Gulf, 175
Peter Lougheed (Hustak), 261
Peters, Rob, 234
PetroCan, 54, 63-65, 73, 93, 97, 106,
    113, 139, 142-143, 145, 149ff., 181,
    191, 287, 294
  Alberta Gas Trunk Line and, 140,
    154-55
  dismemberment of, proposed, 158,
    164
  Dome Petroleum and, 140, 154-55,
    170
  formation, 140-41, 151
  Husky Oil and, 124ff., 140, 157ff.
  Pacific Petroleums Ltd. and., 158ff.
  Syncrude and, 82, 156
PetroCanada. See PetroCan.
Petrofina, 43, 79, 275, 287

Petroleum Club, The, 42, 85, 92, 94, 107-108, 129, 150, 166, 172, 174, 207, 292ff.
Petroleum Industry Monitoring Board, 91
Petromark, 211, 237
PetroSar refinery, 53
Pew, John Howard, 85
Peyto, 237
Phillips, J. C., 73
Phillips Petroleum Co., 158-59, 191
Pierce, Bob, 266, 275
Pierce, Jack, 283
Piercy, George, 25, 66
Pitfield, Mackay, Ross, 123-24, 137, 159
Pitfield, Michael, 126
Pitfield, Ward, 124-26, 129-30, 137
Podpechan, Frank, 239
Polar Gas, 155
Power Corp., 144, 147, 192
Powis, Alf, 196, 211
Pratt, Wallace, 100, 188
Progressive Conservative Party, 163, 299
Prudhoe Bay field, 38, 42, 54, 63, 71, 109ff., 122, 152, 175, 247

Qaddafi, Colonel Muamer, 23
Q&M Pipelines. See Quebec and Maritimes Pipelines.
Quebec and Maritimes Pipelines, 136, 154, 156-57, 178-79
Quebec North Shore and Labrador Railway, 261

Rainbow field, 62, 229, 238
Ranchman's Club, The, 38, 174, 292-93
Rankin, Bill, 133, 135
Rasmussen, Merrill, 158, 162, 275
Redwater field, 172, 285-86
Regent Drilling, 268
Richards, Bill, 167ff., 173-74, 180
Richfield Corp., 85
Rieber, Torkild "Cap", 76
Ripley, Wilder, 249
Ritchie, Ced, 135
Rockefeller Foundation, 145
Rockefeller, John D., 21, 58-59, 169
Rockingham, J. M., 267n.
Roeschinger, Dr. Helmut, 236-37
Rosario Resources, 221
Ross, Al, 296
Rostland Corp., 249
Rostoker, George, 231-32
Rothschild, L. F., 131
Royal Bank, 120, 160, 192, 259, 261, 263, 271, 275
Royal Dutch Shell, 79
Royal Insurance Co. of Canada, 267n.
Royalite Oil Co., 84, 147

Sable Island, 151
Sabre Petroleums, 207, 266
Sangster, Robert, 249
Salomon Brothers, 137
Saskatchewan tar sands, 80, 124
Saudi Arabia, 13, 22, 25, 87, 182, 230, 280
Sceptre Resources, 274
Schiff, Sigma, 231-32

Scott & Eastern United Securities Ltd., 267n.
Scott, Brent, 83
Scrymgeour, John, 282, 296
Scully, Sister Jane, 71
Scurfield, Ralph, 224
Seagull Resources, 284
Seaman, B. J., 270-71, 283
Seaman, Daryl K. "Doc", 108, 263, 267-68, 270ff., 283
Seaman, Donald, 270-71
Seaman Engineering and Drilling Co., 273
Seaman family, 247, 267
Securities and Exchange Commission, 70, 132
Seven Sisters, The, 21-24, 27-28, 59, 65, 90, 169
Seven Sisters, The (Sampson), 22, 58, 64, 66
Seymour, Jim, 262
Shah of Iran, 23, 26, 87
Sharp, Mitchell, 133
Shell Canada, 43, 52, 72, 79, 81-83, 85, 111n., 112, 153, 162, 286
    Shell Oil Co. and, 78
Shell Oil Co., 21-22, 49, 55, 73, 78, 151, 169, 211
Shepard, Clarence, 71-72
Shoyama, Tommy, 161
Siebens, Bill, 180, 226, 229-31, 247, 267-69, 282
Siebens, Harold, 180, 226-29, 231-32, 247, 267-69, 282
Siebens Leaseholds Ltd., 229
Siebens Minerals Ltd., 229
Siebens Oil & Gas Ltd., 179-80, 227, 229, 267, 282
Siebens Oil Producers Ltd., 229
Siegert, Rudi, 236-37, 239
Simon, Bill, 33
Sinclair, D'Alton, 273
Sinclair, Ian, 178, 180
Skye Resources, 236, 239
Smith, Dave, 210
Smith, Ken, 97
Smith, Syd, 97, 100
Socal. See Standard Oil of California.
Social Credit Party (Alberta), 36ff., 109, 114, 300
Sohio. See Standard Oil of Ohio.
Southern, Ron, 266-67, 283
Spragins, Frank, 82
Sproule, J. C., and Associates, 216
Spruce Meadows, 267
Stabback, Jack, 119, 133
Standard Oil of California, 21-22, 32, 55, 58, 76, 88
Standard Oil of Indiana, 88, 221-22
Standard Oil of New Jersey, 169-70, 216
Standard Oil of New York, 216
Standard Oil of Ohio, 114, 120
Standard Trust, 90
Steel Company of Canada, 208
Stelco. See Steel Company of Canada.
Stephenson, William, 262
Stewart, Sam, 153
Stoik, John, 71-73, 80
Strom, Harry, 39
Strong, Maurice, 140, 143ff., 157, 164, 215, 249

320

Sulpetro, 211, 214, 216, 247, 249, 283
Sun Oil Co., 81, 85
Superior Oil Corp., 80, 93
Super Pipe (Gray), 119n.
Syncrude tar sands project, 45, 66-68, 73, 81ff., 152, 258, 298
Syracuse Oils, 274

Tar Sands, Syncrude and the Politics of Oil, The (Pratt), 82-83, 254
Taylor, E. P., 229, 282
Taylor, John, 178, 180
Taylor, Nick, 300
Teheran Agreement (1971), 24
Texaco, 21-22, 32, 49, 55, 75-76, 210-11
Texaco Canada, 43, 52, 73ff., 81, 100
  Texaco and, 77
Texaco Exploration Canada, 74, 77
Texas Eastern Transmission Corp., 111n.
Thomson Industries, 266
Thomson, John, 266
Tiber Ltd., 240
Tiger Resources, 247
Tokyo Stock Exchange, 243
Toronto, 67-68
Toronto-Dominion Bank, 275
Toronto Stock Exchange, 101-102, 123, 135-37, 167, 243, 245, 276
Torstar, 248
Total Petroleum (N.A.), 211
TransAlaska Pipeline, 110, 111, 114, 120, 152
TransAlta Company, 231-32
TransCanada PipeLines Ltd., 40, 111n., 112ff., 155, 173, 178ff., 197ff., 225, 290
TransMountain Pipeline, 261
Transport Commissioners, Board of, 191
Travis, Ken, 277
Trimac, 263-64, 267-68
Tripoli Agreement (1971), 24
Tristar, 237
Trudeau, Pierre E., 36, 42, 82, 91, 110, 121, 126, 141, 143, 150, 169, 270, 288, 299
Tuktoyaktuk, 176
Turbo Resources, 263, 276-77
Turner, John, 43-44, 299
Turner Valley field, 27, 194, 197, 285, 289-90

Twaites, Bill, 51, 60, 62-63, 70, 78, 119, 275
Tye, Bill, 158

Ukalerk, 176
Ulster Petroleums, 247
Union Gas Ltd., 111n., 112
Union Oil, 225
United Nations, 148
United States, 21-22, 24, 31-32, 51, 82, 106, 110, 117
U.S. Pacific Gas & Lighting, 113
Universal Gas, 247, 283
University of Calgary, 204, 291
Upitis, Uldis, 62, 237, 240

Vangus Resources Corp., 215
Van Rensaeller, Harry, 274
Van Wielingen, Gus, 211, 214-15, 217-18, 247-49, 283
Venezuela, 22
Voyager Petroleums, 224, 226

Walcott, Don, 154, 162, 172-74
Walwyn, Stodgell Ltd., 134, 237
Watergate scandal, 70
Waters, Stanley, 267n.
Wayne, John, 103-104
Wellhauser, Fred, 274
Westburne International Industries Ltd., 267n., 282
Westcoast Transmission Ltd., 113, 117-18 162, 189, 192, 197-98
Western Canada Land Co., 285
Western Decalta, 259, 261
Western Leaseholds, 286-87
Western Minerals, 286
Westfort, 237
West Pembina Field, 55, 68-69, 74, 78, 89-90, 94-95, 101-102, 105, 162, 165, 212, 233-34, 241, 244, 290
Whiteford, William, 70n.
Wild, Claude C., Jr., 70
Wilder, William, 71-72, 115, 119
Wilmott, Fred, 262
Wisener, Bob, 134, 212
Woodbine Sands, 245
Wood, David, 259
Wood Gundy, 115, 121, 123-25, 137, 159
Wyatt, Hal, 275

Yamani, Sheik, 12, 14, 25, 58, 66, 124, 281